Kant on the Sources of Metaphysics

In the *Critique of Pure Reason*, Kant famously criticizes traditional metaphysics and its proofs of immortality, free will, and God's existence. What is often overlooked is that Kant also explains why rational beings must ask metaphysical questions about 'unconditioned' objects such as souls, uncaused causes or God, and why answers to these questions will appear rationally compelling to them. In this book Marcus Willaschek reconstructs and defends Kant's account of the rational sources of metaphysics. After carefully explaining Kant's conceptions of reason and metaphysics, he offers detailed interpretations of the relevant passages from the *Critique of Pure Reason* (in particular, the Transcendental Dialectic) in which Kant explains why reason seeks 'the unconditioned.' His book offers a novel interpretation of the Transcendental Dialectic, pointing out its 'positive' side, while at the same time uncovering a highly original account of metaphysical thinking that will be relevant to contemporary philosophical debates.

MARCUS WILLASCHEK is Professor of Philosophy at Goethe University Frankfurt.

Kant on the Sources of Metaphysics
The Dialectic of Pure Reason

Marcus Willaschek
Goethe University Frankfurt

CAMBRIDGE
UNIVERSITY PRESS

University Printing House, Cambridge CB2 8BS, United Kingdom

One Liberty Plaza, 20th Floor, New York, NY 10006, USA

477 Williamstown Road, Port Melbourne, VIC 3207, Australia

314–321, 3rd Floor, Plot 3, Splendor Forum, Jasola District Centre, New Delhi – 110025, India

79 Anson Road, #06-04/06, Singapore 079906

Cambridge University Press is part of the University of Cambridge.

It furthers the University's mission by disseminating knowledge in the pursuit of education, learning, and research at the highest international levels of excellence.

www.cambridge.org
Information on this title: www.cambridge.org/9781108472630
DOI: 10.1017/9781108560856

© Marcus Willaschek 2018

This publication is in copyright. Subject to statutory exception and to the provisions of relevant collective licensing agreements, no reproduction of any part may take place without the written permission of Cambridge University Press.

First published 2018

Printed and bound in Great Britain by Clays Ltd, Elcograf S.p.A.

A catalogue record for this publication is available from the British Library.

Library of Congress Cataloging-in-Publication Data
Names: Willaschek, Marcus, author.
Title: Kant on the sources of metaphysics : the dialectic of pure reason / Marcus Willaschek, Goethe-Universität Frankfurt am Main.
Description: 1 [edition]. | New York : Cambridge University Press, 2018. | Includes bibliographical references and index.
Identifiers: LCCN 2018024263 | ISBN 9781108472630 (hardback : alk. paper) | ISBN 9781108460064 (pbk. : alk. paper)
Subjects: LCSH: Kant, Immanuel, 1724-1804. Kritik der reinen Vernunft.
Classification: LCC B2779 .W55 2018 | DDC 121–dc23
LC record available at https://lccn.loc.gov/2018024263

ISBN 978-1-108-47263-0 Hardback

Cambridge University Press has no responsibility for the persistence or accuracy of URLs for external or third-party internet websites referred to in this publication and does not guarantee that any content on such websites is, or will remain, accurate or appropriate.

This book is dedicated to my dear sons,
Simon and Fabian

Contents

Note on References and Citations		page ix
Preface		xi

Introduction 1
0.1 Beginning at the Beginning(s) 2
0.2 The Rational Sources Account 3
0.3 One Argument, Four Levels 6
0.4 Kant's Two Projects in the Transcendental Dialectic 9
0.5 Overview 12

Part I   From Reason to Metaphysics 17
Introduction to Part I 18

1   Kant's Conceptions of Reason and Metaphysics 21
1.1 Kant's Conception of Reason 21
1.2 Kant's Conception of Metaphysics 36
1.3 Conclusion 44

2   The Logical Use of Reason and the Logical Maxim 46
2.1 The Logical Use of Reason 47
2.2 The Content of the Logical Maxim 56
2.3 The Logical Maxim, Science, and Universal Human Reason 64
2.4 Conclusion 70

3   The Supreme Principle of Pure Reason 71
3.1 'Given' 72
3.2 Real Conditioning 73
3.3 The Unconditioned 87
3.4 The Supreme Principle and the Principle of Sufficient Reason 98

4   Understanding the Transition Passage (A307–8/B364) 103
4.1 Objective Validity 105
4.2 Regulative and Constitutive Use of Principles in the Appendix and in the Resolution of the Antinomy 107
4.3 A Transition in Two Steps 120

5 The Transition from the Logical Maxim to the Supreme Principle of Pure Reason — 127
5.1 Step 1: From the Logical Maxim to the Regulative Supreme Principle — 128
5.2 Step 2: From the Regulative to the Constitutive Supreme Principle — 135
5.3 Why Does the Supreme Principle Hold for Things in Themselves (but Not for Appearances)? — 152

Conclusion to Part I: The Transition from the Logical Maxim to the (Constitutive) Supreme Principle and the Rational Sources Account — 157

Part II The Other Side of the Transcendental Dialectic — 163
Introduction to Part II — 164

6 The System of Transcendental Ideas — 167
6.1 Transcendental Ideas — 167
6.2 On the Metaphysical Deduction of the Transcendental Ideas — 170
6.3 The Concept of the Unconditioned — 177
6.4 The Three Classes of Transcendental Ideas — 182
6.5 Conclusion — 185

7 The Paralogisms and Antinomy Arguments as 'Necessary Inferences of Reason' — 187
7.1 The Psychological Ideas and the Paralogisms — 188
7.2 Transcendental Illusion and Transcendental Realism in the Paralogisms — 195
7.3 The Cosmological Ideas — 202
7.4 The Antinomies — 208
7.5 Conclusion — 216

8 Reason and Metaphysics in the Transcendental Ideal and the Appendix — 218
8.1 The Transcendental Ideal and the Natural Argument for God's Existence — 218
8.2 The Constitutive Use of Ideas and Principles in the Appendix — 237

9 Transcendental Realism and Kant's Critique of Speculative Metaphysics — 243
9.1 Transcendental Realism and Transcendental Idealism — 245
9.2 A Critique of Transcendental Realism — 247
9.3 Limits of Cognition without Transcendental Idealism — 251
9.4 Transcendental Ideas as Empty Concepts — 254
9.5 Conclusion — 262

Conclusion to Part II: Transcendental Illusion and the 'Other Side' of the Transcendental Dialectic — 264

Postscript: Kant's Practical Metaphysics — 270

Bibliography — 276
Index of Names — 291
Index of Subjects — 294

Note on References and Citations

References to Kant's *Critique of Pure Reason* give the page numbers of the A- and/or B-edition(s). All other references to Kant's writings are by volume and page number of the Academy edition (*Kant's gesammelte Schriften*, ed. Königlich-Preußische Akademie der Wissenschaften, now: Berlin-Brandenburgische Akademie der Wissenschaften, Berlin: Walter de Gruyter 1900–). Translations follow the *Cambridge Edition of the Works of Immanuel Kant*, ed. Paul Guyer and Allen W. Wood, Cambridge: Cambridge University Press 1992–2012, sometimes with minor alterations. In case of substantial deviations from the Cambridge Edition, either the German original is given in parentheses or these are explained in a note. In the rare cases of citations from texts not contained in the Cambridge Edition, translations are my own.

The following works by Kant are referred to by short titles:

De Mundi	On the Form and Principles of the Sensible and Intelligible World (1770; 2:385–420)
Dreams of a Spirit Seer	Dreams of a Spirit Seer Elucidated by Dreams of Metaphysics (1766; 2:315–84)
False Subtlety	The False Subtlety of the Four Syllogistic Figures Proved (1763; 2:45–62)
Groundwork	Groundwork of the Metaphysics of Morals (1785; 4:385–464)
Hechsel Logic	Hechsel Logic (lecture transcript not contained in the Academy edition; quoted from *Lectures on Logic*, trans. and ed. J. Michael Young, Cambridge: Cambridge University Press, 1992)
Jäsche Logic	Immanuel Kant's Logik (ed. G. B. Jäsche) (1800; 9:1–150)
Metaphysical Foundations	Metaphysical Foundations of Natural Science (1786; 4:465–566)

Negative Magnitudes	An Attempt to Introduce the Concept of Negative Magnitudes into Philosophy (1763; 2:165–204)
Nova Dilucidatio	A New Elucidation of the First Principles of Metaphysical Cognition (1755; 1:385–416)
On a Discovery	On a Discovery Whereby Any New Critique of Pure Reason Is to Be Made Superfluous by an Older One (1790; 8:185–252)
Only Possible Argument	Only Possible Argument in Support of a Demonstration of the Existence of God (1763; 2:63–164)
Progress	What Real Progress Has Metaphysics Made in Germany since the Time of Leibniz and Wolff? (ca. 1793; 20:253–311)
Prolegomena	Prolegomena to Any Future Metaphysics That Will Be Able to Come Forward as a Science (1783; 4:253–384)

Chapters and Sections from the *Critique of Pure Reason* are referred to with capital initials (e.g. 'Introduction to the Transcendental Dialectic') and sometimes abbreviated in obvious ways (e.g. 'Paralogisms,' 'Antinomy').

Double quotation marks are used for literal quotes with page references, and single quotation marks are used for references to Kantian terms outside longer literal quotes, semantic ascent, scare quotes, etc.

Numbers in brackets such as '(1.3)' and '(5.3.2)' refer to sections in this book (e.g. to Chapter 1, Section 1.3 and Chapter 5, Section 5.3.2, respectively).

Preface

The ideas developed in this book were first presented in rudimentary form at the International Kant Congress 2005 in Sao Paulo. Only two paragraphs from that paper made it into this book, however, which hopefully indicates that some progress has been made. When I started working on the book project during a sabbatical at the University of California, Berkeley, in 2009–10, the book was meant to have two parts, one on the Transcendental Dialectic of the first *Critique* and one on Kant's 'practical metaphysics' (the 'postulates' and the primacy of practical reason). Even though other projects occupied much of my time until 2015, I managed to write several papers mainly on topics from the second part. When I seriously started writing the present book in March 2016, however, it soon became clear that there would not be space for that second part in this book. So now the book is exclusively on Kant's account of reason as the source of metaphysical speculation in the Transcendental Dialectic, and I have added only a short postscript on Kant's 'practical metaphysics.'

In working on this book, I have been helped by a great number of people; first, I would like to mention four friends and fellow undogmatic Kantians whose influence on this book has been particularly important. Volker Gerhardt and Peter Rohs were my academic teachers in Münster. As a first-year philosophy student in 1985, I took my very first class on Kant with Volker Gerhardt. As it happens, it was a course on Kant's account of metaphysics, which makes this book a very late *Hausarbeit*. Between 1986 and 1990, Peter Rohs taught a multi-semester course on the *Critique of Reason*, where I learned much of what I know about Kant's theoretical philosophy. Even though over three and a half years we only made it from the A-Preface to the end of the B-Deduction, our discussions touched on all parts of the first *Critique*. I have continued to learn from Volker Gerhardt and Peter Rohs ever since. Georg Mohr first drew my attention to the originality and importance of Kant's account of the rational sources of metaphysics when we co-authored an introductory text on the first *Critique* in 1997. And finally, since 2010 I have profited from countless discussions on the topics of this book with Eric Watkins, who has been a constant source of encouragement (and constructive criticism, too).

Many people have read and commented on drafts of one, some, or all chapters of the book: Lucy Allais, Stefano Bertea, Claudia Blöser, Angela Breitenbach, Fabian Burt, Ralf Busse, Rosalind Chaplin, Andrew Chignell, Gabriele Gava, Kai Hüwelmeyer, Pauline Kleingeld, Katharina Kraus, Pavle Kufrin, Florian Marwede, Andi Müller, Maria Müller-Hornbach, Andrews Reath, Tobias Rosefeldt, Karl Schafer, Joseph Stratman, Thomas Sturm, Clinton Tolley, Eric Watkins, and Michael Wolff.

Finally, I have received very helpful feedback from the participants of the fifth *Berliner Kant-Kurs* at the Humboldt-Universität (organized by Tobias Rosefeldt in June 2016), where I presented the central ideas of the book (still very much in flux at the time); from the participants of a symposium on a first complete draft at the Gutenberg-Universität Mainz (organized by Eric Watkins in July 2017); from the participants of my research colloquium at Goethe-Universität Frankfurt, of the Frankfurter Kant-Arbeitskreis and of several lecture courses and classes I have taught on Kant's account of metaphysics; and finally from audiences of various talks I have given over the years on the topics of this book.

Maria Russo has taken care of many administrative matters and thus helped me to find the time to write this book. In the final rounds of revisions, Pavle Kufrin and Fabian Burt helped me to locate relevant discussions in the literature on Kant, and Maria Müller-Hornbach checked quotes and compiled the bibliography and the index. Carolyn Benson carefully corrected my English. (All remaining mistakes are my own.) Finally, the research cluster *Normative Orders* funded two extra sabbatical semesters during which I worked on this book.

I am truly grateful to everyone who has helped me write this book; philosophy without many hours alone at one's desk would be empty, but without the continuous exchange with one's friends, peers, and students it would be blind (and so much less fun).

Introduction

This book is about Immanuel Kant's account of reason as the source of metaphysical speculation, as he develops it in the Transcendental Dialectic of the *Critique of Pure Reason*. It has two major aims. First, it will offer a novel interpretation of the Transcendental Dialectic that isolates its constructive side (Kant's account of the rational sources of speculative metaphysics, concerning the soul, the world as a whole, and God), and that distinguishes it clearly from its destructive side (Kant's *critique* of this kind of metaphysics). We will see that Kant himself does not always keep these two projects separate, with the result that there are passages in the Transcendental Dialectic that appear puzzling or even confused but that make perfect sense once the two strands are clearly distinguished. I will offer interpretations of all main parts of the Transcendental Dialectic, and even though I cannot claim to be able to solve all the exegetical problems Kant's texts present (some of his arguments and derivations are extremely brief and cryptic), the reading proposed here unveils a consistent and philosophically attractive account of metaphysical thinking that has so far been widely ignored in the literature on Kant.

Second, this book will reconstruct, and where possible defend, a Kantian account of the rational sources of metaphysical thinking. In particular, it will argue that Kant is right in claiming that metaphysical speculation arises naturally out of principles that guide us in everyday rational thought. On the one hand, the structure of rational thinking is *discursive* and *iterative*, requiring us to ask not only for explanations of empirical phenomena but also for explanations of the phenomena we rely on to explain them (and for their explanations, and so on). On the other hand, as rational inquirers we want our questions to come to a satisfactory conclusion, which they can find only in *ultimate* answers, that is, in answers that do not raise further questions of the same kind. As I will argue, Kant gives us good reason to think that *discursivity*, *iteration*, and striving for *completeness* are fundamental features of rational thinking and that, taken together, they give rise to a specific kind of metaphysical speculation. This is a distinctive and original perspective on metaphysics that deserves to be taken seriously in the current metaphysical and metametaphysical debates. As I will indicate in passing in the course of this book, many

0.1 Beginning at the Beginning(s)

Kant begins the *Critique of Pure Reason*, his treatise on method in metaphysics (Bxxii), with an implicit reference to the beginning of the first book ever to bear that title. Aristotle famously starts his *Metaphysics* with the observation that human beings by their nature desire to know (*eidenai*) (*Metaphysics* 980a1) and then explains that knowledge starts from sense experience and ends with knowledge of first principles and causes. Aristotle calls the science that investigates these principles and causes 'first philosophy'; later, it will be known as 'metaphysics.' Hence, we can sum up Aristotle's line of thought by saying that human beings, because of their rational nature, strive for knowledge, beginning with knowledge from experience and ending with metaphysical knowledge of first principles. Now compare this with how Kant begins the Preface of the first edition of his *Critique of Pure Reason*:

> Human reason has the peculiar fate in one species of its cognitions that it is burdened with questions which it cannot dismiss, since they are given to it as problems by the nature of reason itself, but which it also cannot answer, since they transcend every capacity of human reason. Reason falls into this perplexity through no fault of its own. It begins from principles whose use is unavoidable in the course of experience ... With these principles it rises (as its nature also requires) ever higher, to more remote conditions ... [R]eason sees itself necessitated to take refuge in principles that overstep all possible use in experience ... [I]t thereby falls into obscurity and contradictions ... The battlefield of these endless controversies is called *metaphysics*. (Avii–viii)

On the most fundamental point, Kant agrees with Aristotle: it is part of human nature – Kant speaks of the nature of human reason, but also of human nature (Ax) – to strive for metaphysical cognition and knowledge.[1] This is knowledge of first principles, according to Aristotle, and cognition of higher and highest principles, according to Kant. Kant also agrees, at least in broad outline, that sense experience is the basis for all other knowledge by admitting that reason starts from principles used in experience. As he writes some 300 pages later in the first *Critique*, "[a]ll our cognition starts from the senses, goes from there to the understanding, and ends with reason" (A298f/B355). But where Aristotle presumably thinks that, by rising from experience to reason, metaphysical knowledge is in fact to be gained, Kant, after two thousand years of metaphysical speculation, can only make out a battlefield scattered with the ruins of

---

[1] In this book, the term 'cognition,' if used without further qualification, means 'theoretical cognition.' Note that for Kant, cognition is not the same as knowledge (Willaschek and Watkins 2017 and Chapter 9, note 12 below).

failed theories. According to Kant, human reason, by rising to ever higher principles and more remote conditions, overreaches itself and falls into fallacies and contradictions. The fate of human reason is thus a truly tragic one. The tendency not just to ask metaphysical questions but also to devise answers to them is built into the very structure of rational thought. At the same time, rational thought is limited in ways that make it impossible for us ever to know which answers to these metaphysical questions are correct and that make it seem doubtful that these questions make sense in the first place.

0.2 The Rational Sources Account

So why does Kant hold that human reason inevitably confronts us with metaphysical questions? In the Introduction to the second edition (the 'B-edition') of the *Critique of Pure Reason*, Kant distinguishes between metaphysics "as a science" (which we do not yet possess) and "metaphysics as a natural predisposition" (B22), that is, metaphysics as a natural tendency in human beings to ask metaphysical questions and to come up with answers to them. Kant asks:

How is metaphysics as a natural predisposition possible? i.e. how do the questions that pure reason raises, and which it is driven by its own need to answer as well as it can, arise from the nature of universal human reason? (B22)

There are three claims implicit in this question: (1) pure reason – rational thought independently of any input from the senses – raises metaphysical questions; (2) pure reason is driven by its own need or its nature to answer these questions, even if the answers may not be ultimately warranted ('as well as it can'); and (3) the metaphysical questions do not arise from the minds of individual and perhaps misguided metaphysicians but rather have their source in 'the nature of universal human reason' – that is, they arise from the very structure of rational thinking as such. I will call the conjunction of these three claims 'Kant's account of the rational sources of metaphysics,' or the *Rational Sources Account* for short. The Transcendental Dialectic of the first *Critique* contains Kant's extended argument for this account, with the general framework being developed in the Introduction and Book 1 of the Dialectic and the specifics filled in in the chapters on the paralogisms, the antinomies, and the ideal of pure reason and in the Appendix.

An important aspect of the Rational Sources Account concerns the relation between reason in general and 'pure' reason. According to Kant, even though it is *pure reason* that raises and attempts to answer metaphysical questions, it is reason in general, or *universal human reason*, from which these questions originally arise. This means that even though metaphysical questions take us beyond the bounds of possible experience, they are not willful speculations but arise naturally from features of rational thinking that are at work even in the most ordinary empirical employments of reason in everyday life. It is this latter claim that makes Kant's diagnosis of metaphysical thinking philosophically deep and attractive. Although certain modes of metaphysical thinking may be fundamentally flawed and may have to be abandoned (or, as Kant argues, transformed into a practical mode), they have their ultimate source in something that we cannot possibly abandon, namely, rational thinking. As Kant explains, it is the task of a "critique of pure reason" to determine "the sources, as well as the extent and boundaries" of metaphysics (Axii). His central result in this respect is that the *sources of metaphysics* lie in *reason* itself (A309/B366).

In its broadest outline, this is how the story goes: we begin with principles that work fine within the realm of experience, for instance, the principle that every alteration must have a cause, or that in every change there must be something that persists. "With these principles," Kant says in the A-Preface, reason "rises (as its nature also requires) ever higher, to more remote conditions" (Avii), for example, by asking what caused the *cause* of the original alteration to occur or by wondering whether the very thing that persisted in one situation cannot be transformed into something else in a different situation, thus in turn requiring something that persists. Only much later in his book, in the Introduction to the Transcendental Dialectic, does Kant explain why it lies in the nature of reason to ask these kinds of questions. There, Kant argues that whenever we are confronted with something 'conditioned' (roughly, something calling for an explanation), reason compels us to look for its 'condition' (something that explains it) – a tendency Kant traces back to a core function of human reason: syllogistic reasoning. Just as we can seek premises for given conclusions, and then further premises from which to derive the original premises, we ask not just for conditions of the conditioned but also for the conditions of the conditions, etc. In this way, we find ourselves starting on a regress that is potentially infinite. As Kant says of reason in the A-Preface: "its business must always remain incomplete because the questions never cease" (Aviii). The questions can come to an end only in something 'unconditioned,' for instance in an uncaused cause or a substance that persists throughout every possible change.

In this way, asking for explanations of ordinary phenomena ultimately leads us to assume the existence of something 'unconditioned.' If there is a fire, for instance, we ask what caused it. If lightning caused the fire, we ask what caused the lightning. If electrical charges in the air caused the lightning, we ask what caused the charges, etc.: 'the questions never cease.' But if we assume that there is an answer to each and every one of these causal questions, it seems that there must either be an uncaused cause – a cause that does not raise a further question about its cause – or a series of causes and effects that stretches infinitely back in time. In both cases, Kant argues, we have posited something unconditioned, since neither a first member in a series of causes nor a complete infinite series of causes can itself have a cause that belongs to the same series.

Since everything we experience is conditioned in one way or another (spatially, temporally, causally, etc.), in searching for something *un*conditioned we leave the field of experience and enter the realm of metaphysical speculation: "For that which necessarily drives us to go beyond the boundaries of experience and all appearances is the *unconditioned*, which reason necessarily and with every right demands in things in themselves for everything that is conditioned, thereby demanding the series of conditioned as something completed". (Bxx).[2]

So here we have the outline of an explanation of why metaphysical questions arise from the very nature of rational thought. Rational thinking includes a tendency to move from the conditioned to its condition, a movement innocently at work in syllogistic reasoning and empirical explanation, but one that goes overboard when it aspires to completeness (finding all conditions, giving ultimate answers) because it then leads us to metaphysical claims about uncaused causes, absolute substances, and the like. The concept of the unconditioned that we employ in these metaphysical speculations is not abstracted from experience but based on the reliable activity of syllogistic reasoning and hence comes with the best rational credentials. As Kant argues extensively in the Transcendental Aesthetic and Transcendental Analytic of the first *Critique*, however, human cognition is limited to the realm of possible experience, which implies that we can have no cognition of the unconditioned. Hence, the metaphysical theories that grow naturally out of rational thinking and that seem to provide us with metaphysical cognition and knowledge, according to Kant, lead us into fallacies and contradiction.

Kant's claim that there is a natural disposition toward metaphysics can thus be stated more explicitly as follows:

RS-1   Rational reflection on empirical questions necessarily raises *metaphysical questions* about 'the unconditioned.'
RS-2   Rational reflection (by 'pure reason') on these metaphysical questions necessarily leads to *metaphysical answers* that appear to be rationally warranted.
RS-3   The rational principles that lead from empirical to metaphysical questions and from there to metaphysical answers are principles of '*universal human reason*'; that is, they belong to rational thinking as such.

---

[2] Why Kant restricts this claim to things in themselves will concern us later (5.3). We can set this question aside for now.

The central *philosophical* thesis of this book will be that Kant indeed discovered a source of metaphysical thinking that lies in reason itself. Reason, according to Kant, is characterized by three features that, taken together, lead to metaphysical speculation. First, there is the *discursive* character of human thinking. Human reason, according to Kant, is not intuitive but discursive in that its cognitions result from actively and sequentially processing a multitude of elements. (Contrast sensible intuition, which is passive and holistic.) The need to ask questions and to require grounds and explanations is an expression of this kind of discursivity since it involves the distinctions between question and answer, grounded and ground, *explanandum* and *explanans*, and the active transition from the one to the other. Second, reason-giving and rational explanation are *iterative*. If 'Why A?' is a good question and 'Because of B' is a good answer, then 'Why B?' is a good question too – one that needs to be answered if reason is to be satisfied. And third, there is the rational need for *completeness* – for complete explanations and ultimate answers. As rational inquirers, we cannot be wholly satisfied until we arrive at an answer that does not raise further questions (of the same kind). It is the combination of these three features that takes us, in Kant's words, from the conditioned, through the complete series of conditions, to the unconditioned.

The Kantian account of the sources of metaphysical speculation differs from earlier critiques of metaphysics, e.g. those from empiricist philosophers such as Bacon and Hume, in that it traces both the metaphysical urge and the failure of metaphysics not to the contingent shortcomings of individual thinkers or to aspects of human psychology but rather to the very structure of rational thinking itself. If true, this is a deep and important insight. Uncovering this insight will require some work, however, since Kant's main treatment of this issue in the Transcendental Dialectic of the *Critique of Pure Reason* is highly complex and often difficult to follow.

0.3   One Argument, Four Levels

In the Transcendental Dialectic, we can distinguish four levels on which Kant's Rational Sources Account operates. These levels roughly correspond to the four main parts of the Transcendental Dialectic (Introduction, Book One, Book Two, Appendix). I speak of 'levels' and not 'steps' of an argument because Kant's unfolding of the Rational Sources Account is not best read as consisting of a series of consecutive steps, each of which is foundational to, and independent of, the next. Rather, I suggest that we understand these levels as parts of a complex argument that first lays out a general framework and then fills in the details as it proceeds.

On the first, most general level, there is the transition from the 'Logical Maxim,' which requires us to find a condition for each conditioned *cognition*, to the 'supreme principle of pure reason' (or 'Supreme Principle'), according to which if something conditioned is given, then so is the complete series of conditions, where this series itself is unconditioned. On Kant's view, it is this latter principle that drives human reason to metaphysical speculation. Kant motivates the transition from the Logical Maxim to the Supreme Principle in the second part of the Introduction to the Transcendental Dialectic (A305/B362–A309/B366). At the same time, Kant establishes the general framework he then also applies, *mutatis mutandis*, on the following levels, namely, a move from a 'logical use of reason' to its 'real' or 'transcendental' use and (as becomes fully explicit only in the Appendix to the Transcendental Dialectic) from a 'regulative' use of reason's principles and ideas to a 'constitutive' use of them (more on which soon).

On the second level, Kant derives the *system of transcendental ideas*. Transcendental ideas are concepts of objects that, if they do exist, are unconditioned (such as the soul, the world, and God). According to Kant, these ideas arise naturally out of 'necessary inferences of reason' and can be brought into a system that guarantees the completeness of our account of them. This system consists of the concept of the unconditioned (which is the '*common title* of all ideas of reason'), the three *classes* of transcendental ideas (psychological, cosmological, and theological, corresponding to the ideas of soul, world, and God), and nine *modes* (ways in which objects can be thought to be unconditioned): substantiality, simplicity, personality, and spirituality in the case of the soul (A344/B402; B419); the absolute completeness of composition, division, origin, and mutual dependence in the case of the world (A415/B443); and finally the idea of an *ens realissimum* in the case of God (A571/B599–A583/B611). On this second level, Kant only derives the *systematic order* of transcendental ideas, not these ideas themselves.[3]

On the third level, there are the specific 'dialectical' (that is, fallacious) inferences that purport to provide us with a priori knowledge about the soul, the world, and God (the 'paralogisms,' the arguments leading up to the 'antinomies,' and the (one) argument for the existence of God). These inferences, Kant claims, have their source in human reason itself and must therefore appear compelling to anyone unequipped with the results of Kant's *Critique of Pure Reason*. At the same time, these inferences deliver the specific transcendental ideas that fall into the classes and modes derived on the previous level.

Finally, on the fourth level, Kant argues that even though the transcendental principles and ideas derived at the previous level have a legitimate 'regulative' use in guiding empirical scientific research and our search for unity in the

---

[3] This is not how Kant's derivation of the transcendental ideas is usually understood; I will develop my reading in detail in Chapter 6.

diversity of natural phenomena, they are easily mistaken for being constitutive, that is, for being true representations of objects. Taken together, Kant's reflections and arguments on these four levels are meant to show that metaphysical speculation about the unconditioned, in its various forms, arises naturally and inevitably out of the very structure of human reason.

According to Jonathan Bennett, Kant's argument for the Rational Sources Account and the conception of reason on which it relies "is a clumsy attempt to rationalize a set of problems which reflect not the structure of reason but the preoccupations of German academic philosophers at the time when Kant was writing. Where the theory has an effect, it is by tempting Kant into a brutal and insensitive forcing of his material into unnatural shapes and never by genuinely illuminating it" (Bennett 1974: 258). And indeed, if read as consecutive argumentative steps, Kant's way of developing the Rational Sources Account will not look very convincing.[4] Against readers like Bennett, however, I will argue that in fact Kant offers a highly complex argument for the Rational Sources Account that rests on an equally complex account of human reason. Uncovering the Rational Sources Account as a distinctive line of thought in the Transcendental Dialectic will be the central *exegetical* result of this book.

Specifically, each of the four levels outlined earlier involves a transition from 'logical' concepts and principles to 'transcendental' ones (or, as Kant also puts it, from the 'logical use of reason' to its 'real use'), where logical principles abstract from the objects of cognition and consider only formal relations between them, while transcendental principles consider cognitions in relation to their objects. For instance, the Logical Maxim mentioned on the first level of Kant's account requires us to search, for each cognition, for a more general cognition from which it follows. This is a 'logical' project in that it abstracts from the content of our cognitions and considers only their logical entailment relations. Kant therefore attributes it to the 'logical use of reason.' By contrast, the Supreme Principle requires us to look for a condition for each conditioned *object*, thus moving from mere logical conditioning relations among *cognitions* to 'real' conditioning relations among *things*. This is part of what Kant calls the 'real use of reason.'

In this respect, Kant's leading idea is that there is a natural tendency, first, to move from logical principles implicit in universal human reason to the transcendental principles of pure reason, and second, to misunderstand these principles as 'constitutive' (as implying true claims about objects), while their only legitimate use is 'regulative' (that is, directing our search for systematic cognition and knowledge). Concerning the first aspect, a transition from the

---

[4] For instance, it is only on the second level that the general idea of the unconditioned is introduced, even though it is already employed in the formulation of the principles Kant discusses on the first level.

logical to the transcendental can be found on each of the four levels of Kant's argument. It is modeled on the transition from the table of judgments to the categories (the so-called Metaphysical Deduction) in the Transcendental Analytic, thus revealing the deep structural unity of Kant's overall argumentative strategy in the Transcendental Logic.

On its own, however, the transition from the logical to the real or transcendental use of reason only allows us to ask metaphysical *questions* and does not take us all the way to metaphysical speculation. This comes only when we mistake transcendental principles such as the Supreme Principle for 'constitutive' ones, that is, for true descriptions of the objects they refer to, whereas their only legitimate use is 'regulative,' that is, as hypothetical assumptions from which we derive research hypotheses. Put differently, we mistake 'subjective' principles (which are meant to direct our search for knowledge) for 'objective' principles (which truly describe reality). The tendency to make this mistake is what Kant calls 'transcendental illusion.' He explains it by appeal to a tacit assumption that underlies the speculative use of reason in metaphysics, namely, the assumption of 'transcendental realism.' As I will argue, 'transcendental realism' is here best understood as the claim that the structure of reality corresponds to that of rational thought, or, more generally, that the subjective conditions of thinking rationally about objects are conditions of the objects being thought about. Given this assumption, the regulative principles of reason that govern how we rationally *think* about objects must appear to be constitutive principles that characterize how those *objects* really are. I will maintain that Kant had good reason to think that an implicit commitment to transcendental realism is part of the 'nature' of 'universal human reason,' even though we may be more optimistic than Kant was as to whether we can rid ourselves of this implicit assumption.

0.4 Kant's Two Projects in the Transcendental Dialectic

It is an impression shared by many readers of the *Critique of Pure Reason* that this work falls into two major parts: a constructive one, comprising Kant's account of a priori cognition in the Transcendental Aesthetic and Analytic, and a destructive one, consisting in the demolition of traditional metaphysics in the Transcendental Dialectic. But such an impression can persist only if one ignores both the official structure of the book (which groups the Analytic and the Dialectic together as parts of Transcendental Logic) and the existence of the Doctrine of Method (officially the second main part of the book). Moreover, thinking of the Transcendental Dialectic as merely (or even predominantly) destructive obscures its important *constructive* strand, which is Kant's four-level Rational Sources Account. Kant's aim in the Transcendental Dialectic is not just to criticize traditional forms of metaphysics but equally to show that they arise naturally out of indispensable and epistemically unproblematic employments of reason and are thus inscribed into the very structure of rational thinking itself. As Kant claims, it is his plan to "develop" the Transcendental Dialectic (and with it metaphysical speculation) "from its sources hidden deep in human reason" (A309/B366).

Thus, two projects, and two argumentative strands, are entwined in the Transcendental Dialectic: one constructive, the other destructive. Kant himself notes this at the end of the Transcendental Dialectic when he summarizes its results:

> The outcome of all dialectical attempts of pure reason not only confirms what we have already proved in the Transcendental Analytic, namely that all the inferences that would carry us out beyond the field of possible experience are deceptive and groundless, *but it also simultaneously teaches us this particular lesson*: that human reason has a natural propensity to overstep all these boundaries, and that *transcendental ideas are just as natural to it* as the categories are to the understanding, although with this difference, that just as the categories lead to truth ... the ideas effect a mere, but irresistible, illusion, deception by which one can hardly resist even through the most acute criticism. (A642/B670; emphasis added)

The Transcendental Dialectic is thus both a critique of speculative metaphysics *and* an argument for the claim that there is a 'natural propensity' for metaphysical speculation that has its source in reason itself.[5] This latter 'lesson' is central to Kant's overall project for two reasons. First, Kant wants to criticize not just *some* historically prominent forms of metaphysics but *all possible* forms of *metaphysica specialis* (rational psychology, cosmology, and theology); for this, he needs to show that the proofs and inferences he criticizes are all there can possibly be, which presupposes that they are not contingent products of individual historical thinkers but realizations of a necessary rational structure. (I think that Kant's claim to have covered all possible forms of speculative metaphysics is questionable, and I will not try to defend it.)

But second, and more importantly, Kant aims to explain a fundamental feature of human existence – the urge to go, in thought, beyond the realm of empirical objects and to make claims about 'unconditioned' transcendent objects such as God, immortal souls, ultimate parts, and first causes. According to Kant, human beings have always had (and will always have) "a metaphysics of some kind" (*irgendeine Metaphysik*) (B21). They will always ask metaphysical questions, and certain answers to these questions will always appear plausible, or even irresistible, to them. Why is this the case? One central aim of the Transcendental Dialectic is to answer this question and thus to give a constructive, positive account of the metaphysical urge. If Kant is right, there

---

[5] These two sides of the Transcendental Dialectic have been clearly noted, e.g. in Klimmek 2005 and Pissis 2012.

is a sense in which metaphysics is rationally necessary (even though most of its pretensions may be unwarranted).[6]

In the long history of the reception of Kant's *magnum opus*, the first, destructive aspect of the Transcendental Dialectic has received much more attention than the second, constructive one, partly because it is more prominent in the text but also because its results must have struck Kant's early readers as much more challenging and important. From our present perspective, however, Kant's claim that we cannot prove the existence of God and the immortality of the soul appears less provocative than it did in Kant's own time; indeed, it has become part of enlightened common sense that, as Kant argues, one can only believe but not know that God exists. By contrast, Kant's claim that there is a natural tendency, grounded in reason itself, to ask metaphysical questions and a natural illusion that tempts us to believe that we can answer these questions remains provocative and exciting. I think it is time to pay more attention to this 'other side' of the Transcendental Dialectic, which consists in Kant's extended and highly complex argument for the Rational Sources Account. To the best of my knowledge, there has not yet been a book that focuses exclusively on this topic.[7]

This book appears at a time when the anti-metaphysical scruples that dominated Anglo-American philosophy in the second half of the twentieth century have largely subsided. In Kant scholarship, too, the pioneering work of Karl Ameriks (starting with Ameriks 1982) has led to a renewed interest in the

---

[6] Besides these two main projects in the Transcendental Dialectic, there are two further projects that are subordinated to, and dependent on, the main projects. The first is finding a positive use for the illusory concepts and principles that, according to the Rational Sources Account, arise from reason itself, which Kant attempts in the Appendix. The second consists in showing that Kant's critique of metaphysics does not undermine the logical and epistemic *possibility* of the immortality of the soul, freedom of the will, and God's existence, thus "mak[ing] room for *faith*" (Bxxx) and the postulates of pure reason.

[7] Michelle Grier's study on transcendental illusion (Grier 2001) covers some of the same territory but focuses on Kant's critique of metaphysics. Nikolai Klimmek reconstructs the "genesis of natural metaphysics" in the Transcendental Dialectic (Klimmek 2005: 2) but is primarily interested in Kant's system of transcendental ideas. Besides Grier's and Klimmek's books, there are a number of book-length studies and commentaries on the Transcendental Dialectic (e.g. Heimsoeth 1966–71; Bennett 1974; Pissis 2012), none of which discusses the rational sources of metaphysics for their own sake. R. Larnier Anderson's recent book also covers the Transcendental Dialectic but focuses on Kant's critique of rationalist metaphysics (Anderson 2015). Similarly, James Kreines, although he touches on the Rational Sources Account in his chapter on the Transcendental Dialectic, is primarily interested in how Kant argues for the limits of cognition (Kreines 2015: ch. 4). Susan Neiman's book on the unity of reason (Neiman 1994) overlaps with topics of the present work but does not isolate the Rational Sources Account as a single coherent strand in Kant's thinking (but see also Neiman 1995). In addition, there are important books on individual chapters and parts of the Transcendental Dialectic (e.g. Wood 1978; Ameriks 1982/2000; Malzkorn 1999; Rosefeldt 2000; and Falkenburg 2000, to name just a few) as well as studies with a more general focus (e.g. Guyer 1987; Gerhardt 2002; Höffe 2003; Allison 2004; Mohr 2004) that also cover some of the issues discussed in this book. While I have profited from all of these contributions, none of them focuses on Kant's Rational Sources Account in the way the present book does.

metaphysical aspects of Kant's critical thought (and an awareness of the continuities between the pre-critical and the critical Kant). This book fits into this general development in that it emphasizes the centrality of metaphysics to Kant's project of a critique of pure reason. As the final chapter of this book will show, however, I take Kant's critique of speculative metaphysics to be more radical than some proponents of the metaphysical reading of Kant will be happy to acknowledge, and this attitude will sometimes color my formulations in other parts of the book as well. Note, however, that my reconstruction of the Rational Sources Account in the main parts of this book is meant to be strictly neutral with respect to the extent to which speculative metaphysics is, or is not, compatible with Kant's critical philosophy, since its interest is not Kant's critique of metaphysics but his positive account of the sources of metaphysical thinking. I therefore hope that this book will be seen as a welcome addition to the literature by both proponents and critics of metaphysical interpretations of Kant.

0.5 Overview

This book will discuss the interrelations between two central aspects of Kant's philosophy, namely, his accounts of reason and of metaphysics. It will be obvious to anyone acquainted with Kant's work and the vast secondary literature surrounding it that such a project must be given strict limits. For one thing, I concentrate on Kant's views as developed in the *Critique of Pure Reason*, drawing on his other works only in order to clarify what Kant says in his *magnum opus*. This means that I will have to set aside the development of Kant's views over the course of his long philosophical career, including the pre-history of the Rational Sources Account in Kant's pre-critical writings and notes. I will also not be able to discuss the way in which Kant's understanding of reason and metaphysics develops after the B-edition of the first *Critique*. Moreover, even where the Transcendental Dialectic of the first *Critique* is concerned, I can engage with the chapters on the paralogisms, antinomies, and the arguments for God's existence, as well as the Appendix, only somewhat summarily, since a detailed treatment in each case would require a book of its own. Instead, I will concentrate on those aspects that are essential for an understanding of Kant's account of the rational sources of metaphysics.

The book has two main parts. Part I starts with an overview of Kant's accounts of reason and metaphysics and then offers a detailed interpretation of the first level at which Kant describes the slide from universal human reason to metaphysical speculation, namely, the transition from the Logical Maxim, which requires us to look for unconditioned cognitions, to the Supreme Principle, according to which if some conditioned object exists, there also exists something unconditioned. Chapter 1 offers a brief introduction to Kant's conceptions of reason and of metaphysics. Chapter 2 discusses the logical use of reason, which is guided by the Logical Maxim and aims to transform our manifold cognitions about nature (both empirical and a priori) into a complete system of scientific knowledge and thus to achieve the 'unity of reason.' Chapter 3 turns to the Supreme Principle and the 'real' or 'transcendental' use of reason, which consists in tracking conditioning relations between objects (such as part–whole and substance–attribute relations) akin to what we today call 'metaphysical grounding' (see e.g. Correa and Schnieder 2012). I explain in detail what Kant, in the Supreme Principle, means by 'conditioned,' 'condition,' and the 'unconditioned' and argue that the relevant conditioning relations fall into three classes (corresponding to the three relational categories) without being species of a common genus. The main results of these chapters will be that three essential features of human reason (discursivity, iteration, and completeness) take us from ordinary employments of reason to a metaphysical search for the unconditioned.

Chapter 4 will then discuss the suggestive but cryptic passage (from the Introduction to the Transcendental Dialectic) in which Kant claims that the Logical Maxim 'cannot become' a principle of pure reason unless we 'assume' the Supreme Principle. Based on a close reading of the Appendix to the Transcendental Dialectic, I will argue that what is at issue here is a transition in two steps: first from the Logical Maxim to the regulatively used Supreme Principle, which is metaphysically harmless, and then from the latter to the constitutively used Supreme Principle, which carries with it a commitment to the existence of something unconditioned.

Finally, in Chapter 5, I explain why Kant thinks that both steps of this transition appear to be rationally necessary, even though only the first one really is. The first step *is* rationally necessary because we must go beyond the merely logical use of reason in order to approximate the 'unity of reason' (a complete system of scientific knowledge). The second step *appears* to be necessary because we tacitly assume that the structure of reality must correspond to the principles of reason. This assumption is what Kant calls 'transcendental realism,' and I explain how it follows from Kant's official definition of transcendental realism as the identification of appearances with things in themselves. Given transcendental realism, every regulative principle or concept of reason will appear to be constitutive of nature itself. This appearance is what Kant calls 'transcendental illusion.' Since we are rationally required to use the Supreme Principle regulatively (that is, as a heuristic hypothesis), given transcendental realism it seems to follow that it must necessarily be the case that, if there is something conditioned, there really *is* something unconditioned. As I will argue, Kant was right to assume that transcendental realism is a tacit background assumption that can plausibly be attributed to 'universal human reason.' In this way, Chapters 2–5 reconstruct the first, most basic level of Kant's Rational Sources Account.

At the same time, the transition from the Logical Maxim to the constitutive Supreme Principle provides a general template that is also at work on the other levels of Kant's argument: in moving from *logical* concepts and principles (which concern our cognitions) to real or *transcendental* ones (which concern objects), *transcendental realism* creates the illusion that the constitutive use of the latter is legitimate, since it conceals the difference between a legitimate *regulative* and an illegitimate *constitutive* use of concepts and principles of reason.

In Part II of the book, we will turn to the other three levels of Kant's Rational Sources Account to see how Kant applies this general template throughout the main text of the Transcendental Dialectic. In Chapter 6, we will discuss the second level, Kant's 'system of transcendental ideas' and the place of the 'metaphysical deduction' (subjective derivation) of those ideas. I will argue that the transcendental ideas are not derived from the forms of rational inferences (or the three possible relations a representation can have to its subject and object), as Kant seems to suggest. Rather, the transcendental ideas, which Kant calls 'inferred concepts,' are the result of 'necessary inferences of reason' – namely, the paralogisms, the cosmological arguments that lead up to the antinomies, and the one 'natural' argument for the existence of God that Kant discusses in Section Three of the Transcendental Ideal.

In Chapters 7 and 8, we turn to the third level of Kant's argument, which concerns the 'dialectical' (that is, illusory) inferences of reason and the derivation of the transcendental ideas. In Chapter 7, we discuss the paralogisms and the antinomies and how they allow us to derive specific transcendental ideas. I will argue that Kant provides us with a plausible account of why we tend to think of our souls as simple, persistent, and immaterial substances, and why contradictory claims about the world as a whole (e.g. that it is finite and that it is infinite; that it contains and does not contain simple parts and first causes) appear to be equally justified by rational arguments. As we will see, a reading of the paralogisms and antinomies from the perspective of Kant's Rational Sources Account reveals structural features of Kant's presentation that go unnoticed when the focus, as usual, is on Kant's critique of rational psychology and rational cosmology.

In Chapter 8, we then turn to rational theology and the derivation of the 'transcendental ideal' (the concept of the *ens realissimum*, or most real being) in Section Two of the Ideal of Reason chapter, which is widely considered to be obscure. However, if we read that section as part of Kant's Rational Sources Account (and as following the general pattern of a logical/transcendental transition plus a confounding of the regulative and constitutive uses of principles), many interpretative problems disappear. Concerning Kant's discussion of the three types of arguments for God's existence (ontological, cosmological, physicotheological) in Section Four of the Ideal, I will show that none of them features in Kant's argument for the Rational Sources Account. Instead, the 'natural' argument for God's existence is provided in Section Three of the Ideal of Reason. I will show that Kant makes a plausible case for the claim that the concept of an *ens realissimum* has its source in human reason and that a natural illusion can make us think that such a being must necessarily exist. Also in Chapter 8, we will address the fourth level of Kant's argument, discussed in the Appendix to the Transcendental Dialectic, and see why we tend to mistake regulative principles and ideas (which, according to Kant, are indispensable as heuristic devices in the scientific investigation of nature) for constitutive ones that appear to provide us with metaphysical insight into nature itself. The reason for this 'transcendental illusion,' as in all the other cases, is transcendental realism, which, however, can take a variety of forms.

Finally, in Chapter 9 we will round out our understanding of Kant's Rational Sources Account by asking how it relates to Kant's *critique* of speculative metaphysics. First, I will show that the different forms of transcendental realism appealed to in Kant's account are unified by a common core, which is the idea that reality must conform to the ways in which we necessarily represent it. Next, I argue that Kant's critique of speculative metaphysics is independent of any commitment to his own transcendental idealism. Rather, Kant's critique of the fallacies of rational psychology, cosmology, and theology in the Transcendental Dialectic requires only the rejection of transcendental realism, not the acceptance of transcendental idealism. Moreover, Kant's more general critique of *any* attempt to gain cognition of the unconditioned, or the supersensible, does not presuppose his transcendental idealism either and is instead based primarily on his claim that human cognition is limited to empirical objects. I also argue for a radical reading of Kant's account of transcendental ideas according to which they are cognitively defective ('without sense and significance') as long as we consider them only as part of metaphysical speculation and in abstraction from moral considerations. All in all, Kant mounts a compelling critique of the very kind of speculative metaphysics that his Rational Sources Account shows to be grounded in reason itself.

Each of the two parts of the book is followed by a Conclusion that contains an extensive summary of its main results and highlights the considerable plausibility, even from a present perspective, of Kant's account of the rational sources of metaphysics. The book closes with a brief Postscript on what I call Kant's 'practical metaphysics.' In the *Critique of Practical Reason* and elsewhere, Kant introduces three 'postulates of pure practical reason,' which concern God's existence, freedom of the will, and the immortality of the soul. I briefly discuss whether reason eventually finds in a practical mode what it had been looking for in a speculative mode, namely, the unconditioned. (The answer is: almost, but not quite.)

Part I

From Reason to Metaphysics

Introduction to Part I

According to Kant, engaging in metaphysics is rationally necessary in the following sense: if people reflect on specific features of empirical reality, they will be confronted with questions that, if rationally followed through, will take them to questions about their souls, the world at large, and the existence of God.[1] These questions, if they can be answered at all, cannot be answered empirically, but only a priori, by reason alone. Kant thus maintains that rational thinking, because of its very structure, has a tendency to result in metaphysical questions and purported a priori answers to them. This is what Kant means when he says that there is a 'natural predisposition' or 'natural propensity' to engage in metaphysics (Kant's Rational Sources Account; see Introduction). However, that account does not apply to *every* philosophically respectable use of the terms 'reason' (or 'rational') and 'metaphysics.'[2] Rather, the Rational Sources Account is based on Kant's specific understanding of 'reason' and 'metaphysics.' Before we can try to understand Kant's extended and complex argument for the Rational Sources Account, it will therefore be necessary to look at his conceptions of reason and metaphysics (Chapter 1).

In the chapters that follow, we will look very closely at a passage from the Introduction to the Transcendental Dialectic, which I will call the 'Transition Passage' (A307–8/B364). There, Kant distinguishes between the specific principle of the 'logical use of reason' (the Logical Maxim) and the 'supreme principle of pure reason,' according to which, if something conditioned is given, something unconditioned is also given (the Supreme Principle). Kant claims that the Logical Maxim 'cannot become a principle of pure reason'

---

[1] See A584/B612, where Kant says with respect to the idea of God: "This is the natural course taken by every human reason, even the most common, although not everyone perseveres in it," which implies that every rational human being *would* arrive at the same idea (here the idea of God) if they were to "persevere," that is, to think things through to the end.

[2] I will follow Kant (e.g. A835–6/B863–4) in treating 'rational' as one of the adjectives corresponding to 'reason' (the other, in German, being *'vernünftig'*).

unless we assume the Supreme Principle. We will look at the Logical Maxim in Chapter 2 and the Supreme Principle in Chapter 3 and will then interpret the Transition Passage as a whole in Chapter 4. Finally, we will philosophically reconstruct the transition from reason to metaphysics (i.e. from the logical principles of reason to the constitutive use of its transcendental principles) in Chapter 5.

1 Kant's Conceptions of Reason and Metaphysics

In this chapter, I will offer a first and preliminary outline of Kant's accounts of reason and metaphysics and introduce various themes that will be developed further in later chapters.[1]

1.1 Kant's Conception of Reason

Reason, for Kant, is primarily a mental capacity, or 'faculty of the soul' (*Seelenvermögen*) (5:177) – that is, an ability of thinking beings to be in mental states of different kinds.[2] More specifically, reason is a *cognitive* faculty (*Erkenntnisvermögen*) that allows one to have 'objective representations': mental states aimed either at truly representing things or at actively bringing things about (in the widest possible sense of 'things'). Human beings have various cognitive capacities, distinguished by the kinds of representations to which they give rise (or, more generally, by the cognitive functions they perform): sensibility, understanding, imagination, power of judgment, reason (and more). Kant has different ways of classifying these capacities depending on which of their features he is interested in.[3] With respect to reason, Kant employs two such classifications: on the one hand, cognitive capacities can be classified as resulting either in a priori or in empirical cognition (e.g. A835–6/B863–4); on the other hand, they can be distinguished according to whether they represent things intuitively (in human beings this is the case with sensible

---

[1] Note that my aim in this chapter is not to present an original interpretation, but merely to lay the ground for what follows.

[2] Even though Kant sometimes uses the terms '*Fähigkeit*' (capacity), '*Vermögen*' (faculty) and '*Kraft*' (power) interchangeably, in other places he draws subtle but important distinctions between them. For instance, while 'faculty' (*Vermögen*) involves an activity of the subject, 'capacity' does not (Heßbrüggen-Walter 2004). I will return to the specific connotations of the term '*Vermögen*' in Kant in Section 1.1.2.

[3] In the Introduction to the *Critique of the Power of Judgment*, Kant distinguishes three basic mental faculties: the faculty of cognition, the faculty of desire, and the feeling of pleasure and displeasure (5:177). While Kant sometimes treats *practical* reason as part of the faculty of desire (*Begehrungsvermögen*) (5:24), at other times he regards it as a *cognitive* faculty (*Erkenntnisvermögen*) (5:174), namely the faculty of *practical* cognition (cognition of what one ought to do).

representations) or discursively (in intellectual representations or concepts) (e.g. A68/B93). (As a first approximation, we can say that intuitive representations represent particulars, while discursive representations represent general features of things; 9:91; 8:399.)

Now *reason*, in the sense most relevant to Kant's account of metaphysics, is a capacity of *a priori discursive* cognition. It shares this characterization with the pure understanding (the capacity for a priori conceptual thought and judgment), from which it is distinguished by its characteristic type of activity (and its corresponding type of representation), namely the drawing of mediate (indirect) *inferences*.[4]

1.1.1 Reason as the Capacity for Mediate Inference

Reason, in this sense, is the capacity to logically derive particular cognitions from more general ones by means of intermediary cognitions, as in the inference: 'All humans are mortal; all philosophers are human; thus, all philosophers are mortal.' This inference is based on the schema 'All A are B; all C are A; thus, all C are B,' the validity of which can be grasped a priori. At the same time, all its constituent representations (A, B, C) are concepts and as such are general, not singular. Thus *reason*, in the most fundamental sense, is the capacity for *a priori discursive cognition by means of mediate inference*. It can hardly be denied that human beings possess such a capacity, even though, of course, we are fallible in its employment.

While Kant defines reason in terms of aprioricity, discursivity, and mediate inference (e.g. A298–301/B355–8), this conception of reason must be distinguished from two wider conceptions that Kant also employs without always clearly marking the difference. First, Kant sometimes uses the terms 'reason' (*Vernunft*) and 'understanding' (*Verstand*) interchangeably for the capacity of discursive cognition in general.[5] Second, Kant sometimes defines reason as the capacity for *a priori* cognition (A11/B24) or as the 'entire higher faculty of cognition' (A835/B863) – a characterization that includes not just a priori

---

[4] Guyer and Wood translate '*Vernunftschluss*' as 'syllogism.' Since '*Vernunftschluss*' also includes hypothetical and disjunctive inferences (9:121–2), which are not syllogisms narrowly conceived (as instances of the four syllogistic figures, see Bennett 1974: 259), and in order to emphasize the essential role of reason, I will use 'rational inference' and, depending on the context, 'inference of reason' as translations of Kant's term '*Vernunftschluss*.'

[5] Compare, for instance, Kant's distinction between "the two stems" of human cognition, sensibility and understanding (A15/B29), with his claim that one of these "two stems" is "reason" (A835/B863). Already in his pre-critical writings, Kant distinguishes between reason and understanding without regarding them as distinct cognitive faculties. In *False Subtlety*, he claims that "*understanding* and *reason*, that is to say, the faculty of cognizing distinctly and the faculty of drawing rational inferences, are not different *fundamental faculties*. Both consist in the capacity to judge; but when one judges mediately, one draws an inference" (2:59).

cognitions of the 'pure' understanding (such as the principle that every alteration has a cause), but even those of mathematics (which, according to Kant, are not discursive but intuitive). Thus, Kant sometimes understands reason solely in terms of discursivity, at other times solely in terms of aprioricity.[6] What is at stake in Kant's Rational Sources Account, however, is the narrower conception of reason in terms of discursivity *and* aprioricity (*and* mediate inference).

As we will see later, Kant goes on to enrich this characterization of reason by showing that each of its three features includes further characteristics: discursivity means that any cognition based on reason can relate to its object only indirectly (A320/B377); aprioricity, for Kant, implies necessity and universality (B3); and the logical use of reason in rational inferences gives rise to a priori concepts of 'totalities,' that is, of all the objects of a certain domain (A321/B378). Moreover, the structure of rational inferences is iterative: the conclusion of one inference can be made the premise of another, and so on (A307/B364). By making use of this feature, reason, according to Kant, aims at placing *all* our cognitions in *one* inferential network, thus transforming them into a unified system the structure of which can be determined a priori (A302/B359; A832/B860). But before we turn to this fuller conception of reason (which is already part of Kant's Rational Sources Account), we have to consider what is, and what is not, involved in thinking of reason as a *faculty*.

1.1.2 Reason as a Faculty (Vermögen) and Reason as a System of Principles

Kant's wording can sometimes suggest that he thinks of reason, the understanding, and other 'faculties' as so many agents, each pursuing its own aims and acting in specific ways to realize them. For instance, the understanding is said to use concepts to form judgments (A68/B93); the imagination is said to synthesize a manifold of sensible representations (A78/B103). Similarly, reason is said to aim at bringing systematic unity to the manifold of empirical cognitions (A302/B359). There is something misleading about this way of speaking, but it also contains an important insight. What is misleading is that it can suggest that the cognitive faculties really *are* individual agents – homunculi that are active (in contrast to the human beings whose capacities they are). But of course this is not what Kant means, and nothing in what he says commits him to such a picture. Rather, 'faculties' (*Vermögen*) are always the faculties of a thing or a substance – in this case, the cognitive faculties of

---

[6] On the difference between these conceptions of reason, see Willaschek 2013.

human beings.[7] Thus when Kant says, for instance, that reason tries to bring the greatest manifold of empirical cognitions to the smallest number of principles (A305/B361), he does not want to deny that it is human beings, in virtue of having reason, who 'bring cognitions to principles.' Speaking of faculties as if they were agents can primarily be understood as a literary device meant to facilitate exposition.[8]

But economy of expression is not the only reason that leads Kant to speak of faculties as if they were agents. Another reason, which embodies the insight connected with the faculty idiom, is that this allows him to describe cognitive activity in normative and teleological terms. Rational human beings do not just *happen* to bring cognitions to principles; rather, this is what they *ought* to do. In thinking of cognitive performances as employments of cognitive faculties, Kant attributes a teleological structure to them that combines descriptive and normative elements. The descriptive element is highly complex, consisting in a variety of more specific cognitive dispositions to think in ways that can be characterized as rational. For instance, rational beings tend to draw inferences based on *modus ponens*, *modus tollens*, etc. The normative element is complex too, involving, on the one hand, standards for the correct employment of reason, such as inference rules. (While it is *correct* to infer 'B' from 'If A, then B' and 'A,' it is *incorrect* to infer 'A' from 'If A, then B' and 'B.') On the other hand, according to Kant, reason brings with it its own ends (e.g. A839/B867), needs (e.g. A309/B365), and interests (e.g. A462/B490–A476/B504). Thus, reason *aims* at systematic unity (we will soon turn to why this is the case) and takes an 'interest' in the truth of certain theses. While it may be unclear whether Kant wants to commit himself to an Aristotelian picture of faculties as *dynameis* that are teleologically geared toward their own realization (*energeia*), it is important to understand that in attributing reason to a human being, according to Kant, we not only attribute certain dispositions of thought to her but also hold her to certain standards, attributing specific ends and interests to her – or, more correctly, we normatively *require* her to have them.[9]

Of course, this is a requirement of a rather weak and conditional kind. Thus, Kant does not hold that *every* rational being is *always* required to follow *all* rational principles and pursue *all* of reason's ends. There are ends and principles of reason that are obligatory for everyone and anytime, namely moral ones. But when it comes to non-moral ends, specifically to theoretical ends

---

[7] See Heßbrüggen-Walter 2015. On the metaphysical implications of Kant's account of cognitive faculties, see Heidemann 2017.
[8] For a recent defense of the use of this expository device in psychology, see Kahneman 2011.
[9] For 'Aristotelian' readings of Kant's account of the cognitive faculties, see Kern 2006; Engstrom 2009. On the 'conative' character of reason, see Kleingeld 1998a. For a reading of Kant's conception of reason that emphasizes its teleological features, see Ferrarin 2015.

(such as bringing one's cognitions under ever higher principles), this is obviously something one is only required to do under certain conditions.[10] *If* one reflects on one's empirical knowledge, and *if* one is free to follow through with one's reflection (to 'persevere' with it, as Kant puts it at A584/B612), *then* as a rational being one ought to care about the inbuilt *telos* of this kind of rational reflection. Of course, the plausibility of this claim will depend on the ends attributed to reason. Avoiding inconsistencies and contradictions may not be among the most important things in the world, but in not caring about them at all a rational being may justly be said to make a mistake that he or she *ought to* avoid.[11] Whether this also holds for the systematic unity of cognition and other ends that Kant attributes to reason is a question to which we will return (Chapters 2 and 5). In any case, Kant is committed to such a normative (and teleological) conception of reason, and for him it is part and parcel of thinking of reason not just as a disposition but as a faculty.

A consequence of this normative conception of reason is that reason is not *just* a psychological capacity but can also be viewed as a *body of cognitions and principles*. Kant speaks of reason 'considered subjectively as a human faculty of cognition' (A297/B353), thereby implying that reason can also be considered 'objectively,' that is, with respect to the principles and cognitions it contains – as rules that implicitly guide our thinking and as conclusions we can arrive at solely on the basis of a priori reasoning. No matter what rules of thinking and reasoning a rational being in fact follows, there are those it *ought* to follow. And no matter which conclusion it in fact arrives at, there are (so Kant claims) those it *ought* to arrive at (*if* it follows certain rational trains of thought to their end). Moreover, no matter what ends a rational being in fact pursues, there are those, qua rational, that it *ought* to pursue. Thus, considered objectively, reason is a system of a priori principles and cognitions, as well as ends, needs, and interests (which, when restricted to *pure* reason, Kant calls the "system of pure reason"; A841/B869). Reason in this sense is not distinct from reason as a faculty but rather a different perspective on the same mental faculty: while reason can be considered 'subjectively' as a capacity to think in accordance with certain principles in order to pursue certain ends and thereby to arrive at certain conclusions, it can also be considered 'objectively,' with respect to the principles and ends that guide our use of that capacity and the conclusions to which its employment leads.

---

[10] Kant repeatedly contrasts the conditional character of speculative ends with the unconditional character of moral ends (e.g. 5:5; 5:142; 8:139; 9:87).

[11] But see Kolodny 2005, who argues that there is no normative requirement to care about consistency. It seems that if there is such a requirement, it must derive from an interest in truth, since inconsistency among theoretical attitudes tells us that at least one of them must be false. Kant takes consistency to be constitutive of reason (5:120).

1.1.3 Speculative and Practical Reason, Pure Reason, and Universal Human Reason

Within his conception of reason as a faculty of a priori discursive cognition based on rational inferences, Kant draws two important distinctions: between *theoretical* (and more specifically, *speculative*) and *practical* reason on the one hand, and between reason *in general* and *pure* reason on the other.

Unsurprisingly, while theoretical reason is concerned with theoretical questions (questions about 'what is' the case; 9:86), practical reason is concerned with practical questions (about 'what ought to be'; ibid.). Theoretical reason uses rational inferences to derive theoretical conclusions from theoretical principles, while practical reason derives practical propositions (and 'actions'; 4:412) from practical principles (typically in conjunction with theoretical premises). Instead of 'theoretical reason,' Kant sometimes speaks of 'speculative reason.' Although he does not always seem to distinguish between the two, he uses the term 'speculation' mainly for a specific application of theoretical reason, namely that which results in cognitions that are 'abstract' (not 'concrete') (4:369; 9:27), lack practical applications (9:86), and go beyond the limits of possible experience (A634–5/B662–3).[12] Speculative reason in this sense contrasts with "universal human reason" (B22) or "common human reason" (Aviii; B424)[13] (*allgemeine* or *gemeine Menschenvernunft*), which needs concrete "images" (9:27), is interested in practical consequences, and generally stays within the limits of experience. While all human beings make use of reason, only philosophers (both professional and amateur) engage *speculative* reason. As Kant emphasizes (e.g. Avii; 9:27), however, common human reason and speculative reason are continuous insofar as some of the questions ordinary people ask themselves when thinking about concrete empirical issues of practical relevance (e.g. about what caused the fire that burned down a house) can lead quite naturally to speculative questions (e.g. whether there are uncaused causes). Indeed, this continuity is an essential aspect of the Rational Sources Account, which, as we have seen, is the claim that metaphysical questions "arise from the nature of universal human reason" (B22), which means that they are not the arbitrary inventions of philosophers but rather grow naturally out of ordinary ways of thinking.

The other important distinction Kant draws within the conception of reason is the one between reason in general and *pure* reason in particular. As we have seen, reason itself is the capacity of a priori cognition, which implies that its

---

[12] On these three ways of distinguishing between 'theoretical' and 'speculative,' see Lau 2015.
[13] Guyer and Wood translate "*gemeine Menschenvernunft*" in the A-Preface (Aviii) as "ordinary common sense," thereby obscuring the fact that Kant means the same 'human reason' that is the topic of the first paragraphs of the A-Preface (and of the book as a whole).

own guiding principles are a priori too. Nevertheless, people mostly apply their reason to *empirical* questions, for instance by deriving empirical conclusions from empirical premises. *Pure* reason, by contrast, is concerned exclusively with deriving *a priori* cognitions from *a priori* principles. This general distinction can be spelled out in different ways, however. Thus, in the Introduction to the *Critique of Pure Reason*, Kant first defines reason as "the faculty that provides the principles of cognition a priori" and then adds: "Hence pure reason is that which contains the principles for cognizing something absolutely a priori" (A11/B25). Here, Kant uses the term 'reason' in a wide sense which also encompasses pure intuition and the pure understanding, since both provide us with principles of cognition a priori. But if that is what reason is, what does Kant mean by "*pure* reason"? It seems plausible that he intends his distinction between reason in general and pure reason to parallel the distinction, a little earlier in the text, between a priori cognitions and *purely* a priori cognitions (B3).[14] While a priori cognitions are judgments whose 'objective validity' we can come to recognize a priori, independently of experience, cognitions that are *purely* a priori are those whose constitutive representations are also a priori (that is, not derived from experience). Kant's example is the judgment "Every alteration has its cause" (B3), which we can cognize a priori but which is not *purely* a priori because the concept of alteration is empirical.[15] This would mean that pure reason is the faculty of *purely* a priori cognition – of cognition that is independent of experience in terms of how we acquire its constituent (sub-judgmental) representations and how we can come to recognize their 'objective validity.' Pure reason in this sense is distinguished from reason in general by its more limited scope (*purely* a priori cognitions instead of a priori cognitions in general).

Compare this with the way Kant distinguishes between reason in general and pure reason in the Introduction to the Transcendental Dialectic, in a section entitled "On the Pure Use of Reason":

Can we isolate reason, and is it then a genuine source of concepts and judgements that arise solely from it and thereby refer it to objects ...? In a word, the question is: Does reason in itself, i.e. *pure reason*, contain *a priori* synthetic principles and rules, and in what might such principles consist? (A305–6/B362–3; emphasis added)

As Kant explains, these principles would have to differ from the a priori principles of the understanding in being not only "cognition from concepts" – that is, discursive – but rather cognition "from *mere* concepts" (A307/B364,

---

[14] Parts of this and the next paragraph are adapted from Willaschek 2013; see there for a more detailed interpretation of Kant's two accounts of 'pure reason.'
[15] Unfortunately, Kant says a little later (B5) that this judgment is purely a priori, but we can ignore this here.

emphasis added; see also A301/B357; A302/B258) – that is, independent even of the a priori forms of intuition (space and time). It is in this independence not only from experience but from anything belonging to sensibility and intuition that the purity of reason consists. So while pure reason, according to the Introduction to the *Critique of Pure Reason*, is the faculty of purely a priori cognition, the Introduction to the Transcendental Dialectic defines it even more narrowly as the faculty of a purely *discursive* (i.e. conceptual) a priori cognition. As we will see, it is this narrower conception of pure reason that is most relevant to the Rational Sources Account.[16]

Let me close this section with a remark on Kant's 'multiple' conceptions of reason. Even though Kant often speaks of 'speculative,' 'practical,' 'pure' *reason*, thereby suggesting that these are distinct faculties (or perhaps sub-faculties), Kant just as often speaks of 'speculative,' 'practical,' etc. *uses* of reason, and it seems that he took this to be the philosophically more adequate way of speaking (of which the other formulation is a mere abbreviation). Thus when Kant defines pure reason in the Introduction to the Transcendental Dialectic, the section title reads 'On the Pure Use of Reason' (A305/B362), and he says in the *Critique of Practical Reason* that pure reason, in turn, can be regarded "in its speculative or practical use" (5:107).[17] This shows that Kant thinks of pure, speculative, and practical reason not as distinct cognitive faculties, but rather as different employments of the same faculty, namely the faculty of arriving at cognitions through rational inferences. As Kant emphasizes in the *Critique of Practical Reason*, "it is still only one and the same reason which, whether from a theoretical or a practical perspective, judges according to a priori principles" (5:121).[18] So the overall picture is that human beings have a capacity for logical reasoning that can be applied to different subject matters (including questions about what to do and how to act). Possession of this capacity brings with it certain normative commitments (concerning consistency, systematicity, etc.). Moreover, in its 'pure' aspect it

---

[16] Both ways of distinguishing between reason in general and pure reason offered by Kant in the first *Critique* (1781) seem to be meant to apply only to theoretical or speculative reason, not to practical reason. This should not surprise us since Kant first mentions *pure practical* reason in the *Groundwork* (1785) and fully develops his account of pure practical reason only in the second *Critique* (1788). I discuss Kant's conception of practical reason and his distinction between pure practical reason and empirically conditioned practical reason in Willaschek 1992 and Willaschek 2006.

[17] Thus, 'pure practical reason' is short for 'the pure and practical use of reason.'

[18] It is an open question how pure practical reason and speculative reason, according to Kant, *can* be employments of the same faculty, given that they seem to work in accordance with very different principles and to have different ends. On the problem of the so-called unity of reason, see e.g. Kleingeld 1998b; Timmermann 2009. Note that this 'unity of reason' (*Einheit der Vernunft*) (the unity among the different employments of reason) is different from the 'unity of reason' (*Vernunfteinheit*) that reason is supposed to bring into the manifold of our cognitions (A309/B365).

can be used to derive a priori conclusions from a priori principles, which raises the question whether these principles and conclusions, their lack of sensible content notwithstanding, can be regarded as a priori *cognitions* (assuming, with Kant, that cognitions must relate to objects and that only sensible content bears a direct relation to objects; see Section 9.3).

1.1.4 Two Aspects of Reason: A Historical Digression

Kant's conception of reason is part of a long and highly complex tradition. Before we proceed to Kant's distinction between the logical and the real use of reason, it may be helpful to take a cursory glance at its historical background.

What has traditionally been called reason, or rational thought, comprises two clearly distinguishable aspects whose relation has long been a matter of controversy (Horn and Rapp 2001). On the one hand, there is the intuitive grasp of abstract or general truths (truths that cannot be apprehended by the senses); on the other, there is discursive reasoning (the logical progression from premises to conclusions). Thus, Plato distinguishes between *noêsis* (rational insight into the ideas) and *dianoia* (discursive reasoning), which he seems to have understood as applications of the same faculty, namely the faculty of reason or *logos* (e.g. *Politeia* 511b–e). Building on Plato's distinction, Aristotle distinguishes between a capacity for rational insight into first principles, which he calls *nous*, and a capacity for deductive knowledge (*epistêmê*), which he at least sometimes seems to subsume under *logos* (e.g. *Nicomachean Ethics* 1143a36–1143b1).[19] Later philosophers, writing in Latin, translated *noêsis* as 'intellectus' and *dianoia* as 'ratio,' although terminology in this field is varied and inconsistent (Horn and Rapp 2001). Many early modern authors, particularly of the rationalist tradition, distinguish between insight into principles and logical reasoning as two distinct mental *activities*, attributing these activities not to two different *faculties* but rather to one faculty for which the terms 'intellectus,' 'ratio,' and 'ingenium' are often used interchangeably (Horn and Rapp 2001). As Descartes puts it, there are only two ways of gaining knowledge and certainty through the intellect (*intellectus*), namely intuition (*intuitus*) and deduction (*deductio*) (*Regulae*, Rule 3, §4).

In Germany, starting with the German works of Meister Eckhart, the terms '*Verstand*' and '*Vernunft*' were used to translate '*intellectus*' and '*ratio*,' with some authors translating '*intellectus*' as '*Vernunft*' and '*ratio*' as '*Verstand*,' and others adopting the converse convention (Horn and Rapp 2001). Christian Wolff, for instance, follows Leibniz in defining '*Vernunft*' (reason) as "the faculty of seeing into the connection of truths" (*Deutsche Metaphysik*, §368;

---

[19] While the assumption that *noêsis* is intuitive has been disputed (e.g. Horn and Rapp 2005), it clearly represents the traditional and historically most influential reading.

Watkins 2009: 30), whereas '*Verstand*' (understanding) is more generally defined as "the faculty of distinctly cognizing what is possible" (*Deutsche Metaphysik*, §277; Watkins 2009: 24). For Wolff, as for his critic Crusius (*Entwurf*, §441; Watkins 2009: 176), reason and understanding are not two distinct faculties; rather, reason is a special application of the more general and encompassing faculty of understanding.

Setting the historical and terminological complications aside, we can detect a fairly consistent distinction between two aspects of a priori reasoning. On the one hand, there is (what from a present-day perspective can be characterized as) the capacity for the truth-preserving progression from a given set of propositions to other propositions not included in that set. This capacity is concerned not with the truth of single propositions, but rather with the necessary *relations* between the truth of one or more propositions and the truth of others. In this sense, the knowledge conveyed by this kind of logical reasoning is always *conditional*: given the truth of some propositions, the truth of other propositions follows. On the other hand, there is the capacity to grasp the truth of a principle intuitively. This kind of rational insight is not conditional in the same way logical reasoning is. Rather, it is directed at one proposition at a time. It is the capacity to know whether a proposition is true simply by understanding it, by grasping its content. Descartes, like other philosophers before him, compares this way of coming to know the truth of a proposition to vision (the '*natural light*,' see e.g. the Third Meditation). Like seeing with one's eyes, this purely mental, non-sensible seeing is not discursive (step-by-step, mediated through other cognitions, made up of elements that are available prior to it) but intuitive (instantaneous, immediate, holistic). And it does to the mind of the philosopher just what ordinary seeing (which they say 'is believing') does to the mind of the ordinary person: it commands assent. The paradigm of this kind of rational insight is grasping the truth of mathematical axioms.

We find this distinction at work in a text Kant must have known by heart, namely Meier's *Auszug aus der Vernunftlehre* (Extract from the Doctrine of Reason), on which Kant based his lectures on logic from 1757 until his retirement from teaching almost forty years later in 1796. In §116, Meier defines reason (*Vernunft*) as the "faculty of distinct insight into the nexus of things."[20] Later, in §318, he writes:

In a demonstration from reason all grounds the proof is based on[21] must be completely certain (§§193, 204); hence they are either demonstrable or indemonstrable (§313). In

---

[20] "[E]in Vermögen ..., den Zusammenhang der Dinge deutlich einzusehen" (§116, 16:30); translations are my own.
[21] "[A]lle Beweisthümer," which according to *Grimmsches Wörterbuch* is synonymous with 'Beweisgrund' (on which term see Chignell 2009).

the first case, they in turn must be proven. Consequently, a proof will not become a demonstration [from reason] until I arrive at indemonstrable grounds only. Empty [i.e. tautological] judgments, the fundamental judgments [i.e. axioms] and the postulates, are therefore the first starting points of all demonstrations from reason (§§314; 315). When the proof has been pursued up to judgments of this kind, the understanding finds complete rest.[22]

Thus, Meier distinguishes between derived and underived truths, that is, between truths we recognize on the basis of discursive reasoning and those we grasp immediately. He insists that 'demonstrations from reason' must ultimately rest on the latter. Underived, indemonstrable judgments are such that "their truth becomes clear from themselves, as soon as we have cognized them distinctly" (§313). And while 'reason' is the faculty of logical inference that provides the proofs, it is the 'understanding' that finds rest in indemonstrable judgments.

There are three things I would like to take from this brief historical digression. First, there is a long tradition of distinguishing between two different aspects of reason, namely rational insight into principles and logical reasoning. What both have in common, minimally, is that they are (real or merely purported) sources of non-empirical knowledge. Second, it is controversial whether these two sources of knowledge are fundamentally of the same type, and are thus applications of the same cognitive faculty, or whether they are fundamentally distinct, in that rational insight is intuitive whereas logical reasoning is discursive. Third, while German philosophers of the eighteenth century such as Wolff and Baumgarten use '*Vernunft*' as a name for the faculty of logical reasoning or of cognizing the 'concatenation' of truths, they think of it as an expression of the fundamental faculty of understanding, which also provides rational insight into general truths.

1.1.5 The Logical and the Real Use of Reason

It is only after some 300 pages that Kant, in a book that is, after all, entitled *Critique of Pure Reason*, explains in some detail what he means by 'reason.' And Kant admits: "Since I am now to give a definition of this supreme faculty of cognition [i.e. of reason], I find myself in some embarrassment" (A299/B355).

---

[22] "In einer Demonstration aus der Vernunft müssen, alle Beweisthümer, völlig gewiss sein §. 193. 204; sie sind also entweder erweislich oder nicht §. 313. In dem ersten Falle müssen sie wieder bewiesen werden. Folglich wird ein Beweis nicht eher eine Demonstration, bis ich nicht auf lauter unerweisliche Beweisthümer komme. Die leeren Urtheile, die Grundurtheile und Heischeurtheile sind demnach die ersten Anfänge aller Demonstrationen aus der Vernunft §. 314. 315. Alsdenn beruhiget sich der Verstand völlig, wenn der Beweis bis auf solche Urtheile fortgeführt worden" (§318, 16:91). In his copy of Meier's book, Kant wrote in the margin next to this paragraph the words "mathematical method" (Refl. 3124, 16:670), thereby linking the paragraph to the Cartesian method of deriving all truths from axioms which in turn are certain without demonstration.

The problem is that reason has both a merely formal or logical use, which abstracts from all content, and a real or transcendental use, which is "the origin of certain concepts and principles, which it [reason] derives neither from the senses nor from the understanding" (ibid.). The first use, Kant continues, has "long since been defined by the logicians as [the faculty] of drawing inferences mediately ...; but from this we get no insight into the second faculty, which itself generates concepts" (A299/B355).

What Kant has in mind here is clearly some version of the traditional distinction between *dianoia* and *noêsis*: reason, on the one hand, as the capacity for logical reasoning or, more specifically, mediate inference, and reason, on the other hand, as the capacity for insight into non-empirical principles. To be sure, Kant does not attribute to reason the ability to intuit the truth of non-empirical principles that has traditionally been associated with *noêsis*, *nous*, or *intellectus*; rather, he speaks of reason as containing "the origin of certain concepts and principles" (A299/B355). But this is merely because Kant does not want to commit himself to the view that reason is actually *successful* in its attempt to gain purely rational insight into first principles. By saying that reason is, or contains, "the origin of certain concepts and principles," what he wants to say is that reason, in its real or transcendental use, is at least a *purported* source of (substantial, not just formal) non-empirical knowledge. It is this 'real' use of reason which is at stake in the Rational Sources Account.[23]

Whereas the distinction between the logical and the real use of reason echoes the Platonic distinction between *dianoia* and *noêsis*, Kant regards both as expressions of a single faculty of reason, thereby placing himself more specifically in a *Cartesian* tradition; as we have seen, for Descartes (and many of his rationalist followers) the one faculty of reason or intellect comprises two distinct applications that structurally parallel Kant's logical and real use of reason.

But if reason has these two very different employments, how can it be characterized such that we can understand how these employments are

---

[23] In contrasting the logical and the real use of reason and their respective principles, Kant often uses the word 'transcendental' rather than 'real' (e.g. A299/B356; A306/B363), thus treating the terms 'logical' and 'transcendental' as antonyms. This can be confusing in light of the fact that Kant also distinguishes between general and transcendental logic (A55/B79–80), in which case 'logical' and 'transcendental' are not antonyms. But there is an obvious parallel that explains Kant's usage: while general logic abstracts from the objects of cognition, transcendental logic does not (A55/B79–80); similarly, while the logical use of reason abstracts from objects, the real or transcendental use does not (A299/B355). Thus, when it is contrasted with 'real' or 'transcendental,' Kant uses 'logical' as pertaining to 'general logic.' On the other hand, when Kant speaks of transcendental as opposed to logical principles, he does not necessarily mean that they are 'conditions of the possibility of experience' or part of an explanation of a priori cognition (B25), but rather that they concern objects (see e.g. Caimi 1995: 309; Guyer 2003: 278).

nevertheless two uses of the same faculty? Kant suggests a definition of reason that is meant to cover both its logical and its real use, namely reason as the *faculty of principles*, where 'principle' can mean either the general premise or *maior* of a syllogism ("comparative principles") or "synthetic cognitions from concepts" ("principles absolutely" so called) (A301/B357–8). The latter would be a priori principles based on reason alone. Now this may seem to be a merely verbal maneuver since the two kinds of 'principle' are clearly very different. It is only in what follows that Kant explains how he thinks of the logical and the real use of reason as uses of the same faculty (and how comparative and absolute principles are related).[24] His general idea, which we will explore in detail in later chapters, is that the real use of reason grows naturally out of its logical use and that we inevitably move from using comparative principles to assuming absolute ones.

While the *logical* use of reason (more on which in Chapter 2) abstracts from content and is concerned with the logical entailment relations between judgments, the *real* use of reason (more on which in Chapter 3) "aims at objects" (*auf Gegenstände geht*) (A306/B363). That is, it goes beyond the logical relations between judgments and aims at cognizing objects (in the widest sense of the term). Thus, 'real' (from Latin *res*, thing) here means 'object-related' or 'concerning not just representations but things.'[25] However, both uses of reason share a concern with bringing unity to the manifold cognitions provided by the senses and the understanding: the logical use of reason by searching for its 'principles' (that is, more and more general premises) from which cognitions supplied by the understanding can be derived, the real use of reason by looking for its 'principles' (that is, for fundamental aspects of reality) that ground, or explain, what is less fundamental (conditioned, dependent).[26]

---

[24] Kant does not align the logical use of reason with comparative principles and the real use with principles in the latter 'absolute' sense, thereby allowing for 'comparative' and 'absolute' principles in both the logical and the real use of reason.

[25] Kant's distinction between 'logical' and 'real,' where the former is formal and concerns cognitions in abstraction from their objects and the latter is material and concerns objects, goes back at least to the 1755 essay *Nova Dilucidatio*, where Kant distinguishes between "logical opposition" (contradiction) and "real opposition" (real repugnance) (2:171) and between "logical ground" and "real ground" (2:202). It reappears for instance in Kant's inaugural dissertation, now in the form of a distinction between the "logical use" and the "real use" of the understanding (2:393), which is a direct predecessor of the distinction between the logical and the real use of reason. A late version of that distinction in slightly different terminology can be found in the essay *On a Discovery*, where Kant distinguishes between a "logical (formal)" and a "transcendental (material)" reading of the Principle of Sufficient Reason (8:193), where the original opposition "logical/real" is also used, but only with respect to reasons (8:198).

[26] The term 'principle,' which is the translation of the Greek '*archê*,' can refer to both fundamental premises and reasons (on the 'logical' side) and first causes and grounds (on the 'real' side). See Hebbeler 2012 for a helpful account of Kant's conception of principles in the first *Critique*.

Even though the real use of reason 'aims at objects,' it is meant to work completely a priori and discursively, independently of anything sensible. The a priori principles of the *understanding* depend on something given in sensible intuition insofar as they, according to the Transcendental Analytic, are valid only for objects of possible experience (A158/B197). By contrast, cognition resulting from the real use of *reason* would have to be cognition 'from mere concepts' (that is, completely discursive, independent of even the a priori forms of intuition: space and time; A307/B364). Because of this radical independence from intuition and sensibility, Kant can identify the 'real' use of reason with its 'pure' use (the section title at A305/B362).[27]

At the same time, Kant emphasizes the *synthetic* character of the principles and cognitions in which the real use of reason, if successful, would result. After all, analytic cognitions do not tell us anything specifically about objects, but only about the content of our concepts. If the real use of reason is to consist in gaining cognition and knowledge of *objects* (not just, as with the logical use, of inferential relations between our cognitions), it must result in synthetic principles and cognitions (B18).[28] However, in the Transcendental Analytic Kant had argued that synthetic cognition cannot be purely discursive, but always requires some intuitive element (minimally, a relation to *possible* experience). Reason, by contrast, is a purely discursive faculty for Kant, which means that rational insight into first principles cannot be based on anything intuitive (which in human beings is always sensible), but only on logical reasoning and the discursive principles and concepts that come with it. Already here, at the very beginning of Kant's investigation into the real use of reason in the Transcendental Dialectic, we can therefore foresee that this story will not end well: while according to the Transcendental Analytic there cannot be cognition from concepts alone, according to the Dialectic the cognitions of pure reason would have to be precisely that: purely discursive, cognitions from mere concepts.

In distinguishing between the logical and the real use of reason, Kant does not want to claim that they are unrelated. Rather, the real use builds on the logical use insofar as its concepts and principles correspond to, and perhaps can even be derived from, the forms and principles that characterize the logical use of reason. Conversely, the logical use of reason, when considered in isolation (as we do in formal logic), can be regarded as a mere abstraction from the way we reason about specific objects and events in science and everyday life. The details of this story will concern us in the chapters that follow. For the moment, it is sufficient to note that while the logical use of

---

[27] The meaning of 'pure' in this context is 'without admixture of anything foreign' (A11).

[28] On the emergence of Kant's analytic/synthetic distinction and its relevance to his critique of traditional metaphysics, see Anderson 2015.

reason aims at finding highest principles of *cognition* (principles from which more specific principles and cognitions can be derived, but that cannot themselves be derived from more general ones), the real use of reason, according to Kant, aims at finding first principles of *things* (fundamental sources, elements, or causes that ground other, less fundamental things but are not themselves grounded in anything more fundamental). Kant calls both the highest principles of cognition and the first principles of things "unconditioned" (A307/B364).[29] While the logical use of reason aims at bringing systematic *unity* to the manifold of our cognition by subsuming it under 'unconditioned principles,' the real use of reason aims at cognizing the plurality of objects of cognition by tracing them to their unconditioned grounds or conditions (A322/B379). In this way, the aims of the real use of reason strictly parallel those of its logical use. Both are interested in 'the unconditioned': the logical use of reason in unconditioned cognition, the real use of reason in unconditioned aspects of reality. (We will investigate the relation between the two uses of reason in more detail in the following chapters.)

1.1.6 Pure Speculative Reason

In sum, we can see that *pure speculative reason* – the aspect of reason that is central to the Rational Sources Account – is the faculty of gaining a priori cognition (merely purported or genuine) in a purely discursive way (that is, through mere rational thinking based on a priori concepts, principles, and inferences, independently of sensibility and intuition). Its aim is cognizing a domain of objects, and its hoped-for result is knowledge of its unconditioned conditions.[30] To this real use of reason corresponds its logical use, which consists in drawing mediate inferences and which aims at bringing unity to our cognitions, transforming them into a coherent system of knowledge.

In distinguishing between a 'logical' and a 'real' use of reason, Kant is building on the traditional distinction between rational insight into principles and logical reasoning. However, he is doing so in a way that radically transforms this distinction, since reason can only be discursive for Kant, even in its 'real' employment. Kant famously insists that there are two independent, irreducible 'stems' or 'sources' of human cognition, namely sensibility and

---

[29] I am assuming here that the term "the unconditioned" at A307/B364 refers to an unconditioned cognition. I defend this reading in Section 2.2.2.

[30] In the first *Critique*, Kant uses the term 'pure speculative reason' only in the B-Preface (1787). Kant distinguishes between the "speculative and practical use of pure reason" at A841/B869, but it seems that only after the 'discovery' (implicit in the *Groundwork*, but fully explicit only in the second *Critique*) that pure reason can be 'practical' (in the specific sense of determining the will through the motive of respect for the Moral Law) did Kant feel the need to distinguish clearly between 'pure reason' in general and 'pure speculative reason' in particular.

understanding (in the widest sense, including reason), the former of which is intuitive and the latter discursive (A15/B29; A50/B74). Thus, the only intuitive representations we can have are sensible representations. Since reason, for Kant and for the philosophical tradition, is a non-sensible, purely intellectual capacity, this means that rational insight into first principles, if it is possible at all, can only be discursive. Whether human beings have a capacity for a priori insight into principles is clearly relevant to the question of whether metaphysics is possible. Since Kant does not explicitly argue for his fundamental distinction between sensibility and understanding, it can seem that he rules out the possibility of rational intuition by definition. But, as I have argued elsewhere, the *Critique of Pure Reason* contains the materials for an argument for the claim that human intuition can only be sensible and, by implication, that reason must be completely discursive (Willaschek 2015). Since our main aim here is not to discuss Kant's critique of metaphysics but to interpret his attempt to trace metaphysical speculation to its sources in reason, this is not the place to pursue this issue further.

1.2 Kant's Conception of Metaphysics

Since the beginnings of Neo-Kantianism, interest in Kant's *Critique of Pure Reason* has mainly concentrated on its more 'constructive' parts, the Transcendental Aesthetics and Analytics, which contain Kant's account of space and time as pure forms of human intuition (and the philosophy of mathematics that is based on it), his defense of a priori knowledge of nature as a necessary condition of the possibility of experience, and his account of experience, according to which the latter is the result of the human mind's activity of synthesizing a sensible manifold in accordance with the categories of the understanding. But while the Neo-Kantians tended to emphasize these aspects of Kant's philosophy at the cost of Kant's metaphysical interests,[31] it has long been recognized that Kant's overarching concern in the first *Critique* is not with science, mathematics, or possible experience, but rather with the possibility of *metaphysics*.[32] It is this issue that, according to the A-Preface, motivates the whole project of a critique of pure reason (Axii); the entire book, according to the B-Preface, is "a treatise on the method" of metaphysics (Bxxii). As Kant famously puts it in a letter to Marcus Herz, the *Critique of Pure Reason* is a "metaphysics of metaphysics" (10:269), that is, a metaphysical theory about

---

[31] See e.g. Cohen 1871.
[32] This 'metaphysical turn' after Neo-Kantianism is often associated with Heimsoeth 1924, Wundt 1924, and Heidegger 1929.

the possibility of metaphysics.[33] Such a theory is called for, according to Kant, because of the dismal state of the metaphysics of his time. First, there are no successes in metaphysics that can compare to those in mathematics and the sciences (Bxiv); rather, metaphysics presents itself as a "battlefield of endless quarrels" (Aviii). But second, and more importantly, Kant thinks that these quarrels are not due to the failure of individual philosophers; instead, they have their source in reason itself, which, when it ventures beyond the realm of possible experience, entangles itself in fallacies and contradictions. Thus, in order to investigate whether metaphysics can be a respectable scientific enterprise at all, one must first subject pure reason itself to critical scrutiny to determine the conditions, and limits, of its successful use (Axii).

In this section, I will first outline Kant's conception of metaphysics and its sub-fields, based on the Architectonic section of the first *Critique* (Section 1.2.1). I will then briefly indicate which parts of metaphysics, so conceived, can become successful sciences according to Kant, and which cannot (Section 1.2.2).[34]

1.2.1 Kant's Conception of Metaphysics in the First Critique

In the section entitled 'The Architectonic of Pure Reason' (A832/B860–A851/B879), Kant provides a classification of the 'rational sciences,' that is, sciences based on reason alone. 'Reason' here means the faculty of a priori cognition, including mathematical cognition (A835/B863). A 'science' is a body of knowledge that has the form of a 'system,' that is, that has a hierarchical structure, criteria of completeness, and a set of ends, all of which are given a priori in the 'idea' of that science (A832–3/B860–1). Kant starts by distinguishing philosophy and mathematics as the two 'rational sciences (a priori),' where philosophy is 'cognition from concepts' and mathematics 'cognition from the construction of concepts' (namely construction of mathematical objects in pure intuition; A837/B865). In this way, Kant makes it clear from the outset that philosophy is a purely discursive enterprise, in contrast to mathematics, which essentially involves intuition.[35]

---

[33] Thus, the *Critique of Pure Reason* is an essay in what is now called 'metametaphysics' and is the topic of a growing body of recent literature (e.g. Chalmers et al. 2009; Tahko 2015).

[34] For an overview of the development of Kant's 'critical' account of metaphysics from 1775 to the *Progress* essay, see Ludwig 2017.

[35] One might object that philosophy cannot be purely discursive, according to Kant; after all, the Transcendental Aesthetic discusses space and time as pure forms of intuition, and the Transcendental Analytic essentially refers to the possibility of experience. But this does not show that philosophy itself relies on intuition in the way mathematics does (or in the way the empirical sciences do). Intuition, according to Kant, is not part of philosophical reflection itself, although of course it can be one of its topics (e.g. in the Transcendental Aesthetic).

Within philosophy, Kant then distinguishes between philosophy of nature and of morals, on the one hand, and between "pure" philosophy (or "cognition from pure reason") and "empirical philosophy" (or "rational cognition from empirical principles"), on the other (A840/B868). Metaphysics is 'pure philosophy,' that is, purely rational cognition from concepts, which in turn consists of a 'critique' (of pure reason), which is merely preparatory, and metaphysics proper, which Kant characterizes as "the system of pure reason (science)" and as "the whole (true as well as apparent) philosophical cognition from pure reason in systematic interconnection" (A841/B869). Metaphysics, according to Kant, is therefore characterized by two main features: its 'pureness,' that is, its *discursivity* and complete independence from experience and even from a priori intuition, and its *systematicity* (which it shares with all other sciences).[36] Both features follow directly from Kant's claim that metaphysics is 'cognition from pure reason,' since pure reason is not just discursive and a priori but also, as we have seen, essentially oriented toward systematic unity.[37]

In this way, Kant insists that metaphysics is not defined by the generality of its principles, as metaphysicians from Aristotle to Wolff and Baumgarten had claimed (metaphysics as "the science of the first principles of human cognition," A843/B871, as Kant puts it, effectively quoting §1 of Baumgarten's *Metaphysica*). The generality of metaphysical theses is not sufficient to distinguish them from general empirical claims, and their aprioricity alone cannot distinguish them from mathematics (A843–4/B871–2). Rather, we can have a clear conception of metaphysics only by recourse to its "sources" (A837/B865), "origin" (A844/B872), or "seat" in pure reason: "Thus all pure a priori cognition, by means of the special faculty of cognition in which alone it can

---

Philosophical knowledge is *reflective* knowledge (Bix; 9:12) based on reason and understanding, not knowledge of objects distinct from these faculties themselves. While the understanding brings discursive unity to the manifold of sensible intuitions, reason brings discursive unity to the manifold of judgments. The a priori knowledge provided by reason and understanding is reflective knowledge about the principles that govern the spontaneous activity of the mind in bringing about these two kinds of unity. I think that this is what Kant means when he says at the end of the Transcendental Dialectic that "pure reason is in fact concerned with nothing but itself" (A680/B708); see also Rohs 1987. (I owe this point to a conversation with Clinton Tolley.)

[36] Emphasizing only the 'pure' aspect, Kant characterizes metaphysics in the B-Preface as "a wholly isolated speculative cognition of reason that elevates itself entirely above all instruction from experience, and that through mere concepts (not, like mathematics, through the application of concepts to intuition)" (Bxiv).

[37] Like all sciences, metaphysics requires an 'idea' that provides its a priori 'architectonic' structure and an end at which it is oriented (A832/B860). In the case of metaphysics (which Kant identifies with philosophy "in a genuine sense"; A850/B878), the end is moral and ultimately consists in "universal happiness" (*allgemeine Glückseligkeit*; A851/B879), which I take to be happiness in accordance with universal moral principles, i.e. the 'highest good' (A810/B838). For discussion of the role of the ends in science and philosophy, see Gava 2014 and Sturm (in press).

have its seat, constitutes a special unity, and metaphysics is that philosophy which is to present that cognition in systematic unity" (A845/B873).

Within metaphysics, Kant further distinguishes between "metaphysics of nature" and "metaphysics of morals" (A841/B869). Just as metaphysics is 'cognition from pure reason,' so the distinction between metaphysics of nature and of morals is based on the distinction between the two fundamental uses of pure reason, speculative and practical. In the first *Critique*, Kant sets aside the latter and focuses exclusively on the former. Metaphysics of nature results from the "speculative ... use of pure reason," contains "pure principles from mere concepts," and is concerned with the "theoretical cognition of all things" (A841/B869). It is this "metaphysics of speculative reason ... which has customarily been called metaphysics in the narrower sense" (A842/B870) – and which is the kind of metaphysics with which the Rational Sources Account is concerned.

Within speculative metaphysics, Kant further distinguishes, first, between ontology (which is concerned with all *possible* objects) and physiology of nature (which is concerned with all *given* objects, that is, with all objects that actually exist) and, second, between immanent and transcendent metaphysics, where the former is concerned with objects of possible experience (namely either with material or with thinking beings) and the latter with non-empirical objects (such as God or the world as a whole).[38] Kant sums up his division of metaphysics as follows:

Accordingly, the entire system of metaphysics consists of four main parts. 1. Ontology. 2. Rational Physiology. 3. Rational Cosmology. 4. Rational Theology. The second part, namely the doctrine of nature of pure reason, contains two divisions, *physica rationalis* and *psychologia rationalis*. (A846/B874)[39]

This list, however, does not make explicit that unlike rational cosmology and theology, which are transcendent disciplines, and *physica rationalis*, by which Kant means an immanent discipline (developed in Kant's *Metaphysical Foundations of Natural Science* from 1786), *psychologia rationalis* can be *either*

---

[38] It may seem surprising that rational theology is subsumed under a metaphysics of *nature*, given that God himself is not part of nature. Kant's reason seems to be that God is here considered as a ground of nature (as a being that is in 'connection with,' but 'above' nature; A846/874).

[39] This division is closely related but not quite identical to the traditional distinction between *metaphysica generalis* and *metaphysica specialis*, the former of which was traditionally identified with ontology, while the latter consisted of the three specific branches of metaphysics, namely rational psychology, cosmology, and theology – a distinction that structures the text on which Kant's lectures on metaphysics were based: Baumgarten's *Metaphysica* (§2; see Gawlick and Kreimendahl 2011: xlvii). Although Kant never mentions this widely used distinction explicitly in his published writings, only referring to it in his notes and lectures (e.g. *Refl.* 4851, 18:8–9; 28:617), it clearly underlies the structure of the Transcendental Logic of the first *Critique*, which discusses ontology in the Analytic and rational psychology, cosmology, and theology in the Dialectic.

40   From Reason to Metaphysics

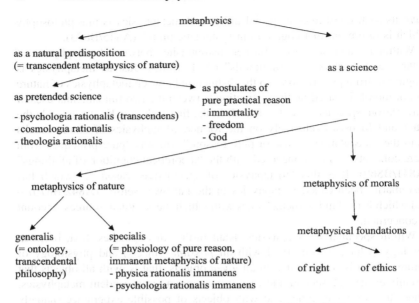

Figure 1.1 The branches of metaphysics according to Kant.

immanent *or* transcendent, since the soul can be considered either as an empirical object or as supersensible.[40] In other words, what is missing in Kant's list is the kind of *psychologia rationalis transcendens* that is the topic of the Paralogisms chapter. If we add transcendent psychology to the list and combine Kant's own division at A846/B874 with his distinctions between (a) metaphysics as a natural propensity and as a science and (b) the metaphysics of nature and of morals, and also take into account that the objects of transcendent metaphysics (immortality, freedom, God) ultimately receive some positive epistemic status as 'postulates of pure practical reason' (see Postscript), we arrive at the division of Kantian metaphysics shown in Figure 1.1.

When Kant claims in the A-Introduction that reason inevitably raises metaphysical questions that it cannot answer (because they go beyond possible experience; Avii), he is thinking not of questions concerning the foundations of morality (which Kant answers in the *Groundwork*, the second *Critique*, and the *Metaphysics of Morals*), nor of *ontological* questions (which he answers in

---

[40] This was at least Kant's view at the time of the A-edition of the first *Critique*, where he seems to have thought that psychology could be a science in the strict sense based on immanent metaphysical (rational) principles. In his *Metaphysical Foundations* (1786), Kant came to deny this (4:471), without, however, revising the relevant passages of the B-edition of the first *Critique*. On Kant's views on psychology as an empirical science, see Sturm 2001 and Kraus (in press).

the Analytic of Concepts of the first *Critique*), nor of questions concerning *immanent* metaphysics (which he answers in the Analytic of Principles and in the *Metaphysical Foundations*). Instead, he is thinking of questions of *transcendent* metaphysics – that is, transcendent psychology, cosmology, and theology. In fact, Kant tends to identify metaphysics with *transcendent* metaphysics (Bxx; B7; B395n). It is metaphysics exclusively *in the transcendent sense*, going beyond the bounds of possible experience, that is at stake in Kant's Rational Sources Account.

1.2.2 Kant on the Prospects and Failures of Metaphysics

When Kant defines metaphysics proper as the "system of pure reason" – that is, as systematic, purely a priori, and discursive – he adds that it comprises both "true as well as apparent" cognition (A841/B869). In this section, I want briefly to survey the different parts of metaphysics that emerged in the previous section, with an eye to the question of whether the cognitions they contain are 'true' or merely 'apparent.' In this way, we will get a better, if still preliminary, understanding of where the Rational Sources Account is located within Kant's overall conception of metaphysics.

Even though metaphysicians before Kant had presented their theories as scientific, Kant claims that they did not succeed, which becomes apparent from the contradictions both within their theories and between different theories that are equally well argued for – contradictions that cannot be resolved by means of the same kind of first-order rational reflection on the subject matter at hand (e.g. objecthood, the soul, the world, God). What has to be asked is the second-order question of how cognition based on this kind of reflection is possible in the first place, which is the project of a critique of pure reason (see Kant's letter to Marcus Herz, February 12, 1772; 10:129–35). Metaphysics without critique (that is, merely on the basis of our 'natural predisposition' to ask metaphysical questions) necessarily ends in fallacies and contradictions. Therefore, metaphysics as (successful) science is possible *only* on the basis of a critique of pure reason.

Now this critique of pure reason has two fundamental results concerning the possibility of metaphysics as a science: first, the claim that cognition requires both intuition and concepts, and second, the distinction between appearances and things in themselves.

First, *any* human cognition (in the demanding sense of 'cognition' relevant here) requires contributions from both sensibility and understanding, intuitions and concepts (A51/B75).[41] Put crudely, while only sensible intuitions relate

---

[41] Kant also uses 'cognition' in a wider sense for any representation that purports to represent something beyond a merely subjective state; see Watkins and Willaschek 2017 on Kant's different uses of the term 'cognition.'

directly to (possible) objects, only the concepts of the understanding allow us to cognize these objects, that is, to attribute properties to them. As Kant famously puts it, "[w]ithout sensibility no object would be given to us, and without understanding none would be thought. Thoughts without content are empty, intuitions without concepts are blind ... Only from their unification can cognition arise" (A51/B75). But from this it seems to follow that metaphysical cognition is impossible, given that it would have to be purely discursive ('cognition from mere concepts').

That this cannot be Kant's considered view is obvious from the fact that he takes himself to have shown that metaphysics *is* possible once we distinguish properly between appearances and things in themselves (e.g. Bxvii–xviii). This is the *second* fundamental result of the *Critique of Pure Reason* concerning the possibility of metaphysics. How to understand the distinction between things in themselves and appearances is a matter of some debate. For now, it will suffice to say that appearances are (all and only) empirical objects, of which Kant claims to have shown that all their empirical properties depend on the way human beings represent them (specifically, on the way we represent them in our human forms of sensible intuition, space and time). By contrast, things in themselves are not represented in space and time and thus do not depend on our forms of intuition. Since, according to Kant, things in themselves cannot be given in human sensibility (because they are not represented in space and time), we cannot have cognitions of them – we can only have cognition of appearances.

Combining the two claims – cognition requires sensible intuition, the objects of which, for human beings, are mere appearances – Kant argues that metaphysical cognition *is* possible if it concerns the "conditions of the possibility of experience" (A158/B197). Because objects of possible experience are mere appearances, they depend on the forms in which we represent them (space, time, categories). For instance, Kant argues that the principle 'Every alteration has a cause' is a condition of the possibility of experience, which means that we can know a priori that it holds for all objects of (humanly) possible experience (B232–4).

These are weighty philosophical claims, and this is not the place to discuss their credentials. But if we accept them for the moment, it follows that we can know a priori that empirical objects are spatiotemporal, that they must exhibit the structure of objecthood specified by the categories, and that they must conform to fundamental principles that follow from applying the categories to objects in space and time. Besides causation and substantiality, these principles concern the quantitative and qualitative structure of empirical reality, as well as the modal properties of our judgments about it. For our purposes, it will not be necessary to go into the details of these a priori principles and Kant's arguments for them. What matters is only that all of these claims and principles are metaphysical in Kant's sense.

More specifically, the categories outline the structure of all possible objects of human experience and are thus the basis for a critical *ontology* (which, according to Kant, includes the system of claims that follows analytically from the categories and the a priori concepts that can be defined on their basis, the so-called predicables; A79–82/B105–8).[42] Applying this structure to objects of possible experience leads to what Kant, in the Architectonic, calls 'immanent metaphysics.' Kant's immanent metaphysics includes the 'principles of the pure understanding' (A158/B197–A235/B287) and his account of matter and physical forces in the *Metaphysical Foundations*.

However, from Kant's limitation of human cognition to the objects of possible experience it also follows that any attempt to develop *transcendent metaphysics* into a science is doomed to fail. After all, transcendent metaphysics would have to consist in a priori claims about non-sensible objects – objects that cannot be given in human intuition, such as an immaterial soul, the world as a whole, and God. It is one of Kant's aims in the Transcendental Dialectic to show in detail how and why the supposed proofs of transcendent metaphysics fail (the other aim, as we have seen, being to argue for the Rational Sources Account, that is, to reconstruct the ways in which rational thinking naturally leads to transcendent metaphysics). But even before the Transcendental Dialectic begins, it is clear according to Kant that transcendent metaphysics can never be a successful science. As Kant writes, looking back at the Transcendental Dialectic: "The outcome of all dialectical attempts of pure reason ... confirms *what we have already proved in the Transcendental Analytic*, namely that all the inferences that would carry us out beyond the field of possible experience are deceptive and groundless" (A642/B670; emphasis added). Thus, for Kant, the failure of transcendent metaphysics already follows from its very definition as a kind of metaphysics that transcends the boundaries of possible experience.[43]

Of the major branches of metaphysics distinguished by Kant, this leaves only the metaphysics of morals, or practical metaphysics, to be discussed. Even though Kant does not apply the distinction between immanent and transcendent metaphysics to the practical realm, it seems appropriate to think of the theory Kant develops in the *Groundwork*, the *Metaphysics of Morals*, and parts of the second *Critique* as being analogous to the immanent

---

[42] Kant sometimes suggests that ontology (or its 'proud name') is to be *replaced* by the results of the Transcendental Analytic (A247/B303), but then, as we have seen, he nevertheless includes it among the sub-disciplines of a scientific metaphysics (A846/B874).

[43] In Chapter 9, I will argue that this result does not presuppose Kant's transcendental idealism, with its distinction between appearances and things in themselves, but only his claim that there can be no cognition without sensible intuition, which, although no doubt contentious, can be defended quite independently of transcendental idealism.

metaphysics of nature unfolded in the Principles chapter of the first *Critique* and the *Metaphysical Foundations*. In both cases, Kant is concerned with metaphysical claims about objects of possible experience – in the moral case, claims about human beings and their moral obligations. Even though the epistemic status of these claims is a matter of some debate (since Kant never develops his 'practical' epistemology in much detail), it is clear that Kant himself thought of this project as (a) metaphysical (abstracting from all empirical knowledge about human beings, based only on reason; 4:388–9) and (b) successful (e.g. 6:216–17). The metaphysical foundations of morality, further subdivided into those of right and ethics, constitute a scientific theory in Kant's sense (which is why Kant begins the Preface of the *Groundwork* with a reflection on the division of the sciences, one of which turns out to be the metaphysics of morals; 4:387–8). By contrast, Kant's so-called doctrine of the postulates concerns 'transcendent' objects, namely God, immortal souls, and freedom of the will, which can never become objects of science. Nevertheless, Kant insists that something analogous to a science is possible even here. Although we cannot have theoretical cognition or knowledge of God, the soul, or freedom, the claims that God exists, that our souls are immortal, and that our wills are transcendentally free can be rationally warranted – although not in the mode of knowledge (*Wissen*), but only in the mode of belief or rational faith (*Glaube*). (We will briefly return to Kant's practical metaphysics and how its success is related to the failure of speculative metaphysics of nature in the Postscript.)

1.3 Conclusion

Kant's conceptions of reason and metaphysics are made for each other. While speculative reason aims at systematic knowledge of the unconditioned, transcendent metaphysics is rational and systematic cognition of the soul, the world, and God (which, as we will see later, are unconditioned objects). This may seem to trivialize the Rational Sources Account, according to which the use of reason necessarily leads into metaphysical speculation. One may suspect that the Rational Sources Account follows directly from Kant's extremely demanding, speculation-prone conception of pure reason. But in fact, this suspicion is unfounded. It is true that, given Kant's conception of pure speculative reason, the Rational Sources Account follows more or less trivially. But Kant's claim is that metaphysical questions raised by pure reason can be traced back to features inherent in 'universal human reason.' Thus, the argumentative work for the Rational Sources Account consists not in showing that the use of pure speculative reason, unsurprisingly, leads to metaphysical speculation, but rather in showing that ordinary employments of reason have a tendency to take us to a speculative use of reason. As we will see in Chapters 4 and 5, Kant's argumentative strategy is to start from the logical use of reason – the use of inferences in non-metaphysical investigations, both in everyday life and in the sciences – and to show that it naturally takes us to the real use of reason, which in turn leads to metaphysical speculation. But first, we must look more closely at Kant's account of the logical (Chapter 2) and real uses (Chapter 3) of reason.

2 The Logical Use of Reason and the Logical Maxim

In a central but opaque passage from the Introduction to the Transcendental Dialectic, Kant writes:

> [T]he proper principle of reason in general (in its logical use) is to find the unconditioned for conditioned cognitions of the understanding, with which its unity will be completed. But this logical maxim cannot become a principle of *pure reason* unless we assume that when the conditioned is given, then so is the whole series of conditions subordinated one to the other, which is itself unconditioned, also given (i.e., contained in the object and its connection). (A307–8/B364)

Kant here distinguishes between (at least) two principles: the 'Logical Maxim' that requires us to "find the unconditioned for conditioned cognitions of the understanding" and a principle that says "when the conditioned is given, then so is the whole series of conditions subordinated one to the other, which is itself unconditioned, also given." A few lines later, Kant refers to the latter principle as the "*supreme* principle of pure reason" (A308/B365; emphasis added); we will call it the 'Supreme Principle.' While the Logical Maxim is concerned with conditioned and unconditioned *cognitions*[1] ('the unconditioned for conditioned cognitions'), the Supreme Principle is about conditioned and unconditioned *objects* ('contained in the object and its connection'). In other words, while the Logical Maxim belongs to reason in its *logical* use, the Supreme Principle is part of its *real* use (Section 1.1.5). According to Kant, the Logical Maxim is a principle of reason that guides rational thinking in general and scientific inquiry in particular; considered on its own, however, it does not have any metaphysical implications. As Kant puts it, it is merely a "subjective law of economy for the provision of our understanding" (A306/B362). By contrast, the Supreme Principle is a metaphysical principle about objects and relations between them. Given that there are conditioned objects (for instance, caused objects

---

[1] Cognitions, in the relevant sense, are representations that determine given objects by attributing general properties to them (Watkins and Willaschek 2017). Cognitions in this sense can, but need not, have propositional form. Those cognitions on which the logical use of reason works, however, are propositional (namely premises and conclusions of inferences).

and wholes conditioned by their parts), the Supreme Principle implies that something 'unconditioned' exists.

Now Kant's claim in the cited passage – a version of the Rational Sources Account (see Introduction, Sections 0.2 and 0.3) – is that the Logical Maxim cannot 'become' a principle of pure reason 'unless we assume' the Supreme Principle. While this formulation is somewhat cryptic – we will be able to explain it in detail only in Chapter 4 – the context makes it clear that Kant's central point is this: if we accept the Logical Maxim as a guiding principle of our cognitive economy, we must also accept the Supreme Principle (and, so it seems, thereby accept the existence of something unconditioned).

This raises a number of questions that we will try to answer in this chapter and the three chapters that follow. What are conditioned cognitions, what are unconditioned cognitions, and why is it an a priori principle of reason ('in its logical use') to search for the latter once the former are given? What does it mean to say that objects are conditioned or unconditioned, and why is a complete series of conditions itself unconditioned? And finally, how can Kant claim that we must accept the Supreme Principle (assuming we must follow the Logical Maxim), even if the Supreme Principle takes us beyond the realm of experience into metaphysical speculation (and ultimately into antinomies and delusions)? Answering these exegetical questions will shed further light on Kant's rich and highly complex account of human reason, a first sketch of which was given in the previous chapter. In the present chapter, we will begin by looking more closely at Kant's account of the logical use of reason and its guiding principle, the Logical Maxim. Even though some aspects of this account may seem outdated, its central elements will turn out to be philosophically important and plausible, even from a contemporary perspective.

2.1 The Logical Use of Reason

As a first approximation, the Logical Maxim can be formulated as follows: 'If there is a cognition that is conditioned, seek the cognition that is its condition. If this condition is itself conditioned, seek *its* condition, and so on, until you find some unconditioned cognition.'[2] According to Kant, the Logical Maxim is the "proper principle of reason in general (in its logical use)" (A307/B364). So what is the logical use of reason? As we have already seen,

---

[2] On the reading of 'the unconditioned' in the Logical Maxim as 'unconditioned condition,' see Section 2.2.2. Kant's own formulation requires us to *find* the unconditioned for every conditioned cognition (A307/B364), but I take this to mean that we should *seek* the unconditioned. 'Finding,' strictly speaking, would imply that the unconditioned exists, which is something the Logical Maxim cannot and need not presuppose. Kant more appropriately speaks of 'seeking' (*gesucht werden*) instead of 'finding' earlier in the same sentence that introduces the Logical Maxim (A307/B364).

Kant distinguishes the logical from the real use of reason in the Introduction to the Transcendental Dialectic:

> As in the case of the understanding, there is in the case of reason a merely formal, i.e., logical use, where reason abstracts from all content of cognition, but there is also a real use ... The first faculty has obviously long since been defined by the logicians as that of drawing inferences mediately. (A299/B355)

So reason in its logical use is characterized by two features: (1) it is formal in that it abstracts from all content, and (2) it draws mediate inferences (i.e. inferences that require two or more premises).

2.1.1 Formality

The logical use of reason is formal, according to Kant, in that it "abstracts from all content of cognition" (A299/B355). Here, Kant is implicitly referring back to the Introduction to the Transcendental Logic, where "logic" is defined as the "science of the rules of understanding in general" (A52/B76) and "general logic" (as opposed to subject-sensitive logics) is said to "abstract from all content of the cognition of the understanding and of the difference of its objects, and has to do with nothing but the mere form of thinking" (A54/B78). A little later, Kant glosses abstraction from the "content of cognition" as abstraction from "any relation of it to the object"; general logic "considers only the logical form in the relation of cognitions to one another" (A55/B79). Transcendental logic, by contrast, does not abstract from all content of cognition (A55/B80) in that it considers "the origin, the domain, and the objective validity" (A57/B81) of pure cognitions a priori, and thus their relation to objects. This precisely parallels the way in which Kant distinguishes between the logical and the real use of reason insofar as the former, like *general* logic, is said to abstract from all content and not to concern objects, while the latter, like *transcendental* logic, is concerned with "the origin of certain concepts and principles" (A299/B355).

While there has been debate about Kant's distinction between general and transcendental logic, as well as the sense in which the former is formal while the latter is not (e.g. Wolff 1995: 197–231; MacFarlane 2002; Tolley 2012), it seems safe to say that the logical use of reason is formal in that it concerns only the (logical) relations among our cognitions and not their relation to objects. Since the logical use of reason is said to consist in the drawing of inferences, the logical form in question is that of syllogisms and other rational inferences. For instance, the inference 'All humans are mortal; Caius is human; therefore, Caius is mortal' has the same logical form as the inference 'All bodies are alterable; the earth is a body; therefore, the earth is alterable,' and this logical form can be expressed by using concept variables: 'All A are B; C is A;

therefore, C is B.' That the logical use of reason abstracts from all content of cognition means that the validity of the inference does not depend on which concepts we fill in for the variables and how their objects (e.g. humans and bodies, Caius and the earth) differ from one another. All that matters are the logical relations among the cognitions in question.[3]

2.1.2 Rational Inference

Kant explains inference in general as the truth-preserving progression from one sentence, or set of sentences, to another (A303/B360) and contrasts the mediate inferences of reason with the immediate inferences of the understanding. By the latter he means inferences that do not require a minor premise because the conclusion follows from the major premise alone. According to traditional syllogistic logic, for instance, both 'Some humans are mortal' and 'Some mortals are human' follow directly from 'All humans are mortal' (A303–4/B360; 9:118–19).

Kant's most general characterization of rational inferences (*Vernunftschlüsse*)[4] is in terms of 'universal rules,' 'conditions,' and 'subsumption': "An inference of reason is the cognition of the necessity of a proposition through the subsumption of its condition under a given universal rule" (9:120). A 'rule,' or universal judgment, according to Kant, consists of a condition and an assertion (9:121). For instance, in 'All humans are mortal,' being human is the condition under which being mortal is universally asserted. We can derive the claim 'All scholars are mortal' by subsuming its condition ('scholar') under the condition of the major premise 'All humans are mortal' ('human'), which requires the minor premise 'All scholars are human.' Thus, the universal principle of all rational inferences is: "*What stands under the condition of a rule also stands under the rule itself*" (9:120). In this sense, the conclusion is *conditioned* by the premises.[5]

---

[3] The fact that Kant characterizes the logical use of reason in terms of formality and abstraction from content shows that he thinks of it as part of general logic rather than transcendental logic. By contrast, it is the *real* use of reason that is characterized as 'transcendental,' that is, as concerning the 'origin' of our concepts and principles and their 'relation to objects.' This explains why Kant tends to use both 'real' and 'transcendental' as exchangeable antonyms of 'logical' in the Introduction to the Transcendental Dialectic; e.g. A299/B355–6; A305–6/B362–3). See also Chapter 1, note 23.

[4] See Chapter 1, note 4, for the choice of 'rational inference' (or, equivalently, 'inference of reason') as a translation of Kant's term '*Vernunftschluss*.'

[5] Within rational inferences, Kant distinguishes between categorical, hypothetical, and disjunctive inferences according to the logical form of their major premises (A304/B361; 9:122) – a distinction that will turn out to be important at subsequent levels of Kant's Rational Sources Account. While categorical inferences have categorical sentences as their major premises (e.g. 'All men are mortal'), the major of a hypothetical inference is hypothetical (e.g. 'If there is an alteration, then there is a cause of the alteration') and that of a disjunctive inference is

Inferences of reason differ from those of the understanding not just in requiring an additional premise but also in requiring a *specific cognitive activity*, namely that of 'determining' the subject term of the minor ('scholar') by applying to it the predicate term of the major ('mortal') (A304/B360–1). This activity differs from concept formation and concept application in individual judgments (which are tasks Kant attributes to the understanding), from subsuming the particular under the universal (faculty of judgment), and from immediate inferences (understanding). The logical use of *reason* in rational inference is a specific cognitive achievement analogous to, but different from, the 'synthesis' involved in concept application. In applying a concept to an empirical object, we must 'synthesize' a manifold of sense impressions into the cognition of the empirical object according to the marks contained in that concept (A105; B137). In drawing an inference from two premises, we must 'synthesize' the assertion of the major premise (e.g. 'being mortal') with the condition of the minor (e.g. 'being a scholar') into the conditioned cognition expressed by the conclusion (e.g. 'All scholars are mortal'). And just as concept application is discursive in that it involves a succession of (at least logically) distinct steps ('going through, taking up, and combining' the given manifold sensations in accordance with the multiple marks contained in the concept; A77/B102), so rational inference is discursive, since it involves the successive synthesis of elements (the premises) that are given prior to their being synthesized.[6]

Kant's theory of syllogistic inference is complex and goes back at least to his 1762 essay on the Aristotelian syllogistic figures (*False Subtlety*). There is no need to engage it here in greater detail (see e.g. Stuhlmann-Laeisz 1976; Malzkorn 1995; Dahlstrom 2015a). There is only one more aspect that will become important in what follows, namely that syllogisms can be combined into *polysyllogisms*, that is, into series of syllogisms where the conclusion of one inference is a premise of another (9:133–4). For instance, we can use the conclusion in our example ('All scholars are mortal') as the major premise from which to derive 'Some philosophers are mortal' with the aid of the minor premise 'Some philosophers are scholars.' Or we can derive the major premise in our original example ('All humans are mortal') as a conclusion from 'All living beings are mortal' and 'Humans are living beings.'[7] Kant calls a syllogism (and more generally a rational inference) whose conclusion serves as a premise of a further syllogism a 'prosyllogism'; he calls the further

---

disjunctive (e.g. 'The world is either finite or infinite,' where the disjunction is supposed to be an exclusive dichotomy).

[6] See Section 0.2 for the concept of 'discursivity.'

[7] But cf. Klimmek 2005: 26, who argues – contra Kant – that in the categorical inferences that interest Kant, the prosyllogism concerns not the major but the minor.

syllogism, which takes the conclusion as a premise, an 'episyllogism' (9:134).[8] While rational inferences as such exhibit the discursivity of reason, polysyllogisms also give expression to its iterative character.

2.1.3 Inferential Concatenation

As Kant points out, rational inferences can be used for two different purposes: (1) to deduce propositions that are not yet elements of our body of cognition or knowledge and (2) to deduce propositions that we already know to be true from more general propositions that are known to be true (A304/B361).[9] The inferences and the relevant cognitive activity are the same in both cases, but they are employed for different tasks. The former task was ridiculed by modern philosophers (such as Bacon) in their critiques of scholastic philosophers, who supposedly restricted their endeavors to deducing conclusions from premises according to the rules of Aristotelian logic (Kneale and Kneale 1984: ch. 5). This made it impossible to attain new insights, the critics argued, because syllogisms can only make explicit what is implicitly contained in the premises.[10] This criticism leaves the second task of syllogistic reasoning unaffected, however. This is the task of articulating the inferential structure of a given body of cognition or knowledge – of explicating what can be derived from what.

Like Wolff and Meier (see Section 1.1.4), Kant sees the main purpose of reason and rational inferences as lying not in gaining new knowledge but in expressing the logical relations between various parts of our body of cognition. The picture Kant suggests in the Introduction to the Transcendental Dialectic looks like this: we start with the 'manifold of cognition' supplied by the understanding, which consists of a priori principles (such as 'Every alteration has a cause'), empirical laws (such as the laws of physics), and empirical generalizations (such as 'Dolphins are mammals').[11] Next, we combine as

---

[8] In the case of a hypothetical inference, we can either derive its minor premise as a conclusion from another hypothetical inference or use its conclusion as a minor premise in a further inference (18:222); analogously for disjunctive inferences.

[9] A third use consists in deriving conclusions (either already known to be true or not) from hypothetically assumed premises; see Section 2.1.4. As Kant makes clear in the Appendix to the Transcendental Dialectic, we can inductively justify a general principle by deriving consequences from it that are already known to be true (A647/B675; see Section 4.2.2).

[10] This objection to the traditional syllogistic logic laid out in Aristotle's *Organon* motivated Bacon's project of a 'New Organon,' which was supposed to provide heuristic principles for the study of nature (*Novum Organon*). Kant admired Bacon (Bxii; 9:32) and took the motto of the B-edition of the *Critique of Pure Reason* (Bii) from the very preface in which Bacon rejects traditional logic ("dialectica") because it "perpetuates error" instead of "opening the way to truth" (Bacon, *Instauratio magna*, Praefatio).

[11] It is unclear to me whether Kant would also include singular empirical judgments such as 'Flipper is a dolphin.' Since he is ultimately interested in a scientific system of cognitions, it seems more plausible that they are not included.

many of these cognitions as possible into syllogisms by looking, for each cognition, for more general cognitions from which it can be derived. Finally, we combine inferences into *polysyllogisms* with the aim of finding, for each cognition, the *most general* cognition from which it can be derived through a series of syllogisms.

Consider an example Kant uses in a similar context: the proposition that all bodies are alterable (A330/B387).[12] Like all general judgments, it consists of a 'condition' (is a body) and an 'assertion' (is alterable). We now "seek whether the assertion of this conclusion is not to be found in the understanding under certain conditions according to a universal rule" (A304/B361). So what we look for is a universal cognition with the same assertion (alterable) but with a different condition, such as 'Everything composite is alterable.' Kant continues: "Now if I find such a condition and if the object of the conclusion can be subsumed under the given condition then this conclusion is derived from the rule *that is also valid for other objects of cognition*" (A304–5/B361). We subsume 'being a body' under the condition of the rule that everything composite is alterable and thus arrive at the minor premise 'All bodies are composite,' which allows us to deduce our original judgment as a conclusion. In this way, we have subsumed a more particular cognition under a more general one ('also valid for other objects of cognition') and have thus taken a step toward unifying our body of cognitions. Moreover, we have given a specific kind of explanation of our original judgment by having shown that bodies are alterable *because* they are composites. We can call this kind of explanation 'inferential explanation,' which consists in the recognition that some seemingly isolated fact turns out to be an instance of something more general (which is also valid for other cases). Inferential explanation is the specific task of reason, since reason is the faculty of cognizing "the particular in the general through concepts" (A300/B357).

But this need not be the end of this process, since we can now ask whether there are even more general cognitions from which to derive our premises. Let us assume that there are: we can derive, say, 'Everything composite is alterable' from 'Everything composite has parts' and 'Everything that has parts is alterable.' And perhaps we can derive 'All bodies are composite' from 'Everything extended is composite' and 'All bodies are extended.' In this way, we have derived our original cognition, 'All bodies are alterable,' from a number of more general cognitions. That they are more general means that they are

---

[12] At A330–1/B387, Kant uses the example differently in that he does not assume that we already know that the conclusion is true, so that we can come to know its truth only by deriving it from more general premises. By contrast, at A304/B360–1 Kant assumes that in searching for premises the conclusion is already known 'through the understanding,' as the final sentence of the section makes clear. This paragraph and the next are adapted from Willaschek 2008.

'also valid for other objects of cognition' besides bodies; adding appropriate minor premises, we can also derive 'All gases are alterable,' 'All souls are unalterable,' etc.

If we repeat this process of inferential concatenation of our cognitions until all cognitions are included, we ideally arrive at a hierarchically ordered system of cognitions, with the most general ones at the top and the most particular ones at the bottom.[13] Thus, Kant can ascribe to reason, in its logical use, the task of bringing "the great manifold of cognition of the understanding to the smallest number of principles (universal conditions), and thereby to effect the highest unity of that manifold" (A305/B361). The unity in question is what Kant calls the "unity of reason" (*Vernunfteinheit*), which he distinguishes from the synthetic unity of the understanding (A302/B358–9). While the latter results from synthesizing a sensible manifold in accordance with the categories, the former results from bringing the manifold cognitions of the understanding under 'principles.'

2.1.4 System and Science

The Introduction to the Transcendental Dialectic makes it sound as if the unity of reason consisted in nothing more than a hierarchical ordering of cognitions according to their generality, which is achieved by placing them in a net of rational inferences. But when Kant returns to the idea of the unity of reason after more than 300 pages in the Appendix to the Transcendental Dialectic, a richer picture emerges. There, the unity of reason is said to presuppose

an idea, namely that of the form of a whole of cognition, which precedes the determinate cognition of the parts and contains the conditions for determining *a priori* the place of each part and its relation to the others. Accordingly, this idea postulates complete unity of the understanding's cognition, through which this cognition comes to be not merely a contingent aggregate but a system interconnected in accordance with necessary laws. (A645/B673)

Thus, the proper task of reason is to achieve "the *systematic* of cognition, i.e. its interconnection based on one principle" (ibid.) – that is, turning our cognitions into a *system* (which Kant defines as "the unity of the manifold cognitions under one idea," A832/B860).[14]

---

[13] 'Ideally' because there are many obstacles, including the fact that there might not be a unique way of ordering our cognitions into a hierarchical system.
[14] Kant's conception of systematicity and its relevance to his conception of science, on the one hand, and to his own philosophical 'system,' on the other, is a complex topic which I cannot adequately address here. On the systematic character of Kant's own philosophy, see the contributions in Fulda and Stolzenberg 2001, as well as Guyer 2000 and Henrich 2001. On systematicity and science, see e.g. Kitcher 1994; Neiman 1994: ch. 2; Sturm 2009: 129–82. On the specific way in

Systems are characterized as having a guiding *idea* (such as the idea of the soul, in the case of psychology; A671–2/B699–700), as being *complete* (which is guaranteed by the guiding idea), as having *unity* (under principles or 'necessary laws'), and as having an *a priori structure* (A832/B860). In the Appendix, Kant attributes the search for systematic unity to the logical use of reason:

[S]ystematic unity or the unity of reason of the manifold of the understanding's cognition is a *logical* principle, in order, where the understanding alone does not attain to rules, to help it through ideas, simultaneously creating unanimity among its various rules under one principle (the systematic), and thereby interconnection, as far as this can be done. (A648/B676)

By identifying 'systematic unity' with the 'unity of reason' (which according to the Introduction is the constitutive goal of the logical use of reason; A305/B361; A307/B364), Kant makes explicit that the latter involves more than ordering given cognitions according to their generality, namely *an idea* that determines the way in which the parts of the system are supposed to hang together. Kant thinks of the logical use of reason, in accordance with his teleological conception of cognitive faculties, as being goal directed. It consists not in drawing inferences for their own sake, as it were, but in doing so with the aim of achieving systematic unity among a given body of cognition, where the logical place of each cognition within the system is defined a priori by a guiding idea.

By emphasizing systematicity, Kant aligns the logical use of reason with striving for scientific knowledge, since science, according to Kant, is characterized by its systematic structure (A832/B860). But scientific knowledge must be not only systematic but also certain (4:468). Accordingly, in the Appendix Kant distinguishes between the apodictic and the hypothetical use of reason (apparently as two varieties of the logical use of reason), where the former proceeds from universal premises that are "certain," while the latter assumes premises that are not certain but "problematic" in order to see whether consequences that are themselves certain follow from them (A646–7/B674–5).[15]

---

which systematicity as a necessary condition of science applies to philosophy, see Gava 2014. The differences between Kant's own system of philosophy as it emerges in the Doctrine of Elements (including the Transcendental Dialectic) and the system sketched in the Architectonic are discussed in Goy 2007. For an overview of the different meanings of 'system' and their functions in Kant's work, see Dahlstrom 2015b.

[15] The relation between the concepts of science and certainty in Kant is more complex than my remarks might suggest, since Kant distinguishes not only different kinds of certainty (e.g. 4:468: "apodictic" and "empirical"; 9:70: "rational" and "empirical") but also different kinds of sciences (e.g. 9:72: "rational" and "historical") and a narrower and wider conception of science (e.g. 4:468). For instance, Kant seems to regard only "empirical certainty," not "apodictic" certainty, as a requirement for empirical or 'historical' sciences, which therefore

The Logical Use of Reason and the Logical Maxim (2.1.4)   55

By invoking the concepts of certainty and inductive confirmation, the distinction between the apodictic and the hypothetical use of reason adds an important *epistemological* dimension to the picture of the logical use of reason painted in the Introduction to the Transcendental Dialectic. While there it looked as if the logical use of reason was only concerned with the logical articulation of the body of our cognitions, it now emerges that it is also concerned with the epistemic status of individual cognitions and relations of epistemic justification between different cognitions. This aspect of the logical use of reason can come into view only once it is made explicit that its ultimate aim is systematicity, and thus science.

Against this picture of the logical use of reason, it might be objected that, strictly speaking, the logical use only concerns the logical articulation of a body of cognitions or knowledge (as portrayed in the Introduction to the Transcendental Dialectic), while epistemological concerns come in only once we also consider the objects of our cognitions and thus make real use of reason (as portrayed in the Appendix).[16] However, as the citations above show, in the Appendix Kant himself attributes the concern with systematicity and certainty not to the real or transcendental but to the logical use of reason (A646–8/B674–6), which also fits the fact that certainty, for Kant and his contemporaries, is a *logical* feature of cognitions (9:65–6; Meier, *Vernunftlehre*, §§9, 29).

Nevertheless, there is a valid point in the objection, which concerns the fact that the logical and the real use cannot always be as neatly separated as the Introduction to the Transcendental Dialectic may suggest. This can be brought out by distinguishing between the logical use of reason *in abstracto*, that is, in abstraction from all content, and *in concreto*, that is, applied to a specific content. The latter characterization may appear to be contradictory, since the logical use of reason is *defined* by its abstraction from content (A299/B355; see Section 2.1.1). But in fact, there is no such contradiction. Compare the logical schema of a syllogism of the *Barbara* figure: 'All A are B; all B are C; therefore, all A are C' with the inference 'All bodies are composites; all composites are alterable; therefore, all bodies are alterable,' as that inference features in a particular person's body of cognitions. While the logical schema expresses the logical use of reason *in abstracto* (as is done for instance in a logic textbook), the latter clearly also involves the logical use of reason, but this time *in concreto*, as applied to a specific subject matter. Despite its application to a concrete content, this is a case of the logical use of reason in that the validity of the inference does not depend on its content, but only on its logical form. Perhaps we can say that Kant's account in the Introduction of the Transcendental Dialectic is (primarily)

---

do not count as sciences in the strictest sense (4:468). On Kant's conception of science and the role of certainty, see Sturm 2009: 146–53.

[16] Thanks to Eric Watkins for pressing me on this.

meant to capture the logical use of reason *in abstracto*, while the account in the Appendix considers the logical use of reason *in concreto* and therefore emphasizes its epistemological aspects more strongly.[17]

2.2 The Content of the Logical Maxim

Given his account of the logical use of reason, Kant arrives at the Logical Maxim in two steps (A306–7/B363–4). First, he reminds the reader that rational inferences do not refer to objects (or to intuitions that refer to objects) directly; instead, they refer to objects indirectly, through the understanding. This means that the 'material' on which the logical use of reason is exercised are (general) cognitions of the understanding. Second, in a syllogism we subsume a condition under a general rule:

> Now since this rule is once again exposed to this same attempt of reason, and the condition of its condition thereby has to be sought (by means of a prosyllogism) as far as is possible, we see very well that the proper principle of reason in general (in its logical use) is *to find the unconditioned for conditioned cognitions of the understanding*, with which its unity will be completed. (A307/B364; emphasis added)

Kant goes on to call this principle a "logical maxim."[18] Before we can ask whether Kant is correct to attribute this principle to the logical use of reason – that is, whether it is plausible to assume that the Logical Maxim should guide the way in which rational beings organize their body of cognitions or beliefs – we must be clear about its content. Kant's formulation ('find the unconditioned for conditioned cognitions of the understanding') raises a number of questions and allows for several different readings.

2.2.1 Conditioned Cognition

First, it is unclear what Kant means by 'conditioned cognitions of the understanding.' In particular, what does it mean to say that a cognition is

---

[17] We can also consider the real use of reason in *abstracto* (that is, in abstraction from the logical use of reason), as a list of concepts and principles that arise from pure reason alone, and in *concreto*, as an inferentially structured system of (real or merely purported) metaphysical knowledge. This shows that it would be a mistake to think of the logical and real uses of reason as necessarily distinct. When we reason about a specific subject matter, we can distinguish between form and matter and consider the form in abstraction from the matter (e.g. in doing formal logic), and we can also consider the matter independently of its logical form (e.g. in writing a metaphysics textbook without the proofs). But of course, both typically *occur* together.

[18] Kant distinguishes maxims, which are "subjective principles," from laws, which are "objective" (e.g. 4:400 n.; 5:19). While in his ethics Kant is interested in practical maxims that are principles of action, the Logical Maxim is a theoretical principle in that it concerns (theoretical) cognition. As Kant explains in the Appendix to the Transcendental Dialectic, "maxims of reason" are "subjective principles that are taken not from the constitution of the object but from the interest of reason in regard to a certain possible perfection of the cognition of this object" (A666/B694).

The Logical Use of Reason and the Logical Maxim (2.2.1) 57

conditioned? Given that Kant introduces the Logical Maxim by appealing to the idea that syllogisms subsume a condition under a general rule and that we must find 'the condition of the condition' by means of prosyllogisms, the most obvious answer is that a cognition is conditioned if it can be derived from more general cognitions by means of a syllogism. Thus, 'All bodies are alterable' is conditioned in this sense, since it can be inferred from 'Everything composite is alterable' and 'All bodies are composites.' Let us call this *'inferentially* conditioned cognition.'

A stronger reading emerges if we assume that a conditioned cognition not only can but *must* be inferred from other cognitions *in order to be cognized*. The passage in which Kant uses the inference to 'All bodies are alterable' as his example suggests such a reading:

Thus suppose I arrive at the proposition 'All bodies are alterable' *only* by beginning with the more remote cognition ... 'Everything composite is alterable,' and go from this to ... 'Bodies are composite'; and then from this finally to ...: 'Consequently, bodies are alterable'; then I arrive at a cognition (a conclusion) through a series of conditions (premises).[19] (A330/B387; emphasis added)

If we take this as our model, then a cognition is conditioned if it can be cognized *only* by being inferred from a set of premises, which serve as its conditions.[20] Such a reading faces a difficulty, however, since it seems to imply that all statements that can be cognized in other ways than by being inferred from general premises (for instance, all empirical cognitions supplied by the understanding) count as *un*conditioned, which surely is not what Kant means.

This difficulty can be circumvented, however, if we assume that the epistemic status at stake is stronger than that of 'ordinary' cognition provided by the understanding. For instance, a cognition might count as conditioned (in the relevant sense) if the only way for it to constitute *scientific knowledge* is by being derived from general premises. As we have seen, Kant mentions an "apodictic use" of reason, which consists in inferring conclusions from premises that are epistemically certain (A646/B674). In this way, certainty can be transmitted from premises to conclusions that, independently of the inference, are not already certain. It seems plausible to read this idea back into Kant's account of the logical use of reason in the Introduction and to say that 'conditioned cognition' includes cognitions whose certainty (or, more generally, positive epistemic status) depends on their being derivable by logical

---

[19] Note that here, as in various other places, Kant calls the premises themselves, and not the subject terms of general sentences, 'conditions.'
[20] See also A331/B388: "we cannot reach it [the cognition] by means of reason except at least on the presupposition that all members of the series on the side of conditions are given ... because only under this presupposition is the judgment before us possible *a priori*."

inference from other cognitions (as their conditions). We can call these cognitions '*epistemically* conditioned.' The conditioning relation is epistemic in that it concerns the epistemic status required for a cognition to be part of a system of scientific cognitions, such as knowledge or certainty.[21]

Both conditioning relations between cognitions, inferential and epistemic, involve kinds of explanation (in the widest sense of the term): while an inferentially conditioned cognition is partly explained by being cognized as a particular instance of a more general principle (what I earlier called 'inferential explanation'; Section 2.1.3), the epistemic status of an epistemically conditioned cognition is explained by deriving it from the epistemic status of some other cognition.[22] Another way of making this point is by saying that conditioned cognitions raise 'why' questions of a specific kind ('Why is it the case that p?'; 'Why is it certain that p?') and that the logical use of reason consists in providing answers to these questions by deriving the cognitions in question from other, more general ones ('p is the case because q, of which p is a specific instance'; 'p is certain because it can be derived from q, which is certain').[23] As we will soon see, even though inferential and epistemic conditions do not necessarily coincide, Kant is particularly interested in the case of cognition that is *neither* inferentially *nor* epistemically conditioned (that is, both inferentially and epistemically *un*conditioned). This will become clear once we ask what Kant, in the context of the Logical Maxim, can mean by 'the unconditioned.'

2.2.2 Unconditioned Cognition

In the A-version of the *Critique of Pure Reason*, the term 'the unconditioned,' which is ubiquitous throughout the Transcendental Dialectic, occurs for the

---

[21] A third possible reading is suggested by what Kant says two paragraphs after introducing the Logical Maxim, where he mentions "objects of a possible experience, whose cognition and synthesis are always conditioned" (A308/B365). Kant does not elaborate on this, but here 'conditioned cognition' might mean a cognition that is 'transcendentally' conditioned by something being given to us in sensibility and by the conditions of sensibility (space and time) and of the understanding (categories). However, this reading does not fit Kant's characterization of the logical use of reason. After all, the logical use of reason connects cognitions (which are representations, not objects) with other cognitions by means of inferences. But the transcendental conditions of cognition are not premises from which the cognitions in question can be derived. They are not logical but *real* conditions, concerning dependence relations between one type of entity (representations that qualify as cognitions) and another type of entity (the mind with its a priori forms). While I do not want to rule out the possibility that Kant may have wanted the Logical Maxim to apply to transcendentally conditioned cognitions, I will not pursue this possibility any further.

[22] The connection between reason and explanation is emphasized in, e.g. Rohlf 2010. For a contemporary account of reason that links reason to explanation, see Schafer 2017.

[23] The close connection between talk of conditions and 'why' questions is emphasized by Proops 2010, who refers to Baumgarten's *Metaphysica* (§14) and Kant's logic lectures (24:921) but does not distinguish between 'logical' and 'real' conditions in this context.

first time in the formulation of the Logical Maxim ("to find the unconditioned for conditioned cognitions of the understanding", A307/B364).[24] Since Kant does not explain what he means by this term, he seems to assume that the reader can gather its meaning from the context. Things are further complicated by the fact that in the German original, the term *'das Unbedingte'* (with a capital 'U') is a noun, which makes it difficult (but not impossible) to read it as an elliptical expression for 'unconditioned cognition.' This might suggest that Kant is talking about an object called 'the unconditioned' (or, somewhat less bewilderingly, an unconditioned object). But such a reading is difficult to square with Kant's view that the logical use of reason is concerned with *cognitions* (in abstraction from their content) and not, like the real use of reason, with objects. Moreover, Kant contrasts this 'unconditioned' with 'conditioned *cognition*,' a term which suggests the possibility of 'unconditioned cognition.' In fact, that Kant uses 'unconditioned' as a noun here does not exclude the possibility that the unconditioned at stake is 'the unconditioned *among our cognitions*,' that is, some unconditioned cognition. Since this seems to be the reading that makes best philosophical sense, I will assume that the Logical Maxim directs us to find some *unconditioned cognition* for each piece of conditioned cognition.[25]

But what does it mean to say that some cognition is *unconditioned*? This of course depends on what one means by 'conditioned cognition.' If we mean *inferentially* conditioned cognition, the unconditioned is a principle (universal premise) from which other cognitions can be derived but that cannot in turn be derived from other premises. If we mean *epistemically* conditioned cognition, the unconditioned is a principle that has some positive epistemic status (e.g. certainty) that is not derived from anything else. We can call the former unconditioned an *inferentially* first principle and the latter an *epistemically* first principle. I now want to suggest that only principles that are *both* inferentially *and* epistemically first principles are unconditioned in the sense required by Kant's conception of an (ideal) system of scientific knowledge.[26]

---

[24] In B, the term "the unconditioned" is also used in the Preface (Bxx).
[25] Against this reading, it might be objected that Kant in fact never speaks of 'unconditioned cognitions.' This is correct, but it does not rule out the reading suggested here. First, as mentioned in the text, Kant does speak of 'conditioned cognitions,' which seems to require, as a logical contrast, the possibility of cognitions that are not conditioned. Thus, at least in this indirect sense, Kant does speak of 'unconditioned cognitions.' And second, in the *Jäsche Logic*, Kant defines 'principles' as judgments (cognitions) that are (1) self-evident ('immediately certain') and (2) not derivable from more general premises (not 'subordinated' to others) (9:110). Thus, they are neither epistemically nor inferentially conditioned (in the sense explained in the previous subsection), which means that Kant acknowledges that there is a specific type of unconditioned cognition, even if he does not use that expression for them.
[26] Anticipating a discussion in Chapter 3, a comparison between the 'logical' and the 'real' use of reason might suggest that first principles are not the only candidates for unconditioned cognitions because, on the side of the real use of reason, there are *two* ways in which something can

Note that inferentially first principles need not necessarily be epistemically first principles; conversely, cognitions whose positive epistemic status does not depend on other cognitions may not be the most general ones. These two things will come apart, for instance, in empiricist epistemologies such as Locke's, since the epistemically first principles will be something like sensations or perceptions, which obviously are not inferentially first principles (that is, most general cognitions). In some rationalist epistemologies, by contrast, inferential and epistemic priority will tend to coincide: for Baumgarten, for instance, the principle of non-contradiction is both an inferentially first principle, since it cannot be derived from any other cognition, and an epistemically first principle, since it is self-evident, which means that its epistemic status (certainty) is underived (*Metaphysica*, §7). Might it be the case that Kant did not explicitly distinguish between inferential and epistemic conditions of cognition because he accepted such a rationalist conception of science?

Not quite. First, even though Kant does not seem to distinguish between inferentially and epistemically conditioned cognitions in the Introduction to the Transcendental Dialectic, he does draw what is essentially the same distinction in a different context. Thus, in the introductory passages to the section entitled "System of all Principles of Pure Understanding," Kant points out:

> A priori principles bear this name not merely because they contain in themselves the grounds of other judgments, but also because they are *not themselves grounded in higher and more general cognitions*. Yet this property *does not elevate them beyond all proof*. For although this could not be carried further objectively, ... yet this does not prevent a proof from ... subjective sources ... from being possible, indeed even necessary, since otherwise the proposition would raise the *greatest suspicion of being a merely surreptitious assertion*. (A148–9/B188; emphasis added)

So here Kant distinguishes between an a priori principle's not being grounded in 'higher and more general cognitions,' that is, its status as inferentially unconditioned, and its being in need of a proof, that is, its status as being epistemically conditioned. While Kant's further distinction between objective and subjective proofs complicates matters in ways we need not discuss here, it is clear that he allows for the possibility that inferential and epistemic unconditionality can come apart.

---

be unconditioned: either by being a first (unconditioned) condition or by being the (possibly infinite) totality of (conditioned) conditions (Section 3.3.4). Similarly, a cognition might be unconditioned either by being an inferentially and/or epistemically first principle or by being the totality of inferential/epistemic conditions. In the latter case, the system of cognitions as a whole would count as unconditioned, even if none of its constituent conditions would. Even though Kant does not seem to consider this possibility, it fits the holistic aspect of Kant's account of systematicity.

Second, we saw before that the logical use of reason, according to Kant, aims at a scientific system of cognitions, which is characterized by unity, completeness, a priori structure, and certainty. But Kant distinguishes between empirical and rational certainty (9:70–1). While the former is based on experience (either one's own or that of others), the latter is a priori and accompanied by the "consciousness of necessity." Empirical certainty based on testimony is called "historical certainty" (9:71). Accordingly, Kant distinguishes between "historical" sciences and "sciences of reason" (9:72). But this distinction between empirical and rational certainty is not exclusive: "our cognitions can concern objects of experience and the certainty concerning them can still be both empirical and rational at the same time, namely, insofar as we cognize an empirically certain proposition from principles *a priori*" (9:71). For instance, we may have empirical reasons to believe that all bodies are alterable, but we can also derive this proposition as a conclusion from a priori premises (e.g. 'All bodies are composite' and 'Everything composite is alterable').

This suggests the following picture. In empirical/historical sciences, inferentially first principles and epistemically first principles can (and presumably will) come apart. But in rational sciences such as metaphysics, even empirical cognitions (that is, cognitions that *can* be arrived at empirically), if they are admitted at all, must be 'cognized from' epistemically first principles by being derived from them, because only in this way can they be rationally certain. In this case, the epistemically first principles will also be inferentially first principles. The 'consciousness of necessity' that accompanies rational certainty derives from the fact that the cognitions in question are either 'principles a priori' or (directly or indirectly) inferred from them. (Recall that an inference, according to Kant, is the "cognition of the necessity of a proposition," 9:120.)

So the reason why Kant did not explicitly distinguish between inferentially and epistemically (un)conditioned cognition in the Introduction to the Transcendental Dialectic may have been that, in the context of his discussion of the logical use of reason, he was only interested in 'rational sciences,' in which certainty (or, more generally, positive epistemic status) is transmitted 'downward,' from principles that are *both inferentially and epistemically* first principles to other cognitions that are *both inferentially and epistemically* conditioned. Empirical cognitions may find a place in such a rational system, but they will count as rationally certain only insofar as they can be inferred from a priori principles.

If this is correct, it brings Kant's conception of the logical use of reason very close to Meier's account of reason. As we saw in Section 1.4, Meier, on whose book Kant based his logic lectures, posits the following:

In a demonstration from reason all grounds the proof is based on must be completely certain (§§193, 204); hence they are either demonstrable or indemonstrable

(§313). In the first case, they in turn must be proven. Consequently, a proof will not become a demonstration [from reason] until I arrive at indemonstrable grounds only. (*Auszug*, §318)

In other words: reason requires certainty (which can be either rational or empirical; §157), and cognitions are certain if they are either demonstrable (that is, epistemically conditioned and proven) or indemonstrable (that is, epistemically unconditioned).[27] The chain of proofs of demonstrable cognitions must ultimately end in indemonstrable ones. Meier also claims that syllogistic reasoning serves to transform a manifold of cognitions into a systematic unity (e.g. §413), which he calls 'science' (§434). A body of cognition (*Lehrgebäude*, doctrinal edifice) is a 'system' (*systema*; §104); if it is presented according to the 'synthetic method,' according to Meier, all cognitions can be derived from one supreme principle, so that the edifice is characterized by unity, coherence, and completeness (§431).[28]

Thus, Kant found in Meier's logic textbook a model for his own account of a scientific system of cognitions and of the logical use of reason, just as he found in the logic textbooks of his time (A70–1/B96) a model (albeit an imperfect one) for his account of judgment and the "logical use of the understanding" (A67/B92). Kant's overall strategy in the Transcendental Logic – in both the Analytic and the Dialectic – is to take the uncontentious 'logical use' of the understanding (forms of judgment) and reason (rational inference) as a 'guiding thread' or 'clue' (*Leitfaden*; A66/B91) for finding their corresponding 'real' or 'transcendental' use (the categories in the case of the understanding, the Supreme Principle and the transcendental ideas in the case of reason). For this purpose, it is important for Kant that his account of the logical use of reason is not just his own invention but is based on the standard logic of his time.[29] At the same time, the parallels between Meier's account of rational proof, syllogistic inference, and science and Kant's account of the logical use of reason confirm that Kant indeed seems to have thought of the logical use of reason as aiming at a scientific system of cognition, and thus as including not just inferential but also epistemological conditioning relations.

---

[27] Note that indemonstrable or self-evident cognitions do not have to be thought of as *self-justifying* (in which case they would not be epistemically *un*conditioned, but *self*-conditioned); rather, they can be regarded as not standing in need of justification. We will see in Section 3.4 that Kant thinks of at least some 'real' conditioning relations as irreflexive.

[28] For a comparison between Kant's conception of science and systematicity and those of his predecessors, in particular Wolff and Meier, see Hinske 1991; Baum 2001; Sturm 2009: 139–46; and Gava (in press), who seem to agree that, despite many similarities, only Kant requires that a system be based on a guiding 'idea.'

[29] This is why Kant explicitly mentions "the logicians" when he introduces the concept of a logical use of reason (A299/B355), just as he does after presenting the table of judgments (A70–1/B96).

In sum, we can see that the distinction between conditioned and unconditioned cognition, as it features in the Logical Maxim, has to be understood against the background of Kant's conception of rational science, which is a hierarchically structured body of cognitions, all of which are linked by inferential relations (expressed in syllogisms and other rational inferences). Ideally, in such a system there is only one supreme principle from which all others can be deduced. This principle is *both* inferentially and epistemically unconditioned; that is, it is the most general principle under which all other cognitions can be subsumed and at the same time self-evident, so that it can transmit rational certainty to all other cognitions (by means of rational inference). When Kant attributes to the logical use of reason the task of bringing "the great manifold of cognition of the understanding to the smallest number of principles" (A305/B361), the aim is such a system of scientific knowledge. Therefore, 'conditioned cognition' should be understood to consist of cognitions that are *either* inferentially *or* epistemically conditioned, and unconditioned cognition as consisting of principles that are *both* most general (inferentially unconditioned) *and* self-evident (epistemically unconditioned).

2.2.3 The Logical Maxim: The Full Formulation

Our reflections so far result in the following version of the Logical Maxim:

Logical Maxim	If there is some piece of cognition that is inferentially or epistemically conditioned, seek the cognitions that are its inferential or epistemic conditions, respectively. If these conditions are themselves inferentially or epistemically conditioned, seek the cognitions that are *their* inferential or epistemic conditions, and so on, until you find cognitions that are both inferentially and epistemically unconditioned.[30]

Kant does not tell us to whom the Logical Maxim is addressed – to each individual rational being or to all rational (human) beings collectively. Correspondingly, it is unclear whose 'manifold cognitions' are to be systematized by following this maxim – those of an individual thinker or those of rational (human) beings in general. As Kant repeatedly emphasizes in the *Critique of Pure Reason*, science in general, and philosophy in particular, is a communal enterprise; it can be successful only if many individuals and even many generations of researchers cooperate (e.g. A820/B848; A856/B884). On the other hand, this cooperation must ultimately consist in the efforts of individual

---

[30] For an alternative reading, cf. Klimmek 2005: 23, who suggests three specific versions of the Logical Maxim, one for each of the three relational categories (categorical, hypothetical, disjunctive); see also Grier 2001: 119–21.

people. Therefore, I will assume that the Logical Maxim addresses each rational being individually but concerns not their private and accidental sets of beliefs but rather those that can possibly be integrated into a rational system of scientific knowledge that can be shared by all rational beings.[31] Moreover, the aim at which the Logical Maxim is directed is not one that any individual is supposed to realize alone. Rather, the task of the individual in following the Logical Maxim is to *contribute* to realizing (or approximating) a complete system of scientific knowledge.[32] Put differently, nothing in what Kant says suggests that the Logical Maxim requires that each individual person should try to transform their own body of cognitions into a scientific system.

Two further restrictions should be noted. First, the Logical Maxim is not a categorical imperative: it does not direct us to find or look for unconditioned cognitions come what may, like moral imperatives (which on Kant's view hold without exception). Rather, Kant points out repeatedly that the speculative interest of human reason is only 'conditional' (5:5; 5:142; 8:139; 9:87), which means that we are rationally required to pursue it only when doing so is morally permitted and pragmatically feasible.[33] Second, the Logical Maxim directs us to turn our cognitions into a unified system, but only "as far as possible" (A307/B364; "as far as this can be done," A648/B676). So the aim is to *approximate* such a system, not necessarily to realize it fully (A647/B675). The general idea behind that maxim is to turn a body of cognitions (alternatively: representations, beliefs, doxastic attitudes, statements), through a series of steps (inferences, justifications), gradually into an inferentially structured whole, so that ideally each element of that whole receives some positive epistemic status (e.g. certainty, justification, knowledge) from occupying a specific place within that whole.

2.3   The Logical Maxim, Science, and Universal Human Reason

According to Kant, the Logical Maxim is "the proper principle of reason in general (in its logical use)" (A307/B364). Like other "maxims of reason," it is

---

[31] These beliefs need not be 'scientific' in our current sense of the term. Rather, they can include all general statements about reality ('cognition of the understanding').

[32] This is meant to be analogous to the way in which, according to Kant, every individual moral agent ought to "advance" (*befördern*) the realization of the highest good (5:114).

[33] It is therefore misleading for Allison to call the Logical Maxim an "intellectual categorical imperative" (Allison 2004: 312; 331). Proops, on the other hand, claims that the Logical Maxim (his prescription 'P') is subjective in depending on a contingent desire: "Should one not wish to proceed rationally in inquiry, one will stand under no obligation" in this respect (Proops 2010: 456). This seems too weak, since according to Kant we ought to proceed rationally in inquiry, whatever our desires. (This follows from Kant's account of imperatives according to which one *ought* to do what is *rational* for one to do; 4:412–13.) Thus, the resulting obligation is conditional on a 'desire' (or 'need'), but the desire is one that is internal to reason and is in this sense necessary.

a "subjective" principle in that it is taken "from the interest of reason in regard to a certain possible perfection" of our cognition (A666/B694). To this 'subjective' Logical Maxim there corresponds an 'objective' principle – the Supreme Principle – that applies not to cognitions but to objects and that not only requires us to *strive* for the unconditioned but also positively asserts its existence (under the assumption that something conditioned exists). As we will see, Kant questions the objective validity of the Supreme Principle, but he does not question the 'subjective' validity of the Logical Maxim, if by that we mean that the Logical Maxim normatively guides the way rational beings (qua scientists) organize their body of cognitions (or beliefs). Kant clearly thinks that the Logical Maxim is a *legitimate* principle of reason precisely because it only concerns cognitions (and not their objects) and only requires us to approximate systematic unity (and does not claim that we can fully realize it).

However, the Logical Maxim is supposed to be a "principle of reason in general," albeit only in its "logical use" (A307/B364). In other words, it is supposed to be valid not only for 'speculative reason' but for 'universal human reason.' This point is central to Kant's overall argumentative strategy in defending the Rational Sources Account, according to which metaphysical questions arise from ordinary uses of reason in everyday life (Section 0.2). The transition from the Logical Maxim to the Supreme Principle constitutes the most general of the four levels on which Kant argues for this claim (Section 0.3). This means that Kant's argument can be fully successful only if the Logical Maxim is a principle not only of speculative reason but also of metaphysically innocent uses of reason that can be attributed to 'universal human reason' or 'reason in general.' This point, however, may seem to conflict with the fact that the Logical Maxim directs us toward the goal of a scientific system of cognition, which clearly goes beyond what can plausibly be required of rational beings as such. Moreover, Kant's conception of science, with its emphasis on systematicity and certainty, can seem outdated in a time where most scientists and philosophers of science would deny that scientific theories are hierarchically structured in the way Kant assumes and that scientific knowledge is certain. We must therefore ask whether it is plausible to consider the Logical Maxim as a guiding principle of human reason in general. I think that even though some aspects of Kant's account of reason and science may no longer be plausible, the claim that some version of the Logical Maxim is valid for rational beings as such can be defended even from a current perspective.

2.3.1 *The Logical Maxim and Science*

Let us first turn to the inferential aspect of the Logical Maxim. One problem is that the inferential relations captured by syllogisms and other rational inferences (that is, relations of conceptual containment and hypothetical reasoning) are not always the most relevant for scientific understanding and explanation. In biology, we may be interested in a taxonomy with the highest genera at the top and the lowest known species at the bottom. But even within biology, theories such as genetics and neurobiology will not easily lend themselves to being represented in this way. Perhaps it is *possible* to represent our current genetic knowledge as a hierarchical system. But not much would be gained by such a representation because it would not capture the explanatory relations between the statements of the theory.

However, this is not to deny that all scientific theories contain both general principles or laws and more specific claims that fall under them, with the latter standing in some form of logical subordination to the former. And perhaps that is enough to validate the Logical Maxim's requirement to search, for any given cognitions, for higher principles. After all, the Logical Maxim does not presuppose, or even claim, that this search will be successful in each case; rather, it requires us to *look* for unconditioned principles that unify our body of cognition.

That the ideal of a hierarchically ordered system of scientific knowledge is still very much alive today can be seen from the fact that many physicists subscribe to the search for a theory that unites quantum mechanics and general relativity theory. Given that such a theory would explain phenomena from the smallest scale (e.g. quarks) to the largest (e.g. galaxies), and presumably all phenomena in between, scientists like Stephen Hawking have claimed that it would be a 'theory of everything' (Hawking 2005).[34] The quest for such a theory is obviously driven by the idea that different pieces of scientific knowledge must ultimately be subsumed under very few general laws from which every aspect of nature can be explained. Perhaps such a system does not have to be structured by inferential relations in the Kantian sense. But it clearly would be hierarchically structured in the sense that the more specific principles and claims are subsumed under more general ones, from which they can be derived (in a sufficiently wide sense of the term). In other words, it would be a theory that brings "the great manifold of cognition of the understanding to the smallest number of principles" (A305/B361), which is just what the Logical Maxim is supposed to achieve. Now such a 'theory of everything' may just be a mirage, given that the sciences are actually highly fragmented and that all attempts to 'reduce,' e.g. biology to chemistry and chemistry to physics seem to face serious objections.[35] But the intuitive appeal of the ideal of a comprehensive theory of nature in which all specific theories are integrated is not undermined by the current fragmented state of scientific research or by the

---

[34] See Stevenson 2011a for critical discussion from a Kantian point of view.
[35] See e.g. the classic papers Fodor 1974 and Dupré 1983.

admission that this fragmentation is likely to continue. We gain a deeper understanding of particular facts, laws, and theories by relating them to other facts, laws, and theories; in particular, we deepen our understanding by viewing seemingly distinct phenomena as instances of the same underlying principles. (The paradigm for this is Newton's theory of gravitation, which showed for the first time that the same laws that govern falling objects on Earth also govern the movement of the planets.) Kant's Logical Maxim does not claim that the search for this kind of unification and systematicity will always be successful, but only that we should pursue it 'as far as possible.' The current fragmentation of the sciences does not imply that this is not a meaningful goal.[36]

Concerning the epistemic aspect of the Logical Maxim, it must be admitted that very few scientists or philosophers of science working today would consider certainty to be the epistemic standard that scientific theorems must live up to (at least outside mathematics). One reason for this is a lesson from the history of science, which shows that many scientific theorems that once seemed certain later turned out to be false. The Euclidian character of physical space is but one example among many: while Kant thought that it was an a priori truth that space is Euclidean, relativity theory (and many experiments that confirm it) has shown not only that physical space is not Euclidean but, ipso facto, that this claim has never been certain. Given the history of scientific theories, which has borne witness to the overthrowing of many supposedly certain beliefs, and taking into account the empirical character of scientific theories, which implies that any such theory can be falsified by future experience, certainty just does not seem to be the appropriate epistemic standard for science.[37]

Moreover, even if we apply a less demanding epistemic standard (perhaps something like 'empirically better confirmed than all rival theories'), the idea that the epistemic justification of scientific theorems flows from unjustified justifiers in a succession of steps to all other parts of the theory is incompatible with the holistic character of scientific theories, which makes it impossible to determine the epistemic status of individual claims independently of the empirical adequacy of the theory as a whole. As Quine famously puts it: "our statements about the external world face the tribunal of sense experience not individually but only as a corporate body" (Quine 1953: 41). While such epistemological holism may be contentious when applied to the beliefs of

---

[36] See Philip Kitcher's Kantian account of scientific explanation as maximizing the number of phenomena explained by one explanatory pattern (Kitcher 1994).

[37] This is not to rule out that scientific claims can be a priori in a suitably relativized sense that detaches aprioricity from (apodictic) certainty and infallibility. For relativized accounts of the a priori, see e.g. Friedman 2001. For a fallibilist reading of Kant's philosophical methodology, see Gava 2016.

individual people, it seems undeniable with respect to current scientific theories, with their complex apparatus of theoretical terms and principles.

But note that even though the downward transmission of epistemic justification through inferential chains ('polysyllogisms') introduces a foundationalist aspect into Kant's account of science and the logical use of reason, due to Kant's emphasis on systematicity it also has a holistic aspect. After all, Kant's point is that the epistemic status of a given cognition (e.g. its status as scientific knowledge) depends on its place in a unified system. The Logical Maxim requires us to look, for *every* epistemically conditioned cognition, for a set of cognitions from which it can be derived (or, more generally, by appeal to which it can be justified), which is just what a holistic understanding of epistemic justification requires. Moreover, Kant himself seems to allow for 'upward' justification in science with his account of a 'hypothetical use of reason,' mentioned earlier, where hypothetically assumed principles are inductively justified by the fact that more specific cognitions one already possesses can be derived from them (A646–7/B674–5; see also Section 4.2.2). In this way, the search for more general principles from which more specific ones can be derived can be part of a holistic conception of epistemic justification in the sciences.[38]

In sum, the idea that there is a rational requirement to look for general principles from which specific cognitions can be derived can be detached from an exclusively foundationalist conception of epistemic justification and the idea that scientific knowledge must be certain. This means that even though Kant's account of science may contain elements that are no longer plausible, this does not undermine the status of the Logical Maxim as the expression of a valid rational requirement.

2.3.2 The Logical Maxim and Universal Human Reason

But even if one admits that the Logical Maxim expresses a rational requirement, one may object to the claim that it is part of 'reason in general' in the sense that *every* rational human being is required to search for the conditions of her inferentially and epistemically conditioned cognitions. After all, most people are not scientists and thus simply not in the business of transforming their body of cognitions into a unified system. It may be plausible to assume a universal rational requirement to avoid contradictions in one's body of beliefs and cognitive commitments. But it would be absurd to claim that ordinary people stand under an obligation to look for conditions for each and every one of their inferentially and epistemically conditioned cognitions. For instance, if

---

[38] For a reconstruction of Kant's account of science that emphasizes its holistic aspects, see Gava 2014.

someone who is not a meteorologist believes that summer in Europe is typically warmer than winter, there does not seem to be any rational pressure to look for a more general principle from which to derive, and thereby epistemically justify, the belief in question. Epistemic justification, at least in everyday contexts, mostly follows a default-and-challenge pattern, which means that we count as justified in our beliefs unless we are confronted with relevant challenges to them (see Williams 2001; Willaschek 2007, 2012; Matthiessen 2014). And even if we are challenged, we do not have to climb the ladder of epistemic conditions up to the unconditioned (to something self-evident or otherwise indubitable); we need only appeal to beliefs that are unchallenged in the present context. As Peirce once remarked, it makes no sense "to argue a point after all the world is fully convinced of it" (Peirce 1992: 115). Thus, the Logical Maxim with its requirement to search for conditions for *every* inferentially and epistemically conditioned cognition (even if 'all the world is fully convinced of it') does not seem to hold for ordinary people in ordinary situations. If it holds at all, it only applies to scientists (in the widest sense, including philosophers and other people interested in what Kant calls 'speculation').[39]

But even if this is correct, it does not undermine the idea that the Logical Maxim is rooted in universal human reason. After all, the Logical Maxim gives expression to three features of the logical use of reason which seem to hold universally: first, its *discursive* or *inferential* character, leading by a series of steps from one claim to another; second, its *iterative* character, allowing the same discursive operation (e.g. syllogistic inference) to be applied to the result of previous instances of that operation; and third, the requirement that this process must come to an end somewhere (*completeness*) (Section 0.2). Each of these features is intuitively appealing and has legitimate applications.

First, rational inference is a powerful tool of thought that can transmit credence and epistemic justification from premises to conclusions. And even where epistemic justification does not take the form of a syllogism, it is often conveyed in a stepwise manner from one belief to another. Second, iteration is also an important cognitive tool. The conclusion of one syllogism can be made the premise of another, leading us further and further in articulating the logical consequences of our beliefs and in transmitting epistemic justification. And again, even where epistemic justification is transmitted not by inference but by other means, we often do ask not merely for justification but also for the justification of the justifying belief. (We ask, for instance, 'How do you *know* that?,' the answer to which we follow with 'And how do you know *that*?'). And, third, it is certainly correct that any such series of questions must end

---

[39] For a helpful discussion of Kant's own philosophical claims as having an 'in between' status between common sense and science, see Ameriks 2001.

somewhere (completion), even if this need not involve principles that are underivable and self-evident, but perhaps only ones that cannot be reasonably unchallenged in the present context. Assuming that discursivity, iteration, and completion are features of universal reason, we can understand the Logical Maxim as grounded in universal reason, since it gives normative expression to these three features.

This still leaves us with the question of why the Logical Maxim, even though it is grounded in universal human reason, nevertheless typically applies not to ordinary people but only to scientists (in the widest sense of the term). An answer can start from the restricted validity of the Logical Maxim, which, as we have seen, is not a categorical imperative but only applies under the condition that no other, more urgent concerns prevent us from following it (Section 2.2.3). For people who are not scientists, this condition may typically not be satisfied. If someone believes that summer is warmer than winter, the reason why they are not required by the Logical Maxim to search for other cognitions from which to derive and justify the belief in question might just be that for them, there will always be other, practical concerns that are more pressing than the rational interest in scientific explanation. Seen from this angle, the Logical Maxim does hold for everyone, but vacuously so for most, since a necessary condition of its making substantive requirements on us and our cognitive activity is not satisfied in most cases.

2.4 Conclusion

In this chapter, we have seen how Kant thinks of the Logical Maxim as guiding the 'logical use of reason.' The latter consists in the drawing of rational inferences with the aim of unifying our body of cognitions into a system of scientific knowledge. Ideally, in such a system all our inferentially and epistemically conditioned cognitions could be derived by chains of rational inferences (polysyllogisms) from a small number of principles that are both inferentially and epistemically unconditioned. The Logical Maxim directs us to approximate such an ideal system by seeking conditions for our inferentially and epistemically conditioned cognitions. While such a requirement may have some pull only for scientists (in the widest sense of the term), but not for most other people most of the time, the Logical Maxim can nevertheless be plausibly regarded as part of 'universal human reason' since it gives expression to three features (discursivity, iteration, and completeness) that characterize rational thinking as such.

3 The Supreme Principle of Pure Reason

In the previous chapter, we gained a better understanding of the Logical Maxim, which is the "proper principle" of the logical use of reason (A307/B364). It requires us to search for inferentially and epistemically unconditioned cognitions in order to transform our body of cognitions by means of inferential reasoning into a system of scientific knowledge. In this chapter, we will now turn to the fundamental metaphysical concept in Kant, the concept of the 'really' (not just logically) *unconditioned*, and to the conditioning relations between objects that speculative metaphysics tracks. Kant's Rational Sources Account (his argument that the sources of speculative metaphysics lie in reason itself) rests on the claim that in following the Logical Maxim, we are naturally led to accept a quite different principle, the "supreme principle of pure reason" (A308/B365):

[W]hen the conditioned is given, then the whole series of conditions subordinated one to the other, which is itself unconditioned, is also given (i.e., contained in the object and its connection). (A307–8/B364)

In the present chapter, we will try to clarify this principle by asking what Kant, in the context of the Supreme Principle, means by 'given' (Section 3.1), by 'the conditioned' and its 'conditions' (Section 3.2), what it means for something to be 'unconditioned,' and why Kant thinks the series of subordinated conditions is supposed to be unconditioned in this sense (Section 3.3). Finally, we will ask how the Supreme Principle relates to the Principle of Sufficient Reason (Section 3.4). This will lay the ground for reconstructing, in the following two chapters, Kant's complex account of why we are naturally led from the Logical Maxim to the Supreme Principle.[1]

---

[1] Readers should be warned that this chapter contains discussion that some may find rather abstract and technical. Those not interested in the details of Kant's account of real conditioning may consider reading only Sections 3.1, 3.2.5, and 3.3.4.

3.1 'Given'

When 'the conditioned is *given*,' according to the Supreme Principle, the unconditioned 'is also *given*.' This can be read in at least two ways, corresponding to the two central meanings of the philosophical term 'given' in Kant, which can either mean 'exist' or 'made cognitively accessible to a finite epistemic subject.'

The first meaning is employed, for instance, when Kant says that in the case of things in themselves, the condition of the conditioned is not just "given as a problem" (*aufgegeben*), but "given" (*gegeben*) (A498/B526). Because individual things in themselves are not cognitively accessible to us, in this case 'given' cannot mean 'given to us'; rather, it means 'exists.'[2] By contrast, it is the second meaning that is operative when Kant says, in the Transcendental Aesthetic, that objects are "given to us" in intuition (A19/B33), which means that they are made cognitively available to us, so that we can represent, refer to, and think about them.[3] We can call the first the ontological and the second the epistemic meaning of 'given.'[4]

Consequently, the Supreme Principle can be taken to say very different things. On the epistemic reading, it says something like 'If the conditioned is cognitively accessible to us, then the unconditioned is cognitively accessible to us too.' On the ontological reading, it says, 'If the conditioned exists, then the unconditioned exists too.'[5]

---

[2] See also A594/B622, where Kant, in a different context, renders 'exists' as 'is given.' In German, '*es gibt*' ('there is'), like '*gegeben*,' is a form of '*geben*' (to give).

[3] Kant uses both of these senses in the same sentence when he claims that "a divine understanding ... would *not* represent *given* objects, but through [its] representation the objects would themselves at the same time be *given*, or *produced*" (B145; emphasis added). Since Kant says of the same objects first that they are not given and then that they are, two senses of givenness must be in play. Kant's point seems to be that for God, it is not the case that independently existing objects are made cognitively accessible to him ('given' in the epistemic sense), but rather that they come into existence (are 'given' in the ontological sense) by being represented.

[4] See Klimmek 2005, who first claims that 'given' in the Supreme Principle has an epistemological meaning (36) but then admits that it can also be read ontologically as 'exists' (37). That '*x* is given' in the epistemic sense implies '*x* exists' is argued by Stang 2016: 290 and Watkins and Willaschek 2017; for contrary views, cf. Stephenson 2015; Chignell 2017; Grüne 2017. For present purposes, however, we can set this question aside. If the epistemic sense of givenness implies existence, then the difference between the two meanings is less stark than it may appear.

[5] There are further readings if one allows that the two occurrences of 'given' in the Supreme Principle can have different meanings or if one allows for further meanings of 'given.' For instance, something may be 'given' if it exists in such a way that its existence depends on our cognitive access to it. Thus, Kant claims that "the objects of experience are *never* given *in themselves*, but only in experience, and they do not exist at all outside it" (A492/B521). While 'given' in the phrase 'never given in themselves' can either mean 'exists' (simpliciter) or 'is made cognitively available to us,' when Kant says that objects of experience are 'given *in*

It may seem natural to read the antecedent of the Supreme Principle ('if the conditioned is given') in an epistemic sense; after all, we only start looking for conditions if something conditioned is given *to us* and makes us wonder about its condition. But why should reason assume that if the condition is made cognitively accessible to us, then the unconditioned is made accessible to us too? Perhaps the idea could be that the unconditioned is accessible to us *through the series of conditions* that lead up to it. As we will see, however, Kant allows for the series of conditions to be infinite, in which case it would be impossible for us (finite beings) to access the unconditioned in this way. Moreover, Kant repeatedly says that the Supreme Principle is true of things in themselves (A498/B526; 18:223; 20:290). We will have to return to the question of how Kant can make such a claim later (Section 5.3). For now, it is sufficient to note that this claim effectively rules out the epistemic reading, since things in themselves, according to Kant, are not epistemically given (that is, cognitively accessible) *to us* – either as conditioned or as unconditioned.

Therefore, I take the basic sense of 'given' in the context of the Supreme Principle to be ontological, since the Supreme Principle is supposed to be the guiding principle of the 'real use' of reason, which is the use of pure reason specific to metaphysics. In fact, Kant's own formulation of the Supreme Principle explains what it means for the unconditioned to be 'given' in purely ontological terms ("i.e., contained *in the object* and its connection"; A307-8/B364; emphasis added). Thus, the point of the Supreme Principle is an ontological one: if something conditioned *exists*, then something unconditioned must also *exist*.[6] Given that there are conditioned objects, the Supreme Principle implies the existence of something unconditioned. But what does it mean to say of an object that it is conditioned, and what is the unconditioned? These are the questions to which we will turn next.

3.2 Real Conditioning

If something is conditioned and something else is its condition, both stand in a specific *relation*, which we may call 'conditioning.'[7] Since we are dealing with a conditioning relation that (unlike logical conditioning) does not hold

---

experience' and 'do not exist outside it,' he means that they *do* exist, not in themselves but rather 'in experience' – that is, in a way that makes their existence dependent on our cognitive access to them. Note that in the context of transcendental idealism, it follows from an appearance's being given in the epistemic sense that it is also given in this third sense. (Thanks to Ralf Busse and Clinton Tolley for suggesting this third sense of 'given.')

[6] See also Stang 2016: 290. – Since there can be conditioned states of affairs (facts), events, etc., for which it can seem inappropriate to say that they 'exist' (and more appropriate to say that they 'are the case,' 'take place,' or 'happen'), 'existence' here should be taken to stand for a whole family of ontological terms. Thanks to Michael Wolff for pointing this out to me.

[7] This section and the next in part overlap with Willaschek 2017.

between cognitions or judgments but is instead "contained in the object and its connection" (A308/B364) and is the topic of the 'real use of reason,' we can call this relation 'real conditioning.'[8] It takes as its relata *objects* (in the widest sense of the term), including appearances, things in themselves, representations, events, actions, possibilities, moments in time, regions in space, human beings, and parts of material objects. Thus, in order to understand what Kant means by 'the conditioned' and its 'condition' in the Supreme Principle, we have to ask what it means for two objects to stand in a relation of real conditioning.

Kant himself, however, does not seem to bother with this question at all, since neither in his published nor in his unpublished writings do we find any explicit explanation of the conditioning relation at issue in the Supreme Principle. What we do find is an astounding variety of relations that Kant appears to regard as *specific instances* of real conditioning: the relation between a thinking subject and its representations (18:226), between substance and attribute (4:333), parts and whole (A413/B440), prior and later moments in time (A411–12/B438–9), regions in space (A412–13/B439–40), the necessary and the contingent (A415/B442; A419/B447), empirical causes and their effects (A194/B239; A419/B447), intelligible causes and their effects (A419/B447), causally interacting objects (A211/B256), parents and their children (A511–12/B539–40), and the *ens realissimum* and the possibility of objects in general (A573/B602). (This list is not exhaustive.)

In what follows, I will start with Eric Watkins's suggestion that the conditioning relation at issue in the Supreme Principle is a generic relation of metaphysical dependence which takes the various relations discussed by Kant as its species (Watkins 2016a; Watkins in press). According to Watkins, the specific instances are differentiated by features of the objects to which they apply, and we can come to understand the generic relation by considering its species. Real conditioning would then be a close cousin of what in current metaphysics is called '(metaphysical) grounding' (e.g. Fine 2001; Rosen 2010; Correia and Schnieder 2012).

This is an elegant proposal, and Kant himself points us in this direction, for instance when he reportedly says in a lecture: "the relation of substance to accident is not the same [as that between ground and consequence], even though they are both closely related" (28:510). But while Watkins is right that we can best understand the real conditioning relation through the diverse relations that fall under it, his proposal may still overestimate the internal

---

[8] I have lifted this term from related works by Eric Watkins. My own reading of the Supreme Principle and Kant's conception of real conditioning has developed in exchange with Watkins's developing views on the same topic.

unity of real conditioning by treating it as a unitary relation of ontological dependence.[9] In this section, I will argue that there is no unified genus that all these relations share, but rather a disjunction of three different basic types of conditioning relations, corresponding to the three relational categories. I will first discuss the question of which formal features are shared, and which are not, by all of the real conditioning relations that Kant acknowledges (Section 3.2.1), and I will point to some dissimilarities between different relations of this sort (Section 3.2.2). Next, I will explain how Kant thinks of real conditioning as comprising three distinct conditioning relations that correspond to the three relational categories but do not fall under any common genus specific to them (Section 3.2.3). Finally, at the end of this section, I will discuss whether the relation between the conditioned and its condition is analytic or synthetic (Section 3.2.4). In the rest of the chapter, I will then turn to the unconditioned (Section 3.3) and the Principle of Sufficient Reason (Section 3.4).

3.2.1 The Formal Features of Real Conditioning

According to Watkins, "Kant seems to be operating with a generic notion of real conditioning that involves an *asymmetrical, transitive,* and *intelligible* relation of metaphysical dependence" (Watkins 2016a: 5; emphasis added; see also Watkins in press).[10] Starting with '*intelligibility*,' I agree that real conditioning in Kant is always explanatory or 'intelligible,' since by asking for the condition of something conditioned we acknowledge that the conditioned stands in need of an explanation of some kind, and by stating its condition we contribute to its explanation. Put differently, if something is conditioned in some respect, this raises the question of why it is the way it is (in that respect), and naming its condition provides an answer to this question. For instance, if something is an event that is causally conditioned, we can ask why it occurred, and naming its cause will provide an answer. Or if something is a whole that is conditioned by its parts, we can ask why it exists, and naming its parts will answer that question. In this sense, real conditioning is explanatory.

Moreover, I agree that real conditioning is *transitive*: if C_1 is a condition of C_2 and C_2 is a condition of C_3, then C_1 is also a condition of C_3.[11] However, as

---

[9] I have adopted the term 'unitary relation' from Bliss and Trogdon 2014, who use it (with respect to grounding) to express the idea that there is a single relation that underlies (either as genus or as determinable) its different specific forms (species or determinates).

[10] That a relation is asymmetrical means that from *aRb* (*a* stands in relation *R* to *b*) it follows that *b* does not stand in relation *R* to *a*. ('Greater than' is an example of an asymmetrical relation.) A relation is transitive if from *aRb* and *bRc* we can infer *aRc*. (Again, 'greater than' is an example.) And a relation is intelligible, according to Watkins, if the fact that *aRb* means that *a* in some way explains *b* or makes it intelligible (Watkins in press).

[11] Watkins qualifies his claim that real conditioning is transitive by saying that there are cases where transitivity does not 'apply' or is 'irrelevant,' such as the relation between a subject and

I will argue now, only some of the conditioning relations that Kant recognizes are *asymmetrical*, while others are not. Relatedly, only the asymmetrical conditioning relations are *irreflexive*, while the symmetrical ones are not.[12] Thus, even at the level of 'formal' (i.e. topic-neutral) features there is less unity than Watkins assumes.

A first example of a *symmetrical* conditioning relation recognized by Kant is what he calls 'community,' that is, mutual causal interaction. On Kant's account in the Third Analogy, every object in space stands in a relation of causal interaction (e.g. mutual attraction) with every other (A211/B256), which is a symmetrical relation. Watkins acknowledges this but points out that community or interaction is built out of causal relations that are asymmetrical: if *A* and *B* interact (which is a symmetrical relation), then *A* acts on *B* and *B* acts on *A* (which are asymmetrical relations). But even if that is granted, community, according to Kant, is a *fundamental* type of conditioning relation (after all, it is a category) that cannot be reduced to causation: community "is an *entirely different kind of connection* from that which is to be found in the mere relation of cause to effect (of ground to consequence), in which the consequence does not reciprocally determine the ground" (B112; emphasis added). Thus, Kant is clearly committed to the claim that community differs from causation in being a *symmetrical* relation of determination and thus a symmetrical conditioning relation.[13]

---

its representations and that between God and the possibility of things (Watkins in press). His point seems to be that transitivity is not relevant because in these cases the relation does not allow for iteration. But note, first, that the relation between subject and representation may well be iterative. Consider, for example, a metaphysical view according to which finite subjects with all their properties are themselves (nothing but) representations of some underlying infinite subject. On this kind of view, if a finite subject *S* has some representation *R*, then both *S* and *R* are representations of the underlying subject *S**. Thus, in this case, the relation between subject and representation is iterative (*S* is a bearer of representations but is itself a representation of *S**) and transitive (if *S** represents *S* and *S* represents *R*, then *S** represents *R*). Relatedly, in the *Prolegomena*, we read (in a section about the soul): "Pure reason demands that for each predicate of a thing we should seek its appropriate subject, but that for this subject, which [because it is a mere appearance] is in turn necessarily only a predicate, we should seek its subject again, and so forth to infinity (or as far as we get)" (4:333). Hence, the relation between subject and predicate (of which the relation between subject and representation is an instance) is clearly transitive for Kant. In the case of God and the possibility of things, the relation is transitive in that, if God grounds the possibility of O_1 and the possibility of O_1 grounds the possibility of O_2, then God also grounds the possibility of O_2. Thus, it does not seem to be necessary to qualify the claim that all real conditioning relations are transitive in the way Watkins does.

[12] A relation *R* is irreflexive if *aRb* implies that $a \neq b$.

[13] As Watkins himself argues in his book on Kant's account of causation, community consists of asymmetrical causal relations but is nevertheless "symmetrical" and "not reducible" to the notions of substance and causation (Watkins 2005: 285). In conversation, Watkins has added the thought that in the case of community, the symmetry might hold between what is conditioned (the objects that stand in a symmetrical relation), while the conditioning relations are asymmetrical. But this does not seem to be the way Kant thinks of community, which

Another example of a symmetrical real conditioning relation recognized by Kant (albeit only in the *Critique of the Power of Judgment* and not in the first *Critique*) is that among the parts of an organism (e.g. my heart and my lung), about which Kant says that "the preservation of the one is reciprocally dependent on the preservation of the other" (5:371). Clearly, the relation among the different parts, or organs, of an organism that Kant is speaking of is a real conditioning relation, not a merely logical one. And this relation is symmetrical in that no organ can function without the other (e.g. the functioning of the heart requires that of the lung, and vice versa).

This example also shows that in some cases of real conditioning, two or more conditioning relations can overlap. First, there is the symmetrical relation between the organs, which Kant considers a relation of "reciprocal determination" (B111) and thus a symmetrical real conditioning relation. Second, there is the relation between the parts and the whole, where the whole is constituted by its parts, which is an asymmetrical real conditioning relation. And third, there is the relation between the whole and the parts, where in the case of an organism the parts can only be explained by recourse to their function in the whole organism, which relation, again, is asymmetrical.[14] This also further confirms the previous point that the fact that community involves two mutual asymmetrical conditioning relations does not imply that community itself is asymmetrical. Rather, as in the case of organisms, community consists in symmetrical and asymmetrical relations that necessarily occur together.

Now consider the question of whether real conditioning is irreflexive. Can something be its own real condition? At least for some cases of real conditioning, Kant clearly denies this. For instance, in his essay *On a Discovery*, he argues against the view that God might be his own ground by saying: "the ground of the existence of a thing, as real ground, must always be distinguished from this thing and this must then necessarily be thought as dependent upon another" (8:198). Being a real ground is a case of real conditioning in Kant's sense. Thus, there are real conditioning relations that, according to Kant, are irreflexive. On the other hand, if a conditioning relation is both symmetrical and transitive, it cannot be irreflexive.[15] In an organism, for instance, the organs mutually condition each other: the organism's heart conditions its lungs, and its lungs condition its heart. But if this relation is transitive, it follows that the heart also conditions itself (by conditioning the

---

apparently is meant to be a *conditioning* relation (a relation of mutual 'determination'). For further discussion of symmetrical conditioning relations, see Willaschek 2017.

[14] See Kant's distinction between a *totum* and a mere *compositum*. Whereas in a *totum* the parts are conditioned by the whole, in a *compositum* the whole is conditioned by the parts (A438/B466).

[15] While *reflexivity* requires that aRa holds for all relata, denial of *irreflexivity* only means that there are possible cases of aRa.

lungs, which condition the heart). Thus, Kant seems to recognize real conditioning relations that are not irreflexive.[16]

In sum, even though many details may remain unclear (since Kant does not explicitly discuss real conditioning as such and its formal features), it seems plausible that all real conditioning relations are transitive and explanatory, while there are some conditioning relations that are symmetrical (and not irreflexive) and others that are asymmetrical (and irreflexive). These relations differ substantially with regard to how the conditioned depends on its condition (reciprocally or not, allowing for reflexivity or not). While this does not rule out that there is a uniform relation of real conditioning, it at least indicates that if there is such a relation, its species are more varied than Watkins's proposal allows for.[17]

3.2.2 Necessary and Sufficient Conditions and Real Conditioning as a Disjunctive Concept

It seems that Kant originally reserved the term 'condition' (*conditio*) for *necessary* conditions and the term 'reason/ground' (*ratio*) for sufficient conditions (e.g. 17:28; König 2015).[18] But the examples of real conditioning relations that he discusses in the Transcendental Dialectic show that no such clear-cut terminological distinction is at work in the *Critique of Pure Reason*. As Watkins also emphasizes (Watkins in press), while in some cases of real conditioning conditions are sufficient but not necessary for what they condition, in others they are necessary but not sufficient. According to Kant, a cause is necessarily followed by its effect (e.g. A200–1/B246), which in turn means that the cause is sufficient for bringing about the effect. By contrast, each part of a mereological whole is necessary for the existence of the whole (since a mereological whole is uniquely constituted by its parts), but no part alone is sufficient.

---

[16] Here I deviate from the position defended in Willaschek 2017, where I say that all real conditioning relations are irreflexive. Thanks to Eric Watkins for prompting that correction.

[17] There is a further formal feature, discussed in the literature on metaphysical grounding, that real conditioning might or might not have, which is 'well-foundedness' (see e.g. Rosen 2010: 116; Schaffer 2010: 37). Real conditioning is well founded if any series of real conditions (conditions, conditions of conditions, etc.) ends in something unconditioned. We will discuss well-foundedness later, in Section 3.3.

[18] The use of 'condition' also varies in the notes and lectures. Baumgarten uses 'condition' as a synonym for 'ratio' (e.g. *Metaphysica*, §14). Kant is critical of this and distinguishes between condition ("quo non posito non ponitur aliud") and ratio ("quo posito neccessario ponitur aliud") (17:28; 18:695–6). According to this definition, a 'condition' is a necessary condition, while a 'ratio' is a sufficient condition. On the other hand, Kant sometimes seems to think of 'condition' as the logical equivalent of 'reason': "every judgment contains a ground [*Grund*], since it has something determining. Logic puts it this way, every judgment has its condition. Everything has in general its ground and its ground of cognition" (28:489).

This means that even though the notion of real conditioning clearly bears some similarity to the notion of a sufficient reason or ground, it cannot simply be identified with it. At best, a sufficient reason is a special case of a real condition, since real conditions can, but need not, be sufficient for what they condition. In fact, there may even be real conditioning relations that are neither necessary nor sufficient. For instance, if we think of the part–whole relation not along strictly mereological lines (according to which two wholes differ if they differ with regard to at least one part) but rather in the way we do in everyday contexts (where a house remains the same object even if we exchange a window or tear down a wall), then parts are neither necessary nor sufficient for the whole, although they still seem to be 'real conditions' in Kant's sense. (We will discuss the relation between the Supreme Principle and the Principle of Sufficient Reason later, in Section 3.4.)

Given that real conditioning can be either sufficient, necessary, necessary and sufficient, or neither necessary nor sufficient, it seems doubtful that Kant viewed real conditioning as a generic but unitary relation of metaphysical dependence. After all, the way in which something depends, e.g. on its necessary but insufficient conditions can be very different from the way in which it depends on its sufficient but not necessary conditions.[19]

In light of these considerations, I want to suggest that we regard Kant's notion of real conditioning (the kind of conditioning relation at stake in the Supreme Principle) not as a substantial generic notion with various species under it but rather as a disjunctive concept built out of substantially different relations. This would explain why Kant does not give a general account of real conditioning and, in fact, does not even have a name for it. On the reading suggested here, there is no substantive account of real conditioning in general. As I will now argue, this does not rule out there being some unity among all real conditioning relations; at the same time, we will find further reason to deny that this unity is substantial.[20]

---

[19] One might respond that Kant thinks of real conditions, even if they are merely necessary conditions, as 'positive' in some sense. But first, it is extremely difficult to say precisely what a 'positive' condition consists in. Even apart from that difficulty, there are cases of real conditioning for which it is questionable that the condition makes any positive contribution to the conditioned. For instance, the parts may make a positive contribution to the existence of the whole, but it seems implausible to say that each part makes a positive contribution to the existence or determination of the other parts. Nevertheless, according to Kant the parts condition each other (B112). Moreover, even if it were granted that real conditioning must be 'positive' in some sense, this still might not be enough to turn real conditioning into a unitary genus. See Willaschek 2017 for additional discussion.

[20] The question whether real conditioning is a generic but substantive and unitary relation or a mere disjunction of different, more specific relations parallels a question discussed among current metaphysicians about what has come to be called 'metaphysical grounding,' or just 'grounding' (see Bliss and Trogdon 2014 for an overview). While Kant's conception of real conditioning bears some similarity to the concept of grounding, it differs from it in various

3.2.3 Real Conditioning and the Relational Categories

If real conditioning is disjunctive, this raises the question of what accounts for the unity and limits of that notion. Why are material constitution and parenthood part of the disjunction that constitutes real conditioning, but simultaneity and brotherhood not?[21] An answer suggests itself once we remember the structure of Kant's overall project in the Transcendental Logic, which is to derive 'transcendental' concepts and principles from 'logical' forms: the unity comes not from substantive features of these relations, but from the way in which they correspond to features of the logical use of reason and understanding. In an important *Reflexion* (from 1778 to 1780) that reads like a preparatory sketch of the Introduction and chapter 1 of the Transcendental Dialectic, Kant writes: "the relational concepts are nothing but the unity of the conditioned and its condition [*Einheit des Bedingten und seiner Bedingung*]" (*Refl.* 5553; 18:222). By 'relational concepts' Kant is referring to the three 'relational' categories (inherence/subsistence, causation, community; A80/B106), which in turn correspond to the three logical forms of relational judgments (categorical, hypothetical, disjunctive; A70/B95, A73–4/B98–9). Thus, what Kant says in the *Reflexion* is that the concepts of substance/inherence, causation and community capture three kinds of real conditioning: a substance is the condition of the properties that inhere in it, a cause is the condition of its effect, and any two things in space stand in causal interaction (or 'community') with each other such that each is a condition of the other.[22]

Note that the categories, according to Kant's account in the Transcendental Analytic, come in two different forms, which in the literature on Kant have come to be called 'schematized' and 'unschematized' categories. While the former are the fundamental concepts of the understanding insofar as they are

---

respects, most strikingly in that causation is typically not thought of as a case of grounding, while according to Kant it is a case of real conditioning. On the other hand, it seems plausible to assume that Kant would have recognized all cases of grounding as cases of real conditioning, so that perhaps we can think of grounding as a special case of real conditioning. Now one question discussed among current metaphysicians is whether grounding is a unitary relation (e.g. Fine 2001; Rosen 2010) or a mere disjunction of more specific relations (e.g. Wilson 2014). While Eric Watkins's reading of real conditioning in Kant is similar to the view held by proponents of grounding who take grounding to be a unitary relation, the view I have suggested here resembles that of critics of grounding who take grounding to consist in a disjunction of specific grounding relations without metaphysical unity, where the specific relations alone are relevant to metaphysical explanations. See Willaschek 2017 for additional discussion.

[21] With respect to grounding, this is a question Jesssica Wilson, in her impressive paper mentioned in the previous footnote (Wilson 2014), neither asks nor answers. As I will argue, Kant is in a position to answer it without undermining Wilson's main point that there is no metaphysically unified notion of grounding (or real conditioning).

[22] From now on, when referring to the respective conditioning relation, I will speak of 'inherence' instead of 'inherence/subsistence' (following Kant's own example at A335/B393; see also 18:228 and below).

applied to objects in space and time, the latter are those same concepts considered independently of human forms of intuition (space and time). In the case of categorical judgments, the 'unschematized' category has as its content the relation between subject and predicate; in the case of hypothetical judgments, its content is the relation between ground and consequence (*Grund und Folge*); and in the case of disjunctive judgments, it is the relation between the parts of a whole (e.g. 4:311). According to Kant, each 'schematized' category comes with its own 'transcendental schema,' which is something like an a priori temporal pattern corresponding to the conceptual content of the category (A142–5/B181–5).[23]

Only by using schematized categories do we get cognition of objects and their relations. But even though we cannot cognize objects through unschematized categories, we can still use them to 'think' (B146; Bxxviii), that is, to entertain general thoughts about how the world might be. For instance, we can use the unschematized category of causation to contemplate the possibility of an uncaused cause. And we can use the unschematized category of inherence to think about the possibility of a substantial immaterial soul. In this way, we can reflect about non-empirical real conditioning relations.[24]

Since the metaphysical inferences Kant discusses in the Transcendental Dialectic abstract from the conditions of sensibility, the basic concepts they employ are not schematized but unschematized categories. Thus, the relation between the thinking subject and its representations (as discussed in the Paralogisms chapter) is an instance of the unschematized category of subject and predicate (but not of its application to space and time, which is the relation of substance and attribute). The relation between successive moments in time, between encompassing regions of space, between a spontaneous cause and its effect, and between the necessary and the contingent (as discussed in the Antinomy section) are instances of the unschematized category of ground and consequence.[25] And the relation between the predicates that together constitute the sum total of possibility (*omnitudo realitatis*)

---

[23] Karin de Boer argues that the 'unschematized' categories are mere abstractions from the schematized ones (de Boer 2016; also see Ferrarin 2015: 294–307 for discussion of a similar point). I am sympathetic to that proposal and intend what I say in the text to be compatible with it.

[24] According to Kant, however, this kind of thinking is severely limited by the fact that it lacks "sense and significance" (e.g. B149). I discuss these limitations later, in Section 9.4.

[25] How can temporal succession (or spatial inclusion) be a case of an unschematized category, given that we can cognize these relations but cannot gain cognition by using unschematized categories? In fact, we are speaking of two different relations here. Moments in time that stand in a relation of temporal succession thereby *also* stand in a relation of real conditioning. While we can cognize moments in time succeeding each other (because that is a relation that can be represented in the a priori form of inner sense), according to Kant we cannot cognize the real conditioning relation in which they thereby stand (because this relation cannot be represented in sensibility).

(discussed in the Ideal of Reason section) is an instance of the unschematized category of community.[26]

In accordance with Kant's general strategy of deriving the real use of the understanding and of reason from their logical use, these cases of real conditioning are indirectly based on the logical forms of relational judgments (A73–4/B98–9). Thus, the relation between a thinking subject and its representations instantiates the logical form of categorical judgments ('*a* is *F*'; 'All *A* are *B*') insofar as 'having' a representation is predicated categorically of the subject. Similarly, the relations between successive moments in time and between what exists necessarily and what exists contingently both instantiate the same logical form of judgment, namely that of hypotheticals ('If *x*, then *y*'). Finally, the relation between the concepts that constitute the '*omnitudo realitatis*,' but also the relation between parts that make up an aggregate whole, instantiates the logical form of disjunctive judgments ('Any part or element of *x* is either p_1 or p_2 or ... p_n') (B112–13; A73–4/B99).

According to Kant, each of the categories is a fundamental concept, not reducible to others, and there is no common genus specific to the three relational categories.[27] If real conditioning comes in three types that correspond to the three relational categories, this confirms the suggestion that the real conditioning relations that interest Kant in the Transcendental Dialectic do not fall under a unified genus and that the concept of real conditioning is the disjunction (as we can now see) of *three* fundamental relations (between subject and predicate, ground and consequence, and among the parts of a whole), each of which is primitive: "pure reason has no other aim than the absolute totality of synthesis on the side of conditions (*whether they are conditions of inherence, dependence, or concurrence*)" (A336/B393; emphasis added).[28]

Each of these fundamental relations has more specific conditioning relations under it. In the case of inherence, these include the relations between substance and attribute and between thinking subject and representations (4:333–4); in

---

[26] The *omnitudo realitatis* can be represented as a (possibly infinite) *disjunction* of predicates: 'Every (transcendentally positive, fundamental) property a thing might have is either F_1 or F_2 or F_3 ... or F_n.' The disjuncts condition each other insofar as each one "excludes" (B112) all others (if some property is F_1, it is not $F_2, F_3, \ldots, F_n$). Moreover, all disjuncts together condition the whole they constitute by completely exhausting its sphere. Again, we see different conditioning relations overlap. For more on the *omnitudo realitatis*, see Section 8.1.3.

[27] 'Relation' cannot be that genus, since there are other relations besides the ones thought in the categories, such as 'earlier/later,' 'left of,' and 'superior to.'

[28] See also 18:228, where Kant mentions the same three relations as types of the *un*conditioned. 'Concurrence' (from the Latin *concurrere*, to run together) means 'causal co-contribution' (Baumgarten, *Metaphysica*, §314). But note that Kant here seems to use the word in a more general and abstract sense, corresponding to the category of community and including non-causal relations modeled on the logical form of disjunction.

the case of dependence, they include empirical causation (A194/B239; A419/B447), noumenal causation (A419/B447), material constitution (that is, the dependence of a material object on its parts; A413/B440), temporal succession (A411–12/B438–9), spatial limitation (A412–13/B439–40), and the dependence of the contingent on the necessary (A415/B442; A419/B447). In the case of concurrence, we have community (interaction) (A211/B256), the relation among the parts of a whole (B113), and the relation between the predicates that together constitute the *omnitudo realitatis* in the case of complete determination (A573/B602).

There are some characteristics shared by all real conditioning relations (transitivity and intelligibility) and others shared by all conditioning relations that fall under the same relational category. For instance, it seems plausible to assume that all inherence and dependence relations are asymmetrical (and irreflexive), since they concern what Kant calls "subordinated" conditions (A409/B436) (where subordination is clearly asymmetrical), while all concurrence relations are symmetrical (and not irreflexive), because they concern "coordinated" conditions (B112). Nevertheless, there are deep differences even within each of the three types of real conditioning. Consider empirical causation and temporal succession, both of which are instances of dependence (ground and consequence). While an empirical cause can be sufficient to produce its effect without being necessary for it, an earlier moment in time is necessary and sufficient for its successor (at least on some ways of interpreting this relation) without in any sense producing it. It seems questionable, then, that we find unitary concepts of metaphysical dependence (in the current metaphysical sense of the term) even at the level of the three fundamental relational categories.

3.2.4 Is There an Analytic Link between Condition and Conditioned?

What has been said so far may suggest that we can define being 'conditioned,' in the sense relevant to the Supreme Principle, as standing in at least one relation R to something else (its 'condition'), where R falls under one of the three basic types of conditioning relations that Kant calls 'inherence,' 'dependence,' and 'concurrence.' However, things are not that straightforward. If they were, the existence of an R-condition would analytically follow from the existence of something R-conditioned.[29] Kant may seem to say as much in the passage immediately following the formulation of the Supreme Principle: "Such a principle of pure reason, however, is obviously *synthetic*; for the conditioned is analytically related to some condition, but not to the

---

[29] Talk of 'R-conditions' is adapted from Bennett 1974: 265; see also Wood 2010: 249.

unconditioned" (A308/B364).[30] In his discussion of the antinomies, however, Kant appears to deny that the existence of something conditioned in the realm of empirical objects (which are 'mere appearances') analytically implies the existence of its condition:

> [A]ppearances, in their apprehension, are themselves nothing other than an empirical synthesis (in space and time) and thus are given only *in this synthesis*. Now it does not follow at all that if the conditioned (in appearance) is given, then the synthesis constituting its empirical condition is thereby also given and presupposed; on the contrary, this synthesis takes place for the first time in the regress, and never without it. (A499/B527)

It is unclear whether 'given' in this passage is meant in the ontological or the epistemic sense (Section 3.1). In any case, however, if appearances 'are nothing other' than syntheses (of a given sensible manifold), and if the synthesis that 'constitutes' a condition 'takes place only in the regress' (from the conditioned to its condition), that is, depending on some contingent cognitive activity, then it is clear that from the existence of an appearance that is R-conditioned, it does not follow *analytically* that its R-condition exists. Thus, even if 'given' here means 'made cognitively accessible to us,' the passage seems to exclude an analytic link between condition and conditioned for appearances. However, Kant continues: "But in such a case one can very well say that a *regress* to the conditions, i.e., a continued empirical synthesis on this side, is demanded or *given as a problem*, and that *there could not fail to be conditions given through this regress*" (A499/B527; last emphasis added). A page before, Kant had pointed out that the sentence "If the conditioned is given, then through it a regress in the series of all conditions is *given* to us *as a problem*" is "analytic" (A497–8/B526).

Thus, Kant commits himself to the following four claims: (1) even among appearances, for anything conditioned there is a condition ('there could not fail to be conditions'), which is guaranteed by the three Analogies of Experience, which are *synthetic* principles a priori that correspond to the three relational categories and thus to the types of conditioning relations; (2) the link between the existence of the conditioned and the existence of its condition is not analytic but synthetic (requiring, in the case of appearances, an 'empirical synthesis'); (3) if there is something conditioned among appearances, we are

---

[30] One may wonder how the existence of a condition can follow from the existence of the conditioned given that there are conditioning relations such as causation, where the condition is merely sufficient but not necessary for the existence of the conditioned. Thus, in this case no specific condition is implied. But note that Kant only says that the conditioned "is analytically related to *some* condition" (emphasis added), which is compatible with the conditioning relation's being merely sufficient.

required to look for its condition (which is 'demanded or given as a problem'); and (4) this latter claim (3) is analytic.

If we now look back to what Kant says about the analytic link between conditioned and condition in the Introduction, we can see that it is compatible with these four claims, since there Kant does not say that the existence of the conditioned analytically implies the existence of the condition, but only that 'the conditioned is analytically related to some condition.' This is similar to what Kant says later in the Antinomy section, according to which the conditioned must be actively "related to a condition" (*auf eine Bedingung bezogen wird*) and that this condition is merely "*given* to us *as a problem*" (A498/B526). Thus, we can read Kant as saying that the analytic link between conditioned and condition, at least in the case of appearances, takes a prescriptive form: if there is something conditioned, look for its condition. It is only with respect to things in themselves that, from the existence of something conditioned, the *existence* of its condition follows: "If the conditioned as well as its condition are things in themselves, then when the first is given not only is the regress to the second *given as a problem*, but the latter is thereby really already *given* along with it" (A498/B527). If this latter claim is supposed to be analytic (Kant does not say whether or not it is), it cannot be analytic merely in virtue of the meaning of the term 'conditioned,' but rather because it is part of the concept of a thing in itself (*noumenon* in the positive sense) that all its conditions must exist. (We will return to this point later, in Section 5.3.)

But if the existence of a condition does not in general follow analytically from that of the conditioned, this raises the question of what it means for something to be conditioned.[31] We cannot assume that 'conditioned' can be *defined* as standing in a relation of real conditioning to some condition, since there is no analytic link to the *existence* of a condition. Rather, what is analytic is the link between the conditioned and the *search* for its condition. Since real conditioning, according to Kant, is an explanatory relation, this suggests that something is conditioned if it is in need of an explanation for which we must search and which would be provided by stating some condition. More specifically, something is conditioned relative to some conditioning relation R if it calls for an explanation in terms of its R-condition. For instance, something is causally conditioned if it requires an explanation in terms of its cause; something is modally conditioned (or contingent) if it requires an explanation by appeal to something necessary (and similarly for the other real conditioning relations). There may be reason to assume that for everything conditioned, there is a condition that explains it. But if what I have said so far is correct, the

---

[31] Thanks to Eric Watkins for pressing me on this point.

existence of an explanation does not follow *analytically* from the fact that there is something that is in need of explanation.

3.2.5 Real Conditioning: Conclusion

Something is 'conditioned' in the sense relevant to the Supreme Principle if it stands in need of explanation with respect to at least one real conditioning relation. Conversely, something is a 'condition' in the sense relevant to the Supreme Principle if there is something it explains by standing in at least one real conditioning relation to it. A relation is one of real conditioning if it falls under one of the three types Kant distinguishes, namely inherence, dependence, and concurrence.[32] We can 'think' of each of these relations by using one of the three relational categories. These categories come in two forms: schematized and unschematized (that is, applied to relations in space and time or abstracting from space and time). Each of the three basic relations covers a large variety of more specific relations but does not fall under a common genus specific to it. While all of these relations are transitive and explanatory, some are asymmetrical (and irreflexive), while others are not. Moreover, conditions in some conditioning relations are necessary but not sufficient, while in others they are sufficient but not necessary, both necessary and sufficient, or neither. Therefore, there does not seem to be any substantial unity among the three forms of real conditioning. Rather, 'real conditioning' is a disjunctive concept that covers a variety of diverse relations. What nevertheless allows Kant to speak of 'condition' and 'conditioned' in the general way he does is that each real conditioning relation instantiates at least one relational category and can thus be expressed by one of the logical forms of relational judgments.

This last feature also links real conditioning with logical conditioning. As we have seen, Kant distinguishes between three types of rational inference (that is, three types of logical conditioning) according to the three forms of relational judgments, depending on whether the major premise is categorical, hypothetical, or disjunctive. While all three species of *logical* conditioning instantiate a common genus (namely truth-preserving transition from premises to conclusion), there does not seem to be a substantive generic notion of conditioning that covers both logical and real conditioning. What both share, however, is a logical form derived from the three relational forms of judgment.[33]

---

[32] Note that the conditioning relations themselves are not defined in terms of explanation. Thus, 'real conditioning' is an ontological, not an epistemological relation, even if the terms 'condition' and 'conditioned' as they appear in the Supreme Principle are defined in terms of explanation.

[33] The "*conditions of the possibility of experience*" that figure so prominently in the Transcendental Analytic (e.g. A158/B197) are, I think, best understood as real conditions, since they concern

3.3 The Unconditioned

Given this account of real conditioning, it is easy to give at least a first formal characterization of what Kant, in the context of the Supreme Principle, might mean by 'the unconditioned,' namely something that is an unconditioned condition (UCC):

UCC   For all x, x is R-unconditioned (i.e. unconditioned with respect to some real conditioning relation R) if (1) there is a y such that x is an R-condition of y and (2) there is no z such that z is an R-condition of x.[34]

For instance, according to UCC, an uncaused cause is *causally* (but perhaps, because something precedes it, not temporally) unconditioned; a first moment in time is *temporally* (but perhaps, as caused by God, not causally) unconditioned; only God, if he exists, would be unconditioned with respect to all conditioning relations.

Since real conditioning is not a unitary relation but a collection of at least three basic relations (inherence, dependence, concurrence), there are, according to Kant, three basic ways in which something can be unconditioned: "1. The unconditioned of inherence (or of the aggregate). 2. That of ~~consequence~~ dependence or of the series. 3. That of the concurrence [*concurrentz*] of all possibility in one and of one for all" (18:228; see also A323/B379, A336/B393).[35] Even though the connections are far from obvious (and will concern us later; see Chapter 6), Kant claims that there is a correspondence between the unconditioned of inherence and the *soul* (as the unconditioned condition of one's representations), the unconditioned of dependence and the *world* (as the sum total of empirical objects), and the unconditioned of concurrence and *God*

---

the dependence of one type of object (appearances or empirical objects) on something else (subjective forms of cognition). While this clearly is not a case of empirical causation, it still seems to fall under the unschematized category of ground and consequence and hence to instantiate a conditioning relation of the dependence type. (But cf. Allison 2012, who reads these conditions as methodological and thus not as 'real' conditioning relations.)

[34] Clause (1) is necessary to avoid making everything that is not apt to stand in the conditioning relation R count as R-unconditioned. For instance, without clause (1), any moment in time would count as unconditioned in at least one respect, simply because it is not spatially conditioned. However, as Rosalind Chaplin and Joe Stratman have pointed out to me, clause (1) may be too strong, since it would mean that a God who chose not to create a world would not count as causally unconditioned. While one possible reaction might simply consist in acknowledging this consequence, a different solution might be to change clause (1) to 'there is a possible y such that, if y is actual, x is an R-condition of y.'

[35] That Kant here aligns 'aggregate' with 'inherence' is confusing (and perhaps simply a mistake), since at B112 he seems to think of an aggregate (more appropriately) as corresponding to the parts of a whole (and thus as a case of 'concurrence').

(as the unconditioned condition of all possibility) (e.g. A334/B391).[36] God, soul, and world, however, are not the only candidates for unconditioned objects. Whereas the specific ways in which the soul might be unconditioned (as substance, as simple, as unity, and as spiritual; A344/B402, see Section 7.1) do not lead to positing additional unconditioned *objects*, there might be more specific objects in the world that are unconditioned (e.g. first moments in time, smallest parts of matter, first causes; A415/B442). The latter would also be unconditioned objects 'of dependence or of the series.' We will return to the different forms of the unconditioned in Chapter 6. For now, as long as we are concerned with the Supreme Principle (which is meant to apply to all of them indiscriminately), we can abstract from the differences and concentrate on what they share.

3.3.1   Unconditioned Series

UCC is not the only sense in which Kant speaks of the unconditioned, however, or even the one most relevant to the Supreme Principle. Kant explicitly distinguishes between two ways in which we can "think" the unconditioned:

either as subsisting merely in the whole series, in which thus every member without exception is conditioned, and only their whole is absolutely unconditioned, or else the absolutely unconditioned is only a part of the series, to which the remaining members of the series are subordinated but that itself stands under no other condition. (A417/B445)[37]

Thus, we must distinguish a UCC (mentioned in the second part of the quote) from something that is unconditioned because it is the 'whole series' of *conditioned* conditions. Kant explains why such a series is unconditioned in a footnote: "The absolute whole of the series of conditions for a given conditioned is always unconditioned, because outside it there are no more conditions regarding which it could be conditioned" (A417/B445). As we will see, however, this explanation is problematic. While I will argue that there is a sense in which a complete series of conditions is unconditioned, it will become clear that it is very different from the sense of 'unconditioned' captured by UCC.

Kant's thought seems to be this: if we consider the 'absolute whole' of R-conditions of something conditioned C, W_{RC}, then W_{RC} cannot be

---

[36] Strictly speaking, the world as such is not unconditioned, since as an aggregate whole it is conditioned by its parts. It is only in certain respects that the world is, or might possibly be, unconditioned, for instance with respect to its temporal and spatial extension (see Section 6.1).

[37] By 'absolutely unconditioned' Kant does not seem to mean 'unconditioned with respect to every conditioning relation' (causal, temporal, modal, etc.), but rather 'completely unconditioned with respect to one specific conditioning relation.'

R-conditioned, because any R-condition that might condition it would have to be part of W_{RC}. Here is a possible argument for this claim: given that real conditioning is transitive, it follows (or at least seems to follow) that any R-condition of W_{RC} is also an R-condition of C, and thus has to be included in W_{RC}. But given that real conditioning in the case of subordinated conditions (that form a series) is irreflexive (Section 3.2.3), which precludes anything's conditioning itself, it follows that W_{RC} cannot contain its own R-condition. Thus, the thought that W_{RC} has an R-condition is contradictory, which means that W_{RC} does not have an R-condition and is thus R-unconditioned. Consider as an example the complete series S_{CE} of causes of some event E. Causation is transitive in that the cause of a cause of E is also a cause of E itself. Therefore, if S_{CE} were to have a cause, this cause would thereby be a cause of E, and thus a part of S_{CE}. But if nothing can cause itself (irreflexivity), then the cause of S_{CE} cannot be a part of S_{CE}, so that a contradiction ensues. Thus, there cannot be a cause of S_{CE}, which means that S_{CE} is causally unconditioned.

But this argument is flawed. That a given conditioning relation R is transitive does not imply that an R-condition of the complete series of R-conditions of x is therefore an R-condition of x. Transitivity works only among the conditions contained *in* the series. It does not mean that an R-condition *of* the series of conditions of x would thereby be part of that series and thus a condition of x.

Consider material constitution (as discussed in the Second Antinomy) and assume a series S_{PM} of material parts (and parts of parts, etc.) that constitute some material object M. The object M and its parts have material parts. A *series* of parts, by contrast, cannot itself have material *parts*. A series is a whole of members or elements, and these elements may happen to be material parts, but that does not mean that the series is a material whole with its elements as its material parts. So the idea that the series of conditions is itself conditioned in the same respect as its elements are conditioned (as a material part of the whole) does not apply. At least in this kind of case, the series of R-conditions is not the kind of object that *can* itself have an R-condition.

If we now return to the case of causation, we can see that even there the idea of a cause of a complete series of causes is problematic. Assume that the complete series of causes of some effect E is caused by God. Given that causation is irreflexive, God cannot be both the cause of the complete series of causes of E and a part of that series, because that would mean that God causes himself. But then, God cannot be a causal condition of E in the same sense as the causes that constitute the complete series.[38] As in the case of material constitution, the idea of being an R-condition does not apply to the

---

[38] God could be a causal condition in some other sense. For instance, if God is a (divine) cause$_d$ of the series of (finite) causes$_f$ of E, it does not follow that God is a member of that series.

complete series of R-conditions. If that series is conditioned at all, it must be conditioned in some respect other than R. But then, it becomes questionable in which sense a series of R-conditions can be said to be R-unconditioned at all.[39]

In what is his final statement on the issue, the unfinished prize essay on progress in metaphysics (1793), Kant himself seems to have recognized this problem and appears to have revoked his distinction between two conceptions of the unconditioned: "To think the concept of an absolute whole of the merely conditioned as unconditioned, involves a contradiction; the unconditioned can thus be considered only as member of the series, which delimits the latter as ground, and is itself no consequence of another ground" (20:287). This directly contradicts the view in the first *Critique*, where, as we have seen, Kant held that a "whole series, in which ... every member without exception is conditioned, ... is absolutely unconditioned" (A417/B445) and that "the totality of conditions is always itself unconditioned" (A322/B379).[40] So it seems that Kant eventually came to see that a complete but infinite series of conditions cannot be considered unconditioned.[41]

Since our goal here is to understand Kant's Rational Sources Account in the Transcendental Dialectic of the first *Critique*, we need to interpret Kant's view there, according to which an infinite but complete series of conditioned conditions is itself unconditioned. On the other hand, for the reasons developed earlier, we must acknowledge that there is something semantically odd about calling a series of conditioned items unconditioned. (As Kant puts it rather starkly in the *Progress* essay: it 'contains a contradiction.') In light of

---

[39] We can arrive at the same conclusion if we make the plausible assumption (A) that in order for something to be potentially R-conditioned it must be a potential R-condition. For example, for something to be a potential effect, it must be the kind of thing that can, at least in principle, also be a cause. Now, the series of R-conditions of *x* is not an R-condition of *x*; nor, it seems, can it be the R-condition of anything else. For instance, the *series* of all causes of *E* is not a cause of *E* and presumably cannot be a cause of anything else. Therefore, it follows from assumption (A) that, if a series of R-conditions is not a potential R-condition, it is not apt to be R-conditioned. But then, its not having an R-condition does not mean that it is R-*un*conditioned (in any interesting sense), but only that it is not one of the things that can be R-conditioned. For a similar worry, see Malzkorn 1999: 86, n. 203.

[40] In the *Progress* essay, Kant adds in a footnote: "The proposition: The whole of all conditioning in time and space is unconditioned, is false. For if everything in space and time is conditioned (internally), no whole thereof is possible. So those who assume an absolute whole of mere conditioned conditions contradict themselves, whether they take it to be bounded (finite) or unbounded (infinite), and yet space must be regarded as such a whole, and so must elapsed time" (20:288 n.). Now this may suggest that the supposed 'contradiction' only concerns thinking of a whole of conditions *in space and time* as unconditioned, which would be compatible with what Kant says in the first *Critique*. But the sentence from 20:287 quoted earlier does not contain such a restriction, which, moreover, would be incompatible with the consequence Kant draws, namely that the unconditioned can only consist in a first member of the series.

[41] On *Progress* and its place in the development of Kant's account of metaphysics, see the essays collected in Hahmann and Ludwig 2017.

this situation, I think we must admit that Kant's own distinction between two ways in which we can think the unconditioned (A417/B445) goes deeper than he himself seems to have acknowledged at the time he wrote the *Critique of Pure Reason*. We must distinguish between *two distinct senses* in which Kant speaks of the unconditioned in the first *Critique*: a sense according to which something unconditioned is an *unconditioned* condition (UCC) and a sense of 'unconditioned' that is applicable to a complete series of *conditioned* conditions.

Before we discuss the latter sense of unconditionality further, let me point out that even if there is something semantically odd about calling a complete series of conditioned conditions *un*conditioned, there are two reasons that explain why Kant thought it appropriate to treat a totality of conditions as one form of the unconditioned. First, one can think of something as R-unconditioned with respect to something R-conditioned, C, if it provides a *complete explanation* of C – that is, if it explains C and does not allow for further questions about R-conditions of C. For instance, something might plausibly count as *causally* unconditioned with respect to some effect E if it causally explains E and does not allow for further questions about the causes of E (and their causes, etc.). But then, a complete series of conditioned conditions is unconditioned in this sense. Second, even if a series of R-conditions lacks an R-condition only in the sense that it is not apt to be R-conditioned, it remains true (although uninformative) to say that it is R-unconditioned insofar as it does not have an R-condition. Thus, it is not inappropriate to treat a complete series of conditions as unconditioned.

3.3.2 Completeness and Totality

While the Supreme Principle identifies the unconditioned with the whole or complete series of subordinated conditions (which may be either finite or infinite), in other places Kant claims that it is "the *totality* of conditions" that is "always itself unconditioned" (A322/B379; emphasis added). While talk of a complete series of subordinated conditions and talk of a totality of conditions may come to the same thing in many contexts, there are some important differences between these formulations.[42]

---

[42] Even though the formulation of the Supreme Principle in terms of a 'series of subordinated conditions' is not entirely inappropriate for the Paralogisms and the Ideal, because the real conditioning relations under discussion there are transitive and thus allow for a series of conditions (see Section 3.2.1), it is clearly written with an eye to the antinomies. A possible reason for this is that, having 'discovered' the antinomies as early as 1769 (see 12:258), Kant seems to have planned for some time to incorporate the discussion of rational psychology (which became the Paralogism chapter) and rational theology (which became the Ideal chapter) into his discussion of the antinomies, with the immateriality of the soul as a topic of the Second

First, totality is a more demanding concept than mere completeness. Kant does not define what he means by completeness in this context, but he does define 'totality' or 'allness' as "nothing other than plurality considered as unity" (B111). If we think of completeness as true universal quantification (a set S is complete with respect to some property F iff it contains all Fs), then a totality of Fs is more demanding than mere completeness of Fs in that it requires not just all Fs but also that they be *considered as a unity*. For instance, let there be a plurality of apples – say, three – on the table and nothing else. While the three apples are all the things on the table, this does not yet make them a totality. For that, we need to *consider* them *as* a unity, e.g. *as* all the things on the table. But if totality is plurality *considered* as unity, then it is possible for there to be a plurality of Fs that in fact contains all Fs, e.g. all the things on the table, which is still not a totality because it is not considered *as* a unity (e.g. *as* all the things on the table). That there is a difference between completeness and totality is confirmed by the fact that there are truths about all the things on the table considered 'distributively,' as it were, that are not truths about them considered 'collectively,' as a totality. For instance, each of the things on the table is an apple, while their totality is not an apple.[43]

We can think of this difference either as merely 'notional' or in an ontologically robust way: on the first option, a totality is not an object over and above the members or elements it contains, but merely a way of considering them as a unity. Ontologically speaking, there is no difference between completeness and totality. On the second, it is an 'additional' object distinct from its members or elements. Kant's wording (*'considered* as unity') suggests that he is thinking of totality in the first, merely 'notional' way. This is confirmed by the fact that Kant repeatedly moves from the claim that 'all' conditions are given or not given (or that the series of conditions is 'complete' or 'not complete') without further argument to the claim that the totality of conditions is given (e.g. A331/B388) or not given (A499/B527). This makes sense if the difference between completeness and totality is merely 'notional' but would appear problematic if that difference is ontologically weighty. Hence, even though the situation is less than clear, I tentatively conclude that Kant draws a distinction between completeness and totality, but that it merely concerns the way in which we conceive of the complete set in question.

Antinomy (soul as simple) and the existence of God as a topic of the Fourth Antinomy (God as necessary being) (Guyer and Wood 1998: 64). But even after Kant gave up on that plan, remnants of it found their way into the published text. Thus, Kant mentions the indivisibility of the soul in connection with the Second Antinomy (A443/B471), and we find an echo of the Antinomy section's contrast between ideas that are either "too big" or "too small" (A486/B514) in the Transcendental Ideal (A613/B641).

[43] For a similar distinction between completeness and totality, see Levey 2016.

The Supreme Principle of Pure Reason (3.3.2)

Second, talk of a *totality* of conditions (e.g. A337/B394) seems to be more general than that of a complete *series* of conditions that Kant uses in the Supreme Principle. For instance, consider a substance S and its first-order property F. If F is conditioned by S insofar as F inheres in S (and thus depends on S), then there is a *totality* of conditions of F (which in this case consists only of S).[44] But there does not seem to be any 'series of conditions subordinated one to the other,' as the Supreme Principle has it. Similarly, if some objects consist of first-order parts which do not likewise consist of parts, then there is a totality of parts, but not a series. This difference can be minimized, however, if we take into account that all real conditioning relations are transitive and at least in principle allow for iteration. Thus, even if a substance S is the ultimate bearer of some property and does not in turn inhere in anything else, there is at least a *potential* series, since S might have inhered in something else (and thus might have been a substance only relatively speaking). Similarly, even if the parts of M do not have further parts, there is a potential series insofar as they might have had parts.

Third, the Supreme Principle speaks of conditions '*subordinated* one to the other.' This raises a question about 'coordinated' conditions, such as the same-order parts of a material object. Recall that Kant claims that the members of a disjunction are "*coordinated* with one another, not *subordinated*, so that they do not determine each other *unilaterally*, as in a series, but *reciprocally*, as in an *aggregate*" (B112). Does a totality of *coordinated* conditions automatically count as unconditioned (because it is a totality)? It seems not. Consider again the case of a material object M consisting of first-order parts that do not in turn have any parts. Each part is 'unconditioned' insofar as it is a condition of M but not conditioned by any further parts. But a totality of first-order parts that makes up M is not *necessarily* unconditioned in this respect. In case the first-order parts of M do have parts, we can still talk about the *totality* of first-order parts, but that totality would clearly not count as unconditioned with respect to the part–whole conditioning relation, since each first-order part is conditioned by its parts. This shows that a totality of *coordinated* conditions counts as unconditioned only if its members are unconditioned.

Finally, a complete series of *subordinated* conditions (parts and their parts, etc.) of something conditioned (e.g. a material object M) is not necessarily the same as the *totality* of its conditions (parts). Since any divisible object has more than one part that conditions it, there will also be *more than one series* of

---

[44] This may seem to conflict with Kant's definition of totality as "plurality considered as unity." However, since Kant seems committed to the claim that God is also a 'totality' (because God is unconditioned and everything unconditioned is a totality; see also A578/B606), it is obvious that this definition has to be amended, e.g. by allowing for the plurality to be merely potential (i.e. there could in principle have been more than just one condition).

subordinated conditions (of parts of parts, etc.), *each of which*, if complete, is a totality which is unconditioned (because it is not again conditioned in the same respect). By contrast, the *totality of conditions* (parts) of M consists of *all* its conditions (parts, their parts, etc.), considered as a unity, that is, in *all* series of subordinated parts. This means that the concept of the totality of conditions of something is broader than that of a particular complete series of its *subordinated* conditions.

I would like to draw the following conclusion from our discussion in this section: since what matters for Kant's conception of the unconditioned is that it consists of *all conditions* of something conditioned, *considered as a unity*, it seems more appropriate to formulate the Supreme Principle simply in terms of a '*totality of conditions*' rather than, as Kant in fact does, in terms of a complete series of conditions.[45]

3.3.3 Totality of Conditions and the Principle of Comprehension

Kant's conception of totality (as plurality considered as unity) provides us with a simple explanation of how, in reconstructing the thoughts of the speculative metaphysician, he can assume without argument that the existence of something conditioned requires not just some condition but the *totality* of its conditions. For instance, Kant claims: "the possibility of something conditioned presupposes the totality of its conditions, but not the totality of its consequences" (A337/B394; see also A409–12/B436–8). While Kant in this context argues for the asymmetry between the 'ascending' series of conditions and the 'descending' series of consequences (A331/B388; A336/B394), he does not *argue* for the claim that reason requires the *totality* of conditions for everything conditioned (which is just another expression of the Supreme Principle) but seems to take this for granted.

This can seem problematic because it is not obvious how to get from the existence of something conditioned to the existence of the totality of its conditions. Some of Kant's formulations might suggest that we arrive at the idea of the totality of conditions (or the conclusion that there must be such a totality) by some kind of reasoning that proceeds from the conditioned to its condition, and from there to its condition, etc., for instance in a series of prosyllogisms (e.g. A331–2/B388–9). But this kind of reasoning would not work in the case of an infinite series of conditions (which Kant allows for),

---

[45] Kant speaks of a "totality of conditions," for instance, at A322/B379, A324/B380, A326–7/B383–4, A340/B398, A411/B437, and A533/B561, as well as 5:104 and 5:107. Note that Kant often calls this totality 'absolute' (e.g. A326/B382; A499/B527), which presumably means that the totality in question really contains *all* conditions and not just a certain subset (see Kant's explanation of his use of 'absolute' at A326/B382).

The Supreme Principle of Pure Reason (3.3.3)

since in this case we would never complete the series of inferences necessary to arrive at the totality of conditions. Similarly, there is no valid inference from

P1 There is something R-conditioned

and

P2 For everything R-conditioned there is at least one R-condition

to the conclusion that there is a *totality* of R-conditions (cf. e.g. Allison 2004: 332), because it only takes us to the conclusion that either there is some unconditioned R-condition or the series of R-conditions is infinite. But in the infinite case, we cannot simply assume that the series is *complete* (because P2 only takes us to the next condition, and to its condition, etc.), so that it does not follow that the *totality* of conditions exists.

This claim follows trivially, however, if we take Kant's definition of 'totality' to express the naïve principle of set formation (sometimes called the 'principle of comprehension'). According to this principle, for every (instantiated) predicate (i.e. a predicate that applies to at least one object), there is a (non-empty) set of all objects that fall under it. Kant's definition of totality can be understood as saying just that: for every (actual or potential) plurality of objects that are F, there is the totality of Fs. For instance, if 'is red' is an instantiated predicate, there is a non-empty set of *all* red things – that is, *the totality* of red things.[46]

Equally, if 'is a condition of x' is an instantiated predicate, it follows that there is a *totality of conditions of x*. Since 'is an R-condition of' is transitive (Section 3.2.1), this totality includes the conditions of the conditions of x, and their conditions, etc. (which is why Kant, in this context, often appeals to a

---

[46] Thus, I take Kant's concept of a totality to be roughly equivalent to Cantor's concept of a set, which Cantor famously defines (in a way that echoes Kant's concept of a totality) as "jede Zusammenfassung M von bestimmten wohlunterschiedenen Objecten n unsrer Anschauung oder unseres Denkens ... zu einem Ganzen" (any collection M of well-defined objects of our intuition or thought into a whole) (Cantor 1895: 481). As is well known, this 'naïve' concept of a set leads into paradoxes (such as Russell's paradox), since it allows us to speak of the set of all sets that do not contain themselves, and thus must be restricted in appropriate ways (e.g. by distinguishing between sets and classes and/or restricting the principle of comprehension to first-order predicates, that is, predicates that do not quantify over sets). Neither Kant nor the metaphysicians whose thoughts he reconstructs could have been aware of these difficulties. Note, however, that the inference from the existence of the conditioned to the existence of a totality of conditions does not invoke higher-order predicates, and thus appears to be valid even if the principle of comprehension is appropriately restricted. On the other hand, since Kant himself wants to *deny* that for empirical objects there is a totality of their conditions (A499/B527), Kant might be read as implicitly rejecting that principle for the domain of appearances; see Section 5.3. For a discussion of Kant's conception of the world (as the totality of objects) in relation to Cantor's set theory, see Kreis 2015.

'series of conditions'; see again e.g. A331–2/B388–9). Thus, if we presuppose the principle of comprehension, which is highly intuitive (after all, thinkers such as Frege and Cantor took it for granted), the existence of a totality of conditions of x (including all members of a series of subordinated conditions) follows immediately from the existence of at least one condition of x.[47]

3.3.4 Conclusion: The Unconditioned and the Supreme Principle

As we have seen, we must distinguish between two senses in which Kant speaks of 'the unconditioned' (on the side of the 'real use' of reason, that is, concerning real conditioning relations). First, there is the concept of an *unconditioned condition* (UCC), and second, that of a *totality of conditioned conditions*:

TCC   For all x, x is unconditioned (with respect to conditioning relation R) if x is the totality of R-conditions of something R-conditioned, each of which R-conditions is itself R-conditioned.

Finally, there is the concept of the *unconditioned as a totality of conditions* (UTC) that comprises both UCC and TCC:

UTC   For all x, x is unconditioned (with respect to conditioning relation R) if x is the totality of R-conditions of something R-conditioned.

This is the concept of the unconditioned Kant must have in mind when he claims that "the totality of conditions is always itself unconditioned" (A322/B379; see Section 6.3.1 for discussion of that passage). While UCC and TCC are mutually *exclusive*, UTC is the generic conception of something unconditioned in Kant. While in the case of an infinite series of R-conditions UTC takes the form of TCC, in the case of a finite series that ends in an unconditioned R-condition there are *two* unconditioned items: one consisting in the unconditioned R-condition (UCC), the other in the totality of conditions (UTC), which in this case is finite. Since the Supreme Principle posits something unconditioned for both finite and infinite series of conditions, the unconditioned mentioned in the Supreme Principle can only be a UTC.[48]

This may seem surprising (particularly in light of Kant's emphasis on UCC in the *Progress* essay), but philosophically speaking it makes good sense.

---

[47] Thanks to Annette Werner for helping me to see this.

[48] By allowing for infinite series of conditions without UCC, Kant commits himself to the view that real conditioning is not well founded (see note 18 above). This is true even for his position in *Progress*, where he only denies that infinite series of conditions are unconditioned, not that they are possible.

The Supreme Principle of Pure Reason (3.3.4)

Kant repeatedly insists that what is relevant to the status of being unconditioned is *totality* – the "totality of the series of conditions" (e.g. A412/B439), "the totality of the synthesis of conditions" (e.g. A326/B382), the "totality of conditions" (e.g. A322/B379; 5:109; 5:254). When Kant says that we can think the *unconditioned* in one of two ways, it is really this *totality* he is speaking of, since, as far as 'subordinated' conditions are concerned, we can think of it as consisting either in an infinite series of conditions or in a finite series ending in an unconditioned condition. Thus, what reason is interested in is not primarily unconditioned conditions as such but the *totality* of conditions. Therefore, the sense of unconditionality most relevant to the Supreme Principle is that of UTC, not UCC or TCC.

Moreover, UTC covers two kinds of cases that differ on a different dimension than UCC and TCC, namely (1) a complete series of subordinated R-conditions of something conditioned, considered as a totality, and (2) the totality of *all* conditions of something conditioned. Of these two cases, the second is more fundamental, because it includes, but is not included in, the first. (If there are any complete series of subordinated conditions of x, e.g. causal chains leading up to x, the totality of conditions of x will encompass *all* of them.)

This finally takes us to the following formulation of the Supreme Principle:

Supreme Principle   If there is something R-conditioned, then there is the totality of its R-conditions (UTC).

This means that if there exists some object x that is conditioned with respect to some real conditioning relation R (which is an instance of inherence, dependence, or concurrence), then the totality of its R-conditions also exists (which, in the case of 'subordinated' conditions, consists either of one or more infinite but complete series of such conditions or of one or more complete finite series ending in some UCC).

Kant does not offer an argument for the Supreme Principle. Nevertheless, the results of this chapter may suggest a very simple and straightforward argument for it that is implicit in what Kant says in the Introduction to the Transcendental Dialectic:

P1   If something R-conditioned exists, then the totality of its R-conditions exists.
P2   Any totality of R-conditions is itself R-unconditioned (in the sense of UTC).
C   If something R-conditioned exists, then something R-unconditioned (UTC) exists.

As we have seen, Kant seems to accept P1 by saying that "the possibility of something conditioned presupposes the totality of its conditions" (A337/B394; although he *may* not be speaking in his own voice here, but merely reconstructing the thoughts of the speculative metaphysician). Moreover, P1 follows from the 'principle of comprehension' (Section 3.3.3), assuming that there is at least one condition for everything conditioned. (This latter assumption is one Kant also accepts, even though, as I have argued, he may not think of it as an analytic truth; see Section 3.2.4). Given the definition of UTC, P2 is an analytic truth (Section 3.3.4). Thus, there is a valid inference to the Supreme Principle from premises Kant (seems to have) accepted. As we will see later (Section 5.3), however, Kant thinks that this argument (and hence the Supreme Principle) is not valid for appearances, but only for things in themselves.

For now, I would only like to point out that in the Transcendental Dialectic, even though Kant explicitly discusses the premises of this argument, he neither puts them together *as an argument* for the Supreme Principle nor suggests in any way that the principle might be based on this (or any other) argument. Rather, the only motivation for the principle offered by Kant consists in his claim that the Logical Maxim cannot become a principle of pure reason unless we accept the Supreme Principle (the 'Transition Passage'). This lack of argument is not an oversight but part of Kant's general strategy in the Transcendental Dialectic. After all, Kant does not accept the Supreme Principle, in its unrestricted form, as objectively valid, but rather denies its validity for empirical objects. Instead, Kant presents it as the 'supreme principle of pure reason,' which suggests that it cannot be derived from premises that are more general or independently certain. (We will return to this issue later, in Section 5.3.)

3.4 The Supreme Principle and the Principle of Sufficient Reason

When Kant calls the Supreme Principle the "supreme principle of pure reason" (A308/B365), he is of course aware that this title had previously – in the Leibniz-Wolffian tradition – been bestowed upon either the Principle of Non-Contradiction (PNC) or both the PNC and the Principle of Sufficient Reason (PSR). The former says that 'nothing is both A and not-A' (e.g. Baumgarten, *Metaphysica*, §7). According to the latter, 'nothing is without a sufficient reason/ground (*ratio*)' (e.g. *Metaphysica*, §22). Leibniz famously calls these the "two great principles" on which all our reasoning is based (*Monadology*, §31). While according to Leibniz both the PNC and the PSR are supreme principles of reason, Wolff (at least in certain writings) and Baumgarten had claimed that the PSR can be derived from the PNC (*Metaphysica*, §§20–22), which is thus an even 'higher' (or alternatively, more fundamental) principle.[49] In this section, it is not my aim to discuss Kant's

---

[49] For an overview of the history of the PSR and the different versions of it defended by different rationalists, see e.g. Engfer 1989; for recent defenses of the PSR, see e.g. Della Rocca 2010; Levey 2016.

complex and changing attitude toward the PSR, but only to indicate how the PSR relates to the Supreme Principle.[50]

In the *Critique of Pure Reason*, Kant insists that it is impossible to derive synthetic judgments from the PNC, which, however, is the "supreme principle of all analytic judgments" (A150/B189). Kant also formulates a "supreme principle of all synthetic judgments": "Every object stands under the necessary conditions of the synthetic unity of the manifold of intuition in a possible experience" (A158/B197). This means that for every object, it must be possible for it to be intuitively given in space and time and to be thought according to the categories. But as Kant insists, this principle is valid only for 'appearances' (empirical objects), not for 'things in general' (including things in themselves).

The Supreme Principle, by contrast, even though it is equally meant to be a principle of synthetic cognition, is not restricted to empirical objects: "Different synthetic propositions must arise from it [the Supreme Principle], of which the pure understanding knows nothing, since it [the understanding] has to do only with objects of a possible experience, whose cognition and synthesis are always conditioned" (A308/B364–5). This suggests that by calling it the 'supreme principle of reason,' Kant meant it to replace the PSR, and not the PNC, since it is only the former and not the latter that, according to Kant, is a (real or purported) source of purely rational synthetic cognition.[51]

In fact, the connection between the Supreme Principle and the PSR seems to be even closer than that, since the former can be understood as Kant's transformation of the latter in response to an objection Kant himself had raised against the universal validity of the PSR. As early as 1755, in his *Nova Dilucidatio*, Kant had insisted that the PSR cannot be true when it comes to God: since God cannot have a ground of existence that is external to him, the PSR would imply that God is, or contains, his own ground, which according to

---

[50] On Kant and the PSR, see e.g. Eidam 2000; Longuenesse 2005a; Chignell 2009; Hicks 2013; Boehm 2016.

[51] Omri Boehm argues that the Supreme Principle just is (a formulation of) the PSR, and the Logical Maxim just is a 'subjective formulation' of the PSR (Boehm 2016: 559; see also Kreines 2015: 115). But as saw earlier, in Section 3.2.2, Kant's notion of real conditioning is wider than the notion of a sufficient reason in that it also includes necessary conditions and perhaps even conditions that are neither necessary nor sufficient. Moreover, as I will indicate presently, most real conditioning relations, according to Kant, are irreflexive, while Kant reads the PSR as implying the reflexivity of grounding. The two principles therefore cannot be identical, according to Kant. This is not to deny that Kant places the Supreme Principle within the same region of discourse as the PSR in the Introduction to the Transcendental Dialectic. This can be seen from the fact that in a paragraph leading up to the Logical Maxim and the Supreme Principle, he contrasts rational cognition with the cognition of the understanding by claiming that the principle of causation ("everything that happens must have a cause") is a principle not of reason but of the understanding (A307/B363). In the Second Analogy, Kant had explicitly identified the principle of causation with the PSR (A200–1/B246; also see A217/B265), since he thinks of it as the legitimate application of the PSR to empirical objects.

Kant is absurd (1:394). Kant's reason for this latter claim is that a ground of existence is a cause, and a cause must be "earlier" than its effect. If God were the ground of his own existence, he would have to have existed earlier than himself, which is impossible (1:394). Now this argument might seem problematic since if God is thought of as timeless, the distinction between 'earlier' and 'later' does not apply. But perhaps what Kant means by saying that a cause is 'earlier' than its effect is not a temporal relation but simply the notion that both must be distinct.[52] Kant could therefore be read as insisting, against those 'modern philosophers' (1:394), such as Spinoza, who claim that God is *causa sui*, that the grounding relation, at least in the case of 'real' grounds (grounds of existence as opposed to grounds of cognition), is irreflexive.[53] Nothing grounds itself.[54]

We find what is fundamentally the same point in an essay published thirty-five years later (*On a Discovery*, from 1790), in which Kant criticizes his Leibnizian critic Eberhardt for (among other things) his misguided proof of the PSR. In close analogy with his distinction between the logical and the real use of reason, Kant distinguishes between two versions of the PSR, a 'logical (formal) principle of cognition' and a 'transcendental (material) principle.' According to the former, "Every sentence must have a reason [*Grund*]," while the latter, which is the one Kant is interested in, holds that "Every thing must have its ground [*Grund*]" (8:193–4). (Here, all 'grounds' are assumed to be sufficient.) Now Kant's fourth and final objection to Eberhardt's proof is that

> the proposition itself [the PSR], in the unlimited universality in which it there stands, is, if it is to be valid of things [and not just, like the logical principle, of sentences], obviously false; for according to it, *there would be absolutely nothing unconditioned*; but to seek to avoid this embarrassing consequence, by saying of the supreme being that it does, indeed, also have a ground of its existence, but that this lies within it, leads to a contradiction; for the ground of the existence of a thing, as real ground, must always be distinguished from this thing and this must then necessarily be thought as dependent upon another. (8:198; emphasis added)

Kant's objection can be restated as follows:

1. If x is a ground of y, x is distinct from y (irreflexivity of grounding).
2. Now assume that (necessarily) every object has a ground (PSR).
3. Then it follows that (necessarily) for every object x there is a ground y that is distinct from x (from 1, 2).

---

[52] In the lecture transcript *Metaphysics Herder*, Kant makes this point by saying that "to have a ground is to be a consequence," where the consequence is "aliud" (something else); 28:13.
[53] See also Watkins 2016b: 122.
[54] Irreflexivity is also usually assumed in the current literature on grounding. For references and critical discussion, see Jenkins 2011.

4. Having a ground distinct from oneself is a way of being conditioned (by definition).
5. It would follow from the PSR that (necessarily) every object is conditioned (from 3, 4).
6. It is possible that there is an object (God) that is unconditioned (assumption).
7. Hence, the PSR is false.

The fact that Kant can move from 4 to 5 (or rather, in the quote, suppress 4 and simply claim 5) confirms our earlier observation that 'condition,' for Kant, is a more general term than 'ground' (Section 3.2.2), unless in the quote, and unlike in the first *Critique*, Kant simply equates the two. In any case, we can see that he takes the PSR to be incompatible with the existence of something unconditioned.[55] Thus, to arrive at an unrestrictedly valid version of the PSR, the principle would have to be revised in order to accommodate the irreflexibility of grounding and thus to allow for something unconditioned. This can be done by explicitly distinguishing between ground and grounded and by restricting the PSR to those things that do have a ground:

PSR$_{an}$ For all objects x, if x is grounded, there is some y such that $x \neq y$ and y is the ground of x.

If we assume with Kant that 'being grounded' analytically implies 'has a ground distinct from itself,' then PSR$_{an}$ is an analytic truth. But now consider the question whether y is itself grounded. If it is, PSR$_{an}$ has the consequence that for y, there must be some z such that $y \neq z$ and z is the ground of y – and so on. It follows from the principle of comprehension (Section 3.3.3) that there is the totality of all grounds of x, which totality, because of the transitivity of grounding, also includes all grounds of grounds of x, and their grounds, etc. Put differently, it follows from PSR$_{an}$ that for everything that is grounded, there is the totality of its grounds.

If we now assume that the totality of grounds of x must be ungrounded (in the relevant respect) because it contains *all* the grounds of x, we arrive at:

PSR$_{ung}$ For all x, if x is grounded, there exists the totality of grounds of x, which is itself ungrounded.

---

[55] Boehm claims that the central assumption in Kant's rejection of the PSR is the claim that existence is not a real predicate (Boehm 2016). But the claim that grounding is irreflexive seems sufficient for his critique and, unlike the claim about existence, is actually appealed to in Kant's argument.

And if we think of grounding as a special case of real conditioning (more specifically, a case of either inherence or dependence, which are both irreflexive), we have arrived at a version of the Supreme Principle:

Supreme Principle   For all x, if x is conditioned, there exists the totality of conditions of x, which is itself unconditioned.

The point of this 'derivation' of the Supreme Principle from the corrected PSR is not to show that the Supreme Principle is valid, of course, but merely that there is a plausible route from the one to the other, which consists of steps Kant is committed to either by his criticism of the PSR or by what he says in the first *Critique* about the Supreme Principle and its components.

Kant himself does not tell us why the Supreme Principle should be considered the 'supreme principle of pure reason' or how he arrived at it. The line of thought developed in this section suggests a plausible answer to both questions: the Supreme Principle can be regarded as the 'supreme principle of reason' because it replaces the PSR (and because, on Kant's view, the only other candidate for that title, the PNC, is only the supreme principle of analytic judgments, and thus of the understanding). And Kant arrived at this idea by recognizing (as early as 1755) that the PSR violates the irreflexivity of grounding and thus has to be restricted in a way that naturally leads to the Supreme Principle.

4 Understanding the Transition Passage (A307–8/B364)

Having investigated the Logical Maxim (Chapter 2) and the Supreme Principle (Chapter 3), we are now in a position to return to the quote from the beginning of Chapter 2 and ask why, according to Kant, accepting the Logical Maxim leads naturally to accepting the Supreme Principle. Thus, the question is why, in attempting to turn the plurality of empirical cognitions into a unified system of scientific knowledge, we must assume that something unconditioned exists. While we will be able fully to answer this question only in the next chapter, in this chapter we will prepare an answer by interpreting what in Chapter 2 I had called the Transition Passage:

this logical maxim can become a principle of *pure reason* only through one's assuming [*dadurch, dass man annimmt*] that when the conditioned is given, then so is the whole series of conditions subordinated one to the other, which is itself unconditioned, also given (i.e., contained in the object and its connection). (A307–8/B364)[1]

In the first section of the Introduction to the Transcendental Dialectic, Kant had explained that the metaphysical fallacies to be analyzed in the Transcendental Dialectic rest on a specific kind of illusion, a "transcendental illusion," which consists in the tendency to mistake "subjective principles" for "objective" ones (A297–8/B353–4; see Section 5.2.1). If the transition from the Logical Maxim to the Supreme Principle Kant mentions in the Transition Passage is meant to be an instance of this kind of illusion, that might suggest that the transition consists in mistaking the merely subjective Logical Maxim for the objective Supreme Principle.[2] But such a reading does not accord with Kant's wording in the Transition Passage, which contains the claim:

T   The Logical Maxim can *become* a principle of pure reason (PPR) only *by our assuming* the Supreme Principle.

---

[1] Translation altered in order to stay closer to the German original.
[2] That is how the transition is often presented in the literature (e.g. Renaut 1998: 356; Grier 2001: 122, 269; Allison 2004: 339; Proops 2010: 543; Kreines 2015: 115; Stang 2016: 290).

This suggests not that we mistake the Logical Maxim for something it is not, but rather that the Logical Maxim is *transformed* into something else (a principle of pure reason).[3] While this may sound somewhat mysterious, we will see that it is possible to read it in a way that makes perfectly good sense. Moreover, neither the Logical Maxim itself nor the principle it 'becomes' is mistaken for the Supreme Principle; rather, the latter must be *assumed* for the Logical Maxim to become such a principle. So something more than just mistaking the one for the other must be at issue.

The Transition Passage raises a number of questions. Does Kant intend the antecedent to be satisfied ('The Logical Maxim becomes a PPR, which is possible only by assuming the Supreme Principle,' from which it follows that we assume the Supreme Principle)? Or is the whole sentence meant to be hypothetical, or even counterfactual ('*If* the Logical Maxim becomes/were to become a PPR, *then* it does so only by assuming the Supreme Principle')? What does it mean for a maxim to become a principle of pure reason, and which principle does the Logical Maxim become? Why is this possible only by assuming the Supreme Principle, and what exactly does it mean to 'assume' such a principle? And finally, is Kant here *endorsing* the transition from the Logical Maxim to the Supreme Principle (and thus the Supreme Principle itself), or is this meant to be a case of transcendental illusion, so that Kant is really saying that it must *appear as if* we have to accept the Supreme Principle?

To answer these questions, it will prove helpful to look, first, at the final paragraph of the Introduction, where Kant raises the question of whether the Supreme Principle is 'objectively valid' (Section 4.1), and then at the Appendix to the Transcendental Dialectic, where he, in close parallel to the Transition Passage, claims of various 'logical principles' that they presuppose 'transcendental principles,' which we must therefore 'assume' (Section 4.2). We will see that in light of the distinction between the regulative and the constitutive use of principles, there are two very different ways of understanding what it means to 'assume' a principle. In the resolution of the Antinomy of Reason, Kant himself applies the regulative/constitutive distinction to the Supreme Principle (or a close relative of it). This will finally allow us to answer the earlier questions concerning the Transition Passage (Section 4.3). We will see that the transition to the metaphysical Supreme Principle involves two steps that are not made explicit in the Transition Passage: one from the Logical

---

[3] R. Lanier Anderson rightly emphasizes the fact that the Logical Maxim is supposed to *become* a principle of pure reason (Anderson 2015: 281–3). According to him, the Logical Maxim becomes a principle of reason by being transformed into a universal and unifying principle. Since Anderson is mainly interested in the synthetic character of the Supreme Principle, however, he discusses neither *why* the Logical Maxim should become a principle of pure reason nor why, in the Transition Passage, Kant says that we must *assume* the Supreme Principle.

Maxim to the regulative use of the Supreme Principle, and another from the regulative use of the Supreme Principle to its constitutive use. While in this chapter we will try to understand what exactly it is that Kant claims in the Transition Passage, in the next we will turn to possible *arguments* for this claim.[4]

4.1 Objective Validity

One paragraph after the Transition Passage, Kant ends the Introduction to the Transcendental Dialectic with a series of questions:

whether the principle that the series of conditions ... reaches to the unconditioned, has *objective correctness* or not; what consequences flow from it for the empirical use of the understanding, or whether there rather is no such *objectively valid* sentence of reason [*Vernunftsatz*] at all, but only a *logical prescription* in the ascent to ever higher conditions to approach completeness in them ...; whether, I say, this need of reason has, through a misunderstanding, been taken for a transcendental principle of reason, which overhastily postulates such an unlimited completeness in the series of conditions in the objects themselves ...: All this will be our concern in the transcendental dialectic which we will now develop from its sources hidden deep in human reason. (A308–9/B365–6; emphasis added)[5]

Kant is asking here whether the Supreme Principle 'has objective correctness' or not, whether it is 'objectively valid,' and whether it really is a 'transcendental principle of reason' or only mistaken for one. The Logical Maxim, by contrast, does not seem to raise such questions, since it is only 'a logical prescription.' As Kant had pointed out earlier, it is "merely a subjective law of economy for the provisions of our understanding" (A306/B362) that does not apply to objects, so that we are not justified "to give objective validity to that maxim" (A306/B363). But what does it mean to say that a principle has 'objective validity'?

Kant's terminology can be confusing in this respect, since he sometimes uses the terms 'objective validity,' 'objective reality,' and 'objective correctness' interchangeably, while at other times he seems to draw more or less subtle distinctions between them.[6] As a general rule, it can be said that

---

[4] This means that the present chapter will primarily be concerned with rather thorny interpretative issues. Readers primarily interested in the philosophical questions at issue in the Transition Passage may therefore consider skipping to the next chapter.
[5] I deviate from Guyer and Wood in various ways in order to stay closer to the original. Among other things, Guyer and Wood take "objectively valid" (*objectivgültigen*) at A309/B365 to refer to possible empirical consequences of the Supreme Principle, whereas the expression "*objectivgültigen Vernunftsatz*" is more naturally understood as referring to the Supreme Principle itself.
[6] See Redaktion 2015 on objective reality; Seeberg 2015 on objective correctness; and Nenon 2015 on objective validity; see also Meerbote 1982; Zöller 1984.

'objective' in these expressions means something like 'concerning objects' (in the widest sense: something other than merely a representational state of the subject), while 'subjective' means 'concerning (merely) the subject of cognition' (e.g. A320/B376). Now if a principle is 'valid' (or 'correct'), this presumably means that it (or its use) is rationally justified or legitimate. Consequently, a principle is 'objectively valid' if it can be *legitimately* applied to *objects*.

Compare the case of the categories. The transcendental deduction of the categories is meant to answer the question of whether the categories have "objective validity" (e.g. A89/B122; see also A84/B116–17).[7] This question arises because the categories are not derived from experience, so that it is unclear how they can refer to objects at all (A85/B117). Thus, the question is not which judgments are true, but whether a certain type of concept can be legitimately applied to objects in the first place. Only if the categories have 'objective validity' can the question of whether particular judgments containing them are true arise.

Things are different when the objective validity not of concepts but of judgments (e.g. principles) is at issue, since in many cases proving that an a priori judgment (such as the principle of causation) is legitimately applicable to objects ipso facto establishes its truth.[8] But even so, the question of whether a judgment or principle is legitimately applicable to some domain of objects is distinct from the question of whether the principle is true.[9] And indeed, as we will see in the next section, Kant claims that there are principles of reason that have (as Kant qualifies, 'indeterminate') objective validity and thus can be legitimately applied to objects in nature even though we cannot know them to be true (or, put differently, even though for all we know they may be false).

So by asking whether or not the Supreme Principle is 'objectively valid,' Kant is asking not whether it is true of some domain of objects, but whether we can be rationally justified in applying it to objects in the first place. This is an open question at the beginning of the Transcendental Dialectic for the same

---

[7] When Kant introduces the project of the transcendental deduction of the categories by raising the question *quid iuris* (by what 'right' do we use the categories, or what legitimates this use?), he first speaks of "objective reality" (A84/B117) but then quickly moves to "objective validity" (e.g. A87/120; A89/B122), which suggests that he is using these terms interchangeably.

[8] The principle of causation, for instance, has objective validity with respect to all empirical events because, according to the Second Analogy argument, we can have empirical cognition of events and their objective temporal order only if they are related as causes and effects (B234). So every event we can cognize (i.e. every empirical event) must be governed by the principle of causation. But then, by showing that the principle of causation is legitimately applicable to empirical objects, we at the same time show it to be true of them. This might explain why Kant sometimes seems to identify objective validity with truth (e.g. A788/B816).

[9] See e.g. A760/B788, where Kant contrasts the truth of the principle of causation with the objective validity of the concept of a cause and implies that the latter is a presupposition of the former.

reason that the objective validity of the categories and the principles of pure understanding is an open question at the beginning of the Transcendental Analytic, namely because it is unclear how concepts and principles that are purely a priori (and thus spring from our own minds) could relate to mind-independent objects. Thus, our a priori concepts (the categories, but also the transcendental ideas and the concept of the unconditioned) might turn out to be "without objective validity and without sense and significance" (A156/B195), so that any attempt to use them in judgments about objects will be illegitimate and doomed to fail.

It is therefore important to see that *purported* objective validity is not objective validity. Since the Supreme Principle belongs to the real use of reason and thus does not, like the Logical Maxim, abstract from the content of our cognitions, it *purports* to be applicable to objects. Put differently, rational cognizers naturally *take* the Supreme Principle *to be* objectively valid. But this in itself does not mean that it *is* objectively valid – that is, that we can *legitimately* apply it to objects.

By contrast, the Logical Maxim is *valid* in that there is indeed a rational demand on cognitive subjects to search for premises from which to derive their conditioned cognitions until they arrive at unconditioned cognitions (Section 2.3). But this validity is merely subjective in that it abstracts from objects and only concerns the way in which a subject organizes its cognitions. Therefore, from the Logical Maxim alone nothing follows about the objects of our cognitions and how the world is structured.[10]

In sum, in the Introduction to the Transcendental Dialectic, Kant *claims* that the Logical Maxim *is* (merely) *subjectively* valid and that the Supreme Principle (as a principle of the real use of reason) *purports* to be *objectively* valid, and he *asks* whether the Supreme Principle *is* objectively valid, announcing that an answer will be given in the course of the Transcendental Dialectic.

4.2 Regulative and Constitutive Use of Principles in the Appendix and in the Resolution of the Antinomy

Kant explicitly returns to the question of the objective validity of principles of reason in the Appendix to the Transcendental Dialectic, where he claims that various transcendental principles (including a version of the Supreme Principle) indeed have (as Kant usually qualifies, 'some,' 'indirect,' or

---

[10] While Kant explicitly speaks of 'objective validity' with respect to the Supreme Principle, he does not use the term 'subjective validity' in the context of the Logical Maxim, but simply says that it is a "subjective law" (A306/B362) and that maxims of reason in general are "subjective principles" (A666/B694) in that they express a need of reason rather than features of objects. It seems plausible, though, that Kant thinks that the Logical Maxim is not just subjective in this sense but also subjectively *valid* (a legitimate requirement on rational beings) (see Section 2.3).

'indeterminate') objective validity, but only when used regulatively, not when used constitutively. Moreover, in preparing the resolution of the antinomies of pure reason, Kant applies this latter distinction to the Supreme Principle (as applied to appearances). Interpreting the regulative/constitutive distinction in these passages will finally allow us to understand the Transition Passage and the status Kant assigns to the Supreme Principle.

4.2.1 Logical and Transcendental Principles in the Appendix

The official aim of the Appendix to the Transcendental Dialectic is to sketch the positive and legitimate use we can make of the ideas and principles of pure reason, following the unveiling, in the main body of the Dialectic, of the metaphysical fallacies inherent in pure reason (A642–3/B670–1; A669/B697). This positive use consists in their role in science, which is why the Appendix is one of the central texts for understanding Kant's philosophy of science.[11] While the Appendix is one of the more obscure chapters of the first *Critique*, and its structure and arguments are sometimes difficult to follow, it is obvious that Kant finally returns to some of the issues he had raised in the Introduction (e.g. Horstmann 1998: 527). In particular, in the first part of the Appendix (entitled "On the Regulative Use of the Ideas of Pure Reason"; A642/B670), Kant again contrasts logical and transcendental principles of reason and claims that the former presuppose the latter. While the Logical Maxim and the Supreme Principle are not explicitly mentioned, Kant claims that there is a "*logical* principle" that requires us to *strive* for unity of reason among our cognitions "as far as this can be done" (A648/B676) but that this does not yet imply the claim that the objects themselves must exhibit such a unity. This latter claim "would be a *transcendental* principle of reason, which would make systematic unity not merely something subjectively and logically necessary, as method, but objectively necessary" (A648/B676). Kant claims that this "law of reason to seek unity" is "objectively valid and necessary" (A651/B679). Even though Kant does not explicitly identify the 'logical principle' with the Logical Maxim and the 'transcendental principle' with the Supreme Principle mentioned in the Introduction, it is obvious that he has the same principles in mind in both passages.

In addition, Kant introduces three principles of reason, each of which comes in a 'logical' and a 'transcendental' variety. These are the principles of *homogeneity* ('For every two species, there is a common genus') (A651–4/B679–82), *specification* ('For every species, there is more than one subspecies') (A654–7/B682–5), and *continuity* ('For every two species, there is

---

[11] See e.g. Kitcher 1986; Friedman 1991; Sturm 2009: ch. 3; Massimi 2017.

a mediating species') (A657–8/B685–6; A660–1/B688–9).[12] All three are "principles of systematic *unity*" (A662/B690). The relation between the logical and the transcendental principles is characterized in terms already familiar from the Introduction. The logical principles concern only our "concepts" (e.g. A652/B680; see also A655/B683) and the unity among our cognitions; they are subjective and methodological (A648/B676), economical (A653/B681), and prescriptive (A652/B680). The transcendental principles, by contrast, concern objects (of nature) (e.g. A653–4/B681–2) and are objective and descriptive (A648/B676). Even though the logical and transcendental versions of the three principles differ in various ways from the Logical Maxim and the Supreme Principle, respectively (e.g. by not directly concerning the unconditioned), the distinction between the logical and transcendental principles in the Appendix clearly parallels that between the Logical Maxim and the Supreme Principle.[13]

With respect to each of the three principles, Kant claims in closely parallel formulations that the logical version presupposes its transcendental analogue (A654/B682; A656/B684; A660/B688; see also A648/B676; A650/B678). For instance, Kant writes:

In fact it cannot even be seen how there could be a logical principle of rational unity among rules [= homogeneity] unless a transcendental principle is presupposed, through which such a systematic unity, as pertaining to the object itself, is *assumed* [*angenommen*] *a priori* as necessary. (A650–1/B678–9; emphasis added)

Note that the word for 'assumed' (*angenommen*) is the same word Kant uses in the Transition Passage with respect to the Supreme Principle (*annimmt*). As I will argue in what follows, passages like these from the Appendix can serve as a model for interpreting the relation between the Logical Maxim and the Supreme Principle in the Transition Passage. Understanding the relevant passages from the Appendix will require considerable interpretative work, however. Unfortunately, it will not be possible to provide a comprehensive interpretation of the first part of the Appendix here. Instead, I will have to restrict my discussion to those aspects that are relevant to understanding the Transition Passage. In particular, I will concentrate on what Kant says about

---

[12] By 'species,' Kant means not only biological species but natural kinds more generally, e.g. metals and other chemical elements (A652–3/B680–1).

[13] While the three logical principles are easily discernible as specific instances of the Logical Maxim (in that they concern logical relations among our cognitions and contribute to transforming them into a unified system of scientific knowledge), it is not obvious how the three transcendental principles fall under the Supreme Principle. Perhaps Kant's idea is that while species in one respect are conditioned by their genera, in a different respect genera are conditioned by their species, so that both higher genera and lower species are, in different respects, conditions of something conditioned (and similarly for mediating species); see Watkins 2013: 293–5 for a similar suggestion.

the *principles* of reason and bracket his related but distinct discussion of the *ideas* of reason. (We will return to the Appendix in Chapter 8.)

4.2.2 Regulative and Constitutive (Use of) Principles in the Appendix: Two Readings

Kant's extended discussion of the principle of the unity of reason and of the three principles of homogeneity, specification, and continuity (A648/B676–A663/B691) is framed by reflections on the distinction between the *regulative* and the *constitutive* use of reason and its principles. Kant had first introduced the regulative/constitutive distinction in the Transcendental Analytic in order to distinguish between different types of principles of the understanding (A179/B222). He returns to this distinction in the Transcendental Dialectic (A509/B537; see Section 4.2.3) and in the Appendix, where he applies it first to transcendental ideas (A644/B672), then to uses of reason (apodictic/hypothetical) (A646–7/B674–5), and finally, after a discussion of the three principles, to principles of reason (A664/B692).[14] For present purposes, we can concentrate on the latter two applications. While Kant does not explicitly introduce or define the distinction between regulative and constitutive principles, it emerges that to use a principle regulatively is to use it 'heuristically' (A663/B691) as a rule that guides our search for unity in nature (A665/B693), whereas a constitutive principle contributes to the possibility of empirical concepts, and thus of experience itself (A664/B692). While Kant denies that principles of reason are constitutive, he claims that their regulative use is possible and legitimate, which lends these principles at least "some objective validity" (A664/B692).[15]

Kant applies the regulative/constitutive distinction to principles only *after* his discussion of the three principles of homogeneity, specification, and continuity and without explicitly distinguishing between logical and transcendental principles. *Within* the discussion of the three principles, by contrast, he only distinguishes between logical and transcendental principles, without mentioning the regulative/constitutive distinction. Thus, the question arises of how these two distinctions are related.

According to one possible reading, the two distinctions ultimately coincide in that all and only logical principles are regulative and all and only transcendental principles are constitutive.[16] This identification can be motivated by the

---

[14] On the different applications of the regulative/constitutive distinction, see e.g. Friedman 1992 and Birken-Bertsch 2015.

[15] In what follows, I will also speak of regulative and constitutive principles, although strictly speaking I mean the regulative or constitutive *use* of principles.

[16] E.g. Pissis 2012: 203. Bernhard Thöle argues that this identification is mandated by Kant's conception of transcendental proofs (Thöle 2000: 119) but then discusses ways in which Kant

Understanding the Transition Passage (4.2.2)

following considerations. First, by calling a principle 'transcendental,' Kant seems to be saying that it is a 'condition of the possibility of experience' and thus constitutive of experience and its objects (in a way similar to the principles of the understanding) (e.g. Horstmann 1998: 530; Thöle 2000: 119). Conversely, to say that a principle is constitutive of experience seems to imply that it has 'transcendental status' (Thöle 2000: 119). Second, many commentators take Kant's claim that principles of reason have 'objective validity' to imply that these principles 'hold for' (are true of) empirical objects (which, given that they are synthetic principles a priori, would mean that they must be constitutive of objects of experience) (e.g. Thöle 2000: 119; Allison 2004: 435). Third, both regulative and logical principles seem to be prescriptive, while constitutive and transcendental principles appear to be descriptive (e.g. Grier 2001: 274). Taken together, these three considerations suggest that a principle of reason can be transcendental, and have objective reality, only by being constitutive (and regulative by being a logical principle). Let us call this the 'identification reading.'

This kind of reading is reinforced by the fact that Kant, in two much-discussed passages in the Appendix, seems to claim that the transcendental principles are indeed 'conditions of the possibility of experience.' For instance, Kant says that "without it [uniformity of nature, as assumed in the transcendental principles] no empirical concepts and hence no experience would be possible" (A654/B682; see also A651/B679). Claims like these have puzzled many readers, since they seem to conflict with Kant's general account of experience in the Transcendental Analytic (according to which concepts or principles of *reason*, as pertaining to things that cannot be given in experience, cannot be constitutive of experience). Nevertheless, they seem to confirm that Kant identifies transcendental with descriptive constitutive principles (and hence logical ones with prescriptive regulative ones) in the Appendix. Given this identification, the sense in which Kant claims that we must 'presuppose' or 'assume' the transcendental principles can only be that we take them to be true claims about the objects of nature (in the same way that we must take the principle of causation to be true of the objects of nature).

While the identification reading clearly has some basis in Kant's text, it faces severe problems, the most important of which is that it has Kant contradicting his own account of experience in the Transcendental Analytic.[17] As Kant himself reminds us, principles of reason cannot be constitutive of

---

might avoid this consequence. Rolf-Peter Horstmann concludes from the fact that the principles of reason cannot be constitutive that they must be merely logical, thereby effectively conflating the two distinctions (Horstmann 1998: 531).

[17] See Thöle 2000, who discusses five different interpretative strategies for resolving this contradiction and then argues that Kant found a consistent position only in the *Critique of the Power of Judgment*; for a similar claim, see Allison 2004: 436–7.

experience because they lack a sensible schema that allows us to apply them to empirical objects directly (A664/B692). Moreover, collapsing the regulative/ constitutive and logical/transcendental distinctions cannot explain how Kant can claim that the logical principles presuppose that we assume the corresponding transcendental ones, since on the identification reading that would mean that there is a necessary and thus legitimate use of *constitutive* principles of reason, which Kant denies. Finally, that reading is incompatible with Kant's insistence that logical principles are merely subjective and concern only our concepts and cognitions but not their objects, since the regulative use of the principles of reason obviously *does* concern objects. After all, the regulative use directs us to find order in *nature* (not just among our cognitions), which means that we must apply the relevant principles to natural objects.

Given these problems, many commentators have tried to resist the identification reading by allowing that transcendental principles can be regulative.[18] But note that this is not so easy, given the considerations that motivate the identification reading. In fact, some commentators who officially reject the identification reading seem nevertheless tacitly to rely on it. For instance, Michelle Grier officially distinguishes between a principle's being constitutive and its being transcendental but identifies the regulative use of the principle of systematic unity with the Logical Maxim (her 'P1') and claims that it presupposes a transcendental principle (her 'P2'), which, however, is illusory (Grier 2001: 273–5). But why should this transcendental presupposition be illusory if it is not taken to be constitutive? Surely its regulative use would not be illusory. It thus seems that Grier tacitly identifies logical with regulative and transcendental with constitutive principles (see also Allison 2004: 432).

The reason why the identification reading is so difficult to avoid is that it seems to be required by the considerations that motivate it. If principles of reason are conditions of the possibility of experience and therefore 'hold for' objects of experience, it is hard to see how they could fail to be constitutive. And if regulative principles are prescriptive while transcendental ones are descriptive, it makes little sense to claim that a principle can be both transcendental and regulative.

I will therefore suggest a different approach, which rejects not only the identification reading but also the three assumptions mentioned earlier as its motivation. First, it is doubtful that when Kant talks about transcendental principles in the Appendix he intends 'transcendental' to mean something like 'condition of the possibility of experience' (Thöle 2000: 119) or 'being indispensable for the proper functioning of the understanding' (Allison 2004: 432). As is generally recognized, Kant uses that term in a variety of senses (e.g.

---

[18] E.g. Caimi 1995; Grier 2001: 274; Allison 2004: 432; Mudd 2013; McLaughlin 2014; Massimi 2017.

Understanding the Transition Passage (4.2.2) 113

Hinske 1998; Knoeppfler 2001; Dohrn 2015). For instance, Kant speaks of the 'transcendental use' of the categories of the understanding, by which he means not their constitutive role in experience but rather the illegitimate attempt to apply them to objects in general, including non-empirical objects (e.g. A238/B298; A247–8/B304–5; see Grier 2001: 76–86). And as we saw earlier, when Kant contrasts the 'logical' with the 'real' or 'transcendental' use of reason (A299/B356–7), he clearly does not want to claim that the latter in general is a condition of the possibility of experience but rather that, unlike the logical use, which abstracts from objects, the transcendental use concerns objects and not just cognitions.[19] Given the thematic continuity between the Introduction to the Transcendental Dialectic and the Appendix, it seems likely that the logical/transcendental distinction in the Appendix also has to do with the question of whether a principle is concerned only with our cognitions and their logical interrelations, in abstraction from their objects, or with these objects themselves.[20] As we saw, this is precisely how Kant characterizes transcendental as opposed to logical principles in the Appendix.[21]

Second, as we saw in Section 4.1, assigning objective reality to a principle does not necessarily mean that that principle is a true claim about some range of objects, but only that it can legitimately be applied to those objects.

Third, it does not seem that regulative principles in general must be understood as prescriptive. This becomes clear from Kant's distinction between the 'apodictic' and the 'hypothetical' use of reason (A646–7/B674–5; see Section 2.1.4).[22] While the apodictic use of reason consists in deriving conclusions from principles that are known to be true ("*in itself certain* and given"), with the hypothetical use a universal principle or rule "is assumed only

---

[19] See also Chapter 1, note 23.
[20] See Guyer 2003: 278, who also reads 'transcendental' in this context as 'purports to relate to objects.'
[21] This is not to deny that there are passages in the Appendix where 'transcendental' seems to connote something like 'condition of the possibility of experience.' The passages mentioned earlier where Kant seems to claim that transcendental principles of reason are necessary for experience (A651/B679; A654/B682) particularly point in that direction. But these passages, if understood in the way just indicated, conflict with some of Kant's most fundamental commitments in the first *Critique* (see e.g. Guyer 1990; Thöle 2010). Thus, if they are read in such a way as to support the claim that transcendental principles of reason are conditions of the possibility of experience, it seems they cannot represent Kant's considered view. By contrast, if they are read in some other way (as I will indicate later, see note 30), they do not support the claim that 'transcendental' in 'transcendental principle of reason' means 'condition of the possibility of experience.' Either way, they do not lend much support to the identification reading.
[22] This distinction is generally regarded as a predecessor of the distinction between the determining and reflecting power of judgment in the third *Critique* (5:179f.); e.g. Guyer 1990: 17.

problematically" (A646/B674) in order to test whether a variety of particular cases, each of which is "certain," can be derived from, and thus understood as instances of, the general principle. If the individual cases can be derived from the hypothetically assumed principle, we can inductively infer the truth of the principle and then derive further particular cases besides those already known to be true. For instance, from the hypothetically employed transcendental principle of homogeneity ('For any two species there is a common genus') in conjunction with the empirical finding that gold and silver are different species or natural kinds, we can deduce the research hypothesis that there is a genus that includes both. Given the overall aim of the unity of reason, this hypothesis implies a prescription to *search* for this common genus. Once we have found this genus (*noble* metals), we continue and deduce the further hypothesis that noble metals and other metals have a common genus (which, trivially, is *metals*). From there, we proceed to, say, metals and gases, until we end with *chemical elements* as the supreme genus. While the regulative transcendental principle of homogeneity generates hypotheses about higher genera, reason's interest in a complete system of scientific knowledge generates prescriptions to search for the genera thus hypothetically assumed.[23]

But Kant warns us:

The hypothetical use of reason ... is not properly *constitutive*, that is, not such that if one judges in all strictness the truth of the universal rule assumed as a hypothesis thereby follows ... Rather, this use of reason is only regulative, bringing unity into particular cognitions as far as possible and thereby *approximating* the rule to universality. (A647/B675)

The hypothetical use of reason is not constitutive (that is, resulting in descriptive statements we can know to be true), because strictly speaking the truth of the problematically assumed universal principle does not follow from the truth of a finite number of particular instances. Rather, it is regulative in that it guides our search for unity among our particular cognitions. This does not mean that regulatively used principles such as the principle of homogeneity are *false*, but only that we would not be warranted in taking them to be true (and that we do not have to in order to use them regulatively). By deriving empirically confirmed consequences from a regulatively used principle of reason, we are 'approximating the rule to complete universality,' even though we will never be able to establish its truth conclusively.

If we take this account of the hypothetical use of reason as our model for the regulative use of principles, we can draw three important conclusions. First,

---

[23] See A652/B680 for Kant's own use of chemical elements as an example of the unity of reason. The periodic table of elements, first published in 1869, is a stunning example of the kind of 'systematic unity' that reason seeks, and in this case finds, in nature.

using a principle regulatively does not mean that it is prescriptive; after all, the principle or 'rule' must be able to serve as a major premise in syllogisms that have particular cases as their conclusions. If the 'rule' were prescriptive, no such consequences would follow. Thus, Kant uses the word 'rule' here in the sense of the Introduction to the Transcendental Dialectic, that is, for any general judgment or sentence that serves as a premise in an inference (A304/B360–1; see also 9:121). By finding more and more instances of it, we 'approximate the rule to universality' – that is, we approximate a state in which we would be justified in asserting the rule in its full universality. This is not to deny that the regulative use of a principle has prescriptive force, but only that the principle itself is a prescriptive sentence. Instead, the regulative *use* of a principle is prescriptive in that reason requires us to investigate the hypotheses that follow from the principle.

Second, this requires a distinction between *logical* principles (which are prescriptive) and regulatively used *transcendental* principles (which are descriptive). While both logical principles and regulatively used transcendental principles direct us to seek the greatest possible unity among our cognitions, the former abstract from the objects of our cognition and concern only the logical relations (e.g. genus/species) between them. They are valid principles of reason, but their validity is merely subjective, that is, restricted to how we organize our cognitions (Section 2.3). The latter, by contrast, apply the same logical relations to objects. They serve as hypothetically assumed premises from which we derive conclusions that can then be empirically checked with regard to their truth.

Third, this kind of hypothetical 'assuming' of a principle is not a case of what we today would call 'belief'. Rather, assuming a principle or rule 'problematically' consists in using it as a hypothesis, which does not require that we commit ourselves to its truth.[24] Compare a detective who entertains the hypothesis that the butler was the murderer. She asks herself what would follow if the hypothesis were true (e.g. there would have to be blood on the butler's gloves) and thus generates more specific hypotheses, the truth of which she can investigate. In order to do so, however, she does not have to *believe* that the butler is the murderer (and, as a good detective, she will not believe this unless she finds convincing evidence). Similarly, in order to derive and test hypotheses about metals, we do not have to *believe* that there is a

---

[24] In the *Jäsche Logik*, Kant defines a hypothesis as the "taking to be true of a presupposition as a ground" (9:84; cf. Sturm 2015). According to Andrew Chignell, a scientist's working on a hypothesis to be confirmed or disconfirmed counts as a case of 'opinion' and thereby also as a case of assent (Fürwahrhalten) for Kant (Chignell 2007, 332). But note that this kind of assent is different from what in philosophy today is called belief in that we do not commit ourselves to the truth of what we hypothetically assume.

common genus under which any two species fall. We only need to 'problematically assume' this.[25]

If we take these points together, we arrive at a reading of Kant's regulative/constitutive distinction in the Appendix that differs substantially from the identification reading. According to this alternative reading, we cannot simply identify transcendental and constitutive principles, because it is *transcendental* principles that can be employed either regulatively or constitutively.[26] If we use them regulatively, we do not accept them as true (nor, of course, do we reject them as false) but rather hypothetically employ them in order to generate hypotheses about objects in nature. By contrast, if we use them constitutively, we take them to be true generalizations about these objects.[27]

This alternative reading also explains how Kant can consistently claim that principles of reason have 'objective validity.'[28] As indicated earlier, by this Kant does not mean that these principles 'hold' of nature and its objects, but rather that they can be legitimately applied to these objects (which initially is unclear because of their merely subjective origin). They can thus be applied not in order to "determine" objects (A665/B693), that is, assertively to attribute properties to them, but only to serve as hypotheses that direct our search for unity in nature. As Kant explains, the regulative use of these principles is *necessary* to achieve the greatest possible unity among our cognitions, the 'unity of reason' (Section 2.1.4), while it does not involve any claims that would be empirically false or even falsifiable (A671/B699). Thus, the principles of reason have 'objective validity' because they contribute to the unity of reason and therefore relate to objects at least indirectly (through the cognitions of the understanding they systematize). The principles in question can only be transcendental principles because the corresponding logical principles abstract from objects and only concern our 'concepts' and 'cognitions' (Section 2.1.1). But the objective validity of these transcendental principles is 'indeterminate' in that they can only be used heuristically, as part of the

---

[25] See Kant's related distinction between assuming something relatively and assuming something absolutely (*suppositio relativa* and *absoluta*) (A676/B704), for which, however, it is not clear from what Kant says whether a relative assumption is merely hypothetical or not.

[26] Transcendental and constitutive principles are clearly distinguished (although not always in the same way that I do here), e.g. in Caimi 1995; Mudd 2013; McLaughlin 2014; Massimi 2017.

[27] That Kant distinguishes between (subjective) logical principles and (objective) transcendental principles, the latter of which can be used either regulatively or constitutively, is also clear from the following passage from the Appendix, where Kant states the "result of the entire Transcendental Dialectic" as follows: "The unity of reason is the unity of a system, and this systematic unity does not serve reason objectively as a principle, extending it over objects, but subjectively as *a maxim*, in order to extend it over all possible empirical cognition of objects. Nevertheless, ... the principle of such a systematic unity *is also objective* but in an indeterminate way ..., *not as a constitutive principle ... but rather as a merely regulative principle*" (A680/B708; emphasis added).

[28] That Kant can consistently claim this has been denied (Allison 2004: 436–7).

Understanding the Transition Passage (4.2.2) 117

hypothetical use of reason, to 'indicate a procedure' of which it is indeterminate how far nature will comply with it, and not in order to 'determine' objects, that is, to cognize them (A665/B693).[29]

This reading of the regulative use of transcendental principles thus steers a middle course between what might be called 'objectivist' and 'fictionalist' readings of the Appendix. According to the former, we must commit ourselves to the truth of these principles; according to the latter, we must take them to be false but employ them as heuristically necessary fictions.[30] On the alternative reading suggested here, we can, and must, remain neutral on whether these principles are true or false.[31]

The alternative reading thus avoids the serious problems of the identification reading without incurring similarly vexing problems. Moreover, as I will argue later, it also allows us to develop a plausible interpretation of the Transition Passage and, more generally, of Kant's account of the transition from the innocuous logical to the metaphysically loaded real use of reason.

But if transcendental principles can be used either regulatively or constitutively, this means that Kant's discussion of the logical and transcendental principles in the Appendix is ambiguous in this respect, since he does not explicitly relate the logical/transcendental distinction to the distinction between regulative and constitutive principles. Thus, when Kant says that we must 'presuppose' or 'assume' the transcendental principles of homogeneity,

---

[28] Kant qualifies the objective validity of principles (and ideas) of reason in three different ways. He says that they only have "some" objective validity (A664/B692), that their objective validity is "indirect" (A665/B693), and that it is "indeterminate" (A663/B691). It is possible that Kant means different qualifications in each case. For instance, the objective validity of transcendental principles is *indeterminate* also in the sense that they do not determine the extent to which we will be able to find unity in nature (e.g. A653/B681; A654/B682; A665/B693; A668/B696). My claim is only that at least one such qualification derives from the fact that regulative principles are not used to determine objects, that is, to attribute properties to them.

[29] See e.g. Wartenberg 1992 for an objectivist reading and Grier 2001: ch. 9 for a fictionalist one.

[30] The alternative reading might also help with the puzzling passages where Kant seems to claim that principles of reason are necessary for experience, such as the following: "For the law of reason to seek unity is necessary, since without it we would have no reason, and without that, no coherent use of the understanding, and, lacking that, no sufficient mark of empirical truth; thus, in regard to the latter we simply have to presuppose the systematic unity of nature as objectively valid and necessary" (A651/B679). Kant goes on to call this a "transcendental presupposition." While various aspects of this quote are striking, they do not prevent us from reading the 'presupposing' of systematic unity as hypothetical, the 'objectively validity' as indeterminate, and the term 'transcendental' as meaning 'concerning objects,' and thus as an antonym of 'logical.' Therefore, I do not think that Kant is claiming here – inconsistently – that the unity of reason is a transcendental condition of experience in the same sense that the principles of the understanding are (similarly for A654/B682). Note that I am restricting my discussion here to the first Critique, bracketing the development of Kant's views in the Critique of the Power of Judgment. That Kant is justified in treating the principle of unity (systematicity, purposefulness) of nature as a transcendental condition of experience has been argued (mostly with reference to the third *Critique*) e.g. by Wartenberg 1992; Kitcher 1994; Caimi 1995; Thöle 2000; Geiger 2003; and Ginsborg 2017. For a more critical view, closer to my own, see Guyer 1990.

specificity, and continuity this means *either* that we must make constitutive use of them, and thus accept them as true (which would then presumably be a case of transcendental illusion), *or* that we must use them regulatively, assuming them only 'problematically,' as hypotheses (which would be legitimate). On the one hand, the fact that Kant does not explicitly restrict his claim that we must necessarily assume transcendental principles by saying that this holds only for their regulative use may suggest that he has their constitutive use in mind, since that would clearly be the more natural reading of these passages. On the other hand, Kant later clarifies that principles of reason have objective validity only when used regulatively, which suggests that the way in which we must 'presuppose' or 'assume' them can only be as regulative principles. In any case, in the passages in question Kant does not explicitly indicate how his claims about 'presupposing' or 'assuming' transcendental principles are to be understood. We will return to this ambiguity shortly.

In sum, in this subsection I have argued that we should not collapse the distinctions between logical and transcendental and between regulative and constitutive principles. Rather, the latter distinction is applied specifically to transcendental principles, the only legitimate use of which, according to Kant, is regulative. When using them regulatively, we 'problematically' assume these principles as heuristic devices within the hypothetical use of reason. When using them constitutively, by contrast, we use them to make determinative judgments about nature, thereby accepting them as true.

4.2.3 The Regulative Use of the Supreme Principle

That the regulative/constitutive distinction applies to transcendental principles is confirmed by the fact that in the context of the resolution of the Antinomy of Reason, Kant applies it to the Supreme Principle, which we know is a transcendental principle (A306/B363):

> Thus the principle of reason [i.e. the Supreme Principle] is only a *rule*, prescribing a regress in the series of conditions for given appearances, in which regress it is never allowed to stop with an absolutely unconditioned. Thus it is *not* ... *a constitutive* principle of reason for extending the concept of the world of sense beyond all possible experience; rather it is a principle of the greatest possible continuation and extension of experience ... that, as a rule, postulates what should be effected by us ... Hence I will call it a *regulative* principle of reason, whereas the principle of the absolute totality of the series of conditions, as given in the object itself (in the appearances), would be a constitutive cosmological principle the nullity of which I have tried to show through just this distinction, thereby preventing ... the ascription of objective reality to an idea that merely serves as a rule. (A508–9/B536–7)

Here Kant explicitly distinguishes between a regulative and a constitutive version of the Supreme Principle (or, more precisely, of a 'cosmological' version of the Supreme Principle that concerns specifically conditioned *appearances*; see A497/B525). The regulative version is a mere 'rule' that prescribes a regress from everything conditioned to its conditions, never allowing us to stop at something unconditioned (since *within* the series of conditions that starts from appearances we can never arrive at something unconditioned). The latter, by contrast, claims that 'the absolute totality of the series of conditions' is 'given in the object itself (in the appearances).' It is illegitimate (a 'nullity'), since it lacks 'objective reality.'[32]

Note that the regulative version of the principle cannot be the same as the Logical Maxim because it prescribes a regress 'for given appearances,' that is, for empirical objects. Thus, it does not abstract from content and is not restricted to the logical relations between cognitions. It "cannot say *what the object is*" (since it is not constitutive), but it can say "*how the empirical regress is to be instituted* so as to attain to the complete concept of the *object*" (A510/B538; final emphasis added). While Kant does not mention the Logical Maxim in the context of the resolution of the antinomies, he makes clear that the regulative version of the cosmological Supreme Principle is concerned with *objects* and must therefore be distinguished from the Logical Maxim.

While Kant's formulations may suggest that the regulatively used cosmological Supreme Principle is prescriptive, we have seen earlier that it does not have to be read this way. Rather, what Kant says is compatible with the reading of the regulative use of principles outlined earlier, according to which these are hypothetically assumed descriptive statements. While the principle itself is descriptive, it receives prescriptive force through its connection with reason's interest in a unified system of cognitions. Indeed, Kant explicitly claims that the principle is valid not as an 'axiom,' but as a 'problem':

> the principle of pure reason we are thinking of retains its genuine validity only in a corrected significance: not indeed as an *axiom* for thinking the totality in the object as real, but as a *problem* for the understanding, thus for the subject in initiating and continuing, in accordance with the completeness of the idea, the regress in the series of conditions for a given conditioned. (A508/B536)

Thus, it is clear that Kant does not think that we must take the Supreme Principle to be true, but rather that we treat it as a 'problem.' While one may be normatively required to solve a problem (e.g. to answer a question or to prove a theorem), this does not mean that the *solution* to the problem (the answer or theorem) is prescriptive. If the Supreme Principle is treated as a problem, this means that we are required to 'approximate it to universality' by finding as many conditions for conditioned objects as possible (this being the

---

[31] Although it sounds in the quote as if Kant wants to deny that even the regulative principle has 'objective reality,' the Appendix suggests that he grants it at least 'some' ('indefinite') objective validity/reality.

'problem' or task). To this end, we must hypothetically assume that principle and generate hypotheses about particular conditioned objects and their conditions, which means that the principle itself is descriptive, not prescriptive.[33]

4.3 A Transition in Two Steps

We can now return to the questions concerning the Transition Passage with which we started this chapter. The passage's central claim is:

(T)   The Logical Maxim can become a principle of pure reason (PPR) only by our assuming the Supreme Principle.

As we noted earlier, this raises the following questions. First, does Kant intend the antecedent to be satisfied ('The Logical Maxim becomes a PPR')? Second, what does it mean for a maxim to *become* a principle of pure reason, and which principle could this be? Third, why should the Logical Maxim become a PPR, and why is this possible only by assuming the Supreme Principle? Fourth, what exactly does it mean to 'assume' such a principle? And finally, is Kant here endorsing an inference (in the widest sense) from the Logical Maxim to the Supreme Principle (and thus the Supreme Principle itself), or is this meant to be a case of transcendental illusion? Our findings from the Appendix and the Antinomy chapter will help us to answer these questions.

4.3.1 A Reading of the Transition Passage

First, considering the parallel passages about logical and transcendental principles in the Appendix, it seems obvious that Kant does not intend the Transition Passage to be merely hypothetical or even counterfactual ('*If* the Logical Maxim were to become a PPR'). Rather, Kant is committed to the idea (1) that there is a legitimate logical use of reason, guided by subjectively valid logical principles such as the Logical Maxim and the logical versions of the principles of homogeneity, specification, and continuity, and (2) that this use

---

[32] The term 'problem' is a technical term of logic in Meier and Kant (see *Auszug*, §§325, 327–37, and *Jäsche Logic*, 9:112). Every problem or task (*Aufgabe*) has three parts: (1) a question, (2) a solution, and (3) a demonstration that the solution is sufficient to answer the question. When Kant says that we must think of the Supreme Principle as a problem, this seems to be short for saying that we must look for the condition for everything conditioned (which is the 'question' or task). This does not imply that the regulatively used Supreme Principle itself is prescriptive. Meier points out (§328) that the solution can be regarded as a condition for answering the question, so that the whole problem can be treated as a conditional theorem (*Lehrsatz*). Applying this to the case at hand, we might say that the hypothetically assumed Supreme Principle is the condition under which it is possible to solve the problem of finding conditions for everything conditioned.

of reason and its logical principles *presupposes* a real or transcendental use and corresponding transcendental principles. (We will consider why that is so in the next chapter.)

Second, while in the Appendix we do not find a parallel formulation according to which a logical principle *becomes* a transcendental one, the correspondence between logical and transcendental principles suggests a plausible way of reading this aspect of the Transition Passage. A transcendental principle corresponds to a logical principle in that it concerns the same logical relations as the logical principle but applies them to the objects of our cognitions rather than to cognitions in abstraction from their objects. For instance, where the "logical principle of the unity of reason among rules" tells us to look for ever higher principles among our cognitions, the corresponding transcendental principle assumes "such a systematic unity as pertaining to the objects themselves" (A650–1/B679–80). To the logical law of *continui specierum (formarum logicarum)* (continuity among logical forms) there corresponds a transcendental law of *continui in natura* (continuity among species in nature) (A660/B688). Thus, the transcendental principle is the logical principle, first, in its descriptive form (whereas the logical principle is prescriptive), and second, as applied to objects (whereas the logical principle abstracts from objects). Put differently, a transcendental principle is the descriptive version of the corresponding logical principle plus purported objective validity. Thus, a logical principle 'becomes' a transcendental one *by being used as a descriptive principle for objects.*[34]

That this is what Kant has in mind in the Transition Passage is confirmed by the fact that the principle that the Logical Maxim 'becomes' is called "a principle of *pure reason*," while the Logical Maxim itself is a principle of "reason in general (in its logical use)" (A307/B364). 'Pure reason,' in the context of the Introduction, is short for 'the transcendental use of reason' (as opposed to 'the logical use of reason'; see Section 1.1.5). Hence, a 'principle of pure reason' is one that, unlike principles of the logical use, does not abstract from objects. That the Logical Maxim becomes a principle of pure reason therefore means that its descriptive analogue is applied to objects, or, in other words, that it is *taken to be* objectively valid. (This raises the question of how, precisely, the Supreme Principle is the descriptive and objective analogue of the Logical Maxim, a question to which we will return in Chapter 5.)

---

[33] Compare the Categorical Imperative, which requires us to act in such a way that one can will one's maxim "to become a universal law" (e.g. 4:402). That a maxim 'becomes' a universal law means that there is a principle that has the same content as my maxim (e.g. 'not to lie') but is valid not just for me (as my maxim is) but for everybody. Important differences between practical and theoretical principles notwithstanding, in the practical case a subjectively valid principle's 'becoming' an objectively valid one likewise consists in applying the same content to a new domain.

Thus, when Kant says in the Transition Passage that the Logical Maxim becomes a PPR by our assuming the Supreme Principle, he is not talking about three different principles (the Logical Maxim, a PPR, and the Supreme Principle). Rather, the Transition Passage must be understood on the model of sentences such as 'A bachelor can become a husband only by marrying someone' or 'A bill can become a law only by an act of legislation,' or, more generally, 'X can become Y only by way of Z,' where X's becoming Y just consists in Z's taking place. Similarly, the Logical Maxim's becoming a PPR just consists in our assuming the Supreme Principle. This means that the PPR in question can be nothing other than the Supreme Principle itself. The Logical Maxim becomes a PPR by being used as a descriptive principle for objects, that is, by 'becoming' the Supreme Principle.[35]

Third, since transforming the Logical Maxim into a PPR *consists in* assuming the Supreme Principle, the Logical Maxim must become a PPR for the same reason that we must assume the Supreme Principle. Now consider why the logical principles of homogeneity, specificity, and continuity 'presuppose' transcendental principles. The reason is that looking for unity among our cognitions somehow presupposes the assumption that there is unity in nature. We will have to postpone a critical discussion of this claim to the next chapter. In any case, we can plausibly assume that Kant thought of the relation between the Logical Maxim and the Supreme Principle in a parallel way: searching for unconditioned cognitions involves the assumption that there are unconditioned objects. Therefore, the Logical Maxim must be transformed into a PPR – that is, it must be applied to nature itself and thus take on the form of the Supreme Principle.

If we take these three points together, we arrive at the following interpretation of the Transition Passage:

Transition$_i$ Following the Logical Maxim presupposes the assumption that nature itself is structured in a way that is analogous to a system of cognitions that would result from following the Logical Maxim. Now the Logical Maxim is a subjectively valid principle of reason in its logical use, which means that we are rationally required (in some appropriately weak sense; Section 2.3.2) to follow it. Therefore, the Logical Maxim *must become* a principle of pure reason in the sense that we must apply

---

[34] Michelle Grier likewise holds that the Logical Maxim and the Supreme Principle are one and the same principle, but she does so for a different reason, namely because both "express the very same demand of reason ... P$_2$ [the Supreme Principle] just is P$_1$ [the Logical Maxim] when it is conceived by reason in abstraction from the conditions of the understanding" (Grier 2001: 124). There is no indication in the Kantian text, however, that the Logical Maxim, unlike the Supreme Principle, is restricted to the conditions of the understanding (the categories as applied to objects in space and time). Kant merely says that it is applied to the cognitions provided by the understanding.

its descriptive analogue to nature itself, which means that we assume that the structure of objects in nature corresponds to the very structure that reason looks for among our cognitions. Since the Logical Maxim requires us to look for the conditions of every conditioned *cognition* up to unconditioned cognitions, applying it to nature itself means that we assume that for every conditioned *object* there is a condition, up to the unconditioned among objects.

Various aspects of Transition$_i$ require further investigation. In particular, we will have to ask (in Chapter 5) whether the Supreme Principle is the descriptive analogue of the Logical Maxim and why it is necessary to assume the former if we want to follow the latter. First, though, let us turn to the final two questions concerning the Transition Passage, namely what Kant means by 'assuming' the Supreme Principle and whether this is a case of transcendental illusion.

4.3.2   The Transition Passage and Transcendental Illusion

As we have seen, the term 'assuming' is ambiguous in this context. It can mean 'taking something to be true' (e.g. A771/B799), or it can be short for 'problematically assuming,' as in the passage on the hypothetical use of reason (A646/B674).[36] If 'assuming' in the Transition Passage is read in the first sense, then the passage would seem to represent a case of transcendental illusion, since it then says, 'We must follow the Logical Maxim, which makes it necessary to accept the Supreme Principle as true.' Since we know that accepting the Supreme Principle as true goes beyond the limits of cognition (according to the Transcendental Analytic) and leads to antinomies and metaphysical fallacies (according to the Transcendental Dialectic), the Transition Passage would have to be read not as expressing Kant's own considered point of view but as articulating the point of view of the traditional metaphysician who falls prey to transcendental illusion.[37]

Alternatively, 'assuming' the Supreme Principle might be read as 'hypothetically employing it in reasoning,' which does not include a commitment to its truth. As we know from the passage from the resolution of the antinomies quoted at the end of the previous section, this is how Kant thinks the Supreme Principle must be understood, which may suggest that this is also what he wants to say in the Transition Passage. But if that were so, it would be strange that Kant goes on to ask whether the Supreme Principle is objectively valid (A308/B365). If the Supreme Principle is used hypothetically, and thus regulatively, it should be objectively valid at least in the same limited sense

---

[35] The term for 'assuming' that Kant uses (*'annehmen'*) is ambiguous in present-day German in just this way since it can mean either 'take to be true' or 'hypothetically suppose.'
[36] This is how Grier and Allison read this passage (Grier 2001: 127; Allison 2004: 433).

('indirectly' and 'indeterminately') in which other regulative transcendental principles are. Moreover, the distinction between the regulative and the constitutive use of principles, and with it the idea of indeterminate objective validity, is not mentioned at all in the Introduction (even though Kant might well have introduced it here as part of his account of the real use of reason).

What this suggests is that Kant is being *deliberately ambiguous* in the Transition Passage. He plans to introduce the distinction between a legitimate regulative and an illegitimate constitutive use of the Supreme Principle only in the course of the Transcendental Dialectic, and only in the Appendix will he argue that transcendental principles indeed have some objective validity when used regulatively. Therefore, his strategy in the Transition Passage is to present the transition from the Logical Maxim to the Supreme Principle in a way that leaves open whether it is legitimate. There is a reading of the passage according to which it represents Kant's own considered view, namely when 'assuming' the Supreme Principle means making regulative use of it. But there is also a reading – in fact, the more natural one, which will automatically suggest itself to the uninitiated reader – according to which moving from the Logical Maxim to the Supreme Principle turns out to be a case of transcendental illusion, namely when 'assuming' is read as 'taking to be true.' It seems that Kant carefully avoids resolving this ambiguity in the Transition Passage and the passages that surround it.

We find the same ambiguity at work in the Appendix, when Kant repeatedly claims that the three logical principles 'presuppose' a corresponding transcendental principle. Each of these passages suggests, but does not state explicitly, that *presupposing* or *assuming* a transcendental principle consists in using it *constitutively*. As we have seen, it is only after these passages (A663–6/B691–4) that Kant invokes the distinction between the regulative and the constitutive use of principles and clarifies that the only sense in which transcendental principles can be *legitimately* presupposed is as regulative principles, not constitutive ones. I think that this ambiguity and its belated clarification explains many of the problems encountered by readers of the Appendix.

But even though this ambiguity can be misleading and thus creates problems for the reader of the first *Critique*, we can understand why Kant allowed it to enter into his text. The reason is that Kant weaves two strands of thought into one in the Transcendental Dialectic: his account of reason as the source of metaphysical speculation (the Rational Sources Account) and his critique of the resulting form of metaphysics as fallacious and contradictory. In the Appendix, these two strands are enriched by a third, namely securing a legitimate use for those aspects of reason that, when used uncritically, give rise to metaphysical fallacies and illusions. With respect to the Supreme Principle and the three transcendental principles from the Appendix, this means that Kant has three distinct goals in view. First, he wants to explain

Understanding the Transition Passage (4.3.2) 125

how these principles grow naturally out of the metaphysically innocent logical use of reason. In order to achieve this goal, the transition from the logical to the transcendental principles must at least *appear* compelling. This is why Kant argues for the claim that the logical principles *presuppose* the transcendental ones in the Appendix. Second, Kant must leave room for his critique of traditional metaphysics. This means that the transition from the logical to the transcendental principles cannot actually *be* compelling – if the latter are used constitutively. And third, Kant wants to allow for the possibility that there is a legitimate use of the transcendental principles, which he does by distinguishing their 'natural' constitutive reading from their 'critical' regulative one. Suggesting that there is a natural transition from logical to transcendental principles and distinguishing between their regulative and constitutive use only later therefore serves a clear expository purpose: it makes us feel the pull of the illusory constitutive reading of transcendental principles, thus contributing to Kant's argument for the Rational Sources Account. Kant introduces the Supreme Principle as a natural presupposition of the logical use of reason, goes on to raise the question of its objective validity, and briefly returns to its status in the context of the resolution of the antinomies, only to finally distinguish between its legitimate regulative and its illegitimate constitutive use some 400 pages later.[38]

4.3.3 Understanding the Transition Itself

Even though the wording of the Transition Passage may suggest otherwise, we have seen that there are only two principles involved in that transition, namely (1) the Logical Maxim and (2) the Supreme Principle. The latter allows for two different employments, however, namely as (2a) a regulative and (2b) a constitutive principle. On Kant's own considered view (which only emerges at the very end of the Transcendental Dialectic), there is a legitimate transition from (1) to (2a), while the transition from (2a) to (2b) is natural but illegitimate.

Both the Logical Maxim and the regulative Supreme Principle fall under Kant's definition of "maxims of reason" in the Appendix, according to which

---

[37] That Kant deliberately left his readers in the dark about his true intentions for so many pages may seem unlikely. This is precisely what he did, however, in one of the last works published before the *Critique of Reason*, *Dreams of a Spirit Seer* from 1766 – in this case without showing his hand at all. Moreover, Kant's critique of the paralogisms and antinomies likewise consists in first presenting apparently cogent arguments, only then to disclose the ambiguity on which they rest (Chapter 7). Admittedly, with respect to the paralogisms and antinomies, however, Kant makes it clear beforehand that the proofs will turn out to be invalid, while in the Transition Passage and the Appendix (and, as I will argue in Chapter 8, in the Transcendental Ideal section) Kant gives conflicting hints as to the validity of the arguments he presents without clearly taking sides.

these are "subjective principles that are taken not from the constitution of the *object* but from the interest of reason in regard to a certain possible perfection of the cognition of this object" (A666/B694). Kant here uses the subjective/objective distinction in a sense that is orthogonal to the distinction between subjective and objective *validity*. Thus, there is a sense in which transcendental principles such as the Supreme Principle are *subjective* even though, when used regulatively, they have some indeterminate *objective validity* (and, when used constitutively, *purport* to have objective validity). They are subjective in that they are not derived from features of the objects of our cognition but are based solely on the interest of reason in the unity of cognition. Thus, when Kant says that transcendental illusion consists in mistaking subjective principles for objective ones, this means that the transcendental illusion surrounding the Supreme Principle does not concern the transition from the Logical Maxim to the latter (since both are subjective in the sense of merely reflecting the interest of reason); rather, it concerns mistaking the subjective Supreme Principle for an objective principle *by using it constitutively*. By contrast, in using the Supreme Principle regulatively, one does not mistake it for an objective principle (even though it *does* then have some objective validity, i.e. is legitimately applied to objects), since in so doing one does not take the principle to be true of the objects to which it is applied.

In sum, we can see that the transition from the Logical Maxim to the metaphysically loaded Supreme Principle can best be understood as involving two logically distinct steps.[39] While the first, legitimate step takes us from the Logical Maxim to the regulative Supreme Principle, the second, illegitimate step leads us from the regulative to the constitutive version of the Supreme Principle. This means that the logical structure of the transition itself differs from that of the Transition Passage. While in the latter Kant moves from the Logical Maxim to a generic version of the Supreme Principle (which only later turns out to be ambiguous between a regulative and constitutive reading), the transition itself can best be understood as leading first (legitimately) to the regulative and then (illegitimately) to the constitutive Supreme Principle. It is this latter two-step transition to which we will turn in the next chapter.

---

[38] Proops (2010: 456) also divides the transition from the Logical Maxim to the Supreme Principle into two steps, which, however, correspond to the transition from the regulative to the constitutive Supreme Principle, since Proops does not seem to take into account the distinctively 'logical' character of the Logical Maxim.

5 The Transition from the Logical Maxim to the Supreme Principle of Pure Reason

According to Kant's Rational Sources Account, rational thinking naturally leads into metaphysical speculation. The fundamental level at which Kant argues for this claim is the transition from the Logical Maxim to the Supreme Principle. As we saw in the previous chapter, the latter can be used in two different ways, namely regulatively or constitutively. Since we do not have to take a principle to be true to use it regulatively, the regulative use even of transcendental principles is metaphysically harmless. It is only the constitutive use that brings with it metaphysical commitments. As we have seen, Kant thinks that logical principles such as the Logical Maxim presuppose the regulative use of transcendental principles. But there is a natural tendency to mistake these principles for constitutive ones, which leads us into metaphysical speculation.

This means that if we want to understand why rational thinkers, according to Kant, are naturally led to accept the Supreme Principle as true (and thus to entangle themselves in metaphysical speculation), we must answer two questions: Why does the Logical Maxim have to become a principle of pure reason – that is, why is it rationally necessary to make *regulative* use of the Supreme Principle (Section 5.1)? And why does this lead to the illusion that the Supreme Principle is an objectively valid *constitutive* principle (that is, a true descriptive statement about everything there is) (Section 5.2)? The latter question will require a discussion of Kant's account of transcendental illusion (Section 5.2.1) and the role of transcendental realism in bringing about this kind of illusion (Section 5.2.2). The central idea is that transcendental realism implies that there is a correspondence between reason and reality; therefore, a tacit commitment to transcendental realism can explain why regulative principles of reason will naturally be taken to be constitutive principles that are true descriptions of reality itself (Section 5.2.3). We will see that even though transcendental realism is a weighty metaphysical claim, it can plausibly be attributed to common sense or 'universal human reason,' as Kant's Rational Sources Account requires (Section 5.2.4). This reading of transcendental illusion as based on transcendental realism will allow us to formulate a general template for the way in which Kant, in the different parts of the Transcendental

Dialectic, argues for his Rational Sources Account (Section 5.2.5). We will close with a discussion of why, according to Kant, the Supreme Principle is valid for things in themselves (Section 5.3).

5.1 Step 1: From the Logical Maxim to the Regulative Supreme Principle

The Logical Maxim is a subjectively valid prescriptive principle of the logical use of reason. It directs us to find, for every cognition C_1 that is inferentially or epistemically conditioned, a more general cognition C_2 from which (in conjunction with additional premises) C_1 can be derived and epistemically justified (see Chapter 2). Ideally, the result of this procedure would be a complete hierarchical system of cognitions with one or few highly general and epistemically certain principles at the top and all other cognitions, in order of decreasing generality, under them as their logical consequences. Such a system would exhibit what Kant calls "unity of reason" (e.g. A302/B359) or "systematic unity" (e.g. A651/B679). Since "systematic unity is that which first makes ordinary cognition into science" (A832/B860), we can think of the unity of reason as an ideal system of scientific knowledge (Section 2.1.4). So the question is why transforming the manifold of our cognitions into a system of scientific knowledge by following the Logical Maxim should presuppose the regulative use of the Supreme Principle.

5.1.1 Why the Logical Maxim Presupposes the Regulative Supreme Principle

A first reason why the Logical Maxim presupposes the regulative Supreme Principle – not explicitly mentioned by Kant himself – is that one cannot turn the 'manifold cognitions provided by the understanding' (that is, the immense wealth of information about nature that we possess) into a unified system of scientific knowledge if one abstracts from their content and restricts oneself to the logical relations between them. Rather, the relations between the objects themselves have to be taken into account, since the logical relations among cognitions underdetermine their place in a system of scientific knowledge. Consider, for instance, pairs of co-extensive concepts such as 'is a mammal' and 'has hair,' or 'has lungs' and 'has a heart.' While something's being a mammal is the 'real ground' of its having hair, having hair is only a 'ground of cognition' for being a mammal. By contrast, having a heart and having lungs are interdependent properties of animals (because, from an evolutionary perspective, hearts and lungs have co-evolved), so that neither is more basic than the other. If we want to systematize our knowledge about nature, we therefore have to know whether all mammals have hair *because* they are mammals or whether they are mammals *because* they have hair, and whether having a heart *explains* having lungs or having lungs explains having a heart (or neither). But these questions cannot be answered if we abstract from the content of our cognitions and consider only their inferential relations. Hence, it is necessary to go beyond the Logical Maxim and apply to nature itself the idea that for every conditioned cognition we must search for its condition – that is, for everything in need of explanation, we must seek something that explains it.[1]

But this is only a first step toward an answer to our question, since it only takes us to a version of the Logical Maxim that no longer abstracts from objects but is still prescriptive in that it requires us to look for the conditions of conditioned objects. Even though, as noted earlier, Kant does not mark this distinction very clearly, such a prescriptive principle still differs from the Supreme Principle – even in its regulative use – in that the latter is a *descriptive* principle that says something about nature, namely that for every conditioned object *there is* the totality of its conditions. So why do we have to make regulative use of this descriptive principle if we follow the Logical Maxim?

A possible answer is suggested by some of the passages in the Appendix, where Kant repeatedly claims that logical principles *presuppose* transcendental ones. There, the reason Kant gives seems to be that if we do not assume that nature conforms to the transcendental principles, following the logical principles may lead us astray:

This logical law of the *continuum specierum (formarum logicarum)* presupposes, however, a transcendental law *(lex continui in natura)* without which the use of the understanding through the former prescription would only mislead, since the prescription would perhaps take a path directly opposed to nature. (A660/B688; see also A651/B679)

So the worry seems to be that if we do not assume that nature itself conforms to the (transcendental) principles of reason, following its logical principles might lead to a false picture of nature. The problem with this suggestion is that presupposing the transcendental principles only postpones that worry, which immediately reappears in the form of the thought that we are mistaken in assuming the *transcendental* principles if nature itself does not conform to them. Simply presupposing the truth of the transcendental principles does not respond to that worry.[2] Perhaps all Kant wants to say is that *given* that we are

---

[1] The same point can be made if we consider the relation between parts and wholes. Whereas in inanimate bodies the parts unilaterally determine the whole, in an organism the whole (also) determines its parts (5:376). Thus, while it is true that rocks exist because their parts exist and not vice versa, it is false to say that trees exist because their parts exist and not vice versa. This difference must somehow be reflected in a complete system of scientific knowledge, but it can come into view only if we go beyond the logical relations between concepts and look at the real conditioning relations among the objects of our cognitions.

[2] For a related point, see Guyer 1979: 50; Thöle 2000: 122.

rationally required to follow the logical principles, we are thereby *committed* to assuming that nature itself conforms to the transcendental principles, because otherwise we would have to admit that it is *possible* that the logical principles will lead us astray. But that cannot be right either, because the possibility of an error of this kind is something we have to admit anyway, given that Kant rejects any constitutive use of those principles as illegitimate (A664/B692). It is precisely the legitimacy of the *constitutive* use that is required if the reason for moving from the logical to the transcendental principles is to allay the worry that the logical principles may mislead us.[3] Thus, we still lack an answer to the question of why following the Logical Maxim should presuppose the *regulative* use of the Supreme Principle.

A different answer suggests itself if we recall the criticism raised by modern philosophers against Aristotelian syllogistic logic, namely that it is unable to generate any new insights (Section 2.1.3). After all, the conclusion of a syllogism can only make explicit what is already implicitly contained in the premises. Similarly, the Logical Maxim itself does not direct us to expand our body of cognitions and does not tell us how to do so. All it can do, as a principle of the logical use of reason, is to direct us to systematize the cognitions *we already have*. As Kant points out, the logical use of reason gives systematic form to "*given* cognitions" (A305/B362; emphasis added); the Logical Maxim is a "subjective law of economy for the provision [*Vorrate*] of our understanding" (A306/B362; emphasis added), which means that it is not concerned with *discovering* cognitions that have not yet been given or with *enlarging* the provision of the understanding.

On the other hand, though, the Logical Maxim directs us to find the condition for *every* conditioned cognition, including those for which we do not yet possess the cognition that conditions it. Since the logical use of reason as such does not lead us to discover new cognitions, we thus see that, considered in isolation, it cannot succeed in achieving the unity of reason, since at any given point in time many of the pieces required for full systematic unity will still be missing. Hence, the aim at which the logical use of reason is directed – systematic unity – points us beyond a merely logical use and toward a real use of reason, which in this case consists in providing hypotheses that allow us to search for new cognitions that fix the holes in the system of cognition (A646–7/B674–5). This is why Kant remarks in the Appendix that transcendental principles, when used "with good success"

---

[3] This suggests that, when Kant claims that we must accept the transcendental principles because otherwise we would have to allow that the logical principles are misleading, this is a claim he makes not on his own behalf but as part of his account of transcendental illusion and his argument for the Rational Sources Account; see Section 4.3.2.

(that is, regulatively), are "heuristic" devices (A663/B691), that is, means of generating new cognitions.

Recall that the regulative use of transcendental principles consists in using them as premises that generate empirical hypotheses which can then be confirmed (or disconfirmed) by the understanding (A647–8/B675–6; see Section 4.2.2). Applying this thought to the Supreme Principle, we can see that this principle can be used to generate, for any conditioned *object* (in the widest sense of the term), the (hypothetical) conclusion that it must have a condition, which we can then search for empirically. In this sense, following the Logical Maxim requires the regulative use of the Supreme Principle: in order to find the condition for *every* conditioned cognition, we must in many cases go beyond our present body of cognitions and search for as yet undiscovered conditions. And for this, we must *hypothetically* assume that they exist, which is what the regulative Supreme Principle entails.[4]

5.1.2 How the Supreme Principle Corresponds to the Logical Maxim

But even if we now have an answer to the philosophical question of why one must presuppose the Supreme Principle if one follows the Logical Maxim, we still face an exegetical problem. Earlier, we said that for Kant the Supreme Principle is the descriptive version of the Logical Maxim as applied to objects (Section 4.3.1). But while it is more or less obvious how the transcendental version corresponds to the logical one when it comes to the three principles of homogeneity, specification, and continuity, this is not so clear for the Logical Maxim and the Supreme Principle. The logical principle of homogeneity, for instance, requires us to look, with respect to each pair of species concepts, for a more general concept that covers both, while the corresponding transcendental principle applies what is recognizably the same logical structure to nature itself by positing that there is a common genus for every pair of species. By contrast, it is not obvious how the search for conditions of conditioned *cognitions* (required by the Logical Maxim) corresponds to the search for conditions of the conditioned *objects* of our cognitions. The problem stems from the ambiguity of the term 'condition.' The conditions that the Logical Maxim directs us to find are inferential and epistemic conditions of conditioned *cognitions*. These conditions are themselves cognitions. By contrast, the Supreme Principle is concerned with *real* conditions – with 'objects and their conjunction' (A308/B364; see Chapter 3). But it is unclear what in nature itself could correspond to the inferential and epistemic relations

---

[4] Also recall that the distinction between the logical and the real use of reason rests on an abstraction and that the logical use *in concreto* always applies to one subject matter or another (Section 2.1.4).

between our cognitions. It seems that the conditioning relations between cognitions that would constitute the unity of reason (relations of logical inference and transmission of epistemic status) do not map directly onto the conditioning relations between objects covered by the Supreme Principle (e.g. part–whole, causation, inherence). This raises the question of why Kant thought that the Supreme Principle corresponds to the Logical Maxim in the same way that the logical principle of homogeneity corresponds to its transcendental counterpart.[5] Kant himself does not explicitly address this question, but rather seems to take the correspondence between the Logical Maxim and the Supreme Principle for granted.

In order to make some progress in this respect, it will help to return to the distinction between the logical and the real use of reason. As we saw earlier, that distinction is best understood as concerning the form and matter of rational cognition (Section 2.1.1). While the logical use of reason consists in drawing inferences whose validity depends only on their form, the real use of reason consists in gaining a priori cognitions about conditioning relations among objects (which objects are the matter of our cognitions). Both 'uses' can be considered in isolation, but this does not mean that they are completely distinct activities. On the one hand, the real use of reason will typically consist in drawing rational inferences from a priori premises (e.g. the paralogisms and the proofs of the antinomies). On the other hand, the cognitions on which the logical use of reason operates (in order to unify them into a coherent and complete system) will include the a priori cognitions (or putative cognitions) provided by the real use of reason, with the Supreme Principle serving as their most general premise.

Assume, for instance, that lightning is a causal condition of thunder, and electrostatic discharge a causal condition of lightning. These conditioning relations can be represented in our system of cognitions by the empirical principles 'Whenever there is thunder at t_2, it was caused by lightning at t_1' and 'Whenever there is lightning at t_1, it was caused by an electrostatic discharge at t_0.' In this way, the laws and principles governing the real conditioning relations among objects are represented as general premises in our system of cognitions. The Supreme Principle then serves as the most general premise in this system insofar as all specific conditioning relations represented in our system of cognitions fall under it as special cases. This fits with Kant's claim that it is the "supreme principle of pure reason" (A308/B365), which seems to imply that it must have a special place in any rational

---

[5] That Kant assumes that the relation between the Logical Maxim and the Supreme Principle is the same as that between each of the three specific logical principles (homogeneity, specification, continuity) and their transcendental counterparts is clear from the Appendix, where Kant describes that relation in completely parallel ways; see A648/B676–A663/B691 and Section 4.2.1 above.

The Transition to the Supreme Principle (5.1.2) 133

system of cognitions. Thus, even though the conditioning relations between cognitions do not map directly onto the conditioning relations between objects, there is a clear sense in which the Supreme Principle corresponds to the Logical Maxim, namely insofar as the former is the most general substantive principle of reason while the latter is the most general methodological principle, and in that the conditioning relations captured by the former are represented in the system of cognitions governed by the latter.[6]

There is a second way in which the Supreme Principle corresponds to the Logical Maxim, namely in that both concern *ultimate* answers to a certain type of question. The Logical Maxim requires us to find answers to questions concerning our cognitions and their epistemic status by deriving them from a set of premises. The Supreme Principle asserts that there are answers to questions concerning the real conditions of objects. These kinds of questions, and their respective answers, may differ more radically than Kant (particularly in the Introduction and Book One of the Transcendental Dialectic) acknowledges. But what the Logical Maxim and the Supreme Principle share is an interest in *ultimate* answers, where an answer is ultimate if it does not raise further questions of the same kind. For instance, naming the cause of an event answers the question of why that event happened, but it does not necessarily provide an ultimate answer, because there is a further question concerning the cause of the cause, etc. Thus, an ultimate answer would be one that does not raise (or even allow for) further questions concerning the causes (and causes of causes, etc.) of the original event. Similarly, deriving some cognition C from a more general premise P may provide an answer to the question of how we know that C is the case, but it raises the further question of how we know that P is the case. Again, an ultimate answer would be one that does not raise (or even allow for) a further question of the same kind. The Supreme Principle thus corresponds to the Logical Maxim in that both concern ultimate answers, the latter concerning the inferential and epistemic status of our cognitions, the former concerning the real conditioning relations among objects.

In sum, we can see that the correspondence between the Logical Maxim and the Supreme Principle is less direct than Kant's formulations may suggest since, as Kant is of course well aware, logical conditions differ from real conditions.[7] Thus, the search for logical (inferential, epistemic) conditions instigated by the Logical Maxim does not map one-to-one onto the search for ontological conditions guided by the hypothetical assumption of the

---

[6] That there is a structural correspondence between scientific theories and the reality they describe is an idea that can be found in current metaphysical theories as well. Thus, Jessica Wilson writes: "The fundamental is, well, *fundamental*: entities in the fundamental base play a role analogous to axioms in a theory" (Wilson 2014: 560).

[7] That logical and real grounds must be distinguished is one of Kant's central insights of the pre-critical period and goes back at least to his essay *Negative Magnitudes* from 1763.

Supreme Principle. Nevertheless, the connection between the two principles is close enough to explain why Kant treats them as corresponding to each other. First, while the Logical Maxim is the most general methodological principle of reason, the Supreme Principle is reason's most general substantive principle. Thus, an ideal system of cognitions would be governed by the Logical Maxim, but it would also include the Supreme Principle. And second, just as the Logical Maxim directs us to find ultimate answers to all 'logical' questions (concerning inferential and epistemic relations between cognitions), hypothetically assuming the Supreme Principle amounts to assuming that there are ultimate answers to all 'real' questions (concerning real conditioning relations).[8]

5.1.3 Conclusion to Step 1

This concludes the first step from the Logical Maxim to the metaphysical Supreme Principle, namely the step from the former to the *regulative* use of the latter. In short, we must hypothetically assume the Supreme Principle because this is necessary for approximating the end at which the Logical Maxim – and ultimately any use of reason – aims, namely systematic unity among our cognitions. In making regulative use of the Supreme Principle, we do not commit ourselves to its truth; rather, we employ the thought that there is a condition for everything conditioned (and thus something unconditioned) to generate empirical hypotheses about real conditioning relations. We are thus not committing ourselves to any metaphysical claims about nature or the world at large; in particular, we are not claiming that something unconditioned exists.[9]

---

[8] But note that this kind of correspondence between the Logical Maxim and the Supreme Principle, while clearly assumed by Kant, is not strictly necessary for his argument for the Rational Sources Account, which only requires that we must presuppose the latter if we are to follow the former (Section 5.1.1).

[9] Does the regulative use of the Supreme Principle commit one to the existence of something unconditioned even hypothetically? As Kant says in the passage from the Antinomy chapter (quoted in Section 4.2.3): "Thus the principle of reason [= Supreme Principle] is only a *rule*, prescribing a regress in the series of conditions for given appearances, in which regress it is *never allowed to stop with an absolutely unconditioned*" (A508–9/B536–7; emphasis added). This means that the regulative use of the Supreme Principle requires us to treat every particular condition as conditioned. However, this does not mean that the Supreme Principle (the very principle we hypothetically assume when we make regulative use of it) does not imply the existence of something unconditioned. If the existence of something conditioned requires the existence of the totality of its conditions, and if any such totality is itself unconditioned (in the sense of UTC; see Section 3.3.3), then the regulative use of the Supreme Principle commits us to *hypothetically* assuming something unconditioned. (We will return to this issue in Sections 5.3 and 6.3.)

5.2 Step 2: From the Regulative to the Constitutive Supreme Principle

According to Kant's Rational Sources Account, there is a natural and unavoidable tendency to move from the metaphysically innocent regulative use of the Supreme Principle to a metaphysically committed constitutive use, which then drives the different metaphysical inferences Kant reconstructs in the Transcendental Dialectic. As he says explicitly of the Antinomy, "the entire antinomy of pure reason rests on this dialectical argument: If the conditioned is given, then the whole series of all conditions for it is also given; now objects of the senses are given as conditioned; consequently, etc." (A497/B525). Even though the importance of the Supreme Principle to the Paralogisms and the Transcendental Ideal is less obvious, it plays a role even there (see Chapters 7 and 8). And it is of course the constitutive Supreme Principle – as a claim we take to be true – that plays this fundamental role in metaphysical thinking, not just its regulative counterpart. Thus, it is essential to the Rational Sources Account and to the project of the Transcendental Dialectic as a whole that we understand why the constitutive Supreme Principle appears to be rationally compelling. So far, we have only seen how following the Logical Maxim commits us to the *regulative* use of the Supreme Principle. The question now is why, according to Kant, we cannot just leave it at that. Why does the Supreme Principle, which we legitimately use as a regulative principle of reason, appear to be constitutive, that is, a true principle about everything that is?

A natural place to look for an answer to this question is Kant's account of transcendental illusion (*transzendentaler Schein*), since, as Kant insists again and again, at the bottom of the dialectical fallacies of reason lies the natural and unavoidable misleading appearance of rational cogency that he calls 'transcendental illusion.' As we will see in the next subsection, however, 'transcendental illusion' is only a name for the phenomenon we are trying to understand (namely the fact that illegitimate principles appear legitimate), not an explanation of it.

5.2.1 Transcendental Illusion

In the first part of the Introduction to the Transcendental Dialectic, Kant introduces his conception of transcendental illusion by comparing it with logical illusion, on the one hand, and perceptual illusion, on the other:

Logical illusion ... arises solely from a failure of attentiveness to the logical rule. Hence as soon as this attentiveness is focused on the case before us, logical illusion entirely disappears. Transcendental illusion, on the other hand, does not cease even though it is uncovered and its nullity is clearly seen into by transcendental criticism (e.g. the illusion in the proposition: 'The world must have a beginning in time'). The cause of this is that in our reason (considered subjectively as a human faculty of cognition) there lie fundamental rules and maxims for its use, which look entirely like objective principles, and through them it comes about that the subjective necessity of a certain connection of our concepts on behalf of the understanding is taken for an objective necessity, the determination of things in themselves. [This is] an *illusion* that cannot be avoided at all, just as little as we can avoid it that the sea appears higher in the middle than at the shores. (A296–7/B353–4)

Thus, transcendental illusion is characterized by the following features: (1) it rests on mistaking subjective necessity (concerning concepts) for objective necessity (concerning objects), or, as Kant also puts it, in "subjective principles" being "passed off" as "objective" ones (A298/B354); (2) unlike logical illusion, it arises from human reason itself and is thus "*natural* and unavoidable" (A298/B354); and (3) unlike logical illusion, and like perceptual illusion, it does not disappear once it is discovered. Thus, the best we can do is to protect ourselves "from being deceived by it" (A297/B354). It is important to keep in mind that an illusion, according to Kant, is only the 'enticement' (*Verleitung*) to error, not the error itself (A293/B350).[10]

In the 'subjective principles' mentioned in the quotation above, we can easily recognize the maxims of reason Kant mentions in the Appendix, which include the Logical Maxim and the logical principles of homogeneity, specification, and continuity. But their transcendental counterparts, including the Supreme Principle, are also subjective in the relevant sense, in that they are "taken not from the constitution of the *object* but from the interest of reason in regard to a certain possible perfection of the cognition of this object" (A666/B694; emphasis added). Transcendental illusion consists in mistaking these subjective principles of reason for objective or constitutive ones, that is, for true descriptive statements about objects.

In Kant's example, "the illusion in the proposition: 'The world must have a beginning in time'" (A297/B353) arises from taking the Supreme Principle to be constitutive, from which it follows that there is either an infinite series of past moments or a first moment in time. Assuming with the thesis side of the first antinomy (as Kant seems to do in his example) that an infinite series of past moments in time is impossible, it follows that there must be a first moment in time. This is a case of transcendental illusion because the disjunction between 'infinite series' and 'first moment,' according to Kant, is complete only if we take the Supreme Principle to be an objective principle that is true of empirical objects, while really it is only a subjective principle that should guide us in approximating the unity of reason (A508–9/B536–7). If we had an explanation of this kind of illusion, this would presumably take us a long

---

[10] The importance of this point has been emphasized by Michelle Grier (e.g. Grier 2001: 116).

The Transition to the Supreme Principle (5.2.1) 137

way toward understanding why the transition from the Logical Maxim to the Supreme Principle appears rationally compelling.[11]

But while some of Kant's formulations in the earlier passage ('the cause of this,' 'through which it comes') may suggest that he is offering an *explanation* of the phenomenon he calls 'transcendental illusion,' if we look closer we can see that all Kant is giving here is a *description* of that phenomenon. What would be required for an explanation is an account of *why* the subjective principles in question unavoidably appear to be objective and *why* this illusion does not disappear even when we become aware of it. But in the first section of the Introduction, no such account is given.[12] Nor does Kant offer an explanation of transcendental illusion in any other part of the first *Critique*. The only further explanation we are given is that transcendental illusion rests on "dialectical inferences" (A405/B432; see also A397). These inferences are the inferences to the existence of something unconditioned: the "unconditioned unity of *subjective* conditions of all representations in general" (the soul), the "unconditioned unity of objective conditions in appearance" (the world in its unconditioned aspects), and "the unconditioned unity of objective conditions of the possibility of objects in general" (God) (A406/B432–3). But given that these inferences are 'dialectical' – which here means 'illusory' (A63–4/B88) – this raises the question of *why* they appear to be valid even though they are not. An explanation of transcendental illusion would have to explain just that. Kant does not offer such an explanation. Nor does Kant explain why, as with perceptual illusions, we remain under the spell of the transcendental illusion even when we see through it.[13] So we will have to look in a different place in order to understand why Kant thinks that the transition from the regulative to the constitutive Supreme Principle appears rationally compelling.[14]

---

[11] The standard account of the transcendental illusion involved in the transition from the Logical Maxim to the Supreme Principle (e.g. in Grier 2001) is that we somehow mistake the prescriptive Logical Maxim for the descriptive Supreme Principle (or in any case do not properly note the difference between them) (see Chapter 4, note 2, for further references). But even if this were correct, it would not provide an explanation of transcendental illusion and in turn calls out for an explanation. After all, we typically do not mistake a prescription to look for something ('For every sock in the laundry pile, look for its partner') for its descriptive analogue ('For every sock in the laundry pile, there is a partner').

[12] The account in terms of the undue influence of sensibility on the understanding given at the beginning of that section (A293–5/B349–51) is an account not of transcendental illusion but of the errors that can result from it (Grier 2001: 116).

[13] That there are cognitive illusions that resemble optical illusions in being cognitively impenetrable is an important aspect of Daniel Kahneman's 'heuristics and biases' theory (Kahneman 2011). Kahneman argues that the heuristics that lead to cognitive illusions are hard-wired in our brains. It is an interesting question whether a similar psychological-physiological explanation would be available to Kant (see Butts 1997). In any case, he does not offer one.

[14] My interpretation of Kant's account of transcendental illusion and its role in the Transcendental Dialectic differs in various ways from Michelle Grier's influential reading (Grier 2001; see also Allison 2004 and Proops 2010, who follow Grier in this respect). According to Grier,

5.2.2 Transcendental Realism as the 'Key' to Transcendental Illusion

Kant explicitly introduces his famous doctrine of transcendental idealism rather late in the *Critique of Pure Reason*, in a section entitled "Transcendental Idealism as the Key to the Resolution of the Cosmological Dialectic" (A490/B519). There, he explains that transcendental idealism is the "doctrine" according to which

> everything intuited in space or in time, hence all objects of an experience possible for us, are nothing but appearances, i.e., mere representations, which, as they are represented, as extended beings or series of alterations, have outside our thoughts no existence grounded in itself ... The realist, in the transcendental signification, makes these modifications of our sensibility into things subsisting in themselves, and hence makes *mere representations* into things in themselves. (A490–1/B518–19)

Thus, while the transcendental realist identifies empirical objects with things in themselves (see also A369), the transcendental idealist insists that empirical objects are appearances (and thus mere representations) and not things in themselves. How to understand the distinction between things in themselves and appearances, and thus how to understand Kant's transcendental idealism, is a much-debated issue among readers of the first *Critique*.[15] For present purposes, let us rest content with what Kant says in the quote, namely that appearances are representations inherent in a representing subject, while things in themselves are thought of as 'subsisting in themselves.' Thus, while according to transcendental idealism empirical objects depend on a representing subject, according to transcendental realism they are independently existing things.

---

transcendental illusion consists in accepting the Supreme Principle (which she calls "P_2") (e.g. Grier 2001: 144), which is an "application condition" for the Logical Maxim (which she calls "P_1") (126; see also Allison 2004: 330). However, she fails to distinguish between the regulative and constitutive use of the Supreme Principle; instead, she takes the Logical Maxim to be the regulative version of the Supreme Principle (137). And why should the constitutive use of the Supreme Principle be an application condition for the Logical Maxim (or of the regulative use of the Supreme Principle)? Allison argues that this is because the Logical Maxim requires us to look for conditions that are guaranteed to exist by the analytic link between condition and conditioned, which link, if iterated, implies the Supreme Principle (Allison 2004: 332; for critical discussion, see Rohlf 2010: 207 and Section 3.3.3 above). But this argument ignores the difference between 'logical' and 'real' conditions and between the regulative and the constitutive use of the Supreme Principle, which, if I am correct, is the key to understanding Kant's transition from the Logical Maxim to the Supreme Principle. These differences notwithstanding, I am indebted to Grier in many ways, for example when it comes to the inevitability of transcendental illusion (e.g. Grier 2001: 128) and the distinction between illusion and error (e.g. 116, 128). Most importantly for me, her pioneering work has provided an important background against which I have developed my own interpretation.

[15] See e.g. the essays collected in Schulting and Verburgt 2011.

The Transition to the Supreme Principle (5.2.2) 139

In what way, then, is transcendental idealism the 'key' to resolving 'the cosmological dialectic' – that is, the key to resolving the antinomies (which consist in pairs of contradictory theses about the world at large, for each of which there appears to be an a priori proof)? As we will discuss in more detail later (Section 7.3.1), Kant thinks that the antinomies rest on a 'dialectical argument' that starts from the Supreme Principle as its first premise: "If the conditioned is given, then the whole series of all conditions for it is also given; now objects of the senses are given as conditioned; consequently, etc." (A497/B525) – where 'etc.' obviously stands for the conclusion 'The whole series of all conditions (of objects of the senses) is also given.' But as Kant points out:

> the major premise of the cosmological inference of reason takes the conditioned in the transcendental signification of a pure category, while the minor premise takes it in the empirical signification of a concept of the understanding applied to mere appearances; consequently there is present in it that dialectical deception that is called a *sophisma figurae dictionis*. This deception is, however, not artificial, but an entirely natural mistake of common reason. (A499–500/B527–8)

We will discuss Kant's diagnosis in more detail later (Section 7.4.2). For present purposes, it will suffice to note that a '*sophisma figurae dictionis*' is an inference that is fallacious because it rests on the ambiguity of its middle term (9:135). As Kant had pointed out immediately before, the Supreme Principle (as the major premise) is true only of things in themselves, but not of appearances (A498/B526). (We will ask why this is so later, in Section 5.3.) So the sense in which transcendental idealism is the 'key' to the resolution of the antinomies is that the antinomies rest on an ambiguity of the term 'conditioned' that can only be detected once we accept transcendental idealism and acknowledge that empirical objects are mere appearances rather than things in themselves. And this means that the 'entirely natural mistake of common reason' involved in this inference rests on the tacit assumption that empirical objects *are* things in themselves, that is, on the assumption of transcendental realism.

If transcendental idealism is the key to the resolution of the 'cosmological dialectic,' then transcendental realism is the key to understanding the transcendental illusion involved in that dialectic. And if that is the case, perhaps transcendental realism is the key to understanding transcendental illusion in general, including the transcendental illusion involved in the transition from the regulative to the constitutive Supreme Principle. In the next subsection, I will argue that this is indeed the case.[16]

---

[16] Many authors have noted in a general way that transcendental illusion depends on the assumption of transcendental realism (e.g. Malzkorn 1999: 103; Klimmek 2005: 37; Watkins 2010), although they do not explain in detail how this dependence is supposed to work. That transcendental illusion rests on transcendental realism has been denied by Grier 2001: 101.

5.2.3 Transcendental Realism and the Transition from the Regulative to the Constitutive Supreme Principle

At first sight, the hypothesis that transcendental realism motivates the transition from the regulative to the constitutive Supreme Principle may not seem very promising. Why should the identification of empirical objects with things in themselves tempt us to make an illicit move from the regulative to the constitutive use of a principle? And how could such a demanding philosophical thesis be part of a 'natural mistake of common reason'? In order to make this hypothesis work, we have to look more closely at the thesis of transcendental realism (TR). As we have seen, TR is the claim that empirical objects are things in themselves. Now things in themselves, according to Kant, are 'intelligible objects' or '*noumena*,' that is, things that cannot be perceived by the senses, but only thought by the intellect (*nous*). In this way, Kant aligns the distinction between appearances and things in themselves with the traditional distinction between the sensible and the intelligible, between "phenomena" and "noumena" (A249; B306).

Only in the second edition of the *Critique of Pure Reason*, however, does Kant point out that the term '*noumenon*' is ambiguous:

But right at the outset here there is an ambiguity, which can occasion great misunderstanding ... If by a *noumenon* we understand a thing *insofar as it is not an object of our sensible intuition*, because we abstract from the manner of our intuition of it, then this is a *noumenon* in the *negative* sense. But if we understand by that an *object of a non-sensible intuition*, then we assume a special kind of intuition, namely intellectual intuition, which, however, is not our own, and the possibility of which we cannot understand, and this would be the *noumenon* in a *positive* sense. (B306–7)

As I will now argue, this ambiguity carries over to the thesis of transcendental realism. For this, it will not be necessary to discuss Kant's complex account of *noumena* (and the related account of intellectual intuition) in all its detail. What matters for our purposes is that a *noumenon* in the negative sense is an object with respect to which we *abstract* from the sensible way in which we intuit *it*. Taken literally, this means that only empirical objects can be *noumena* in the negative sense, since it is only of these that we have sensible intuitions from which we can abstract. While I think that this is indeed what Kant wants to say (Willaschek 1998), other commentators have rejected the identification of *noumena* in the negative sense with empirical objects (e.g. Haag 2007: 78–101). In any case, a *noumenon* in the negative sense is either something

---

According to Grier, transcendental realism (which Grier identifies with the transcendental use of the categories; e.g. 150) plays a role in generating not transcendental illusion itself but only the fallacies of traditional metaphysics that result from it (143; see also Grier 2011: 78).

that *is not* an object of the senses (e.g. Emundts 2010: 189) or (as I would prefer) something that is *not considered* as such.[17]

By contrast, *noumena* in the *positive* sense are objects of a hypothetical non-sensible or intelligible intuition – a kind of intuition Kant typically attributes to God. While many details of Kant's conception of intellectual intuition remain obscure (partly because, as Kant repeatedly points out, we cannot have any positive conception of it), an intellectual intuition combines in one cognitive act the immediacy and singularity of intuition with the determinacy and intelligibility that comes with the intellect. Moreover, since being non-sensible means that its representations cannot be dependent on the represented object (because sensibility, according to Kant, just is the ability to receive representations by an impact coming from the object; A19/B33), and since there must be some kind of dependence relation between representation and represented object (A92/B124; see also B72), an intellectual intuition must be "one through which the existence of the *object* of intuition is itself given (and that, so far as we can have insight, can only pertain to the original being [i.e. God]" (B72; emphasis added).[18]

Thus, *if* there is an intellectual intuition, the existence of the objects being represented depends on their being thus represented and not – as is the case with human intuition – the other way around. Note that this does not imply that if there is no intellectual intuition (because God does not exist), then there are no *noumena* in the positive sense.[19] Rather, the notion of an intellectual intuition merely serves to pick out a class of objects that, if they exist at all, might also exist even if there is no intellectual intuition. Kant's main point in introducing the concept of a *noumenon* in the positive sense, apart from distinguishing it from the concept of a *noumenon* in the negative sense, is to highlight that we can consistently *think* of a class of objects that finite, sensible

---

[17] Kant seems to identify *noumena* in the negative sense with empirical objects by saying: "if we call certain objects, as appearances, beings of sense (*phaenomena*) because we distinguish the way in which we intuit them from their constitution in itself, then it already follows from our concept that to these we as it were oppose, as objects thought merely through the understanding, either *these same objects* conceived in accordance with the latter constitution, even though we do not intuit it in them, or else other possible things, which are not objects of our senses at all, and call these beings of understanding (*noumena*)" (B306; emphasis added). Note that Guyer and Wood translate "*dieselbe*" (literally: the same) not as "these same objects" but as "other objects," thus obscuring the fact that it is the same objects that are called appearances and *noumena*. I take the distinction in the quote ("either these same objects ... or else other possible things") to prepare us for the distinction between *noumena* in the negative and the positive sense, which Kant introduces in the following paragraph.

[18] On Kant's conception of an intellectual intuition, see Förster 2011: 150–60, who argues for a distinction between intellectual intuition and intuitive intellect (154), both of which can be understood in two different ways (160). The relevant conception in our context is that of an intellectual intuition as a non-sensible intuition of things in themselves.

[19] This would follow only if an object's depending on being cognized by God were an essential property of that object, which is a claim to which Kant does not seem to be committed.

beings like us cannot *cognize* (B146). These are non-sensible objects or *noumena* in the positive sense.

As becomes apparent, for instance, in Kant's distinction between the empirical and the intelligible character of human beings, this realm of the non-sensible also includes the non-sensible or "intelligible" *properties* of sensible objects (A538/B566). Thus, Kant can speak of a *homo noumenon* in contradistinction to the empirical human being, the *homo phenomenon* (e.g. 6:418), which shows that even human beings can count as *noumena* in the positive sense in virtue of their intelligible properties (such as having free will).[20] Since intelligible objects and properties as such are not cognitively accessible to us, however, we cannot know whether they exist. All we can say (from a theoretical point of view) is that their existence is logically possible.[21]

In sum, while *noumena* in the negative sense are either non-sensible objects or objects in abstraction from their sensible properties, *noumena* in the positive sense are objects that (with respect to some or all of their properties) can be cognized only by an infinite being (God). *Noumena* in both the negative and the positive sense are what Kant calls 'things in themselves.'[22]

But this means that Kant's formulation of transcendental realism as the thesis that empirical objects are things in themselves is ambiguous between the following two claims:

TR_{neg} Empirical objects are *noumena* in the negative sense.

and

TR_{pos} Empirical objects are *noumena* in the positive sense.

Brief reflection shows that by 'transcendental realism' Kant can only mean TR_{pos}. If, as I have indicated, the concept of a *noumenon* in the negative sense is meant to be co-extensive with the concept of an empirical object, TR_{neg} would turn out to be true. Since Kant rejects transcendental realism as false, this cannot be what he means. If, by contrast, we take a 'noumenon in the negative sense' to be a non-sensible object, TR_{neg} would mean that empirical objects are non-sensible (not accessible to our senses), which is so obviously

---

[20] Thus, *noumena* in the positive sense are not necessarily objects that we cannot experience, but rather objects that have at least some properties we cannot experience.

[21] As Kant argues in the Canon section of the first *Critique* (and then in various ways in later writings), from a practical point of view we are rationally committed to accepting the existence of human freedom, God, and immortal souls (A797/B825–A819/B847). We will briefly return to this important point in the Postscript.

[22] See B307, where Kant subsumes *noumena* in both the negative and the positive sense under the concept of an "object in itself [*Gegenstande an sich selbst*]," and B307, where he calls *noumena* in the negative sense "things in themselves."

false that it can hardly be attributed to 'common reason' (as Kant does with respect to transcendental realism).

Thus, what Kant means by 'transcendental realism' can only be TR_{pos}.[23] And indeed, this makes perfectly good sense. Read in this way, transcendental realism is the claim that empirical objects do not depend on our sensible ways of representing them – in particular, on space and time as our human forms of intuition – and are what they are independently of any finite mode of representation. Kant articulates this thought by recourse to the concept of a divine mind that immediately takes in objects as they are in themselves, in their full individuality, but also with all their general properties. This thought has a long tradition. According to many Christian philosophers from Augustine onward, while human knowledge is not only limited in scope and depth but also distorted by sensibility, God's knowledge is complete and undistorted knowledge of everything there is.[24] With this traditional thought comes the assumption that the world as known by God must be unified, true, and good (the traditional *transcendentalia*). Put differently, since the divine mind is supremely rational, the world created and cognized by it must be a rational order.[25] Accordingly, for Kant, *noumena* in the positive sense are members of an 'intelligible world,' or *mundus intelligibilis*, which is a world "in which therefore everything would be real merely because it is (as something good) possible" (5:404; see also 4:451–62).[26]

While in his dissertation *De Mundi* Kant tries to explain how we can have cognitive access to such a world through the 'real use' of our intellect (2:393), in the first *Critique* he famously denies that we can have cognition of an intelligible world, or that we can know that it exists. As he puts it in a note from the 1770s, however:

It is a necessary hypothesis of the theoretical and practical use of reason ... that an intelligible world grounds the sensible one, of which the soul as intelligence is the subjective prototype [*Urbild*], but an original intelligence its cause. (*Refl.* 5109, 18:91)

Put differently, we must represent an intelligible world as a rational order, because we must project our own 'intelligence' onto it and think of it as the creation of a divine (and thus supremely rational) intellect.

---

[23] On this reading, transcendental realism is a weighty metaphysical claim. For a methodological and non-metaphysical reading of transcendental realism, see Allison 2004; 2012.
[24] One variant of this view is Wolff's claim – interesting also because of its terminological proximity to the title of Kant's *magnum opus* – that only God's reason is "pure," while human reason cannot be "pure" (Wolff, *Natürliche Gottesgelahrtheit*, 1742, §288). By 'pure reason,' Wolff means the 'unbounded' (*uneingeschränkte*) faculty of reason only God can have.
[25] See e.g. Wolff, *Natürliche Gottesgelahrtheit*, who claims that God cognizes the "entire rational world" (*ganze vernünftige Welt*) (§289).
[26] See A811/B839, where Kant seems to identify an "intelligible" with a "moral" world ("einer intelligiblen, d.i. *moralischen* Welt").

In sum, I want to suggest that transcendental realism, according to Kant, is the view that empirical objects are part of a rational order and that human reason is therefore able to cognize these objects and their relations (even though this cognition will always be imperfect, due to the imperfections of human reason compared with divine reason):

TR$_C$ There is a necessary *correspondence* between the principles of reason and the principles of reality.[27]

Transcendental realism in this sense is a fundamental background assumption of Western philosophy from Plato to Wolff and Baumgarten. It can take many different forms, depending, among other things, on the respective conceptions of reason and reality. TR$_C$ is meant as a generic formulation that underlies the different forms of transcendental realism. Some very general remarks will have to suffice here to illustrate this historical point.[28] The most influential form of transcendental realism is Aristotle's thesis that there is a formal identity between knowledge and what is known (e.g. *De anima* III 4, 430a3–5), a thesis he also applies to *nous* and what is cognized by it (*Metaphysics* XII 9, 1074b38–1075a5).[29] This means that the very properties and principles that characterize reality are present, although in a different way, in the mind that cognizes them. Thanks to thinkers such as Albert the Great and Thomas Aquinas, this Aristotelian thesis became an integral part of the mainstream medieval and early modern philosophy that was dominant in Europe up until Kant's own time. Another important variant of transcendental realism is Cartesian rationalism, according to which reality is correctly and completely characterized by quantitative properties and laws in a mathematical language, which can be discovered by reason (and reason alone) (e.g. *Principles* 2.1). In Spinoza, transcendental realism takes the form of Spinozian parallelism: "The order and connection of ideas is the same as the order and connection of things" (*Ethics* 2p7).[30] In Leibniz, transcendental realism is the claim that the world created by God (because it is the best possible world) must be a rational order (Rutherford 1995). The same thought also underlies the metaphysics of Wolff and the Wolffian school, with which Kant was deeply familiar from

---

[27] Susan Neiman identifies a view similar to TR$_C$ ("the idea of the complete intelligibility of the world as a whole") with Kant's conception of "the Unconditioned" (Neiman 1994: 64–5).

[28] Unfortunately, I am not aware of any sustained discussion of the role of transcendental realism (in the sense of TR$_C$) in the history of Western philosophy.

[29] I am grateful to Friedemann Buddensieck for helping me to locate the relevant passages in Aristotle; see also Charles 2000: ch. 5 and Hafemann 1998, who reads Aristotle as a transcendental realist in Kant's sense of the term.

[30] On Kant's understanding of Spinoza as a transcendental realist, see Messina 2014.

decades of lecturing on Baumgarten's *Metaphysica*.[31] Of course, I am not claiming that all these different philosophical perspectives are fundamentally the same. Rather, the precise meaning of TR$_C$ in the philosophy of thinkers as different as Aristotle, Descartes, and Leibniz will differ widely depending on various other aspects of their views. It is possible to discern a common underlying idea, however, which is the notion that there is a necessary correspondence between the principles of rational thinking and the principles of reality.[32]

Given this understanding of transcendental realism as TR$_C$, how does it explain the transition from the regulative to the constitutive Supreme Principle? As we have seen, the regulative use of the Supreme Principle consists in using the latter in a hypothetical and metaphysically neutral way that does not commit one to the truth of the Supreme Principle. However, the aim of the regulative use of the Supreme Principle is to approximate an ideal system of scientific knowledge. This system would have to contain the Supreme Principle (in its *constitutive* form) as one of its supreme principles, since such a system would have to represent all real conditioning relations between objects, with the Supreme Principle as their most general principle. The Supreme Principle will thus be a true constitutive principle *if* nature allows itself to be truly represented in a rational system of knowledge. Now TR$_C$ is the assumption that the structure of reason and that of reality correspond to each other, so that rational cognition of reality is possible. Thus, given TR$_C$, from the fact that the Supreme Principle is a necessary hypothesis of reason and a necessary part of an ideal rational system of knowledge it follows that the Supreme Principle is true of nature itself. Put differently, against the background of transcendental realism, any regulative principle of reason must appear to be constitutive of nature itself.

That according to Kant it is TR$_C$ that drives the transition from the logical to the real or transcendental use of reason is confirmed by a passage from the Appendix, where Kant claims that chemists ('analysts,' *Scheidekünstler*) follow the principle of homogeneity ('there are common genera for different kinds') and therefore cannot resist the thought that 'earths' and 'salts' must belong to a common genus. And Kant adds:

One might have believed that this is merely a device of reason for achieving economy, for saving as much trouble as possible, and a hypothetical attempt that, if it succeeds, will through this unity give probability to the grounds of explanation it presupposed. Yet such a selfish aim can easily be distinguished from the idea, in accordance with

---

[31] According to Baumgarten, it is necessarily the case that the world is a rational order (*Metaphysica*, §§356–60).

[32] Note that this idea is by no means dead. See e.g. Sider 2011 for a spirited defense of a form of transcendental realism (which he calls "realism about structure").

which *everyone presupposes that this unity of reason conforms to nature itself*, and here reason does not beg but commands, though without being able to determine the bounds of this unity. (A653/B681; emphasis added)

Chemists cannot rest content with the logical principle of homogeneity, since this principle only concerns our concepts and not nature itself. But neither can they restrict themselves to the 'hypothetical attempt' of a regulative use of the principle of homogeneity. Rather, they assume that *there really is* a common genus shared by 'earths' and 'salts,' thus making constitutive use of the principle of homogeneity and thereby accepting it as true. What motivates the transition from the regulative to the constitutive use of that principle is the 'idea, in accordance with which *everyone presupposes that this unity of reason conforms to nature itself*.' As we have just seen, this 'idea' is nothing other than transcendental realism – the thought (shared by 'everyone') that there is a necessary correspondence between reason and reality.

Similarly, in Section Seven of the Antinomy, Kant explains the transcendental illusion involved in the 'cosmological inference' that underlies the antinomies by appeal to TR_C. The inference in question has the Supreme Principle as its major premise and the claim that there are conditioned empirical objects as its minor premise, from which it seems to follow that there must be something unconditioned (the complete series of conditions). As we have already seen (Section 5.2.2), Kant thinks that this inference rests on the ambiguity of the middle term ('conditioned'), since the conditioned mentioned in the major can only be a thing in itself, while that in the minor is a mere appearance (A499/B527):

This deception is, however, not artificial, but an entirely natural mistake of common reason. For through common reason, when something is given as conditioned, we presuppose (in the major premise) the conditions and their series as it were sight unseen *because this is nothing but the logical requirement of assuming complete premises for a given conclusion* ... Further, it is likewise *natural* (in the minor premise) *to regard appearances as things in themselves* and likewise as objects *given to the mere understanding*, as was the case in the major premise, where I abstracted from all conditions of intuition under which alone objects can be given. But now in this we overlooked a remarkable difference between the concepts. (A499–500/B528; emphasis added)

Kant is here appealing to transcendental realism in order to explain the 'natural mistake of common reason' involved in the 'cosmological inference.' In fact, he is invoking TR_C with respect to both premises of the dialectical inference. First, he explains why we take the first premise (the Supreme Principle) to be true by saying that this is 'the logical requirement of assuming complete premises for a given conclusion.' This is somewhat elliptical, but it can be understood as the thought that we naturally take the Logical Maxim (or its descriptive analogue) to be a constitutive principle of

The Transition to the Supreme Principle (5.2.3)

nature itself – an assumption that will appear natural if we assume that nature must correspond to the requirements of reason (that is, if we assume TR_C). Second, Kant explains the fact that we do not notice the ambiguity on which the inference rests by saying that 'it is natural (in the second premise) to regard appearances as things in themselves,' which is his generic formulation of transcendental realism, from which, as we have seen, it follows that empirical objects are parts of a rational order (TR_C). Notice that Kant himself claims that common sense tacitly identifies empirical objects with *noumena* in the *positive* sense by saying that they are 'objects given to the mere understanding,' because the only way in which objects can be *given* to us (finite beings) is through sensible intuition (A19/B33), while the only way in which they can be 'given to the mere understanding' is by being given to an intellectual intuition, which means that they are *noumena* in the positive sense.[33] Thus, although this is not immediately obvious on the surface of the text, Kant explains the transcendental illusion involved in the antinomies by appealing to TR_C.

In sum, I suggest that the transition from the regulative to the constitutive version of the Supreme Principle (and with it the transcendental illusion at the heart of traditional metaphysics) rests on the tacit assumption of TR_C. While I have argued here that TR_C can explain the naïve transition from the regulative to the constitutive use of the Supreme Principle, in the second part of this book I will show how different forms of transcendental realism are at work in transcendental psychology, cosmology, and theology.[34]

Against this suggestion, however, it might be objected that it restricts Kant's Rational Sources Account to a specific form of rationalist philosophy that is committed to TR_C. This objection has two sides, one of which concerns the question of whether TR_C can be part of common sense or 'universal human reason' if it has its home in a certain philosophical tradition. I will discuss this aspect in the next subsection. The other side concerns the question of whether TR_C is a rationalist thesis, which might make it doubtful that TR_C can play a fundamental role on the following levels of Kant's Rational Sources Account, particularly in the context of the antinomies. After all, Kant seems to align the theses of the four antinomies with rationalism, and the antitheses with empiricism (A465–6/B493–4). But this second aspect of the objection can be easily rebutted. First, the kind of 'empiricism' Kant has in mind here includes Aristotle and Locke, who, although empiricists about the "origin of pure cognition of reason," were

---

[33] See also A264/B320: "Leibniz took the appearances for things in themselves, thus for *intelligibilia*, i.e., objects of pure understanding."

[34] See *Refl.* 5961: "The entire dialectic amounts to this. One would know the sensible world as a thing in itself, although it can only be thought in space and time" (18:400).

not as "consistent" as Epicurus in that they (as Kant qualifies: primarily Locke) offered proofs of the existence of God and the immortality of the soul (A854/B882). Second, in accepting the existence of infinite series of conditions and denying the existence of unconditioned conditions (see Chapter 7), the antitheses of the antinomies clearly go beyond what 'consistent' empiricists (such as Epicurus and Hume) would have allowed. Thus, the kind of metaphysics Kant discusses in the Transcendental Dialectic is indeed rationalist in spirit. After all, it is supposed to be a purely a priori enterprise, based on pure reason alone (Section 1.2.1). The fact that TR_C is characteristic of the rationalist tradition (widely conceived) therefore does not tell against the suggestion that it is necessary to generate the transcendental illusion of speculative metaphysics.

5.2.4 Transcendental Realism as Part of 'Universal Human Reason'

I now turn to the other side of the objection just mentioned. A central aspect of Kant's Rational Sources Account is the claim that transcendental illusion is "*natural* and unavoidable" (A298/B354). It consists in the fact that certain metaphysical claims appear to be rationally necessary and well grounded. As we have just seen, for Kant the error resulting from falling prey to this illusion is a "natural mistake of common reason" (A500/B528); it can be avoided only through a 'critique of pure reason.' The illusion itself, together with the urge to ask metaphysical questions in the first place, is part of "universal human reason" (B22). If transcendental illusion rests on the implicit acceptance of transcendental realism, this means that Kant must assume that transcendental realism is likewise 'natural' and part of 'universal human reason.' (As we have just seen, Kant claims that "everyone" is committed to transcendental realism; A653/B681 and Section 5.2.3.)[35]

Against this assumption, one might object that a philosophically demanding claim like TR_C cannot plausibly be attributed to common sense. But note that for TR_C to be part of common sense, it need not be an explicit belief held by every rational person, but only a tacit background assumption that people implicitly rely on when thinking rationally about the world. Many consequences of TR_C are highly intuitive, which can be explained if we assume

---

[35] In the *Groundwork*, by contrast, Kant claims that the distinction between *phaenomena* and *noumena* is part of common sense (4:451–2). This may seem to rule out his attributing TR_C to common sense, but in fact it does not. The common sense distinction between *phaenomena* and *noumena* is one between things or properties that can be perceived and those that can only be thought. Drawing this distinction is compatible with identifying empirical objects with things as cognized by a divine intellect (*noumena* in the positive sense), so that the common sense character of the *phaenomena/noumena* distinction does not tell against the common sense character of TR_C. Thanks to Karl Schafer for prompting this clarification.

The Transition to the Supreme Principle (5.2.4)

that common sense is tacitly committed to TR_C. Consider, first, how TR_C plays out in the antinomies in creating the appearance that both thesis and antithesis must be true (see Section 7.4.1). The relevant background assumption is:

Bivalence$_W$ Of the two cosmological claims 'The world is finite in magnitude' and 'The world is infinite in magnitude,' precisely one is true and the other false.

Kant notes: "Nothing seems clearer than that between the two, one of whom asserts that the world has a beginning, and the other that it has no beginning but has existed from eternity, one of them has to be right" (A501/B529; A504/532). It is this assumption of Bivalence$_W$ that allows the traditional metaphysician to prove both theses and antitheses by apagogic arguments (proof by *reductio ad absurdum*), since the truth of *A* follows from the falsity of not-*A* only if bivalence is presupposed. But according to Kant, Bivalence$_W$ only holds if we assume that the world is a thing in itself: "But if I take away this presupposition, *or rather this transcendental illusion*, and deny that it is a thing in itself, then the contradictory conflict of the two assertions is transformed into a merely dialectical conflict, and because the world does not exist at all (independently of the regressive series of my representations), it exists neither as *an in itself infinite* whole nor as *an in itself finite* whole" (A504–5/B532–3; first emphasis added). The details of Kant's resolution of the cosmological antinomies need not concern us here. What matters is that bivalence is a logical principle of human reason (9:117), and the concept of the world, according to Kant, is a concept of pure reason (A333–4/B390–1; see Chapter 6). If TR_C is presupposed, we will assume that there really is an object corresponding to our rational concept of the world and that bivalence holds for statements about it. In this way, the intuitive character of the antinomies – the fact that we find Bivalence$_W$ intuitively compelling – can be traced back to an implicit assumption of TR_C.[36]

Second, TR_C gives expression to the natural self-understanding of rational thinking. Reason is a cognitive capacity that we exercise in order to know and comprehend things. It is therefore an entirely natural assumption that rational thinking, if done properly, will not lead us astray, but will bring us closer to knowledge and comprehension. But this means that we expect reality to be structured in a way that is *accessible* to rational thinking, which would be the case if TR_C were true.[37]

---

[36] As mentioned before, Michael Dummett identifies realism about some domain with unrestricted acceptance of bivalence for statements about that domain; see Dummett 1978: xxx.

[37] Recall our discussion of the argument, presented in the Appendix to the Transcendental Dialect, that we must assume or presuppose transcendental principles (that apply to objects in nature)

Finally, TR_C implies that things make sense. If reality is a rational order, then life is objectively meaningful and everything that happens happens for a reason. While it is obviously debatable whether these claims are true, it can hardly be denied that they have a strong intuitive appeal and give expression to a naïve but entirely natural attitude. (It seems that for most people, the sheer *possibility* that the world might be devoid of objective meaning is a startling discovery made in adolescence.)

Thus, even while TR_C may not be an explicit component of most people's 'cognitive households,' the intuitive character of various claims about reality in general (Bivalence$_W$, reason as a source of knowledge, reality as objectively meaningful) can be explained if we assume TR_C as a tacit background assumption. In this sense, Kant can plausibly attribute it to common sense or 'universal human reason.'

This does not mean, however, that it is impossible to give up this assumption. As we have seen, Kant claims, on the one hand, that the transcendental illusion created by transcendental realism is natural and unavoidable, while, on the other, he holds that we can see through it and come to recognize it as illusory, thereby avoiding being taken in by the illusion. This means that when Kant claims that transcendental realism is part of human reason, he does not mean that we are rationally committed to holding transcendental realism to be true, but only that there is a natural *tendency*, based on human reason itself, to take it to be true. If Kant's diagnosis in the *Critique of Pure Reason* is correct, we can give up the natural assumption of transcendental realism by accepting transcendental idealism, but we cannot completely overcome the tendency to fall back into implicitly assuming that transcendental realism is true. I do not see, however, how one could argue that it is absolutely impossible for rational beings to rid themselves of any commitment to transcendental realism and thus to overcome the transcendental illusion to which it gives rise. But given that the assumption of transcendental realism naturally accompanies any reliance on reason as a cognitive faculty (and that it requires critical reflection to recognize that this assumption is unwarranted), it seems plausible that simply rejecting transcendental realism as a matter of philosophical doctrine will not be sufficient to free oneself from transcendental illusion.

---

because otherwise the corresponding logical principles would lead us astray (Section 4.2.2). As I have objected, this argument is unconvincing as long as we cannot know that assuming the *transcendental* principles does not lead us astray. I suggested that Kant does not present this argument in his own voice, but rather as an expression of a transcendental illusion to the effect that nature must live up to our rational expectations.

5.2.5 Conclusion

Kant does not explicitly say that transcendental illusion – the appearance of necessity that pertains to the transition from subjective to objective principles underlying the paralogisms, the antinomies, and the proofs of the existence of God – rests on transcendental realism in the sense of TR_C. As we have seen, however, he does say (by implication) that the antinomies rest on the assumption of transcendental realism, and he appeals to the latter to explain the transition from logical to transcendental principles in the Appendix. Moreover, transcendental realism is not just a background assumption at work in much of Western philosophy; it is also highly intuitive and can thus plausibly be attributed to 'universal human reason.' Finally, transcendental realism explains why subjective principles of reason appear to be objectively valid (in their constitutive form). Taken together, these points suggest that Kant indeed thought of transcendental realism as the 'key' not just to the transcendental illusion in the case of the antinomies, but to transcendental illusions in general.

Applied to the transition from the regulative to the constitutive use of the Supreme Principle, this means that the transcendental illusion that motivates this transition rests on the tacit assumption of transcendental realism. According to TR_C, the very principles that guide us in rational thinking also govern reality itself, which means that the Supreme Principle, which we must use regulatively in order to approximate the unity of reason, will appear to be constitutive. If this is correct, we have arrived not only at an interpretation of the first level at which Kant develops his Rational Sources Account – the level of the Logical Maxim and the Supreme Principle – but at a template for understanding the other levels of the transition from the logical to the real use of reason. This template is as follows:

Transition$_{gen}$ (1) We start from a *logical* principle or concept (belonging to the logical use of reason) and make a rationally necessary transition to a corresponding *transcendental* principle or concept (that belongs to the real use of reason). (2) That transition will appear to justify a metaphysically committed *constitutive* use of the transcendental principle or concept (and not just its metaphysically harmless *regulative* use) (3) because of the tacit assumption of some variant of TR.

It will be our guiding interpretative hypothesis in the second part of this book that this template underlies Kant's argument for the Rational Sources Account in the Transcendental Dialectic. While Kant may not always clearly distinguish the three elements (logical/transcendental, regulative/constitutive, transcendental realism), I will argue that they are operative on each of the three levels that follow and indeed structure Kant's argument.

5.3 Why Does the Supreme Principle Hold for Things in Themselves (but Not for Appearances)?

In an intriguing set of notes on the Introduction to the Transcendental Dialectic from around 1780, published as *Reflexion* 5553, Kant writes:

> The proposition that if the conditioned is given, the whole series of all conditions through which the conditioned is determined is also given, is, if I abstract from the objects or take them merely intellectually, correct. (18:223)

If one considers the Supreme Principle but abstracts from objects, the proposition in question is part of the logical use of reason. Kant is therefore saying that, if taken in the sense of the Logical Maxim, the proposition in question is 'correct.' This is in keeping with what he says in the *Critique of Pure Reason* and confirms our reading, according to which the Logical Maxim (1) corresponds to the Supreme Principle in that it concerns the same (or relevantly similar; see Section 5.1.2) logical relations but abstracts from objects and (2) is a 'subjectively' valid principle of reason (Section 2.3). But Kant also says in the *Reflexion* that the proposition in question is 'correct' if the objects are taken 'merely intellectually' – that is, it is true of *noumena* in the positive sense. This is also in keeping with the first *Critique*, where Kant claims the following:

> If one represents everything through mere pure concepts of the understanding, without the conditions of sensible intuition, then one can say directly that for a given conditioned the whole series of conditions subordinated one to another is given; for the former is given only through the latter. (A416/B444)

Thus, Kant is obviously committing himself to the claim that the Supreme Principle is true of things in themselves. Why does Kant think this, and how can he be justified in this claim (given that we cannot have cognition of things in themselves)?

In the context of the resolution of the antinomies, Kant offers the following argument for why the Supreme Principle holds for things in themselves:

> If the conditioned as well as its condition are things in themselves, then when the first is given ... the latter is thereby really already given along with it; and, because this holds for all members of the series, then the complete series of conditions, and hence the unconditioned, is thereby simultaneously given. (A498/B526)

Assuming that 'given,' when said of things in themselves, must have an ontological meaning ('is' or 'exists'; see Section 3.1), and speaking more generally of a 'totality of conditions' rather than a 'whole series of conditions' (Section 3.3.2), this argument can be restated as follows (with x and y ranging over things in themselves):

P1   If x is R-conditioned, then there is at least one R-condition of x.
C1   If x is R-conditioned, then there is the totality of R-conditions of x (from P1).

P2   If y is the totality of R-conditions of x, then y is R-unconditioned (in the sense of UTC).

C2   If x is R-conditioned, then there is the totality of R-conditions of x, which is R-unconditioned (= Supreme Principle) (from C1 and P2).[38]

As we have seen, Kant takes P1 to be an analytic truth. While the analytic link between the conditioned and its condition turns out to be merely prescriptive in the case of appearances (where the condition is not 'given' but only 'given as a problem,' that is, something for us to look for; A497–9/B526–7), Kant seems to accept that P1 is analytic when read as a claim about things in themselves (Section 3.2.4). The move from P1 to C1 follows by the 'principle of comprehension' (or, equivalently, from Kant's definition of a totality as – actual or potential – plurality considered as unity) (Section 3.3.3). According to this principle, if there is at least one object that is F, then there is the set of all Fs – their totality. P2 is analytic because it follows from the definition of UTC: any totality of R-conditions of x is unconditioned insofar as it contains *all* R-conditions of x and therefore cannot again be R-conditioned (Section 3.3.4). But then, the Supreme Principle for things in themselves appears to follow from only two premises that are both analytic.

This may seem to be a problem, however, since the Supreme Principle is synthetic according to Kant (A308/B364–5), and a synthetic principle cannot follow logically from analytic premises. But really, there is no problem here because the argument just considered is meant to apply only to things in themselves and not to appearances, while the Supreme Principle that Kant classifies as synthetic is not restricted in this way. Since, according to Kant, the (unrestricted) Supreme Principle he introduces at A307–8/B365 is true of things in themselves but not of appearances, it cannot be analytic and must be synthetic. But this does not rule out its being analytic when its domain (the set of objects the principle is meant to apply to) is restricted to things in themselves. Consider the sentence 'If x is a parent, then x is a mother.' That sentence is synthetic but false. If we restrict its domain to female parents, however, it turns out to be analytically true. Similarly, the unrestricted Supreme Principle is synthetic and false, but analytic when restricted to things in themselves. However, this means that the reason why the Supreme Principle is analytic when restricted to things in themselves (while it is not analytic without such a restriction) must lie in the concept of a thing in itself (just as 'If x is a parent, then x is a mother' is analytic if restricted to female parents because of what is contained in the concept of a female parent).

I think we can explain this by appeal to the account of transcendental realism developed earlier. First, we must remember that the Supreme Principle is a principle of pure reason (A307–8/B364–5). Second, we may assume that

---

[38] We encountered a slightly simpler version of the argument in Section 3.3.3.

the things in themselves in question can only be *noumena* in the positive sense because we cannot be justified in attributing positive features (such as compliance with the Supreme Principle) to *noumena* in the negative sense (since these are characterized purely negatively by abstracting from, or denying, our sensible access to them). Now Kant, unlike the transcendental realist, cannot claim to know that there are any *noumena* in the positive sense. But he can claim that *if* there are *noumena* in the positive sense, they have to conform to principles of reason, including the Supreme Principle, because by definition they have to be part of a fully rational order of things. Thus, we can see why the Supreme Principle is analytically true of things in themselves: it follows from the concept of a *noumenon* in a positive sense that it must conform to the supreme principle of pure reason.[39] Conversely, the Supreme Principle is not analytically true for appearances because the concept of an appearance (or of an empirical object) does not imply that the objects that fall under it are parts of a rational order (see Section 3.2.4).

But this creates another exegetical problem which I can only mention, but not resolve, here. In the case of appearances, the link between the conditioned and its condition (P1) is not analytic, but synthetic (based on the synthetic principles of the understanding) (Section 3.2.4). Nevertheless, Kant is committed to the truth of P1, given that the principles of the understanding guarantee that for every predicate, there exists a subject; for every effect, there is a cause; and, in general, for every conditioned appearance, there exists its (first-order) condition ("there could not fail to be conditions," A499/B527). But then, P1 will be true (even if not analytically true) when read as a claim about appearances, which seems to mean that the argument from P1 (which is synthetic and true) and P2 (which is analytically true) to the truth of the Supreme Principle will remain valid and sound even when applied to the domain of appearances. But as we have also seen, Kant needs to *deny* that the Supreme Principle holds for appearances in order to resolve the antinomies. When Kant discusses what he calls the 'cosmological inference of reason' (which is the inference, with the Supreme Principle as its major premise, from given conditioned *appearances* to the existence of something unconditioned) (A497/B525; A499–500/B527–8), he rejects this inference as involving a "dialectical deception" (A500/B528). Since Kant cannot deny that there are conditioned appearances, it seems that the only way he can block this inference is by denying that the Supreme Principle is true of appearances. And of course,

---

[39] For a similar point, see Anderson 2015: 302. But Anderson links it to the claim that when applied to things in themselves (or "*intelligibilia*"), the Supreme Principle is really not about "a series of *existing* objects," but about "a series of concepts," which seems to me to be incompatible with Kant's insistence that the Supreme Principle is part of the real use of reason and thus concerned not with concepts but with objects.

The Transition to the Supreme Principle (5.3)   155

that is just what Kant does by claiming that with respect to appearances, it is *not* a constitutive principle, but only a regulative one (A509/B537; see Section 4.2.3). The problem is how Kant can be entitled to this claim, given his other philosophical commitments.

Kant argues against the cosmological inference from conditioned appearances to the unconditioned by appealing to his transcendental idealism and the representation-dependent character of appearances (e.g. A498–9/B527), but it is unclear how this argument is supposed to work and what exactly it entails. Some of Kant's formulations suggest that he wants to deny P1 with respect to appearances after all, that is, to deny that for every conditioned appearance there is a condition. For instance, Kant can at least *seem* to argue that appearances depend on our *actual* "acquaintance with them," so that, as long as we have not made 'acquaintance' with it, the condition does not exist (A499/B527; see also A501/B529). But this would commit Kant to an extreme form of idealism – a view that he himself rejects by allowing that empirical objects exist if they are *possible* objects of experience in the relatively weak sense of standing in empirical conditioning relations to things we *actually* perceive (A225–6/B273; A493/B521; see Wood 2010: 260).

Alternatively, Kant may want to deny the move from 'For every conditioned appearance, there is a condition' to 'For every conditioned appearance, there is the totality/complete series of its conditions' (A499/B527), that is, the move from P1 to C1 in the earlier argument. One reason Kant offers in this context seems to be that, in the case of appearances, the complete series of conditions cannot exist because we can experience neither an infinite series of conditions nor an unconditioned condition, so that the series of conditions can be neither finite nor infinite (A505/B533–A506/B534). But from the fact that we cannot *experience* each member of an infinite series of conditions it does not follow that the infinite series does not exist, unless we revert to the extreme idealism Kant rejects (e.g. Guyer 1987: 404–6).

Therefore, I think that the philosophically most plausible way for Kant to resist the inference from the conditioned to the unconditioned totality of its conditions consists in denying the principle of comprehension, that is, the assumption that for every predicate there is the totality of objects of which it is true (which licenses the step from P1 to C1). From our current perspective, this is a plausible move since we know that the principle of comprehension must be restricted anyway (although in a way that has nothing to do with the distinction between appearances and things in themselves) in order to avoid Russell-style antinomies (e.g. about the set of all sets that do not contain themselves). But of course this cannot be the reason for Kant's rejection of the principle of comprehension. Therefore, we will have to leave the question of how Kant can deny that the Supreme Principle holds for appearances unanswered. But note that such an answer is not required for the purposes of this book, because rejecting the Supreme Principle for appearances is part of Kant's *critique* of speculative metaphysics, not part of his account of why we must ask, and think we can answer, metaphysical questions (the Rational Sources Account).[40]

---

[40] While I think that Kant wanted to reject any inference from appearances to the unconditioned, Eric Watkins argues that Kant acknowledges such an inference (even if its force is limited in that it does not yield cognition of something unconditioned) (e.g. Watkins 2016a; see also Gardner 1999: 289; Ameriks 2006: 290). I do not think that Kant would have been justified in drawing such an inference because even if it is correct that appearances presuppose something that appears, which is a thing in itself, it does not seem to follow that that thing is unconditioned. In particular, one would have to specify the respect in which the thing in itself conditions the appearance. If the thing in itself is the causal condition of the appearance, it does not follow that it is causally unconditioned, since it might well be caused. If the thing in itself is the condition of the appearance by being that which appears, it does not follow that it is not itself an appearance of some underlying thing in itself, etc.

Conclusion to Part I: The Transition from the Logical Maxim to the (Constitutive) Supreme Principle and the Rational Sources Account

According to Kant's Rational Sources Account, rational thinking naturally and inevitably leads into metaphysical speculation. As we saw in the Introduction, Section 0.2, this claim contains three distinct theses:

RS-1 Rational reflection on empirical questions necessarily raises *metaphysical questions* about 'the unconditioned.'
RS-2 Rational reflection (by 'pure reason') on these metaphysical questions necessarily leads to *metaphysical answers* to them that appear to be rationally warranted.
RS-3 The rational principles that lead from empirical to metaphysical questions and from there to metaphysical answers are principles of '*universal human reason*'; that is, they belong to rational thinking as such.

The transition from the Logical Maxim through the regulative to the constitutive Supreme Principle constitutes an argument, on the most general level, for these three theses. Before we turn to the more specific levels of Kant's argument in the following chapters, let us pause and review the transition considered thus far with respect to the question of how it supports Kant's Rational Sources Account. Let us start with a brief recapitulation of the main line of thought that underlies the transition from the Logical Maxim to the constitutive Supreme Principle.

There is a generally recognized logical use of reason that consists in drawing mediate inferences. Insofar as it is not merely a kind of play with regard to forms of reasoning (as in logical exercises), this logical use works on cognitions provided by the understanding (that is, on representations of empirical objects and events). It consists in articulating the inferential and epistemic relations among these cognitions: what follows from what, what epistemic status depends on a cognition's being inferred from some other. In doing so, we abstract from the objects of cognition and only consider their logical form. The ultimate aim of this activity is the 'unity of reason,' that is, transforming the cognitions provided by the understanding into a complete system of scientific knowledge. In such a system, each cognition has a specific place that reflects its relations of inferential and epistemic dependence on other cognitions. In order to approximate such a system, reason must therefore search, with respect to each inferentially or epistemically conditioned cognition, for further cognitions from which it can be derived and epistemically justified.

This is the rational requirement expressed in the Logical Maxim.[1] It gives expression to three basic features of reason, namely *discursivity*, *iteration*, and *completeness*. Because reason is *discursive*, we can have rational insight into a judgment or principle only by inferring it from other, more general or fundamental judgments or principles. Because these inferences are *iterable*, we can try to infer these other judgments or principles from yet other, even more general or fundamental ones. And because reason seeks *completeness*, we are rationally required to try to infer our judgments from general premises and must not stop until we have arrived at absolutely fundamental principles (that cannot be inferred from even more general and independently certain premises).

The Logical Maxim is a principle of reason in its *logical* use. But in order to approximate the unity of reason (and thus to achieve the ultimate aim of the logical use of reason) we must go beyond the Logical Maxim, and this for two reasons: first, inferential relations will often be insufficient to determine the place of a given cognition in the system of knowledge; and second, since the system is supposed to be *complete* (that is, a complete and adequate scientific account of everything there is), we will have to go beyond any number of cognitions we may possess at any given time and find new cognitions not yet included in the current body of cognitions provided by our understanding. In order to do this, we must hypothetically assume another principle – the Supreme Principle – according to which for every conditioned object there exists a condition, and thus (assuming the principle of comprehension) the totality of its conditions. From the Supreme Principle, we can then deduce concrete hypotheses about conditioning relations between objects and about the existence and properties of the relata of these relations, hypotheses we can then try to confirm or disconfirm.

While the Logical Maxim concerns logical conditioning relations between cognitions, the Supreme Principle concerns 'real' conditioning relations among objects that fall into three basic kinds (which Kant calls 'inherence,' 'dependence,' and 'concurrence') and that include, among many others, such diverse relations as those between substance and predicate, cause and effect, and the parts of a whole. According to this principle, for everything

---

[1] I here assume that in an ideal system of scientific knowledge, paths of inferential subordination and paths of epistemic justification coincide and that, when a cognition is derived from others that are epistemically certain, it acquires the status of scientific knowledge; for a critical discussion of these assumptions, see Section 2.1.4.

Conclusion to Part I

conditioned there is the *totality* of conditions – a thought that can at least appear to follow from analytic premises. This totality, according to the Kant of the first *Critique*, is necessarily unconditioned in the sense that it cannot be conditioned in the same respect as the conditioned item whose totality of conditions it is. Thus the thought that there *might* be something unconditioned is a necessary part of reason itself, since it is contained in a principle we must hypothetically employ in order to achieve, or at least approximate, the unity of reason. Moreover, the Supreme Principle is an 'objectively valid' principle of pure reason when used regulatively, that is, in the hypothetical way just indicated. That it is objectively valid means that we can legitimately apply it to objects, albeit only hypothetically, not as a true description of them. Its objective validity derives from its necessary role in approximating the unity of reason (and thus in cognizing empirical reality); it is only limited or 'indeterminate,' however, since it cannot be used to determine or cognize any specific aspect of empirical reality.

There is a tendency, however, rooted in universal human reason itself, to mistake this regulative principle for a constitutive one – that is, to assume that it is valid not just as a heuristic hypothesis but as a true description of reality. The reason for this tendency, and the source of what Kant calls 'transcendental illusion,' is 'transcendental realism': the assumption that empirical objects are things in themselves. More specifically, this is the assumption that empirical objects are *noumena* in the positive sense – potential objects of a divine mind – and, as such, are part of a rational order, an order that corresponds to the principles that govern our own rational thinking, including the Supreme Principle. Transcendental realism can take many different forms, but they all share the thought that there is a necessary correspondence between reason and reality that allows us to cognize reality through rational thinking.

While many forms of transcendental realism that surface in the history of Western philosophy are philosophically demanding and complex, the basic idea is highly intuitive and can plausibly be attributed to common sense. Its intuitively plausible core is the thought that pure reason (rational thinking in abstraction from empirical input) allows us to cognize the basic principles and structures of reality. One way to explain the intuitive character of this thought is to note that it articulates a necessary aspect of how rational thinking must understand itself. Reason is a cognitive capacity, a capacity for objective representation. The natural assumption is thus that its most general principles allow us adequately to cognize the most general aspects of reality. Once we make this assumption (one which, according to Kant, is hard to avoid and of which we can never fully rid ourselves), the regulative Supreme Principle must appear to be a true principle about everything there is, including empirical objects.

If we step back even a little further, we can sum up this story as follows. Rational thinking is characterized by discursivity, iteration, and completeness. *Discursivity* means that in order to rationally understand something we must ask for reasons or explanations. Call the question 'Why *p*?' *rationally necessary* if '*p*' is a fact that stands in need of explanation (i.e. is 'conditioned' in one way or another). *Iteration* means that every answer to a question raises new questions: if 'Why *p*?' is a meaningful question and 'Because *q*' is the answer to that question, then 'Why *q*?' is a meaningful question too. The quest for *completeness* plays out in two different ways that can pull in different directions. On the one hand, we require an answer to *every* rationally necessary question, which, given the iterative character of rational questions, sends us on a potentially infinite regress. On the other hand, we expect there to be *ultimate* answers, where an answer is ultimate if it does not raise further questions of the same kind. We can then understand the transition from the Logical Maxim to the Supreme Principle as reflecting the idea that the three features (discursivity, iteration, and completeness) that characterize reason even in its logical use also drive our rational inquiries into nature, and thus lead into metaphysical speculation. If we apply rational inquiry to real conditioning relations (searching, e.g. for underlying substances, constitutive parts, or efficient causes), we will equally respond with a new question to every answer while still expecting there to be ultimate answers (invoking, for instance, *either* 'absolute' substances, indivisible parts, and first causes *or* infinite but complete series of 'relative' substances, divisible parts, and subordinate causes).

In this way, the Supreme Principle gives expression to the same characteristics of rational thinking as the Logical Maxim. But what is thus rationally warranted is only the *regulative* use of the Supreme Principle, which guides our *search* for ultimate answers without committing us to the claim that they are there to be found. By contrast, the *constitutive* use of that principle consists in the assumption that there must be something unconditioned in (or beyond) nature itself (a totality of conditions) that provides an ultimate answer to our questions. The move from the (legitimate) regulative to the (illegitimate) constitutive use is motivated by transcendental realism, which in this context can be expressed as the claim that there must be true answers to all rationally necessary questions, independently of our means of finding them.

With this account of the transition from the Logical Maxim to the constitutive Supreme Principle at hand, we can now offer a first general argument for the Rational Sources Account. According to RC1, rational reflection on empirical questions necessarily raises metaphysical questions. This is because rational reflection on empirical questions employs the regulative Supreme Principle as a heuristic tool for generating hypotheses that, if confirmed, will bring our system of scientific knowledge closer to completion. The regulative Supreme Principle can thus be understood as a tool for asking questions of the

Conclusion to Part I

following form: 'What is the R-condition of x?' (with respect to any given x that is conditioned in some respect R). But as we have seen, the Supreme Principle implies the existence of something unconditioned and thus also allows us to ask questions of the following form: 'Is there an R-unconditioned R-condition of x?' and 'Is there a totality of R-conditions for x (which totality is itself R-unconditioned)?' Moreover, if we assume, plausibly enough, that the conditioned cannot exist if the totality of its conditions does not also exist, then these are questions reason cannot avoid asking, since they grow naturally out of the regulative use of the Supreme Principle.

As Kant puts it in the first sentence of the A-Preface, these are "questions which it [reason] cannot dismiss, since they are given to it as problems by the nature of reason itself" (Avii). They arise once we follow through with the kind of rational thinking that is completely appropriate and necessary to achieve the unity of reason. Thus, metaphysical questions grow naturally out of rational reflection that starts with empirical questions such as 'What was the cause of the fire?' or 'What do the faculties of perception and imagination have in common?,' since this ultimately leads to questions such as 'Is there, in the series of causes that led to the fire, a first cause, or is this series infinite?' and 'Is there an immaterial soul as the unconditioned condition of all my representations?'

Note that even though these may seem to be perfectly fine questions, they already involve a form of transcendental illusion in that they employ concepts such as 'the unconditioned,' 'first cause,' and 'immaterial soul' – concepts that, according to Kant, arise naturally out of the logical use of reason (Section 6.1) but only *appear* to be concepts of determinate objects (Section 9.4). Instead, they are mere forms of thought that (at least in a purely speculative context, apart from moral considerations) cannot be used to refer to objects.

So much for RC-1. Even if the metaphysical questions that arise from the logical use of reason and the regulative Supreme Principle may not be as unproblematically meaningful as they appear to be (because of the deficiencies of the concepts involved; Section 9.4), at least asking them does not involve any unfounded metaphysical claims. These enter once we consider RC-2, according to which rational reflection on the metaphysical questions that grow out of the logical use of reason naturally leads to metaphysical *answers* that appear to be rationally warranted.

The transition from the Logical Maxim to the constitutive Supreme Principle gives us a first example of this. If the regulative use of the Supreme Principle leads to the question of *whether* there is something unconditioned, the constitutive use of the Supreme Principle appears to warrant a *positive answer* to that question, since from the constitutive Supreme Principle in conjunction with the claim that there is something conditioned it follows that there must be something unconditioned. Thus, we appear to be rationally justified in making at least the very general metaphysical assertion that something unconditioned exists. As we have seen, however, Kant thinks that this inference from the existence of something conditioned (namely empirical objects) to the existence of something unconditioned (which would have to be a thing in itself) rests on the assumption of transcendental realism (here in the form of identifying empirical objects with things in themselves). The only conditioned objects of which we can have cognition, according to Kant, are appearances, not things in themselves. But the constitutive Supreme Principle that we need for the inference to the unconditioned holds only for things in themselves (*noumena* in the positive sense). Hence, the inference is invalid. However, with transcendental realism as a tacit background assumption (according to which empirical objects are *noumena* in the positive sense and thus part of a rational order that conforms to the Supreme Principle), the inference must appear to be valid, and its conclusion, the existence of the unconditioned, must appear to be true. Metaphysical answers to the metaphysical questions raised by reason itself must therefore appear to be rationally warranted, since they *appear* to follow by valid inference from true premises (RC-2).

Finally, the Supreme Principle is a principle of pure reason that grows out of the completely innocent logical use of reason. In fact, according to Kant it *is* the Logical Maxim, applied descriptively to objects and their relations. Moreover, using the Supreme Principle regulatively is necessary for approximating the unity of reason. Since the unity of reason is a necessary goal of reason as such (that is, rational thinking necessarily aims at transforming our body of cognition into a unified system), the Supreme Principle can legitimately be considered part of 'universal human reason.' The same is arguably true of transcendental realism. In any case, Kant is committed to the view that TR is not just a philosophical invention but an entirely natural assumption. And since TR takes us from the regulative to the constitutive use of the Supreme Principle, we can see how the principles from which metaphysical speculation arises are rooted in 'universal human reason' (RC-3).

This, at least in its broadest outline and at the highest level of abstraction, is Kant's account of the rational sources of speculative metaphysics.

Part II

The Other Side of the Transcendental Dialectic

Introduction to Part II

In the second part of this book, we will look at how Kant develops his Rational Sources Account over the course of the Transcendental Dialectic. As we have seen, the guiding idea is that there is a transition from a logical to a real or transcendental use of reason, which is necessary to achieve the unity of reason – that is, to approximate a complete system of scientific knowledge. But the real use of reason is legitimate only when its principles are employed regulatively: when they serve as hypothetical assumptions that help us to structure our body of cognition and generate new hypotheses, which, if confirmed, complement our present knowledge. This hypothetical, heuristic use of reason and its principles is rationally necessary and therefore legitimate, but it does not carry any metaphysical commitments, since we do not have to accept a principle as true in order to use it regulatively. This also holds for the Supreme Principle, which says that for every conditioned object, there exists the unconditioned totality of its conditions (Section 3.3.4).

There is, however, a natural tendency to project reason's regulative principles onto nature itself and thus to use them constitutively, as supposedly true descriptive principles. Kant calls this tendency 'transcendental illusion' and explains it, as I argue in Chapter 5, by appealing to transcendental realism, which is the view that empirical objects are *noumena* in the positive sense and therefore part of a rational order of things. Transcendental illusion and transcendental realism can be regarded as two sides of the same coin: while transcendental illusion consists in the tendency to project subjective or regulative principles of reason onto reality itself, thereby taking them to be objective or constitutive principles, transcendental realism is the view that taking rational principles to be constitutive of nature is not a subjective projection but a metaphysical insight.

By accepting the Supreme Principle and other principles of reason as true, we claim to have cognition of objects and properties that lie beyond possible experience. As we know from the Transcendental Analytic, Kant thinks that such a claim cannot be warranted, since human cognition depends on the human forms of sensibility, space and time, and is therefore limited to empirical objects in space and time (Section 9.3). In the Transcendental Dialectic,

Kant goes on to uncover in detail the metaphysical fallacies and contradictions that result from the natural tendency to make constitutive use of the principles of reason.

Kant's project in the Transcendental Dialectic has two sides: on the one hand, Kant must offer an account of the errors involved in this kind of speculation that goes beyond the generic result of the Transcendental Analytic (i.e. that we can have cognition, including a priori cognition, only of empirical objects) and must show in detail where and why the proofs of traditional metaphysics go wrong. On the other hand, Kant must show that it is reason itself (and not individual mistakes, historical prejudices, and anthropological factors) that entangles us in metaphysical speculation. As indicated in the Introduction to this book, the first side of the Transcendental Dialectic has received much more attention than the second. In the following three chapters, we will pay attention to this 'other side' of the Transcendental Dialectic, which consists in Kant's extended and highly complex Rational Sources Account.

As also indicated in the Introduction, this account is developed by Kant on four different levels, which largely correspond to the consecutive parts of the Transcendental Dialectic (Introduction, Book One, Book Two, Appendix) but without therefore forming a sustained consecutive argument. Rather, all levels reconstruct the same kind of illusion at different degrees of generality and, in part, with respect to different topics. This becomes obvious right from the beginning, since on the first of these levels – the transition from the Logical Maxim to the Supreme Principle (see Chapters 2–5) – Kant already employs the very concept of the unconditioned that is explicitly derived from the logical use of reason only later in the text (on the second level). Since the first level provides the template for the others, and because it contains a highly original self-contained argument for the Rational Sources Account, I have dedicated the previous four chapters to it. It is neither possible nor necessary to progress at the same pace through the other three levels. This means that I will not try to offer complete interpretations of the relevant parts of the first *Critique*. Rather, I will mainly focus my discussion to how the following template plays out on these levels: in moving from logical concepts and principles (concerning cognitions) to real or transcendental ones (concerning objects), transcendental realism creates the illusion that the constitutive use of the latter is legitimate, since it conceals the difference between their legitimate regulative and their illegitimate constitutive use.

Level two comprises Kant's 'system of transcendental ideas': the concept of the unconditioned as the 'common title' of the transcendental ideas, their three basic classes (psychological, cosmological, theological), and the nine 'modes' that fall under them. It is often assumed that the relevant parts of Kant's text also contain the derivation of the transcendental ideas themselves (the so-called metaphysical deduction of the transcendental ideas). Against this,

I will argue that Kant calls these ideas "inferred concepts" (A310/B366) because we arrive at them through rational inferences – the paralogisms, the arguments leading up to the four antinomies, and a 'natural' argument for the existence of God. Thus, it is only on the third level, in his discussion of the three types of dialectical arguments of transcendental psychology, cosmology, and theology, that Kant derives the transcendental ideas. Finally, the fourth level concerns the tendency to make constitutive use of the principles of reason and the transcendental ideas (as outlined in the Appendix to the Transcendental Dialectic).

Chapter 6 will discuss Kant's 'system of transcendental ideas' in Book One of the Transcendental Dialectic. While its focus is primarily interpretative, it also introduces a philosophical point that is central to the rest of the book, namely Kant's claim that there are metaphysical concepts – the 'transcendental ideas' – that any sufficiently persistent thinker will necessarily arrive at by means of rational inferences. Chapters 7 and 8 reconstruct Kant's Rational Sources Account at the level of rational psychology, cosmology, and theology. Chapter 7 will consider the fallacies of rational psychology (the 'paralogisms' concerning the substantiality, simplicity, personality, and spirituality of the soul) and the contradictions of rational cosmology (the 'antinomies' concerning the world as unconditioned in spatial, temporal, mereological, causal, and modal respects), which also contain the derivation of the psychological and cosmological ideas, respectively. Chapter 8 will offer a reading of the Transcendental Ideal – Kant's derivation of the concept of an *ens realissimum* or most real being – and present what Kant considers the 'natural' argument for the existence of God (as opposed to the three philosophical arguments for God's existence he famously criticizes). Also in Chapter 8, we will discuss how the Rational Sources Account features in the Appendix to the Transcendental Dialectic by looking at why, in scientific investigations, we tend to make constitutive use of rational principles and ideas. Finally, in Chapter 9, I will briefly turn to Kant's critique of speculative metaphysics and argue that it does not presuppose a commitment to Kant's contested transcendental idealism but can be understood as reacting specifically to features of speculative metaphysics highlighted by the Rational Sources Account.

6 The System of Transcendental Ideas

A central aspect of Kant's Rational Sources Account is his claim that there are concepts – the transcendental ideas – that necessarily arise from rational reflection. According to Kant, these ideas of reason, like the categories of the understanding, form an a priori system. In this chapter, we will first look at Kant's conception of transcendental ideas and survey the system they form (Section 6.1). Next, I will argue that Kant does not attempt to derive the transcendental ideas in questionable ways from the forms of rational inferences or the possible relations between subject, object, and representation (even though the text suggests this), but rather considers them, much more plausibly, as concepts we arrive at through rational inferences about specific (psychological, cosmological, and theological) subject matters (Section 6.2). The central philosophical point here is that concepts can be the result of (what Kant calls) 'necessary inferences of reason.' A first instance of this is Kant's derivation of the concept of the unconditioned, which we will discuss in Section 6.3. Finally, we will turn to the three classes of transcendental ideas (psychological, cosmological, theological) (Section 6.4).

6.1 Transcendental Ideas

In Book One of the Transcendental Dialectic, Kant introduces his account of 'transcendental ideas,' or 'concepts of pure reason.' 'Ideas,' or 'concepts of reason,' are defined as non-empirical concepts of objects that cannot be met with in experience (A313/B370; A320/B377). Examples of ideas include the concept of virtue (A315/B371), the idea of a perfect (rightful) state (A316/B373), and the idea of humanity (A318/B374). While these are what Kant calls "practical idea[s]" (A328/B385), *transcendental* ideas, or "concepts of *pure* reason" (A311/B368), are "speculative" ideas (A329/B386; see also 18:228), that is, ideas that arise from theoretical reason's attempt to transcend the conditions of experience and to cognize non-empirical objects (A327/B383–4).[1]

Transcendental ideas, according to Kant, are (1) necessary, (2) purely rational and (3) inferred concepts (4) whose object is something unconditioned. They are (1) *necessary* (A327/B383) and (2) *purely rational* in that they arise naturally from the logical use of reason. Transcendental ideas are thus concepts of pure speculative reason in the specific sense Kant lays out in the Introduction to the Transcendental Dialectic (Section 1.1.3). Moreover, as it turns out only later (in the Appendix), they are necessary in a further sense in that they are indispensable in science (for approximating the 'unity of reason,' see Section 8.2.2). While Kant does not explain what it means to say that (3) the transcendental ideas are *inferred* concepts (A310/B366), I will argue in what follows that they are derived by way of what Kant calls 'necessary inferences of reason' (such as the paralogisms). Finally, (4) they are concepts of something *unconditioned* (A311/B367; A322/B379), which makes them *ideas* in the first place, since the unconditioned is not an object of possible experience.

These transcendental ideas form a 'system' in Kant's sense (see Section 2.1.4) in that they can be derived a priori and exhibit a hierarchical structure that guarantees completeness. At the top of this hierarchy is the concept of the *unconditioned* in general, which Kant calls "the common title of all concepts of reason" (A324/B380).[2] Next, all transcendental ideas fall into three "classes" (A334/B391) under three "titles" (A335/B392), which are commonly identified with the ideas of the soul, the world, and God – an identification, however, that does not have a firm basis in Kant's own text. (As we will see, 'psychological,' 'cosmological,' and 'theological' are more plausible candidates for these titles.) Each of the first two titles comprises four "*modi*" (A335/B392), or transcendental ideas, which Kant presents in the first section of the Paralogisms and the Antinomy, respectively, and which capture four different respects in which soul and world, respectively, can be thought of as

---

[1] As the passage at A327/B383–4 shows, Kant does not always strictly distinguish between ideas in general and transcendental ideas and sometimes seems to use the terms "idea" and "transcendental idea" interchangeably. Relatedly, Kant calls the transcendental ideas both "concepts of pure reason" (e.g. A311/B368) and "pure concepts of reason" (e.g. A321/B378). These terms are not equivalent. While the latter are concepts of reason the content of which is completely independent of sensible input, the former are concepts that arise from the real use of reason (which Kant, in the Introduction to the Transcendental Dialectic, identifies with *pure* reason). Since there are presumably pure concepts of reason that are not transcendental ideas (such as the concept of a syllogism, the holy will, or freedom), it seems that 'concepts of pure reason' is the more adequate expression.

[2] Since any system, according to Kant, requires a guiding idea, it seems that the idea of the unconditioned must also serve as the guiding idea of the system of transcendental ideas. Thanks to Fabian Burt for suggesting this.

The System of Transcendental Ideas (6.1) 169

Table 6.1 *Table of Transcendental Ideas*

Title of all Tr. Ideas		The unconditioned	
Classes of Tr. Ideas	Title of first class	Title of second class	Title of third class
	Psychological	Cosmological	Theological
Modes	The soul as substance	The world as containing complete composition	God as *ens realissimum*
	The soul as simple	The world as containing complete division	
	The soul as unity	The world as containing complete origin(s)	
	The soul as spiritual	The world as containing complete dependence	

unconditioned: substantiality, simplicity, unity, and spirituality in the case of the soul (A344/B402); completeness with respect to composition, division, origin, and dependence in the case of the world (A415/B443; see Chapter 7 for further discussion). To these psychological and cosmological ideas corresponds, in the case of the theological idea, the notion of God as *ens realissimum*, which Kant derives in the section on the Transcendental Ideal (A571/B599–A583/B611). This system of transcendental ideas, which is meant to correspond to the table of the categories (A80/B106) – a table which is itself structured by titles, classes, and modes (or 'moments') (see B110–11)[3] – can be represented as shown in Table 6.1.

Thus, according to Kant, there are precisely nine transcendental ideas.[4] There is a conspicuous absence in this table, which concerns the ideas of soul

---

[3] In connection with the table of categories, "*modi*" are explicitly mentioned only with respect to Aristotle's categories at A81/B107; see also 5:65. On the use of the terminology of 'classes,' 'titles,' and 'modes' with respect to the transcendental ideas, see also Klimmek 2005: 50–1. Of course, there are various differences between this table and the table of the categories. For instance, there are only three titles instead of four, but four modes instead of three, with the exception of the third title, where there is only one mode (*Refl.* 5553; 18:223). A further difference may only be superficial, namely that Kant mentions no common title for all of the categories corresponding to the unconditioned as the title of all transcendental ideas. This common title of the categories might be the concept of an object in general, since all twelve categories, according to Kant, are so many ways of thinking something as an *object* (A111; B128) just as the transcendental ideas are so many ways of thinking something as unconditioned. To be sure, the categories seem to be meant as *complementary* ways of thinking something as an object (in the sense that every object must be determined with respect to each title of the table of categories), while the transcendental ideas are *alternative* ways of thinking something as unconditioned.

[4] Klimmek reconstructs four different 'theological ideas' (corresponding to the systems of psychological and cosmological ideas) from a passage at A580/B608 and from *Refl.* 6017; see Klimmek 2005: 182–5. But in a different *Reflexion*, Kant says that in the case of the ideal, it is unnecessary to distinguish different modes (*Refl.* 5553; 18:223). Moreover, in the *Prolegomena*,

(simpliciter), world (simpliciter), and God (simpliciter), which are generally taken to be the prime examples of transcendental ideas.[5] However, in both places where Kant offers a derivation of the three classes of transcendental ideas (A323/B379 and A333–4/B390–1), which would be natural places to introduce the concepts of soul, world, and God, they are not explicitly mentioned. In fact, nowhere in the first *Critique* does Kant explicitly call these concepts 'transcendental ideas.'[6] Moreover, at least in the case of the generic concept of the world, which is defined as the "sum total of all appearances" (A334/B391), it is unclear how it could be a transcendental idea; it is not the concept of something unconditioned, since a sum total is conditioned by its parts or constituents. Accordingly, Kant in one passage distinguishes between the cosmological *transcendental* ideas (complete composition, partition, etc.), which he calls "world concepts" (*Weltbegriffe*), and the concept of the world, which he calls "an idea" (A408/B434) but not a 'transcendental idea.' In sum, the concepts of soul, world, and God are best understood as (speculative) ideas, not as transcendental ideas in the strict technical sense.[7]

6.2 On the Metaphysical Deduction of the Transcendental Ideas

A 'metaphysical deduction' explains the origin of an a priori concept (B159). In analogy to the metaphysical deduction of the categories (which derives the categories from the logical use of the understanding, specifically from the logical forms of judgment; A67–91/B92–124), Kant seemingly attempts to derive all transcendental ideas from the logical use of reason, in particular from the forms of rational inference. He writes:

The transcendental analytic gave us an example of how the mere logical form of our cognition can contain the origin of pure concepts *a priori* ... The form of judgments (transformed into a concept of the synthesis of intuitions) brought forth categories that direct all use of the understanding in experience. In the same way, we can expect that the form of the rational inferences, if applied to the synthetic unity of intuitions under

---

the corresponding section titles are "Psychological Ideas" (4:333) and "Cosmological Ideas" (4:338) (each in the plural), but "Theological Idea" (4:348) (in the singular), which confirms that there is only one theological transcendental idea.

[5] See e.g. Horstmann 1998: 526; Grier 2001: 131; Allison 2004: 320–2; Rohlf 2010: 203.

[6] Admittedly, Kant's wording sometimes suggests that he regards the concepts of soul, world, and God as transcendental ideas (e.g. A337/B394–5). But even in the Appendix, where the regulative function of the ideas of soul, world, and God are discussed (A642–704/B670–732), Kant mentions the three *kinds* of transcendental ideas (*dreierlei transzendentale Ideen*), "psychological, cosmological and theological" (A671/B699), but calls the concepts of soul, world, and God 'ideas,' never 'transcendental ideas.'

[7] For a similar view, see Klimmek 2005: 51–4. Klimmek accommodates the traditional reading by treating 'soul,' 'world,' and 'God' as titles of the three classes of transcendental ideas. I do not see sufficient basis for doing so in Kant's text, given that the titles Kant explicitly mentions seem to be 'psychological,' 'cosmological,' and 'theological.'

the authority of the categories, will contain the origin of special concepts *a priori* that we may call pure concepts of reason or *transcendental ideas*, and they will determine the use of the understanding according to principles in the whole of an entire experience. (A321/B377–8)

So far, this confirms our general line of interpretation, according to which Kant's Rational Sources Account explains how a metaphysically loaded 'real' use of reason grows naturally out of its metaphysically harmless 'logical use.' In this case, this means that the logical use of reason in rational inferences gives rise to transcendental ideas, and Kant already indicates in the final part of the quote that these ideas will have a 'real,' object-related use (which, as we learn only later, in the Appendix, can be either regulative or constitutive). However, it is far from clear how this 'transformation' of logical form into conceptual content is supposed to work. Just how to understand the metaphysical deduction of the *categories*, which serves as the model for the deduction of the transcendental ideas, is a difficult and much-discussed question, and no reading of these difficult passages has gained universal or even widespread acceptance.[8] The situation is even worse when it comes to the metaphysical deduction of the transcendental ideas, partly because the relevant texts are brief and cryptic and offer only hints at a full account of the origin of the transcendental ideas, and partly because much less attention has been paid to it.[9]

6.2.1 Where to Look for the Metaphysical Deduction of the Transcendental Ideas

At least part of the problem with the metaphysical deduction of the transcendental ideas stems from the fact that Kant explains the origin of these concepts in what seems to be three different ways. First, as we have just seen, they are said to originate from applying the forms of rational inferences to cognitions of the understanding (A321/B378), which closely parallels the way in which the categories arise from the forms of judgment. Second, even though they are 'concepts of pure reason,' Kant denies that they are originally generated by reason. Instead, reason "free[s]" a concept of the understanding (a category) from its restriction to possible experience (A409/B435). Similarly, Kant explains that reason turns the category into a transcendental idea by demanding

---

[8] See Caimi 2000 for an impressive overview of debated issues and divergent opinions in the literature.
[9] The most notable exception is the book-length study Klimmek 2005. Other reconstructions of the metaphysical deduction of the transcendental ideas include Renaut 1998; Malzkorn 1999: 7–77; Rohlf 2010; Caimi 2012. For a reading of Book One of the Transcendental Dialectic as a rationally necessary 'metaphysics of ideas,' see Theis 2010.

the totality of conditions of the conditioned (A409/B436); transcendental ideas are thus categories that are "extended to the unconditioned" (A409/B436). Third, Kant claims that we arrive at the transcendental ideas through inferences of reason (A339/B397), which seems to be why he calls them "inferred concepts" (A310/B366). While some passages suggest that the inferences in question are series of prosyllogisms that lead from something conditioned, through the series of its conditions, to something unconditioned (e.g. A323/B379; A331/B388), other formulations indicate that these inferences are the very dialectical inferences discussed in Book Two of the Transcendental Dialectic – the paralogisms, the proofs of the antinomies, and the proof(s) of the existence of God (e.g. A335/B392; A339–40/B397–8).[10]

While for Kant these must have been three aspects of a unified account of the origin of the transcendental ideas, it is unclear how exactly they hang together and what work each of them is supposed to do. Since Kant's remarks on this issue in the *Critique of Pure Reason* (and in other places as well) are sparse and offer only fragments of a full-blown metaphysical deduction of the transcendental ideas, any attempt to provide such a deduction will have to be highly speculative.

Things are complicated even further by the fact that Kant wants to achieve two distinct aims with the metaphysical deduction of the transcendental ideas. First, he wants to show that transcendental ideas are *necessary* and *a priori* concepts possessed, if only implicitly, by anyone who engages in rational inferences. Second, his aim is to make sure that the table of these concepts is complete in the sense of containing neither more nor fewer transcendental ideas than there really are. Kant may have had good reason to think that he could achieve the second aim by relying on his table of categories (and thus indirectly on the table of judgments) in combination with a threefold classification of the forms of inference (categorical, hypothetical, and disjunctive – a classification which in turn rests on the table of judgments). From a contemporary perspective, however, this path does not seem very promising. After all, our understanding of the logical forms of judgment and reasoning has changed significantly since Kant's days. According to post-Fregean logic, Kant's table of judgments is clearly inadequate as a table of the basic logical forms of thinking, for instance in not allowing for 'nested' quantifiers (e.g. 'For all x, there is a y ...'). Moreover, Kant's tripartite distinction does not capture all basic forms of deductive rational

---

[10] The first of these two ways of deriving the transcendental ideas are discussed in Guyer 2000: 80–4, who traces them to different strands of Kantian *Reflexionen* from the 1770s. On their interrelation, see Rohlf 2010: 205–6. Guyer and Rohlf do not discuss the third approach, which to me seems to be the most promising.

inferences, for instance those analyzed in the so-called logic of relations (e.g. the inference from '$x > y$' and '$y > z$' to '$x > z$').[11]

For this reason, in what follows I will not put much emphasis on the completeness and systematicity of Kant's metaphysical deduction of the transcendental ideas, even though it was undeniably important to Kant. Note, however, that the aims of completeness and systematicity are not essential to the Rational Sources Account, since transcendental ideas and dialectical inferences may well arise naturally from rational thinking as such, even if they do not form a system that guarantees completeness. I will therefore concentrate on Kant's other aim in the metaphysical deduction of the transcendental ideas, which consists in showing that the transcendental ideas grow naturally out of ordinary uses of reason. For this aim, what matters most is Kant's insistence that the transcendental ideas are *inferred concepts*.

As I shall argue now, the inferences that lead to the transcendental ideas are the very inferences Kant discusses in the Paralogisms, Antinomy, and Ideal sections of Book Two of the Transcendental Dialectic. For instance, Kant says that it is "only in the complete execution," that is in Book Two, that we will see how reason arrives at the transcendental ideas (A335–6/B392–3). Some pages later, Kant is more specific:

the transcendental (subjective) reality of pure concepts of reason rests on the fact that *we are brought to such ideas by a necessary inference of reason*. Thus there will be inferences of reason containing no empirical premises, by means of which we can infer from something with which we are acquainted to something of which we have no concept [of the understanding], and yet to which we nevertheless, by an unavoidable illusion, lend objective reality ... There are ... only three species of these dialectical inferences of reason, as manifold as the *ideas in which their conclusions result*. In the *first class* of syllogisms, from the transcendental concept of a subject that contains nothing manifold I infer the absolute unity of this subject itself ... This dialectical inference I will call a transcendental *paralogism*. The *second* class of sophistical inference is applied to the transcendental concept of absolute totality in the series of conditions for a given appearance in general; and from the fact that I always have a self-contradictory concept of the unconditioned synthetic unity in the series on one side, I infer the correctness of the opposite unity ... I will call the condition of reason with regard to these dialectical inferences the *antinomy* of pure reason. Finally, in the *third*

---

[11] To be sure, that inference can be transformed into a Kantian inference of reason by adding the inference rule as a premise, but this premise is not necessary for the validity of the inference, which shows that there are basic kinds of inference that are not Kantian inferences of reason. On the limitations of Kant's table of judgments, see e.g. Bennett 1966: 78–83; Strawson 1966: 78–82; Young 1992: 105–6. See Wolff 1995 for a defense of Kant's table of judgments and the exchange between Wolff, Beckermann, and Nortmann on the relation between Kantian and modern logic (Beckermann 1998; Nortmann 1998; Wolff 1998, 2000). On the limitations of the syllogistic logic available to Kant (limitations with respect to proofs in geometry, but also to inferences involving the concept of infinity), see Friedman 1992b: 55–96. On Kant's conception of logic in relation to both traditional and modern conceptions, see Tolley 2007.

kind of sophistical inference, from the totality of conditions for thinking objects in general insofar as they can be given to me I infer the absolute synthetic unity of all conditions for the possibility of things in general ... This dialectical syllogism I will call the *ideal* of pure reason. (A339–40/B397–8; first and second emphasis added)[12]

We will turn to the individual derivations of the transcendental ideas Kant is hinting at in due course. For the moment, what matters is that Kant here suggests that this derivation is *contained in the very inferences* that are the main topic of the sections on the Paralogisms, the Antinomy, and the Transcendental Ideal.[13] As we will see (in Chapters 7 and 8), this is indeed a plausible way to derive the concepts in question.[14]

This means that the metaphysical deduction of the transcendental ideas is to be found not in Book One but in Book Two of the Transcendental Dialectic. But what, then, is the role of Book One, entitled "Of the Concepts of Pure Reason" (A310/B366), and in particular its second and third sections, "Of the Transcendental Ideas" (A321/B377) and "System of Transcendental Ideas" (A333/B390)? I think that they primarily serve to introduce the very concept of a transcendental idea (and the corresponding concept of the unconditioned) and to establish, by recourse to the table of the categories and the forms of rational inference, that the transcendental ideas form a system in analogy to the table of the categories. Thus, what is derived in these sections is not what Kant calls the "transcendental (subjective) reality" of the transcendental ideas (A339/B397), that is, their origin in the structure of thinking (which is the proper aim of a metaphysical deduction), but the systematic order in which

---

[12] Guyer and Wood translate '*so vielfach als die Ideen sind*' as 'as many as there are ideas,' which suggests – against what I earlier argued – that there are only three transcendental ideas. But the German also allows for a reading (although it is not the most natural one) according to which the number of species of ideas is equal to the number of species of inference, which is why I have altered the translation.

[13] While I agree with Klimmek that the metaphysical deduction of the transcendental ideas is to be found in Book Two of the Transcendental Dialectic, Klimmek denies that it is identical to the dialectical inferences (e.g. Klimmek 2005: 118–21).

[14] Kant also seems to suggest that transcendental ideas are the result of a series of prosyllogisms (e.g. A323/B379), which are categorical, hypothetical, or disjunctive inferences, leading to the psychological, cosmological, and theological ideas, respectively (see e.g. Klimmek 2005: 26–8 and Rosefeldt 2017: 236–44 for reconstructions of this thought). But of course this cannot mean that any series of prosyllogisms could ever take us to a transcendental idea. What would be required is a kind of argument like the one Kant gives in the antinomies, which *reflects on* the series of syllogisms and concludes that *for structural reasons*, the series must end in the representation of something unconditioned. Kant seems to acknowledge this when he says that the paralogisms proceed "in correspondence to" categorical inferences and the antinomies "in analogy to" hypothetical ones (A406/B432–3). See also A577/B605, where Kant says that he has "grounded the systematic division of all transcendental ideas, according to which they were generated *parallel* and *corresponding to* the three kinds of inference of reason" (emphasis added) and that reason's use of the transcendental ideal is "analogous" to the use of reason in disjunctive inferences.

they stand.[15] This means that Kant's repeated recourse to the logical form of inferences is not part of the derivation of the transcendental ideas themselves (although admittedly, Kant may seem to suggest this), but merely a means of establishing their systematic order. Since I will not try to defend Kant's claims about the completeness and systematicity of the table of transcendental ideas, I will largely set these passages to the side in what follows.

6.2.2 Transcendental Ideas as Inferred Concepts

I will end this section by briefly reflecting on what it can mean to say that a concept is 'inferred.' While it is possible to locate inferred concepts in Kant's general classification of concepts as 'a priori made concepts' (9:93; Klimmek 2005: 10), Kant does not explain what he means when he calls a concept 'inferred.' We can see what he may have had in mind, however, if we consider that, according to Kant, a concept is a general representation that combines a variety of 'marks,' which in turn are general representations (9:95–6). The concept of a human being, for instance, contains the marks 'rational' and 'living being,' which in turn may contain other, more general marks. Now what is inferred in an inference is not a concept but a judgment (the conclusion); if a concept is said to be 'inferred,' this must mean that a concept that appears in the conclusion of an inference does not yet appear in the premises and in this sense results from that very inference. More specifically, it means that concepts used in the premises are combined in the conclusion into a new concept that contains them as its marks. Here is a simple example:

P1 Kant is a philosopher.
P2 Kant is married.
C   There is at least one married philosopher.

In this way, we 'infer' the concept of *married philosopher*.[16] As the example shows, the derivation of the concept does not depend on the truth of the premises (since Kant in fact never married). What matters is only that the conclusion contains a combination of concepts (or 'marks') that is not yet contained in either of the premises. In this way, the 'new' concept is 'inferred.'

---

[15] Kant's claim that the section on the "System of Transcendental Ideas" (A333/B390) contains a "subjective introduction to [the transcendental ideas] from the nature of our reason" (A336/B393) may suggest otherwise, but it is unclear what Kant means by "introduction" (*Anleitung*) here.

[16] This account of inferred concepts is inspired by Stefanie Grüne's explanation of what Kant might mean when he says that a concept "emerges from a judgment" (20:266; see Grüne 2009: 28).

This derivation also works for concepts for which we already have a primitive expression:

P1 Kant is unmarried.
P2 Kant is an adult male.
C   Kant is a bachelor.

If to be a bachelor just is to be an unmarried adult male, we have shown how this concept *can* be derived by way of inference. But of course, this also shows that *any* (complex) concept can be derived in this way, so this cannot be what Kant means by 'inferred concepts.' What is special about the transcendental ideas – in contrast to concepts such as married philosopher and bachelor – is that they can be derived by way of a "necessary inference of reason" (A339/B397), that is, an inference that is necessary insofar as its premises are a priori.[17] That the transcendental ideas are just "categories extended to the unconditioned" (A409/B436) can then be read as saying that one of the premises of these necessary inferences makes use of a category, while the inference 'extends' this category 'to the unconditioned' by leading to some unconditioned feature of objects thought under that category. In sum, I want to suggest that the specific sense in which transcendental ideas are inferred concepts is that they are contained in the conclusion of a 'necessary inference of reason,' where some appropriate category, but not the transcendental idea itself, is explicitly contained in the premises of that inference.

We will discuss how Kant applies this conception to the transcendental ideas in the chapters that follow. But let me briefly indicate why this appears to be a philosophically plausible approach. Consider the idea of an uncaused cause, which strictly speaking is not a transcendental idea in Kant's sense but a close relative of such an idea (namely the idea of the complete series of causes of an event). Why should this idea be rationally necessary in the sense that rational thinkers, if they are sufficiently persistent, will end up possessing that concept? Kant's answer, as I understand it, is that we start from a given event, ask for its cause, and for the cause of the cause, etc., and then reflect on the fact that in this way – by going back from one cause to the next – we will never get an ultimate answer to our question of what caused the original event, that is, an answer that does not again raise a question of the same kind. Such an answer can only come from reflecting on the *complete series* of causes. But once we do that, we recognize that *either* the complete series of causes is infinite *or* it

---

[17] The inferences in question may be necessary also in the further sense that they are part of the search for the unconditioned and the 'unity of reason.' For instance, Kant says of a "dialectical theorem of pure reason" that it differs "from all sophistical propositions" in that it "does not concern an arbitrary question that one might raise only at one's option, but one that every human reason must necessarily come up against in the course of its progress" (A421–2/B449–50).

ends in a cause that does not again have a cause – an uncaused cause. In this way, we necessarily arrive at the idea of an uncaused cause.

The sense in which the concept of an uncaused cause is an 'inferred concept' in Kant's sense can be brought out even more clearly if we reformulate the final steps of the reasoning just sketched in the following form:

P1   Either the complete series of causes of some event e is finite or it is infinite.
P2   If every cause has a cause, the complete series of causes of e is infinite.
C   If the complete series of causes of e is finite, it is not the case that every cause has a cause, that is, there is an uncaused cause.

Note that the concept of an uncaused cause does not appear in the premises, but only in the conclusion of this inference. Given that both premises at least seem to be analytic truths and that the very idea of a complete series of causes arises naturally from reflecting on the causal history of ordinary events, it seems plausible that this is a 'necessary inference of reason' in Kant's sense. It is by way of this kind of inference that, according to Kant, we arrive at the transcendental ideas.

6.3   The Concept of the Unconditioned

In the section "On the Transcendental Ideas," after explaining the general concept of a transcendental idea as based on the logical form of inferences, Kant introduces the concept of the unconditioned as the "common title" of all transcendental ideas (A324/B380), which presumably means that the transcendental ideas are different ways of thinking of something as unconditioned. Kant first reminds us that "[t]he function of reason in its inferences consisted in the universality of cognition according to concepts, and the rational inference is itself a judgment determined *a priori* in the whole domain of its condition" (A321–2/B378). Kant gives an example (A322/B378):

P1   All humans are mortal.
P2   Caius is human.
C   Caius is mortal.

Here, 'being human' is the condition under which Caius is cognized as mortal. Now 'the whole domain of the cognition's condition' for being mortal is 'living being' (Klimmek 2005: 25–6), which, as Kant explains, in P1 is 'limited under a certain condition':

Accordingly, in the conclusion of a syllogism we restrict a predicate [being mortal] to a certain object [Caius], after we have thought it in the major premise in its whole domain [being a living thing] under a certain condition [being human]. This complete magnitude of the domain, in relation to such a condition, is called *universality* (*universalitas*). In the synthesis of intuition this corresponds to *allness* (*universitas*), or the *totality* of conditions. So the transcendental concept of reason is none other than that of the *totality of conditions* to a given conditioned thing. Now since the unconditioned alone makes possible the totality of conditions, and conversely the totality of conditions is always itself *unconditioned*, a pure concept of reason in general can be explained through the concept of the unconditioned, insofar as it contains a ground of synthesis for what is conditioned. (A322/B378–9)

This is an extremely condensed and difficult argument. Kant's derivation has two clearly discernible steps, which we will discuss in the next two subsections. First, Kant derives the concept of a *totality of conditions* (which is the 'transcendental concept of reason') from the universality of the major premise in a categorical syllogism (Section 6.3.1). Indeed, the phrase 'totality of conditions,' which is ubiquitous in the rest of the Transcendental Dialectic, occurs here for the first time in the *Critique of Pure Reason*. Second, Kant argues that the concept of a *totality of conditions* takes us to that of the *unconditioned* (Section 6.3.2).

6.3.1 Totality of Conditions

Concerning the first step of the argument, Kant's idea seems to be that implicit in the drawing of a categorical syllogism (arguably the paradigm case of a rational inference) is the concept of the universality of the condition to a given conditioned *cognition*. The conditioned cognition is stated in the conclusion ('Caius is mortal'), and the universality of the condition (or the 'whole domain of its condition') is represented in the universally quantified subject term of the first premise ('all humans'). If only *some* humans were mortal, Caius's being mortal would not follow from the condition (his being human). Thus, the condition must be considered to hold universally. So far, this concerns only the logical use of reason.

With the next sentence ("In the synthesis of intuition this corresponds to allness . . ."; A322/B379) Kant moves from logical to real conditions by claiming that the logical concept of the universal domain ('All A are B') corresponds to the concept of totality, which is a category and thus a 'transcendental' and object-related concept. This correspondence is not reflected in the tables of judgment and of the categories, however, since in the former 'universality' is the *first* logical form under 'quantity,' while in the latter 'totality' is the *third* category under that title (A70/B95; A80/B106; see Heimsoeth 1966: 44 n.). It nevertheless seems highly plausible that the concept we employ in thinking of the domain of objects falling under the subject term F in a universal judgment is that of 'allness,' that is, of the *totality* of things that are F.

So far, we have the 'logical' concept of the *universal domain of the condition* of a given conditioned *cognition*, on the one hand, and the corresponding 'transcendental' concept of a *totality of objects* that constitute that universal

The System of Transcendental Ideas (6.3.1)

domain, on the other. What Kant now seems to suggest is that we thereby arrive at the concept of the *totality of conditions* (of a conditioned object). But this move is problematic, since we are speaking of 'conditions' in two different senses here. On the one hand, the subject term of a universal judgment is the *logical* condition of the subsumption of the middle term; on the other, there are the *real* conditions of a conditioned object. Kant's claim seems to be that implicit in the logical form of a universal categorical inference is the idea of a *totality of real conditions*. But his argument only takes us to the quite different idea of a *totality of objects falling under a logical condition*. For this reason, I do not see how Kant can successfully derive the concept of a totality of conditions from the logical form of a universal categorical syllogism.[18]

Perhaps what Kant wants to claim is only that there is an *analogy* between the universality of a major premise and the totality we think in the concept of the unconditioned (just as Kant claims that there is an analogy between the classes of transcendental ideas and the three types of metaphysical fallacies, on the one hand, and the three forms of inferences of reason, on the other).[19] But then, Kant still owes us a metaphysical deduction of the concept of the unconditioned.[20]

As we have seen, Kant's strategy of basing the transcendental ideas on the logical form of inferences of reason primarily serves his aim of providing a systematic and hence complete derivation of the transcendental ideas. What matters for the Rational Sources Account, however, is only the aim of showing that the transcendental ideas are necessary concepts of reason. To achieve this, it is not necessary that the transcendental ideas, including the concept of the unconditioned as their 'common title,' flow from the logical form of inferences of reason, which are (somewhat mysteriously) 'transformed' into a concept. Rather, what needs to be shown is that we arrive at them through a "necessary inference of reason" (A339/B397), that is, through an inference from a priori premises that any rational thinker is bound to accept. I think that the materials for such an inference can be found in Book One of the Transcendental Dialectic.

---

[18] This problem is clearly articulated by Henry Allison (2004: 316). Allison suggests a more charitable reading that emphasizes the distinction between totality as a category (universal quantification) and totality as a concept of reason (totality of conditions). However, this does not help us to understand how to derive the latter concept from the former. Might Kant have intended the derivation of the concept of the unconditioned at A322/B378-9 to reflect some form of transcendental illusion, so that it would not be astonishing if the argument were invalid? Perhaps so. On the reading I will present in the two chapters that follow, the nine specific transcendental ideas are also derived in inferences that, from a critical perspective, turn out to be fallacious and only appear valid if transcendental realism is presupposed. The same is true for the inference to the unconditioned, as I will presently suggest.

[19] See note 14.

[20] Hinske 1993 shows that Kant developed his concept of the unconditioned in the 1770s quite independently of considerations about the logical form of inferences.

As we have seen, Kant insists that the conditioned could not exist if the totality of its conditions (the complete series of its conditions) did not exist: "the possibility of something conditioned presupposes the totality of its conditions" (A337/B394; see also A409–10/B436–7). I have argued that this claim in fact follows from Kant's own conception of a totality, if the latter is understood as giving expression to the principle of comprehension, according to which for any F there is a set of all Fs (Section 3.3.3). This means that one can derive the idea of a totality of real conditions by an inference from the existence of something conditioned to that of the totality of its conditions:

P1　If there is some x that is R-conditioned, then there is some y that is the R-condition of x.
P2　For every instantiated predicate P, there is a totality of things that P can be truly predicated of.
C　If there is some x that is R-conditioned, there is a totality of R-conditions of x.

For the transcendental realist, both premises will appear to be a priori truths. According to Kant, P1 is an analytic truth about things in themselves (see Section 5.3). Since the transcendental realist does not distinguish between things in themselves and appearances, to her P1 will appear to be an a priori truth even if it is not thus restricted. P2 is the principle of comprehension, which follows from Kant's definition of a totality (a multitude considered as a unity) if we assume that *any* (actual or potential) plurality can be considered as a unity (as a set or totality) (Section 3.3.3). Thus, the concept of a totality of (real) conditions is indeed a necessary concept of reason in that it can be derived from a priori premises by means of a rational inference (given the background assumption of transcendental realism).[21]

In this section, we started from the passage in which Kant seems to derive the concept of the unconditioned in two steps: first, the concept of a totality of conditions is derived from the logical form of universal categorical inferences; second, this concept is shown to take us to the concept of the unconditioned. As we have seen, the first step is problematic; it appears to involve an illicit transition from the idea of a totality of objects that fall under the subject term in a major premise to the idea of a totality of real conditions of something conditioned. Drawing on Kant's claim that the existence of something conditioned presupposes the existence of the totality of its conditions, however, we have been able to derive the concept of a totality of real conditions as part of the consequence of a 'necessary inference of reason.' This is a sufficient basis

---

[21] But note that P2 is problematic not only from a modern post-Russellian perspective (see Chapter 3, note 47), but perhaps also according to Kant. After all, for the realm of empirical objects Kant wants to resist the inference from the conditioned to the totality of conditions (A499/B527). As I have indicated (Section 5.3), the philosophically most promising way to block this inference is by denying or restricting P2.

for Kant's claim that the concept of the unconditioned is a necessary concept of reason, assuming that the second step of Kant's argument is convincing. It is to this step that we now turn.

6.3.2 The Unconditioned

Here again is the sentence where Kant moves from the concept of the totality of conditions to that of the unconditioned:

> Now since the *unconditioned* alone makes possible the totality of conditions, and conversely the totality of conditions is always itself unconditioned, a pure concept of reason in general can be explained through the concept of the unconditioned, insofar as it contains a ground of synthesis for what is conditioned. (A322/B379)

Kant appears to make two distinct claims, one of which is supposedly the converse of the other:

(1) The unconditioned alone makes possible the totality of conditions.
(2) The totality of conditions is always itself unconditioned.

On the face of things, however, rather than being the converse of (2), (1) seems to be a different but logically equivalent formulation of (2):

(1*) A totality of conditions is possible only if there is something unconditioned.
(2*) If there is a totality of conditions, then there is something unconditioned.

Ignoring modal complications, (1*) says that if there is no unconditioned, then there is no totality of conditions, which is not the converse but the contraposition of (2*) and thus logically equivalent to it. But if this is so, then Kant's linking these two claims with the term 'conversely' (*umgekehrt*) does not make sense. Moreover, Kant's general point is that we can 'explain' the concept of a totality of conditions by the concept of the unconditioned. But (1*) and (2*) are not sufficient for this purpose. What Kant needs is the claim that the concept of a totality of conditions (which supposedly arises from the logical form of a syllogism) *is* the concept of the unconditioned – that is, the claim that both concepts are equivalent.[22]

There is, however, an alternative reading of (1) which, although less natural, avoids making (1) and (2) logically equivalent. On this reading, that the

---

[22] There is a natural reading of (1) that would make things even worse. According to this reading, what Kant wants to say is that only an unconditioned condition (UCC) makes possible a totality of conditions. But this can hardly be what Kant had in mind, since it would rule out that infinite series of subordinated conditions count as unconditioned, a claim to which Kant is clearly committed in the first *Critique*. (But see Section 3.3.1 for Kant's apparent change of mind in the *Progress* essay.)

unconditioned 'alone' makes possible the totality of conditions means that nothing but the unconditioned is required for there to be a totality of conditions. In other words, the unconditioned is not a necessary but a sufficient condition for a totality of conditions. Read this way, the two claims are really the converse of each other:

(1**) If there is something unconditioned, then there is a totality of conditions.
(2**) If there is a totality of conditions, then there is something unconditioned.

Moreover, this reading takes us to the result Kant intends, namely the equivalence of the concept of the unconditioned and that of a totality of conditions. I therefore think that this is the correct reading of Kant's argument.

We have already discussed (1**) (Section 3.3.4). Following Kant (A417/B445), we distinguished between two senses of 'the unconditioned': an unconditioned that consists in a totality of conditioned conditions (TCC) and one that is an unconditioned condition (UCC). Both of these senses can be subsumed under the *general* concept of something unconditioned as the *unconditioned totality of conditions* of something conditioned (UTC), which is at stake, for instance, in the Supreme Principle. But if the unconditioned mentioned in (1**) and (2**) is UTC, then it is obvious that (1**) and (2**) are true. If there is a UTC, then by definition there is a totality of conditions (because that is just what a UTC is). And if there is a totality of conditions, then there is a UTC, since any totality of R-conditions, according to Kant, is necessarily R-unconditioned (Section 3.3.1). Thus, Kant is correct to insist that the concept of a totality of (real) conditions and that of the unconditioned (understood as UTC) are equivalent.

With this, we have completed the derivation of the concept of the unconditioned as a necessary concept of reason. First, we have derived the concept of a totality of real conditions in an 'inference of pure reason'; second, we have shown that that concept is equivalent to that of the unconditioned. Even though we had to deviate from Kant's official derivation, the argument provided here only uses materials that Kant himself mentions in the Transcendental Dialectic (primarily in Book One).

6.4 The Three Classes of Transcendental Ideas

Having derived the concept of the unconditioned as the "common title of all concepts of [pure] reason" (A324/B380), Kant moves on to three classes of transcendental ideas as so many *kinds* of unconditioned objects:

There will be as many kinds of pure concepts of reason [*so vielerlei reine Vernunftbegriffe*] as there are species of relation represented by the understanding by means of the categories; and so we must seek an unconditioned, first, of the categorical synthesis in a subject, second of the hypothetical synthesis of the members of a series, and third of the disjunctive synthesis of the parts in a system. There are namely just as many species of inferences of reason each of which proceeds by prosyllogisms to the unconditioned: one, to a subject that is no longer a predicate, another to a presupposition that presupposes nothing further, and the third to an aggregate of members of a division such that nothing further is required for it to complete the division of a concept. Hence the pure rational concepts of the totality in a synthesis of conditions ... are grounded in the nature of human reason. (A323/B379–80)[23]

Kant introduces the three classes of transcendental ideas by analogy with the three relational categories (substance/inherence, causation, community) and with the three forms of rational inference (categorical, hypothetical, disjunctive; see A304/B361). Even though he does not make this explicit in the passage under discussion, Kant takes all three tripartite distinctions to be grounded in turn in the logical forms of relational judgments (categorical, hypothetical, and disjunctive, which, in the passage, are mentioned indirectly in the forms of "synthesis" through the relational categories). Kant's idea is clearly to model the classes of transcendental ideas, along with the corresponding relational categories and forms of inferences of reason, on the tripartite structure of the relational judgments.

After these remarks, however, Kant does not pursue this approach further. Instead, he returns to the derivation of the classes of transcendental ideas ten pages later, in the section titled "System of the Transcendental Ideas." After reminding us that the three species of dialectical inference correspond to the three forms of rational inference (categorical, hypothetical, disjunctive), Kant introduces yet another tripartite distinction by saying that "all the relation of representations of which we can make either a concept or an idea are of three sorts: 1) the relation to the subject, 2) to the manifold of the object in appearance, and 3) to all things in general" (A334/B391).[24] And a sentence later he concludes:

Consequently, all transcendental ideas will be brought under *three classes*, of which the *first* contains the absolute (unconditioned) *unity* of the *thinking subject*, the *second* the absolute *unity* of the *series* of *conditions of appearance*, the *third* the absolute *unity* of the *condition of an object of thought* in general. The thinking subject is the object of *psychology*, the sum total of all appearances (the world) is the object of *cosmology*, and

---

[23] I deviate from the Guyer/Wood translation in various ways, most importantly by translating '*so vielerlei reine Vernunftbegriffe*' not as 'as many concepts of reason' but as 'as many *kinds* of pure concepts of reason.' ('*Vielerlei*' in German means 'various, of many kinds.')

[24] This tripartite classification is in turn derived from two binary distinctions, one between the relation of representations to the subject and to objects, the other between appearances and objects of thought.

the thing that contains the supreme condition of the possibility of everything that can be thought (the being of all beings) is the object of *theology*. (A334/B391)

Thus, as has often been remarked in the literature, Kant seems to offer two different and independent derivations of the three classes of transcendental ideas, one from the three forms of inference, the other from the three relations between subject and object. And since the classes of transcendental ideas are widely believed to correspond to the ideas of the soul, the world, and God, he seems also to derive these ideas in two different and independent ways.[25]

Instead of trying to reconstruct Kant's different derivations and how they hang together, let me point out, first, that they are inessential to Kant's argument for the Rational Sources Account, since for this what matters is not that we possess a systematic table of all transcendental ideas, but only that these ideas are in fact "grounded in the nature of human reason," as Kant puts it in the first quoted passage (A323/B379–80). Second, it is not at all obvious that Kant intends to derive the ideas of the soul, the world, and God in either of the quoted passages. A first indication is that the terms 'soul' and 'God' are not used at all in the passages under discussion and that the term 'world' is used only once, in parentheses. Instead, in the first passage Kant speaks only of "a subject that is no longer a predicate," of "a presupposition that presupposes nothing further," and "an aggregate of members of a division such that nothing further is required for it to complete the division of a concept" (A223/B379–80), which are not yet the full-fledged metaphysical concepts of the soul, the world, and God. Similarly for the second passage: the concept of "the absolute (unconditioned) unity of the thinking subject" is not yet the idea of the soul, if by the latter we mean the idea of a simple, personal, immaterial substance (as discussed in the paralogisms). Moreover, the concept of "the absolute unity of the series of conditions of appearance" is different from the concept of "the sum total of all appearances (the world)" that Kant mentions in the next sentence. If Kant had wanted to identify these two concepts, he would have indicated that and would not have used two clearly different formulations. And, finally, the concept of "the absolute unity of the condition of an object of thought in general" is not the concept of God or a supreme being, even though Kant argues in the section on the Transcendental Ideal that the former necessarily leads to the latter.

This confirms the point made earlier in this chapter (in Section 6.2) that it is not Kant's aim in the sections on transcendental ideas and their system to derive any particular transcendental idea, not even the ideas of the soul, the

---

[25] See e.g. Grier 2001: 133–9; Allison 2004: 319; and Rohlf 2010: 204–6, who all argue in different ways that the two trichotomies are two steps of Kant's derivation of the transcendental ideas. Klimmek, by contrast, takes only the second trichotomy to be relevant to the derivation of the *classes* of transcendental ideas (Klimmek 2005: 41).

world, and God (which are not transcendental ideas strictly speaking). Instead, he aims to introduce the very idea of a transcendental idea (and the 'common title' of all transcendental ideas, the concept of the unconditioned) and to provide a systematic basis for the derivation of the nine transcendental ideas that Kant introduces in Book Two of the Transcendental Dialectic, along with the dialectical inferences that lead to them. This is further confirmed by the fact that Kant concludes the second passage by linking the three classes of transcendental ideas to the fields of psychology, cosmology, and theology, thus introducing the 'titles' of the three classes, namely 'psychological,' 'cosmological,' and 'theological.'

This is not to deny that Kant uses the concept of the soul in the formulation of the first three paralogisms (in the A-version) and the concept of the world in each of the thesis and antithesis arguments of the four antinomies. But in each case, this is a rather unspecific concept of a thinking being or the sum total of appearances, respectively, which does not necessarily concern something unconditioned. Rather, it is only in the conclusions of the dialectical inferences that soul and world feature as being unconditioned (see Chapter 7). And in the case of the idea of God, it is only in the course of the 'natural' argument for God's existence (introduced in Section Three of the Ideal) that God is identified with the *ens realissimum* of rational theology (see Chapter 8).

In sum, it would be a mistake to look for a derivation of the transcendental ideas and the ideas of the soul, the world, and God in Book One of the Transcendental Dialectic. Rather, Kant's aim is to show that the transcendental ideals form a system and to lay out its structure. Whether Kant succeeds in proving the completeness and systematicity of the table of transcendental ideas is an open question; in the literature, Kant's arguments have often been viewed as unsuccessful, although they have also found some defenders.[26] But even if the critics are correct, this does not undermine the central point of Kant's Rational Sources Account, which is that the transcendental ideas themselves are necessary concepts of reason. We will turn to this derivation of the transcendental ideas in the two chapters that follow.

6.5   Conclusion

In this chapter, I have argued that Book One of the Transcendental Dialectic is not meant to derive the transcendental ideas from the forms of rational inference, but rather to introduce the very conception of a transcendental idea, to derive the concept of the unconditioned as the 'common title' of all transcendental ideas, and to lay out the systematic structure these ideas will

---

[26] See e.g. Bennett 1974 for a sharp critique and Klimmek 2005 for a defense.

instantiate. Let me close by remarking on how Kant's derivation of the system of transcendental ideas relates to the general template of his argument for the Rational Sources Account.

According to this template, there is (1) a transition from logical to transcendental concepts and principles, the latter of which (2) can be used either regulatively or constitutively, but (3) the distinction between the legitimate regulative and the illegitimate constitutive use is concealed by a tacit assumption of transcendental realism. In Book One of the Transcendental Dialectic, we find Kant arguing for the first of these steps by trying to derive the transcendental concept of the unconditioned from the logical form of the syllogism, and the classes of transcendental ideas (and, according to many readers, also the ideas of the soul, the world, and God) from the three types of rational inference (categorical, hypothetical, disjunctive). While these derivations are problematic in various ways (I have voiced my skepticism as to their cogency), it was clearly Kant's *intention* to argue for a transition from the logical to the transcendental use of reason at the level of the transcendental ideas. By contrast, Kant does not explicitly invoke the regulative/constitutive distinction. This is postponed until the very end of the Transcendental Dialectic, where Kant, in the second part of the Appendix, distinguishes between the regulative and the constitutive use of transcendental ideas and explains the latter by appeal to transcendental realism. Moreover, the derivation of the concept of a totality of conditions we reconstructed earlier (Section 6.3.1) may also presuppose an assumption of transcendental realism, since only under this assumption will its first premise (that if there is something conditioned, then there is some condition) be analytically true (while Kant himself appears to take it to be synthetic when applied to appearances; see Section 3.2.4). However, since this inference, even though reconstructed out of materials Kant himself provides, cannot be found in Kant's text, it remains an open question whether Kant thinks of the derivation of the concept of a totality of conditions (and thus of the unconditioned) as an instance of transcendental illusion. At least on the surface of the text, in Book One Kant is only concerned with the first step of his general template (logical/transcendental), not with the two steps that follow (regulative/constitutive, transcendental realism).

7 The Paralogisms and Antinomy Arguments as 'Necessary Inferences of Reason'

In this chapter, we will turn to the first two of the three metaphysical disciplines whose inferences and conclusions Kant discusses in the context of his Rational Sources Account, namely rational psychology and cosmology. (The third discipline, rational theology, will be the topic of the next chapter.) As Kant argues, we are led by four seemingly cogent inferences from a priori premises (the 'paralogisms') to conclude that our souls are immaterial, simple, and persisting substances. Another set of seemingly cogent inferences take us to four theses about the size and structure of the world at large. Unfortunately, equally compelling proofs of the negations of these four theses can be given, so that we end up with four pairs of contradictory theses about the world as a whole, all of which seem to be backed by a priori proofs (the four 'antinomies'). (As Kant points out, however, this unfortunate inconsistency has the fortunate side effect of alerting us to the illusory character of purely rational inferences and thus motivates a 'critique of pure reason'; 5:107.)

At the same time, the paralogisms and the arguments that lead up to the antinomies deliver the corresponding transcendental ideas. Kant introduces the nine transcendental ideas – four psychological, four cosmological, and one theological (see Section 6.1) – in the introductory sections of the Paralogisms, Antinomy, and Ideal chapters, respectively. In the case of the four psychological ideas, these are presented in two different but substantially identical tables (A344/B402 and A404). Kant also presents a table of cosmological ideas (A415/B443), while the single theological idea is developed in the section on the Transcendental Ideal (A571/B599–A583/B611). The order of the tables is based on the table of the categories, which allows Kant to claim that these are all the transcendental ideas there can possibly be.[1] As we saw in the previous chapter, however, the derivation of the systematic structure of the ideas is not the same as the derivation of the ideas itself, which, according to various already-quoted passages (e.g. A339/B397), is part of the dialectical inferences discussed by Kant. Transcendental ideas are necessary and inferred

---

[1] For a perceptive reconstruction of how Kant bases the tables of psychological and cosmological ideas on the table of the categories, see Klimmek 2005.

concepts, which means that we form them as a result of a "necessary inference of reason" (A339/B397). In other words, the transcendental ideas are concepts that rational thinkers necessarily arrive at by means of rational inferences if they begin to reflect on certain of their a priori cognitions about conditioned objects and proceed from there to the totality of their conditions (as part of their search for the 'unity of reason'). What we will have to ask, then, is which inferences these are and how they lead to the transcendental ideas. As before, I will set aside the question of whether Kant is correct to claim completeness for the system of transcendental ideas and will instead concentrate on showing that they are indeed necessary concepts of reason in the sense just explained.

In this chapter, we will see how the four transcendental paralogisms and the arguments underlying the four antinomies of pure reason can be read as 'necessary inferences of reason' and how they result in the corresponding transcendental ideas. We will consider the paralogisms and the psychological ideas (Section 7.1), discuss the role of transcendental realism in the paralogisms (Section 7.2), look at the derivation of the cosmological ideas (Section 7.3) and the four antinomies (Section 7.4), and reconstruct the role of transcendental realism in the antinomies (Section 7.5). In doing so, we will not be able to discuss the relevant parts of the *Critique of Pure Reason* in detail. Instead, we will have to concentrate on those aspects that are relevant to understanding how Kant develops his Rational Sources Account in the Transcendental Dialectic.

7.1 The Psychological Ideas and the Paralogisms

Kant's table of psychological ideas, which he calls a "topic of rational psychology" (A344/B402), contains four ideas, the first three of which can be read off of Kant's own formulations, namely the soul as (1) substance, (2) simple, and (3) numerically identical over time (that is, a person), where these ideas are taken to apply to a thing in itself (see A344/B402). Unfortunately, it is not clear what the fourth idea is, but I take it to be the idea of the spirituality of the soul.[2]

---

[2] The fourth entry in Kant's table reads "In relation to possible objects in space" (A344/B402), which does not attribute any property to the soul and does not have any obvious bearing on its supposed unconditionality. In the second version of the table (A404), things become somewhat clearer. There, the fourth entry refers to the soul's cognizing itself as "the unconditioned unity of existence in space, that is, nothing [not?] as the consciousness of several things outside itself, but rather only of its own existence, and of other things merely as its representations." This formulation, as well as the corresponding fourth paralogism, clearly refers to the Cartesian proof of the immateriality of the soul (in the Sixth Meditation), according to which we are immediately and infallibly aware of our own existence as thinking beings, but not of the existence of our bodies (of which we are conscious merely through fallible representations within us), from which it supposedly follows that we, as thinking beings, are distinct from our bodies. In the fourth

If these four psychological ideas are supposed to be the result of necessary inferences of reason (see Section 6.2), we will have to turn to the four paralogisms, which, according to Kant, are such inferences. It will not be possible to offer a full discussion of the Paralogisms chapter with its many intricacies. In particular, I will have to set aside many important questions raised by that chapter, including the central question of what, according to Kant, a thinking being *really* is and what we can know about it. Rather, I will concentrate exclusively on the relevance of the paralogisms to the Rational Sources Account and ask why, according to Kant, someone who reflects rationally about thinking beings like ourselves will naturally be led to conclude that they are unconditioned in various ways (as substances, simples, persons, spirits). As we will see, this focus on the Rational Sources Account provides a perspective on the Paralogisms chapter that differs from the approach commonly taken in the extensive literature on the topic.[3]

I will primarily discuss the first paralogism, focusing on how it leads us to the idea of a substantial soul and why it is a 'necessary inference of reason' (Section 7.1.1). I will then address the other three paralogisms (Section 7.1.2). Finally, I will turn to Kant's diagnosis of the fallacy involved in the paralogisms in order to understand the role of transcendental realism in generating the transcendental illusion at work in the paralogisms (Section 7.2). Where the A- and B-versions of the Paralogisms chapter differ, I will mostly follow the latter (even though this means that the explicit formulations of the paralogisms must be reconstructed from Kant's summary at B407–9). However, I take the main lines of the reading suggested here to hold for the A-paralogism as well,

---

paralogism (and the Refutation of Idealism in the B-edition), Kant primarily attacks the *epistemological premise* of this argument, according to which one's own existence is certain, but not the existence of material objects in space. This focus obscures the fact that what is at issue in the fourth paralogism is the *ontological consequence* of this epistemological premise, namely the *immateriality* of the soul (its being distinct from material objects). (See Rosefeldt 2000: 136–9, who claims that the topic of the fourth paralogism is immateriality and who contrasts epistemological and ontological aspects of the Cartesian proof.) The fact that Kant himself links immateriality with the first (A345) and second (A356) paralogisms speaks against immateriality as the fourth psychological idea, however. Rather than immateriality as such, it would seem to be *spirituality* that is at issue (Rosefeldt 2000: 136), which includes but is not the same as immateriality. Following the rationalist tradition, Kant defines a "spirit" or *Geist* as an immaterial *thinking* (or *rational*) being (e.g. 2:321; 20:325). In fact, the intended conclusion of the fourth paralogism in B (which unfortunately is not explicitly formulated as such) appears to be 'I could exist merely as a thinking being (without being a human being)' (B409), which precisely fits Kant's definition of a spirit. I will therefore assume that the fourth transcendental idea is that of spirituality. (But note that spirituality is mentioned at A345/B403 not as the fourth psychological idea but as following from the first three ideas.) For a different reading, see e.g. Klimmek, who claims that the fourth psychological idea is that of the indubitability of the soul (Klimmek 2005: 148–51).

[3] Helpful discussions of different aspects of the Paralogisms chapter include Ameriks 1982/2000; Kitcher 1982; Grier 1993; Klemme 1996; Horstmann 1997; Ameriks 1998; Malzkorn 1998; Sturma 1998; Rosefeldt 2000; Klemme 2010; Proops 2010; Thöle 2010; Wuerth 2010; Dyck 2014; Watkins 2016a; and Rosefeldt 2017.

which suggests that despite the many differences between the A- and B-versions, they do not differ with respect to how Kant argues for the Rational Sources Account in that part of the first *Critique*.

7.1.1 The First Paralogism

The first transcendental paralogism can be formulated as follows:

P1   What must always be represented as a subject, not a predicate, is a substance.[4]
P2   I, as a thinking being (soul), must always be represented as a subject, not a predicate.[5]
C   I, as a thinking being (soul), am a substance (see A348; B407; B410–11).

Although 'substance' is mentioned in P1, and 'thinking being' in P2, it is only the conclusion that combines these marks into the concept of a *substantial thinking being*. In this rather straightforward way, I will argue, Kant explains how one arrives at the concept of the soul as a substantial thinking being, which is the first psychological idea.

As the inference is intended by the rational psychologist, both premises are supposed to be a priori.[6] P1 is supposed to be an analytic truth that follows from the concept of a substance, which is traditionally defined as something that is the bearer of predicates but not itself a predicate of something else (see Aristotle, *Categories*, 2a 12–15).[7] P2 is also analytic in that the rational psychologist, according to Kant, bases P2 not on empirical introspection but solely on the content of the 'problematic' (that is, hypothetically assumed)

---

[4] Kant uses the terms 'subject' and 'predicate' both in a 'logical' and a 'real' sense. In the *logical* sense, both subject and predicate are representations (or linguistic expressions) that feature in judgments (or sentences). They are distinguished by their logical role, the subject term being further determined by the predicate (see 9:103). For instance, in 'All humans are mortal,' 'human' is the subject and 'mortal' the predicate. In the *real* sense, by contrast, a subject is a bearer of properties or attributes, which are its predicates. In the first paralogism, it is the real sense that is at stake, although the minor premise may be thought to be plausible only if one somehow conflates the logical and the real senses. I will turn to Kant's diagnosis of the fallacy involved in the paralogisms in the next section.

[5] I take P2 to be the hypothetical claim that *if* I represent myself as a thinking being, *then* I must represent myself as a subject. For a different reading, according to which P2 means that in *all* my representations I must represent myself as a subject, see Bennett 1974: 73–4.

[6] As Corey Dyck has argued, this insistence on complete independence from empirical input is not a feature of the Wolffian tradition of rational psychology, and not even a feature of Kant's own pre-critical conception of that discipline. Rather, it is first to be found in the *Critique of Pure Reason* (Dyck 2014: 70–81). I think that this development can be explained by Kant's interest, in the first *Critique*, in tracing speculative metaphysics to its sources in reason (the Rational Sources Account), which requires him to reconstruct the thoughts of the speculative metaphysician as purely a priori.

[7] Baumgarten offers a similar definition but weakens the modality: a substance is something that *can* exist without inhering in something else (*Metaphysica*, §191). Cf. also Kant's own definition at B149.

thought 'I think' (A347/B405; see also A343/B401; B407). From these two analytic premises, the rational psychologist infers that the soul is a substantial thinking being and thereby also arrives at the corresponding transcendental idea.[8]

Granting that the first premise is indeed analytic and that the inference at least *appears* to be valid, whether this is a 'necessary inference of reason' will mainly depend on P2. Why should one necessarily think of oneself as an 'absolute' subject (A348) – as something that can only be represented as a subject, not a predicate? The answer Kant suggests is that by thinking of myself as a thinking being, I necessarily place the representation of myself, 'I,' in the subject position, never in the predicate position: "Now in all our thinking the I is the subject, in which thoughts inhere only as determinations, and this I cannot be used as the determination of another thing" (A349; see also B407). While this can be understood in a variety of ways, I think at least one relevant aspect is that the representation expressed by the term 'I' does not function like a predicate and refers to its object not by means of 'marks,' like a concept does, but rather in some other, directly referential way, which makes it impossible to use that expression as a predicate (see Rosefeldt 2017: 225–8).[9] Therefore, the thought that I might be an attribute of something else does not seem to make sense: my thoughts inhere in me, but *I* do not inhere in anything else. This is an entirely natural way to think of oneself, and Kant indeed admits that there is some truth to it: "Thus everyone must necessarily *regard* Himself as a substance, but *regard* his thinking only as accidents of his existence and determinations of his state" (A349; emphasis added).[10]

In the hands of the rational psychologist, however, who combines it with P1, this thought becomes the basis of a supposed proof of the substantiality of the soul. This proof can be understood as part of reason's search for the

---

[8] In the literature, it is common to distinguish between at least two conceptions of substance at work in Kant's discussion of the first paralogism, often called (with Bennett 1966: 182–4) 'substance₁' and 'substance₂,' where the former means a bearer of properties while the latter means something that is sempiternal (unoriginated and indestructible). Bennett identifies the former with the unschematized and the latter with the schematized category of substance in Kant. I think that the central meaning of 'substance' as used in the first paralogism is substance₁. But note that *ultimate* substances₁ (bearers of properties that are not again properties of a bearer) may plausibly be thought also to be substances₂ (see Bennett 1966: 182–3, who in effect attributes this identification to Spinoza). It will not be possible here, however, to trace the different senses of 'substance' through Kant's discussion of the first paralogism.

[9] Of course, one can also think, e.g. looking at a photo, 'That is I.' But even then, the term 'I' functions not as a predicate but as a referring singular term.

[10] Since the paralogisms are supposed to be 'necessary inferences of reason,' it is important for Kant that the premises are a priori. For the purposes of a philosophical reconstruction and defense of the Rational Sources Account, however, it may be sufficient if the premises have strong intuitive appeal, so that rational inquirers will tend to accept them unless they encounter arguments against them.

unconditioned if we consider that a substance (in the required 'absolute' sense of a bearer of predicates that is not a predicate of something else) is the unconditioned condition of its attributes (in the sense that the attributes inhere in the substance, which does not inhere in anything else).[11] Since, as rational thinkers, we are interested in finding unity in the manifold of empirical cognitions, we are also interested in finding the unconditioned condition of the manifold of our representations (all of which are conditioned by inhering in a thinking subject; A397). As Kant indicates in the Appendix (A648–50/B676–8), we can unify the manifold of psychological phenomena by attributing different phenomena to common faculties. Finally, however, we must ask whether these faculties are in turn attributes of one underlying substance. The first paralogism seems to offer an a priori guarantee that this is so. In this sense, it is a 'necessary inference of reason,' not just because its premises are a priori, but also because it is part of our striving for the unity of reason.

While the Supreme Principle does not feature explicitly in the first paralogism, it is clearly at work in the background. This can be brought out by reformulating the first paralogism as follows:

P1   If there is something that is R-conditioned, there is a totality of its R-conditions, which is R-unconditioned (= Supreme Principle).
P2   A totality of conditions is either a case of UCC or a case of TCC.[12]
P3   My representations exist as inherence-conditioned by me (that is, by the thinking being in which they inhere).
P4   I, as a thinking being, cannot properly think of myself as a representation or property that inheres in something else.
P5   What cannot properly be thought of as a representation or property that inheres in something else is not a representation or property that inheres in something else.
C1   I, as a thinking being, am the unconditioned inherence-condition (UCC) of my representations.
P6   Something that is an unconditioned inherence-condition is a substance.
C2   I, as a thinking being, am a substance.

While P4 roughly corresponds to the minor and P6 to the major premise of the first paralogism, without the additional premises, including the Supreme Principle, they do not imply C2 (which is the conclusion of the first paralogism). Thus, if we make explicit the thought that a substance, as understood by the rational psychologist, is something unconditioned (a thought Kant is

---

[11] Moreover, a substance$_2$ (see note 8) is unconditioned also because it continues to exist through all changes to its attributes and therefore does not "naturally arise [or] perish" (A349).
[12] 'TCC' stands for 'totality of conditioned conditions' and 'UCC' for 'unconditioned condition'; see Section 3.3.4.

clearly committed to), we must also make explicit that the inference depends on the Supreme Principle as its major premise.

In sum, Kant arguably makes a plausible case for the claims (a) that there is a natural tendency to conclude that we, as thinking beings, are substances and (b) that we thereby arrive at the concept of a thinking substance (which is the concept of something unconditioned, namely the unconditioned inherence-condition of its representations).

7.1.2 The Other Three Paralogisms

Next, let us briefly consider the other three paralogisms.

Second Paralogism
P1   What cannot be represented as a plurality is simple.
P2   I, as a thinking being (soul), cannot be represented as a plurality.
C   I, as a thinking being (soul), am simple (see B407–8; A351).

Third Paralogism
P1   What must represent itself as identical over time is a person.
P2   I, as a thinking being (soul), must represent myself as identical over time.
C   I, as a thinking being (soul), am a person (see B408–9; A361).

Fourth Paralogism
P1   A thinking being that must be represented as distinct from external objects is a spirit.
P2   I, as a thinking being (soul), must be represented as distinct from external objects.
C   I, as a thinking being (soul), am a spirit (B409).

In each of these inferences, a transcendental idea is derived from premises that, considered individually, do not yet contain that idea, namely the *simplicity*, *personality*, and *spirituality of the soul*. In each case, this idea can plausibly be understood as 'containing the unconditioned' (A311/B367), that is, as representing the soul as unconditioned in some respect. Thus, the soul as simple is not conditioned by any parts, the soul as person is not conditioned by its temporal segments, and the soul as spirit is not conditioned by matter.[13] Moreover, each of the premises in these inferences can be understood as an analytic truth. The major premises can be read such that they follow from the definition of 'simple,' 'person,' and 'spirit,' namely by reading the phrase

---

[13] While the conditioning relation between a subject and its representations at issue in the first paralogism is one of inherence, the conditioning relations at issue in the second, third, and fourth psychological ideas are species (or determinables) not of inherence but of dependence (Section 3.2.3).

'must be represented' as 'can be correctly/truly represented only as' (and 'cannot be represented' as 'cannot be correctly/truly represented'). For example, 'What can be correctly represented only as identical over time is a person' is an analytic truth that follows from the definition of 'person.' By contrast, the minor premises make explicit an aspect of what it is to think of oneself as a thinking being that at least appears to follow from the mere thought 'I think.' It seems to be a truism that in representing myself in the thought 'I think,' I represent myself not as a plurality but as the single subject of a plurality of representations, as thinking different thoughts at different times while still being the same thinker, and as distinct from 'my' body. Given the intuitive appeal of the minor premises and reason's inherent tendency to move from the conditioned (a manifold of representations at a given time; a succession of representations over time; representations depending on the body) to the unconditioned, it seems plausible that these are also 'necessary inferences of reason' in Kant's sense. Again, we can see the Supreme Principle in the background, since the relations of part–whole, temporal succession, and material constitution are all transitive conditioning relations that allow for 'ascending' series of conditions and thus require something unconditioned (in this case, an unconditioned condition or UCC), which we seem to find in the thinking subject mentioned in the minor premise.

The paralogisms are written in the vocabulary of eighteenth-century rationalist metaphysics; terms like 'soul' and 'spirit' are rarely used in current philosophy. This can make the claims the paralogisms argue for and the questions they respond to appear outdated. In fact, however, these questions about the nature of mind and self are very much alive, and the claims Kant reconstructs (in order to criticize them) still have ardent defenders. While the substance dualism of the first paralogism may not be very popular today, it is nevertheless extensively discussed in most introductions to the philosophy of mind (see e.g. Carruthers 2004; Stich and Warfield 2003; Beckermann 2008) and still has its advocates.[14] The unity of consciousness and the self (the second paralogism) is a live problem not only in the philosophy of mind but also in cognitive science (see Brook 2017), while the simplicity of the self or soul has recently been defended as part of an argument against materialism (Barnett 2010). The identity of the thinking subject over time has been intensely debated over the past sixty years (see for instance the papers collected in Martin and Barresi 2003), and philosophers such as Kripke and Chalmers have argued, against the broadly materialist mainstream in current philosophy, for the immateriality of the mind – the topic of the fourth paralogism (Kripke 1980; Chalmers 1996). This goes to show that the paralogisms

---

[14] E.g. Lowe 2006, who defends a 'non-Cartesian' substance dualism and claims that the Strawson of *Individuals* (Strawson 1959) was also a dualist in this sense.

are not arbitrary inventions from a different era but concern questions that, if Kant is right, will remain with us as long as people think rationally about themselves and their place in the world.[15]

7.2 Transcendental Illusion and Transcendental Realism in the Paralogisms

If the paralogisms are apparently valid inferences from analytically true premises, one might wonder why Kant takes issue with them. In this section, I will not try to provide a comprehensive account of Kant's critique of the paralogisms and will instead focus on those aspects of Kant's critique that allow us to reconstruct Kant's positive account of the paralogisms as 'necessary inferences of reason.' In particular, I will show how, according to Kant, transcendental realism is constitutive of the transcendental illusion involved in the paralogisms.

7.2.1 The Paralogisms as Fallacies

Kant's general diagnosis of paralogisms is that they involve a *sophisma figurae dictionis* (A402; see also B411): their middle term is ambiguous (9:135). Here is an example of a *logical* paralogism from Kant's logic lectures: "E.g., no artist is born [= no one is born as an artist]; some men are artists; hence some men are not born. In the *major* the *medius terminus* [artist] means the art, and in the *minor* the man" (*Hechsel Logic*, 410). Note that there are two ways to diagnose such a fallacy: either one can admit that both premises are true, in which case the inference is invalid because of the ambiguity of the middle term ('artist,' which in the major premise means the property of being an artist and in the minor a person who is an artist), or one can admit that the inference is valid, in which case the middle term must have the same meaning in both premises and, since then at least one of the premises turns out to be false, the inference is unsound. (In the example, the major premise is false, since it is untrue that no person who is an artist is born.) As we will see, Kant applies both kinds of diagnosis in the Paralogisms chapter.[16]

---

[15] Also see Kitcher 1990, 2011: ch. 15; Brook 1994, 2016; and the essays collected in Gomes and Stephenson 2017 for the current relevance of Kant's philosophy of mind.

[16] It is therefore misleading to say that according to Kant both premises of a transcendental paralogism are true (see e.g. Stuhlmann-Laeisz 1990; Malzkorn 1998; Proops 2010: 470). Rather, because of the ambiguity of the middle term, it is *possible* to read each premise such that it turns out to be true (but also to read it in a way that makes it false or unwarranted). Note that at A402 Kant does not say that both premises are true, but rather that we can call the paralogisms a '*sophisma figurae dictionis*' "*insofar as* they have correct premises" (emphasis added). There has been some debate about whether the transcendental paralogisms (some or all) are valid (see e.g. Bennett 1974: 72; Ameriks 2000: 48, 68) or, as Kant himself claims, formally

Now the 'transcendental' paralogisms Kant criticizes differ from a merely 'logical' paralogism because in their case there is a "transcendental ground for inferring falsely with respect to form" (*einen transcendentalen Grund: der Form nach falsch zu schließen*), which explains why "a fallacy of this kind will have its ground in the nature of human reason" (A341/B399). In keeping with the general account of transcendental illusion given earlier (Section 5.2.2), I take this to mean that even though the inferences are in fact fallacious, they *appear* valid and sound on the assumption of transcendental realism, since the ambiguity of the middle terms can only be detected if we distinguish between appearances and things in themselves.

It is not obvious, however, how to apply this general diagnosis to the individual paralogisms. In the first paralogism, for instance, the middle term is 'must always be represented as subject, not as a predicate.' What is the ambiguity involved here, and why does transcendental realism render it undetectable?[17]

7.2.2 Which Transcendental Realism for the Paralogisms?

On the interpretation of transcendental illusion developed in Chapter 5, transcendental realism is the view that there is a necessary correspondence between the principles of reason and the structure of (mind-independent) reality (TR_C). A tacit assumption of TR_C makes us mistake the transition from *logical* principles and concepts to the *regulative* use of the corresponding *transcendental* principles and concepts for a transition to their *constitutive* use (see Section 5.2.5). In brief, transcendental illusion consists in the tendency, based on TR_C, to think that the principles that govern rational thinking are true of reality itself.

But while there clearly is a logical/real transition to be found in the paralogisms, it seems to be a transition of the wrong kind for our interpretation of transcendental illusion. Consider how Kant sums up his critical discussion of the individual paralogisms in the B-version: "through the analysis of the

---

invalid (Klemme 2010: 144–7; see also Grier 2001: 154–6; Thöle 2010: 102–3). This debate presupposes that a paralogism must be *either* valid *or* invalid. Given that a paralogism can be diagnosed in the two ways indicated earlier, however, this assumption is mistaken. Read one way, a paralogism is valid but not sound; read another way, it is sound but invalid. Either way, it is fallacious. One might object that on the second kind of diagnosis the ambiguity of the middle term does not play a role and is therefore not compatible with Kant's general claim that the paralogisms rest on a *sophisma figurae dictionis*. That is not the case, however, since on the second kind of diagnosis the ambiguity explains how an otherwise patently false premise can appear to be true. Thanks to Fabian Burt for raising this worry (see also Rosefeldt 2017: 231 for a similar objection).

[17] Recall that Kant does not claim that the dialectical fallacies themselves are inevitable (as Malzkorn 1998: 109–10 seems to assume). What is inevitable is only the *illusion* of their validity, not the *error* involved in accepting their conclusions (see Grier 1993, 2001).

consciousness of myself in thinking in general not the least is won in regard to the cognition of myself as object. *The logical exposition of thinking in general is falsely held to be a metaphysical determination of the object"* (B409; emphasis added; see also A350). The phrase 'logical exposition of thinking' refers to the minor premises of the paralogisms, which only make explicit what is contained in the 'logical' representation 'I think,' which is "wholly empty" of content (A345/B404), while 'metaphysical determination of the object' refers to the conclusion as intended by the rational psychologist. Kant's thought therefore seems to be that in moving from the premises to the conclusion *we make an illicit transition from the logical to a real (transcendental, metaphysical) use of the representation 'I think.'*[18] Specifically, we move from a 'logical' to a 'metaphysical' reading of the middle term in the minor premise of the paralogisms.

If transcendental realism is understood as the claim that the structures of reason and reality are necessarily in agreement, however, this does not explain the transcendental illusion involved in the paralogisms. After all, the 'I think' and its logical properties are not part of the logical use of *reason* specifically, but rather part of what Kant calls the "logical use of the understanding" (A67/B92 and B138–9). When Kant characterizes the 'I think' as merely logical, this is meant to emphasize its 'emptiness' – the fact that it abstracts from all content and merely concerns the form of consciousness, its formal unity.[19] But this does not make the 'I think' part of the logical use of *reason* (even though it must be able to accompany all my thoughts, including all inferences of reason). If the 'I think' and its logical properties are not part of the logical use of reason, however, transcendental realism (TR$_C$), which concerns the agreement between *reason* and reality, cannot explain why we do not recognize that the predicates in question are taken in an empty logical sense in the minor premise and in a robust transcendental or real sense in the major premise and the conclusion.[20]

---

[18] This has been repeatedly noted in the literature; see e.g. Anderson 2015: 289, with references to Grier, Ameriks, and Proops.

[19] Rosefeldt 2017 reads 'logical' in the Paralogisms chapter as meaning something like 'represented in mere thinking, not in intuition.' (I slightly simplify; see Rosefeldt 2017: 236 for his detailed analysis.) I think this reading is too narrow because it does not cover the other parts of the Transcendental Dialectic and, more importantly, misses the central point that 'logical' in the Transcendental Dialectic connotes abstraction from objects (see Section 1.1.5).

[20] Could we perhaps explain the transcendental illusion in the paralogisms by appeal to transcendental realism in its generic form (the lack of a distinction between things in themselves and appearances) by saying that in the *major* the rational psychologist speaks of the soul as a thing in itself, while in the *minor* he is really speaking about an appearance of inner sense (without noticing the difference)? This cannot be correct, however, since on Kant's own considered view the *minor*, if read so as to be true, is not about an appearance of inner sense but rather the 'I think' of transcendental apperception (see e.g. A343/B401), which is neither a thing in itself nor an appearance. Therefore, transcendental realism in its generic form does not help here either.

The solution to this problem lies in the recognition of an even wider and more general sense of transcendental realism than TR_{pos} and TR_C (see 5.2.3). Kant gives us a hint when he says, before turning to the individual paralogisms, that "we must necessarily ascribe to things a priori all the properties that constitute the conditions under which alone we can think them" (A346/B405). Kant appeals to this principle to explain why we think that something we know only from our own case must also hold for all other thinking beings. In fact, however, its relevance is much wider. We naturally take the necessary conditions under which we represent things to be conditions of those represented objects. For instance, if the only way I can represent a thinking being is to represent it as a substance, then I will (tend to) assume that it *is* a substance. Put more generally:

PR   If, in order to represent o at all, S must represent o as being F, then S will (tend to) take o to be F.

This is a 'psychological' principle in that it concerns how subjects tend to objectify the subjective conditions of representation. It explains, for instance, why we naturally attribute colours to objects even though (at least according to the predominant theories of color) they are merely features of how we represent objects, and why we tend to think that an object that makes us feel afraid must be dangerous. To this psychological principle corresponds an ontological one, which, if true, would epistemically justify a subject's functioning according to PR:

TR_{rep} If, to be represented at all (by finite beings like us), some object o must be represented as being F, then o is F.

While PR is a principle to which Kant, as we have just seen, explicitly commits himself as part of an account of how human beings actually think, TR_{rep} is a principle that Kant rejects, at least in its general and unrestricted form.

The Transcendental Deduction of the categories effectively argues that TR_{rep} holds only for objects of possible experience. Even though the categories (for human and other finite beings) are conditions of the possibility of representing objects as such (B128), they are conditions of the possibility not of objects in general but only of those that can be given to us in experience: "The conditions of the *possibility of experience* in general are at the same time conditions of the *possibility of the objects of experience*" (A158/B197; see also B147–8). This principle is a restricted version of TR_{rep} – restricted to objects of experience. For instance, it has the consequence that if I must represent every event that I experience as caused, then it follows that every empirical event has a cause (see B232–4). By contrast, if I must think of everything conditioned as being conditioned by something unconditioned (because that is how reason works), it does *not* follow that there is something unconditioned for everything that is conditioned, because the conditions of *thinking* something are not necessarily conditions of the things that are thought. The reason for this difference is that for Kant empirical objects are mere appearances, the features of which depend (in some appropriate sense) on how we represent them, while this is not true of objects in general. Since appearances are representation-dependent objects, the conditions of representing them 'carry over' to the represented objects. Things in themselves, by contrast, are not representation-dependent; we therefore cannot assume that what holds for appearances according to Kant – namely that "*subjective conditions of thinking* should have *objective validity*" (A89–90/B122) – also holds for things in themselves. Kant's *transcendental idealism*, with its distinction between things in themselves and appearances, can thus be understood as restricting the intuitively plausible (but in its generality unwarranted) principle TR_{rep} to empirical objects and their experience. Viewed from this angle, *transcendental realism* (as the denial of transcendental idealism) is the view that TR_{rep} holds unrestrictedly.[21] Thus even though TR_{rep} is different from TR_{pos} and TR_C, treating the former as a version of transcendental realism does not mean that there is a variety of unrelated doctrines that Kant happens to associate with transcendental realism. Rather, as I will continue to argue later (Section 9.1), TR_{pos} and TR_C can plausibly be viewed as specific versions of TR_{rep}.

7.2.3 Kant's Diagnosis of the Paralogisms

If we now return to the Paralogisms chapter, we can see that it is transcendental realism in the sense of TR_{rep} that underlies the transcendental illusion of the paralogisms. These dialectical inferences of reason rest on the illicit assumption that the conditions under which we must represent something are conditions of the represented object. More specifically, they rest on the assumption that we can infer properties of the soul from the 'logical' conditions of the representation 'I think.' However, as Kant argues in the Transcendental

---

[21] In a *Reflexion* from the early 1780s, Kant insists that his transcendental idealism is meant to avoid the "transcendental *vitii subreptionis*," which consists in "*making one's representations into things*" (18:279, *Refl.* 5642; emphasis added). Kant can also be read as appealing to TR_{rep} in his account of the transcendental illusion involved in the arguments for God's existence: "For, just as with space, ... even though it is only a principle of sensibility, it is necessarily held to be a something subsisting in itself with absolute necessity and an *a priori* object given in itself, so it also comes about entirely naturally that since the systematic unity of nature cannot be set up as a principle of the empirical use of reason except on the basis of the idea of a most real being as the supreme cause, this idea is thereby represented as an actual object" (A619/B647). See also *Progress*, where Kant explains the transcendental illusion involved in the transcendental ideal by saying that we "make this subjective condition of thinking into an objective condition of the possibility of things in themselves" (20:302).

Deduction of the categories (and reminds us right before turning to the individual paralogisms; B406–7), such a move is legitimate only when the object in question is given in intuition and thought in accordance with the (schematized) categories. As Kant points out in his critique of the individual paralogisms, neither of these conditions is satisfied in the conclusions of the paralogisms: the 'I think' is a purely discursive representation that is not based on intuition (A349–50; A356; B408; B413), and the categories invoked in the paralogisms, such as the category of substance, are used "only as a function of synthesis, without an intuition being subsumed under it, hence without an object" (A356; see also A349; B407). This is why we cannot infer properties of the soul from the 'I think.'[22]

That the transcendental illusion involved in the paralogisms is based on TR$_{rep}$, according to Kant's diagnosis, can also be seen from the varying formulations in which he insists that, in the case of the 'I think' (unlike the case of appearances), we cannot infer properties of objects from the conditions of their representation:

[T]he formal proposition of apperception, I think, ... must always be regarded as a *merely subjective condition in general* [of a possible cognition], *which we unjustly make into a condition of the possibility of cognition of objects*, namely into a concept of a thinking being in general. (A354; second emphasis added)[23]

Thus the rational psychologist assumes, in accordance with TR$_{rep}$, that the 'I think,' which according to Kant is only a subjective condition of representing anything at all, is the representation of an object (namely a thinking being). Similarly, Kant's brief critique of each of the four individual paralogisms (B407–9) has as its recurring theme the notion that we cannot infer from how we *represent* ourselves in the merely formal thought 'I think' (namely as a subject, singular, identical over time, and distinct from bodies) the properties of the represented *object* (substantiality, simplicity, personality, and spirituality), because we have no intuition of that object (see also A397–8; B421–2).[24]

This also helps to explain why Kant claims that the middle terms of the paralogisms are ambiguous. In the major premises, the middle term (e.g. 'must be represented as a subject') must be taken as a "metaphysical determination of

---

[22] See Rosefeldt 2017 for a similar reading.

[23] Kant continues: "because we are unable to represent this being without positing ourselves with the formula of our consciousness, in the place of every intelligent being." He thereby refers back to the context in which he had introduced PR, namely as an explanation of why we attribute features we know from our own apperception to all thinking beings (A346/B404).

[24] Ian Proops reads a specific instance of TR$_{rep}$ into the major premise of the first paralogism: "The major premise says, in effect, that if it is impossible to *conceive* of some entity as a property or mode, then that entity cannot *exist* as a property or mode" (Proops 2010: 472). While this is a possible reading of the major premise in B, it does not seem to apply to the A-version.

the object" (B409) if the conclusion is to follow in the sense intended by the rational psychologist. In the minor premises, however, these terms are merely "logical explication[s] of thinking in general" (B409). Kant himself takes the minor premises to be true because they are backed by his account of transcendental apperception (according to which the apperception accompanies all representations and is thus 'always subject,' 'unified,' 'identical over time,' and 'certain'; A106–8; B132–6). But of course, that cannot be why the rational psychologist, whose thoughts Kant reconstructs, takes them to be true. Rather, the rational psychologist must interpret both premises in light of TR_{rep}, such that 'what must be represented as F' is equivalent to 'what is F.' While Kant seems to grant the legitimacy of this reading when it comes to the major premises, he insists that it leads us astray in the minor premises; if the minor premises are supposed to be true a priori, they can only contain 'logical explications,' not substantial predicates.

For this reason, if both premises are true, the inferences are invalid (e.g. A341/B399; B411; A397–8) because of the ambiguity of the middle terms (which are read 'metaphysically' in the major premises and 'logically' in the minor ones). This is the kind of diagnosis that Kant applies in the brief discussion of the four paralogisms at B407–9, where he effectively insists that the conclusions do not follow because the minor premises only concern the "logical exposition of thinking" and not the "metaphysical determination of the object" (B409). Alternatively, if the inferences are valid (because the minor premises are also understood as containing 'metaphysical determinations of the object'), then the minor premises are unwarranted (because we cannot cognize 'real' properties of objects without intuition). Because he is oblivious to the ambiguity of the middle term, however, the rational psychologist does not notice that the minor premise – as he needs to understand it for the conclusion to follow – is unwarranted. This is the kind of diagnosis that Kant is working with when he insists that the correct understanding of the minor premise is only 'logical' (e.g. A349–50; A355), thereby rejecting the premise as false when read 'metaphysically.' Despite this difference, both approaches are versions of the same underlying diagnosis, according to which the inferences do not guarantee the truth of the conclusions because of an ambiguity of the middle term.

In sum, we have seen how Kant derives the psychological ideas, which like all transcendental ideas are 'inferred concepts,' in the four transcendental paralogisms. These are 'necessary inferences of reason' in that their premises are true a priori (and they contribute to achieving the unity of reason). They are fallacious, however, because they rest on the ambiguity of their middle terms, which, according to Kant, can be detected only within the framework of transcendental idealism. Conversely, this means that the transcendental illusion involved in the paralogisms rests on the assumption of transcendental realism, here in the form of TR_rep, which appears to warrant the transition from merely logical features of the representation 'I think' to real or transcendental predicates of the soul. This assumption is entirely natural, but according to Kant it is mistaken. Once transcendental realism is given up, the inferences of rational psychology can be seen for what they are, namely paralogisms.[25]

In this reconstruction of the paralogisms and the transcendental illusion involved in them we find a transition from the logical to the real use of reason in the form of an illicit shift from a 'logical' to a 'metaphysical' conception of the 'I think' (or, relatedly, from a logical to a metaphysical reading of the minor premises; or, alternatively, from a merely 'logical' minor premise to a 'metaphysical' conclusion). As I have argued, this transition or shift is explained by Kant by appeal to a version of transcendental realism (TR_rep). But note that the third element of our general template for Kant's arguments for the Rational Sources Account, the regulative/constitutive distinction, is missing from this reconstruction (and, it seems, from Kant's text). This is because in the context of the paralogisms, as was the case with the transition from the Logical Maxim to the Supreme Principle and the system of transcendental ideas in Book One, Kant postpones the introduction of that distinction until the Appendix. Only there will Kant point out that there is indeed a legitimate use of the idea of a soul as the concept of something unconditioned (substance, simple, person, spirit), but that this use can only be regulative. Even if Kant does not make this explicit in the Paralogisms chapter, however, it is clear that insofar as the paralogisms are supposed to prove the *truth* of their conclusions, these must be understood as *constitutive* claims about the soul, which is why (in accordance with the general template of Kant's argument) they rest on a tacit assumption of transcendental realism. That the same conclusions can also be read regulatively, in which case we use them to generate *hypotheses* about the nature of our souls, is a possibility that Kant does not raise until some 250 pages later (see A672/B700; A682/B710–A784/B712; see also A649/B677).

7.3 The Cosmological Ideas

Kant presents the four cosmological ideas, or "world-concepts" (*Weltbegriffe*; A408/B434), in the first section of the Antinomy chapter. There, his aim is not to derive these concepts themselves but "to enumerate these ideas with

---

[25] I do not want to claim, however, that this is the only way in which Kant criticizes the rational psychologist. Rather, there are various distinct strands of criticism, including the one recently stressed by Dyck (2014: 85–90), according to which the rational psychologist misunderstands the minor premises as empirical claims. I have focused here on the line of criticism that I take to be relevant to Kant's Rational Sources Account.

Table 7.1 *Table of Cosmological Ideas*

1. The absolute completeness of the **composition** of the given whole of all appearances
2. The absolute completeness of the **division** of a given whole in appearance   3. The absolute completeness of the **arising** of an appearance in general
4. The absolute completeness of the **dependence** of the **existence** of the alterable in appearance

systematic precision according to a principle" (A408/B435). As with the "topics" of rational psychology (A344/B402), Kant bases the "system of cosmological ideas" (A408/B435) on the order of the table of categories in combination with the threefold distinction between forms of inferences. According to Kant, the antinomies correspond to a series of hypothetical inferences. This cannot mean, however, that the arguments for the theses and antitheses are themselves *prosyllogisms* (series of syllogisms with hypothetical major premises), which they obviously are not. Rather, it means that reason moves from the fact that something is hypothetically conditioned and that there exists an ascending series of conditions (corresponding to an ascending series of hypothetical inferences) to the conclusion *that the series must be complete*.[26] Now Kant claims that under each of the four titles of the table of categories there is only one category that can generate a regress of hypothetical conditions, namely that of unity, reality, causation, and necessity (A411–15/B438–42). The details of this derivation need not concern us here since, as earlier, we shall set aside the question of the completeness and systematicity of Kant's system of transcendental ideas.[27] In any case, Kant arrives at the table of cosmological ideas (A415/B443) shown in Table 7.1.

While Kant's formulations of the four ideas may be somewhat obscure, the remarks that lead up to the table (and the antinomical arguments that follow) show that the cosmological ideas concern (1a) the complete series (or totality) of past temporal stages of the world and (1b) of surrounding spatial parts of the world, (2) the complete series of parts of a given material object, (3) the complete series of causes of a given event, and (4) the complete series of conditions of something contingent. Each of these ideas involves a series of subordinated conditions (and conditions of conditions, etc.) and has the completeness of that series as its object, which, qua totality of conditions, would have to be something unconditioned. So our question is why, according to Kant, we necessarily arrive at these ideas through inferences of reason.

---

[26] See Chapter 6, note 14.   [27] But see Schmucker 1990; Malzkorn 1999; Klimmek 2005.

7.3.1 The Metaphysical Deduction of the Cosmological Ideas

While the derivation of the four psychological ideas is straightforwardly identical to the four paralogisms, this cannot be true of the four cosmological ideas and the four antinomies because there are *eight* proofs of cosmological theses and antitheses in the antinomies. Nevertheless, in Section Seven of the Antinomy chapter, Kant argues that the cosmological ideas also rest on necessary inferences of reason:

> The entire antinomy of pure reason rests on this dialectical argument: If the conditioned is given, then the whole series of all conditions for it is also given; now objects of the senses are given as conditioned; consequently, etc. Through this inference of reason, whose major premise seems so natural and evident, *a corresponding number of cosmological ideas are introduced*, in accordance with the difference of the conditions (in the synthesis of appearances), insofar as they constitute a series, which *postulate an absolute totality of these series* and thereby put reason into an unavoidable conflict with itself. (A497/B525; emphasis added)[28]

Thus the general paradigm for the derivation of the cosmological ideas, which Kant also calls "the cosmological inference of reason" (A499/B527) and "the common argument (for the cosmological assertions)" (A501/B529), is this:

P1   If the conditioned is given, then the whole series of all conditions for it is also given.
P2   Empirical objects are given as conditioned.
C   The whole series of all conditions (the totality of conditions) for each empirical object is given.[29]

This inference gives us the concept of a *totality of conditions of an empirical object*, which is not explicitly mentioned by Kant in the Antinomy chapter (but

---

[28] See also A462/B490, where Kant, having presented the four antinomies, concludes: "Now we have before us the entire dialectical play *of the cosmological ideas*, which do not permit an object congruent to them to be given in any possible experience ... but which have not been thought up arbitrarily; reason, rather, in continuous progression of the empirical synthesis, *has been led to them necessarily* when it tries to liberate from every condition, and to grasp in its unconditioned totality, that which can always be determined only conditionally in accordance with rules of experience. These sophistical assertions are only so many attempts to solve four natural and unavoidable problems of reason" (emphasis added).

[29] Is P2 meant to be empirical or a priori? The same question arises for the other minor premises that figure in the proofs of the antinomy. If they are empirical, it is hard to see how they can figure in purely rational inferences as part of the Rational Sources Account. As Kant says at the beginning of Book Two, speaking about the dialectical inferences of reason in general, they "do not contain empirical premises" (A339/B397). A possible solution is to read these premises as hypotheticals: 'If empirical objects are given/exist, they are given/exist as conditioned,' which may well be thought to be a priori. Alternatively, one might hold that the rational cosmologist takes it to be an a priori truth that there are conditioned empirical objects. Kant explains that in the context of the antinomies, "appearances are here considered as given" (A416/B443), which can be read in both of the two ways just indicated. Thanks to Gabriele Gava for raising this issue.

see A340/B398) but which we can think of as the 'common title of all cosmological ideas' (in analogy to the concept of the unconditioned as the 'common title' of all transcendental ideas; see Section 6.1). Now this generic inference can be further specified 'in accordance with the difference of the conditions,' that is, in accordance with the different ways in which temporal stages and spatial parts of the world, divisible material objects, empirical events, and contingent existences are conditioned. In this way, we can derive *five* cosmological ideas. (This is one more than Kant himself recognizes, since it makes sense to distinguish between the temporal and the spatial completeness of the world, which Kant, mainly for architectonic reasons, seems to treat as one idea and discusses in one antinomy.) We can thus fill in the corresponding five inferences, which Kant himself alludes to in the quoted passage but does not state explicitly:

Completeness of Composition (Time)
P1   If the conditioned is given, then the complete series of its conditions is also given.
P2.1T   A temporal stage of the world, ts_0, is given as conditioned by a prior temporal stage, ts_{-1}.[30]
C1T   The complete series of temporal stages of the world prior to ts_0 is given.

The temporal stages prior to ts_0 form a series because the relation 'prior to' is transitive: if ts_1 is prior to ts_2 and ts_2 is prior to ts_3, then ts_1 is prior to ts_3. Therefore, any temporal condition of a temporal condition of ts_0 is a temporal condition of ts_0. The series of temporal conditions is complete if it contains *all* temporal stages prior to ts_0. In this way, we arrive at the transcendental idea of a *totality of temporal conditions of a given temporal stage of the world* (see Sections 3.3.2 and 3.3.3 on completeness and totality). Similarly for the other four cosmological ideas.

Completeness of Composition (Space)
P1   If the conditioned is given, then the complete series of its conditions is also given.
P2.1S   A spatial region of the world, r_1, is given as conditioned by a surrounding spatial region, r_2.
C1S   The *complete series of spatial regions of the world* surrounding r_1 is given.

Completeness of Division
P1   If the conditioned is given, then the complete series of its conditions is also given.
P2.2   A material object o is given as mereologically conditioned by its first-order parts.
C2   The *complete series of parts of a material object o* is given.

---

[30] 'P2.1T' stands for: second premise of the first paralogism with respect to time. Similarly for the other inferences.

Completeness of Arising
P1 If the conditioned is given, then the complete series of its conditions is also given.
P2.3 An empirical event *e* is given as conditioned by a cause.
C3 The *complete series of causes of an empirical event e* is given.

Completeness of Dependence
P1 If the conditioned is given, then the complete series of its conditions is also given.
P2.4 An empirical object *o* is given as contingent (i.e. as conditioned by a sufficient ground).
C4 The *complete series of the sufficient grounds of an empirical object o* is given.[31]

In each of these inferences, we derive a transcendental idea (italicized in the conclusion), namely the concept of a totality of conditions – temporal, spatial, mereological, causal, and modal conditions, respectively – of an empirical object. This idea is not explicitly mentioned in either of the premises and only occurs in the conclusion, which explains how Kant can claim that the cosmological ideas are 'introduced' through specific instantiations of the general form of the cosmological inference of reason. Note that while the idea of the world (conceived of as the totality of empirical phenomena) is already presupposed in the first two cosmological inferences, it is only the conclusions that give us the idea of the world as something unconditioned in various respects (temporal, spatial, mereological, causal, and modal).

This derivation of the cosmological ideas is highly intuitive. Its major premise is the (constitutive) Supreme Principle, which, Kant grants, is valid for things in themselves – that is, for objects that belong to a rational order of things. Given the background assumption of transcendental realism (TR_C), one can derive the Supreme Principle from formal features of rational thinking (the 'logical use of reason') (see Section 5.3). Even apart from that, however, the Supreme Principle can at least *appear* to be self-evident. (If something exists and is conditioned, isn't it obvious that all of its conditions must also exist?) The minor premises also look intuitively compelling. For instance, if it is Monday today, this presupposes that the previous temporal stage of the world (i.e. Sunday) has already passed. Also, there are certainly regions in space – such as the region occupied by my office – that depend on there being a region surrounding it – such as the region occupied by the building in which the office is located. Next, all middle-sized dry goods have material parts. Further, there are clearly events that have a cause. And finally, there are

---

[31] For a similar reconstruction of these inferences, see Malzkorn 1999: 104–5 (although Malzkorn does not use them to derive the cosmological ideas).

contingent things (such as myself) whose existence has a direct sufficient reason (e.g. the fusion of a particular ovum with a particular sperm cell). And from these intuitively plausible premises it at least *appears* to follow that *the complete series of conditions* (and conditions of conditions, etc.) for the conditioned empirical object in question must exist as well. For instance, if this region of space depends on there being a space that encompasses it, and that on an even larger region surrounding it, etc., it appears to follow that if the original region exists, then *all* regions that condition it must exist as well. And if I exist, and that presupposes that my parents exist, and their existence presupposes that *their* parents existed, etc., then it appears to follow that *all* my ancestors must have existed; and similarly for the other cosmological ideas. It thus seems plausible that these are ideas rational thinkers will inevitably come up with once they begin to reflect rationally on the world around them.

7.3.2 Transcendental Realism in the Metaphysical Deduction of the Cosmological Ideas

As compelling as the inferences by means of which these ideas are derived may appear, Kant denies that they can be both sound and valid. As in the case of the paralogisms, Kant holds that they involve a *sophisma figurae dictionis* (see A500/B528): their middle term is ambiguous. As is also the case in the paralogisms, Kant claims that this fallacy can be detected only on the basis of his transcendental idealism, while the inferences must appear both sound and valid to the transcendental realist. Since Kant does not discuss the five individual inferences presented earlier, focusing only on the cosmological master argument they instantiate, he formulates his critique with respect to the former, but it clearly applies to the latter too.

Kant's analysis of the cosmological inference formally resembles that of the paralogisms: while the major premise is true only when the conditioned mentioned in it is a thing in itself (a *noumenon* in the positive sense), the conditioned mentioned in the minor premise is an appearance (since according to transcendental idealism, all empirical objects are appearances) (A499/B527). Hence, if both premises are true, the middle term ('the conditioned') is ambiguous; it refers to a different kind of object in each premise, and the inference is invalid. Alternatively, if the inference is to be valid, the minor premise must be read as being about things in themselves, in which case that premise is false, according to Kant, since empirical objects are appearances and not things in themselves (A500–1/B528–9). Thus, as in the case of the paralogisms, if the inference is read so as to be valid, it is unsound: its minor premise is false. The same analysis can be applied to the individual inferences that lead to the five cosmological ideas.

What role does transcendental realism play in generating the transcendental illusion involved in the 'cosmological inference of reason'? Given Kant's diagnosis, the true (illusion-free) form of the cosmological inference is as follows:

P1   If there is some R-conditioned thing in itself, then there is a complete series of its R-conditions.
P2   There are R-conditioned empirical objects.
C   There is a complete series of R-conditions (for each empirical object).

This inference is blatantly fallacious. How can transcendental realism explain why it nevertheless appears to be valid? The obvious answer is that the inference *is* valid if transcendental realism is added as a premise:

P1   If there is some R-conditioned thing in itself, then there is a complete series of its R-conditions.
P2   There are R-conditioned empirical objects.
TR   All empirical objects are things in themselves.
C   There is a complete series of R-conditions (for each empirical object).

Moreover, if TR is read as TR_{pos}, the inference will even appear to be sound, because (as we have already seen) P1 is analytically true for *noumena* in the positive sense (things in themselves that are members of a rational order) (see Section 5.3). Adding TR as a premise is only meant to illustrate the fact that given TR, an otherwise invalid inference turns out to be valid; it is not to say that some form of TR must play the role of an explicit premise in the minds of traditional metaphysicians or others who are prone to engage in cosmological speculation. Instead, TR will typically work as a tacit background assumption. Given that assumption, the two premises of the cosmological inferences will *appear* to refer to the same domain of objects (objects in general, *Dinge überhaupt*). The fact that the only conditioned objects we know of are empirical objects will not seem relevant to someone in the grip of transcendental realism. The transcendental realist will simply subsume empirical objects under the conditioned objects mentioned in the first premise (the Supreme Principle). Thus, TR_{pos} explains why the cosmological master argument and its specific instantiations *appear* valid and sound to the transcendental realist in all of us. At the same time, rejecting transcendental realism is sufficient to show that the cosmological inferences are fallacious, since without TR as a premise they are invalid, and without TR_{pos} as a background assumption their major premises cannot be known to be true.

7.4   The Antinomies

When Kant introduces the 'dialectical inferences of reason' at the beginning of Book Two of the Transcendental Dialectic, after claiming that the transcendental ideas arise from 'necessary inferences of reason' that, alas, involve an "unavoidable illusion" (A339/B397), he goes on to announce the antinomies as follows:

> The second class of sophistical inference is applied to the transcendental concept of absolute totality in the series of conditions for a given appearance in general; and from the fact that I always have a self-contradictory concept of the unconditioned synthetic unity in the series on one side, I infer the correctness of the opposite unity. (A340/B398)

This suggests that the individual arguments for the theses and antitheses of the four antinomies rest on a three-step procedure. In the first step, we derive, by way of the cosmological master argument, the 'transcendental concept of absolute totality in the series of conditions for a given appearance in general,' or what we earlier called the 'common title' of the cosmological ideas. This is the idea of a complete series of conditions of a conditioned empirical object (the concept of an unconditioned totality of conditions, UTC, as applied to empirically conditioned objects). In the second step, not explicitly mentioned by Kant in our quote, we derive the four (or five) cosmological ideas (the idea of a complete series of temporal and spatial, mereological, causal, and modal conditions of a given empirical object). In the third step, we arrive at four (or five) pairs of antinomical theses, because we can think of the complete series of conditions as either finite or infinite. We infer from the fact that we have a 'self-contradictory concept of the unconditioned synthetic unity in the series on one side' – either as finite or as infinite – 'the correctness of the opposite unity.'

As we saw in the previous section, the first two steps, even though they are not explicitly developed in the *Critique of Pure Reason*, can be reconstructed from what Kant says in Section Seven of the Antinomy chapter. Next, we will turn to the third and final step, which consists in the derivation of the pairs of antinomical theses.

7.4.1 The Rational Inferences Underlying the Antinomies

As with the paralogisms, it will be neither possible nor necessary for the purposes of this book to enter into a detailed interpretation and critical discussion of the Antinomy chapter and its arguments.[32] Instead, I will offer a schematic reconstruction of the four antinomies and restrict my discussion to the question of whether they also qualify as 'necessary inferences of reason' in

---

[32] Helpful reconstructions of the Antinomy chapter and of individual antinomies include Guyer 1987: 385–415; Schmucker 1990; Allison 1998; Ertl 1998; Kreimendahl 1998; Watkins 1998; Malzkorn 1999; Falkenburg 2000; Engelhard 2005; Wood 2010; Naeve and Pringe 2015; and Bird 2017.

the sense relevant to Kant's Rational Sources Account. As was also the case with the paralogisms, we will see that this focus on the Rational Sources Account opens up a distinct perspective on the Antinomy section.

Each antinomy consists of a pair of apparently contradictory statements – thesis and antithesis – about the complete series of conditions of a given empirical object. (As it turns out, the pairs of statements *appear* to be contradictory only if one presupposes transcendental realism.) While the theses claim, each with respect to a particular cosmological idea, that the complete series of conditions we think under that idea must be *finite*, the antitheses claim that it must be *infinite*. Put in terms introduced in Chapter 3, the theses claim that there must be an unconditioned condition (UCC), while the antitheses deny this and claim that there can only be an unconditioned consisting in the totality of *conditioned* conditions (TCC), which must therefore be infinite.[33] As Kant indicates in the quoted passage, each side of the antinomy appears to be compelling if we focus on the fact that the other side is self-contradictory. As is also evident from the actual arguments that Kant presents, this means that each side is proven indirectly, by rejecting the other side (which presupposes that the theses and the antitheses indeed form contradictory pairs). The general schema for a transcendental antinomy, represented as a pair of 'necessary inferences of reason,' is therefore as follows:

Thesis
P1   The complete series of R-conditions of an empirical object o exists.
PT   The complete series of R-conditions of an empirical object o cannot be infinite.
CT   There is a complete finite series of R-conditions of an empirical object o.

Antithesis
P1   The complete series of R-conditions of an empirical object o exists.
PA   The complete series of R-conditions of an empirical object o cannot be finite.
CA   There is a complete infinite series of R-conditions of an empirical object o.

Here, 'R-conditions' stands for one of the five conditioning relations that are at issue in the cosmological ideas.[34] Note that 'object' must be read widely here, as including temporal stages and spatial parts of the world as well as material objects and events. Under the initially plausible assumption that the complete series of R-conditions mentioned in P1 exists and must thus be either finite or infinite (an assumption that Kant eventually rejects), CT follows from P1 plus

---

[33] That both the theses and the antitheses assume the existence of something unconditioned is widely (but not universally) recognized in the literature; see Malzkorn 1999: 107, with further references.
[34] In the case of the antinomies, it seems that all four (five) specific conditioning relations are instances of the generic conditioning relation of dependence (see Section 3.2.3).

PT, while CA follows from P1 plus PA. Moreover, under that assumption, CT and CA must appear to be contradictory.

In each individual antinomy, P1, which is the same for both sides of the antinomy, is the conclusion of the inference, reconstructed above, by which the corresponding cosmological idea is derived. In the case of the temporal version of the First Antinomy, for instance, P1 is identical to C1T above, which was derived as follows:

P1   If the conditioned is given, then the complete series of its conditions is also given.

P2.1T   A temporal stage of the world, ts_0, is given as conditioned by a prior temporal stage, ts_{-1}.

C1T   The complete series of temporal stages of the world prior to ts_0 is given.

The corresponding antinomy now takes C1T as its major premise and adds on the thesis side:

PT.1   The complete series of temporal stages of the world prior to ts_0 cannot be infinite.

CT.1   There exists a complete finite series of temporal stages of the world prior to ts_0 ("The world has a beginning in time"; A426/B454).

By contrast, the antithesis side also starts with C1T as its major premise, but continues:

PA.1   The complete series of temporal stages of the world prior to ts_0 cannot be finite.

CA.1   There exists a complete infinite series of temporal stages of the world prior to ts_0 ("The world has no beginning ... but is infinite with regard to ... time"; A427/B455).

We can similarly fill in the specifics for the other antinomies.[35] In his synoptic presentation of the four antinomies (A426–61/B454–89), Kant first states the conclusions of each inference (as "Thesis" and "Antithesis," respectively) and then argues for the minor premises ("Proof").[36] The four (or five) antinomies

---

[35] For a different reconstruction of the 'formal structure of the antinomies,' see Wood 2010: 148–9. Wood sees 'a priori laws of experience' as motivating both the theses and the antitheses (for a similar claim, see Tetens 2006: 211–14). While I agree that Kant does occasionally appeal to laws of experience in his arguments for the antithesis side (e.g. A445–6/B473–4), this cannot be part of his argument for the Rational Sources Account, which requires that the antinomies emerge from the structure of rational thinking as such, independently of laws of experience (even if they are a priori).

[36] On this reconstruction, each thesis and antithesis consists of two subtheses: (i) there is a complete series of R-conditions, and (ii) this series is finite (thesis) or infinite (antithesis). This twofold structure is explicit in some of Kant's formulations of the theses and antitheses, but not

concern the cosmological questions (concerning 'the world' at large): whether there was a first moment in time (1T); whether physical space is finite (1S); whether there are simple objects (2); whether there are uncaused causes (3); and whether there are necessarily existing objects (4) (see A481/B509). These questions have been discussed since antiquity and continue to be controversial today.[37]

A full reconstruction of the antinomies as 'necessary inferences of reason' would have to discuss the Kantian 'proofs' of the theses and antitheses (that is, his arguments for PT and PA), which are meant to show that (under the assumption of transcendental realism) there are compelling a priori arguments for both the thesis and the antithesis of each antinomy. Kant's supposed proofs are highly complex, however, and there has been much debate, not just as to whether they are successful but also concerning how to understand them.[38] It would require a separate study to address them adequately. Instead, in the next section I will try to indicate why it is indeed *plausible* to assume that rational inquirers, because of their tacit commitment to transcendental realism, should find the theses and the antitheses of the antinomies equally compelling.

7.4.2   Transcendental Realism in the Antinomies

In Section Five of the Antinomy chapter, Kant provides a 'sceptical representation' of the antinomy, by which he means a representation that makes perspicuous why something is wrong with *both* sides of each antinomy, thus curing us of our desire for a 'dogmatic' resolution of the antinomy (which would show one side to be true at the cost of the other):

Accordingly, if I could antecedently see about a cosmological idea that whatever side of the unconditioned in the regressive synthesis of appearances it might come down on, it would *be either too big* or *too small* for every concept of the understanding, then I would comprehend that since it has to do with an object of experience, which should conform to a possible concept of the understanding, this idea must be entirely empty and without significance because the object does not fit it no matter how I may accommodate the one to the other. And this is actually the case with all the world-concepts, which is why reason, as long as it holds to them, is involved in an unavoidable antinomy. (A486/B514; emphasis altered)

---

all. In particular, the antitheses of the Second and Fourth Antinomies are formulated as purely negative claims that deny the existence of an unconditioned condition (simples, a necessary being). These formulations can be viewed as elliptical, though – as implicitly containing the corresponding positive claims (that there is an infinite series of parts and of contingent conditions).

[37] For the historical sources of Kant's antinomies, see Al-Azm 1972; Wood 2010; and, particularly for the second antinomy, Engelhard 2005.

[38] See the works referred to above in note 32.

Kant then goes on to apply this schema to each transcendental idea, arguing that if the "unconditioned in the regressive synthesis of appearances" thought under that idea is *infinite*, it is "*too big*" for a concept of the understanding, while if it is *finite* it is "*too small*" (A486–90/B514–18). Kant claims, for instance:

> *First*, [assume] that *the world has no beginning*; then it is too *big* for your concept; for this *concept, which consists in a successive regress, can never reach the whole eternity that has elapsed.* Suppose *it has a beginning*, then once again it is *too small* for your concept of the understanding in the necessary empirical regress. For since the beginning always presupposes a preceding time, it is still not unconditioned, and the law of the empirical use of the understanding *obliges you to ask for a still higher temporal condition*, and the world is obviously too small for this law. (A486–7/B514–15; final emphasis added)

This passage is perplexing in many ways. In particular, it is unclear why Kant focuses here on the *understanding* and its concepts and laws instead of focusing on reason.[39] But if we set this problem aside, we can find in this section the schema for an intuitively compelling explanation of why the idea of a totality of conditions of a conditioned empirical object can set us on a seesaw of contradictory conclusions. The first step is to recognize that 'the unconditioned' (that is, the unconditioned totality of conditions, UTC) can be thought of in one of two ways (A417/B445), namely as finite (terminating in a UCC) or as infinite (TCC) (Section 3.3.4). This means that once we have concluded from the Supreme Principle that, for a given R-conditioned empirical object, there must exist a totality of its R-conditions, the question arises whether this totality is finite or infinite. The second step is the recognition that if it is infinite we will never get a fully satisfactory answer to the question of why the object exists or why it has the R-conditioned property it has. After all, every R-condition we can point to raises the question of what *its* condition is since empirical objects as such, according to Kant, cannot be unconditioned. Thus, if the totality of conditions is infinite, we never reach what I earlier called an *ultimate* answer – one that does not raise further questions of the same kind (see Section 5.2.1). On the other hand, if the series of conditions is finite, we do not get an ultimate answer either, since with respect to *any* member of a series of conditions for an empirical object (including the final member) it makes sense to ask what *its* condition is (because, as Kant says in the quote, we are 'obliged to ask for a still higher condition'). Either way, we end up with further questions rather than an ultimate answer.[40]

---

[39] Kant appears to offer an explanation at the end of the section. He says, somewhat cryptically, that in this way he wanted to emphasize that the problem lies on the side of the idea of reason, not on the side of the concept of the understanding (A489/B517).

[40] Instead of 'ultimate answers,' Kant speaks of 'complete comprehensibility': "Thus the cosmological ideas are concerned with the totality of the regressive synthesis, and go *in antecendentia*, not *in consequentia*. If this latter happens, then that is an arbitrary and not a necessary problem of pure reason, because for the complete comprehensibility of what is given in appearance we

Against this kind of argument, it might be objected that it confuses epistemic and ontological issues. *If* the series of conditions is infinite, of course the series of possible questions of the form 'And what is the condition of *that* condition?' is infinite too. But this does not mean that the series of conditions cannot *be* infinite. And *if* the series of conditions is finite, then there is an unconditioned condition, even if we cannot help asking what *its* condition is. But this objection misses the point of the argument, which is not meant to show that a totality of conditions for a conditioned object is objectively impossible, but rather to explain why we, as rational inquirers, cannot rest content with either a finite or an infinite series of conditions. The reason is that either way, we will not get ultimate answers to our rational questions.

Consider the Third Antinomy (which concerns causation) as an example. Something, e, happens, and we ask *why*. Assume that we find out that e happened because of c, which is its cause. It now obviously makes sense to ask why c happened, since as long as we do not know why c happened we have not *fully* answered the question of why e happened. To fully answer the question of why e happened, we would have to answer *all* questions concerning its causes, the causes of those causes, and so on, because otherwise our answer will only be conditional: *given that* c happened, we understand why e happened, etc. But what we want is an unconditional answer that does not raise further questions of that kind – that is, an ultimate answer.

Now suppose that the series of causes of e goes back infinitely. It then follows that we will *never* have an ultimate answer, because no matter how far back we go in the series of causes, there will always be a further, yet unanswered question that is relevant to understanding why e happened. By contrast, suppose that c is the uncaused cause of e. In this case, *it still makes sense to ask why c happened*. On the one hand, this is because we can never be sure that we have reached an uncaused cause, since for this we must rule out the existence of a cause of c, and it is hard to see how we could achieve this. On the other hand, even if we knew that c was uncaused, this would not provide us with an ultimate answer to the question of why e happened, because it would still make sense to ask why c happened. (Think, for instance, of the Big Bang. Assuming that the Big Bang was itself uncaused and the cause of everything that followed, it seems that we can still meaningfully ask *why* the

---

need its grounds but not its consequences" (A411/B438). By contraposition, this means that the antinomies are necessary, not arbitrary, inferences because they concern something (namely the completeness of the series of hypothetical conditions) that is required for the "complete comprehensibility of what is given in appearance." (In the *Logic*, Kant explains that to "comprehend" is the highest degree of cognition, which is a priori and reserved for reason; see 9:65.)

Big Bang happened.)[41] Either way, our need for an ultimate answer to the question of why *e* happened remains unsatisfied.

This result may be disappointing to those who are interested in ultimate answers (that is, according to Kant, every finite rational being). We want such answers, but we are not going to get them. Things become truly tragic, however, once we add transcendental realism to the picture, which assures us that there must be an answer to every rational question (even if that answer is inaccessible to us) and hence that there will be ultimate answers to our questions about the conditions of empirical objects. In particular, given that bivalence is a fundamental principle of reason (see Section 5.2.4), transcendental realism assures us that for any meaningful claim, either it or its negation must be true: "Nothing seems clearer than that between the two, one of whom asserts that the world has a beginning, and the other that it has no beginning but has existed from eternity, one of them has to be right" (A501/B529). Even if in our time philosophers such as Michael Dummett have questioned the unrestricted validity of the principle of bivalence,[42] it can seem overwhelmingly plausible that for each of the four (five) pairs of antinomical statements about the world (when properly formulated so as to be contradictory), precisely one must be true and the other false.

With transcendental realism as a background assumption, we are forced into an antinomy. If the series of conditions of an empirical object is infinite, then there is no ultimate answer to the question of why it exists and has the properties it has, because its existence and properties are conditioned by an infinite series of conditions, each of which raises new questions as to its existence and properties. But since transcendental realism guarantees that an ultimate answer exists, we must conclude that the series is finite. On the other hand, if the series of conditions is finite, we will not get an ultimate answer either, because with respect to every condition, even if it is unconditioned, we can ask why it exists and has the properties it has. With transcendental realism as a background assumption, it follows that the series of conditions cannot be finite either. In sum, the very idea of an antinomy of reason is plausible and intuitive once we presuppose transcendental realism.

The intuitive character of the antinomies is confirmed by the fact that the cosmological questions Kant discusses are still debated in metaphysics and cosmology today. As a philosopher, I cannot competently speak about the

---

[41] See Kant's staggering claim, in the lecture transcript *Naturrecht Feyerabend*, that if we ask why something has value, the answer 'Because it pleases God' is not sufficient because we can ask 'Why does God's existence have a value?' (27:1321). Here, too, his point seems to be that it is *always* rationally possible to reiterate the original question.

[42] See Dummett 1978: xxx and 1978b, who identifies realism about some domain of objects with the acceptance, and antirealism with the denial, of the principle of bivalence for statements about that domain.

current state of cosmology and the question of whether time and space are finite or infinite, but the fact that there is no generally accepted 'theory of everything' (a theory that combines all four known fundamental physical forces) and that different candidates differ, among other things, in their accounts of space and time, clearly indicates that these questions have not yet been settled. Similarly for the other three antinomies. While some metaphysicians argue for (the necessity or actuality of) simple objects (objects without proper parts) and against 'gunk' (objects whose parts all have proper parts), others argue that gunk is possible or even actual (Hudson 2007). The question of whether there are uncaused causes or whether every physical event is caused is an open question, even if prevalent interpretations of quantum mechanics seem to favor the former option (Keil 2000; Hoefer 2016). Whether everything contingent is grounded in something that exists necessarily is also a question that has recently been taken up again in the debates about metaphysical grounding (e.g. Correia and Schnieder 2012) and the Principle of Sufficient Reason (e.g. Della Rocca 2010; Levey 2016). The currency of these issues (as well as the fact that they go back to antiquity) speaks in favor of Kant's claims that these are questions that arise not from the arbitrary preoccupations of individual philosophers or historical periods but from the very structure of rational thinking and that they will therefore stay with us as long as we reflect on empirical objects and the various ways in which they are conditioned.

7.5 Conclusion

In this chapter, we have seen how Kant reconstructs metaphysical speculation about the soul and the world as arising from and consisting in 'necessary inferences of reason.' Inferences motivated by reason's search for conditions for everything conditioned take us from (really or apparently) a priori premises to conclusions about metaphysical properties of soul and world and at the same time supply us with the 'transcendental ideas' of soul and world as being unconditioned in various ways. As I have argued, these inferences and their conclusions are highly intuitive, particularly when considered with transcendental realism as a background assumption. They reflect the discursive and iterative character of rational questions and reason's interest in completeness (the 'unity of reason,' 'ultimate' answers).

As was the case with the first two levels of Kant's argument for the Rational Sources Account (see Chapters 4–6), on this third level we also found that Kant reconstructs a transition from the *logical* to the *real* use of reason or, in the case of the paralogisms, of the understanding. In this latter case, this was the slide from 'logical' features of the 'I think' to 'metaphysical determinations' of the underlying subject. While this aspect is less prominent in the

Antinomy chapter, we do find Kant arguing that the Supreme Principle as applied to empirical objects expresses "nothing but the logical requirement of assuming complete premises for a given conclusion" (A500/B528), which we mistake for a claim about things in themselves. The principle "If the conditioned is *given*, then through it a regress in the series of all conditions for it is given to us *as a problem*" is a legitimate "logical postulate of reason" (A498/B526). It is only the transcendental and constitutive version of the Supreme Principle, according to which the series of conditions is not just given as a problem but "*given*" (A498/B526), that leads into metaphysical speculation.

Conversely, while transcendental realism and the distinction between regulative and constitutive principles are not explicitly mentioned in the Paralogisms chapter, both play a prominent role in the 'general' account of the resolution of the antinomies. As we saw in Chapter 5, Kant first argues that transcendental idealism is the 'key' to the resolution of the antinomies (which implies that the appearance of their cogency rests on the tacit assumption of transcendental realism) (see A490/B518–A497/B525) and then distinguishes between a legitimate regulative and an illegitimate constitutive version of the Supreme Principle (A508–9/B536–7). Clearly, it is the latter that is at work in the metaphysical speculation about the world that is critically reconstructed by Kant in the Antinomy chapter.

As I have argued, however, transcendental realism is implicitly appealed to even in the Paralogisms chapter in order to explain why the psychological inferences appear to be valid and sound. And while Kant postpones any discussion of a regulative use of the idea of the soul until the Appendix,[43] this is merely a matter of exposition. Concerning the *content* of Kant's account of metaphysical speculation, we find all three elements of the general template outlined earlier at work in the Paralogisms and Antinomy chapters, which at least implicitly appeal to a transition from the *logical* to the real or *transcendental*, the mistake of treating the latter as *constitutive* instead of *regulative*, and *transcendental realism* as the background assumption that makes this latter move seem admissible and even necessary.

---

[43] This raises the question of why Kant does mention the regulative/constitutive distinction in the Antinomy chapter. The answer is that Kant needs the regulative/constitutive distinction for his 'general' account of the resolution of the antinomies (A509–10/B537–8), which includes the claim that a regress from conditioned to condition, etc., is only regulatively required of us but not constitutively given. No such appeal was necessary for uncovering the transcendental illusion involved in the paralogisms.

8 Reason and Metaphysics in the Transcendental Ideal and the Appendix

In the first part of this chapter (Section 8.1), we will push forward to the very heart of speculative metaphysics, its account of God, and the alleged proofs of God's existence. In this way, we will conclude our discussion of the third level at which Kant argues in the Transcendental Dialectic that the sources of speculative metaphysics lie in reason itself (the Rational Sources Account). On this third level, after having discussed the idea of the soul in the Paralogisms and the idea of the world in the Antinomy, Kant turns to the idea of God and the rational inferences that appear to prove his existence. In the second part of the chapter (Section 8.2), we will then return to Kant's discussion of the metaphysical presuppositions of science in the Appendix to the Transcendental Dialectic, which constitutes the fourth and final level of Kant's Rational Sources Account, at which Kant explains the tendency to make constitutive use of transcendental ideas and principles in scientific investigations.

Again, within the limits of this book, it will not be possible to discuss in their own right Kant's treatment of rational theology in the Ideal and his account of science in the Appendix. Instead, I will have to limit my discussion to those aspects that are of immediate relevance to understanding and evaluating Kant's Rational Sources Account.

8.1 The Transcendental Ideal and the Natural Argument for God's Existence

As was the case in the Paralogisms and the Antinomy, Kant begins his discussion of rational theology in the Ideal of Reason with a section on the transcendental idea(s) in question. In this case, it is only one idea, the 'transcendental ideal,' which is the idea of an *ens realissimum* (or most real being). Following a brief section on the term 'ideal,' by which Kant means an idea '*in individuo*' (A568/B596) – that is, a concept that, despite being general (in the sense of representing its object through general marks), necessarily represents precisely one individual object – Kant turns to the derivation of the transcendental ideal in Section Two. In Section Three, he presents the one 'natural' argument for God's existence (on which the three philosophical arguments he famously criticizes try, unsuccessfully, to improve). This argument builds on the concept of an *ens realissimum* and connects it to the idea of a necessary being. I thus suggest that Kant's derivation of the idea of God should be read as falling into two parts: while the first part consists in deriving the concept of an *ens realissimum* (Section Two of the Ideal of Pure Reason), the second part transforms that notion into the idea of God by representing its object as necessarily existing (Section Three).[1]

8.1.1 The Transcendental Ideal

The section on the transcendental ideal is widely considered one of the most obscure and difficult sections in the first *Critique*, mainly, I think, because Kant seems to move back and forth between reconstructing the thoughts of the rational theologian and developing his own critical perspective on the relevant concepts and principles.[2] In what follows, I will be able to present only the main line of Kant's argument, with special attention to the transition from the logical to the real use of reason and the specific role played by transcendental realism, both of which have been largely ignored in the literature thus far.

Kant's derivation of the transcendental ideal comes in five steps, which I will briefly present in broad outline before taking a closer look at some of the individual steps. The first two steps clearly echo the transition from the Logical Maxim to the Supreme Principle, since Kant is contrasting (1) a "logical principle" (A571/B599) with (2) a transcendental principle that "concerns content, and not just logical form" (A572/B600). The former is the "principle of *determinability*," which says that, for all *concepts*, "of *every two* contradictorily opposed predicates only one can apply to it" (A571/B599). The latter is the "principle of *complete* [or 'thoroughgoing,' *durchgängige*] *determination*; according to which, among *all possible* predicates of *things*, insofar as they are compared with their opposites, one must apply to it" (A571–2/B599–600).[3] Now this latter principle (3) "contains a transcendental presupposition, namely that of the material *of all possibility*, which is supposed to contain *a priori* the

---

[1] Michelle Grier rightly rejects Strawson's claim that Kant offers two independent and incompatible derivations of the transcendental ideal (or the idea of God), one in Section Two of the Ideal chapter and the other in Section Three (Strawson 1966: 221–2; Grier 2001: 233). However, I disagree with Grier's understanding of how the two sections are related (see note 22).

[2] For a similar diagnosis, see Klimmek 2005: 164. Helpful discussions of the section on the Transcendental Ideal include Henrich 1960: 137–79; Rohs 1978; Wood 1978: 25–63; Ferrari 1998; Grier 2001: 234–51; Allison 2004; Klimmek 2005: 163–223; Longuenesse 2005b; Ricken 2010; Verburgt 2011; and Callanan 2017.

[3] Recall that Kant uses 'predicate' in both a 'logical' and a 'real' sense, that is, for predicates in judgments and for properties of things (see Chapter 7, note 4). I take this ambiguity to be harmless given that context allows us to disambiguate.

data for the *particular* possibility of every thing" (A572–3/B600–1). This "idea of the *sum-total of all possibility*" (A573/B601) in turn contains (4) the idea of an "All of reality (*omnitudo realitatis*)" (A575–6/B603–4), that is, the idea of a totality of positive predicates a thing can have (where 'positive' means something like 'not consisting in the mere negation of some other predicate'). We finally get to the transcendental ideal by (5) thinking of this totality of positive predicates as being instantiated in one individual object, the *ens realissimum* (A576/B604) or 'most real being,' where 'most real' means that it has all *realitas*, that is, all positive features a thing can possibly have.[4] In this way, Kant claims, the idea of an *ens realissimum* or transcendental ideal is implicit in human reason.[5] Insofar as it is considered the 'ground' of all possibility (A578–9/B606–7), the derivation of the transcendental ideal can also be read as an inference from the conditioned (possibility) to its unconditioned condition. The transcendental ideal is "the supreme and complete material condition of the possibility of everything existing" (A576/B604; see also A334/B391).[6]

Let us now look more closely at the first three steps of Kant's derivation of the transcendental ideal. Next, we will discuss the final three steps and ask whether the transcendental ideal, like the other transcendental ideas, can be considered an 'inferred concept' derived through a 'necessary inference of reason.'

8.1.2 The Principles of Determinability and Complete Determination

The 'logical' principle from which Kant starts, the 'principle of determinability,' can be formulated as follows:

PD   For every concept C and any predicate P (not contained in C), if P is added to the content of C, then not-P cannot also be added to its content (where 'not-P' is the contradictory opposite of P) (A571/B599).

This, Kant says, is "a merely logical principle, which abstracts from every content of cognition, and has in view nothing but the logical form of

---

[4] Kant does not seem to distinguish between *ens realissimum* and *ens perfectissimum*; for an explicit identification of reality and perfection, see A628/B656.
[5] See the four-step reconstruction in Grier 2001: 234–51 and the three-step reconstruction in Allison 2004: 398–405. While Grier's four steps roughly correspond to my steps 2–5 and Allison's three steps to my steps 3–5, Grier's and Allison's steps do not include the move from the logical to the transcendental principle (from 1 to 2).
[6] The derivation of the transcendental ideal is closely related to Kant's pre-critical argument for God's existence in his essay *The Only Possible Argument* from 1763. On that essay and its relation to the Transcendental Ideal, see e.g. Henrich 1960: 140–51; Wood 1978: 73–9; Fisher and Watkins 1998; Chignell 2009; Kreimendahl and Oberhausen 2011; Chignell 2012; Stang 2016: 99–149; Abaci 2017.

cognition"; in fact, it "rests on the principle of non-contradiction" (A571/B599). Assume, for example, that the concept of a human being contains only two marks, namely 'living being' and 'rational.'[7] This concept leaves 'indeterminate' whether a human being is a biped. According to PD, we can add to the concept of a human being either the mark 'biped' or the mark 'non-biped,' but not both.

Kant contrasts PD with a 'principle of complete determination,' which concerns not *concepts* but *objects*, and not *any* predicate but *all* predicates:

PCD For every object x and all predicates $P_1, P_2, \ldots, P_n$: (either P_1 is true of x or not-P_1 is true of x) and (either P_2 is true of x or not-P_2 is true of x) and ... (either P_n is true of x or not-P_n is true of x).

This formulation of PCD makes explicit its connection to the logical form of disjunctive judgments (A577/B605) and reason's preoccupation with completeness and totality since it consists in a supposedly complete list of disjunctions, one for each possible predicate. Thus, according to PCD, every object is "completely determined" (A573/601) insofar as, for every possible property, the object either has that property or lacks it. Put negatively, the principle says that there cannot be an object for which, with respect to a possible predicate, it is objectively indeterminate whether that predicate applies to it.[8]

Kant does not explain how PD and PCD are related; nor does he comment on their status beyond saying that the former is a logical principle and the latter is not. But given Kant's general strategy in the Transcendental Dialectic of deriving transcendental concepts and principles of reason from logical ones, it seems unlikely that mentioning a logical and a transcendental principle at the beginning of the Transcendental Ideal section is not part of that general strategy. In analogy with the transition from the Logical Maxim to the Supreme Principle (Section 4.3.1), this would mean that Kant wants PD to be read as a prescriptive maxim that 'becomes' a transcendental principle (PCD) by being descriptively applied to objects, which in turn can be done either regulatively and legitimately or constitutively and illegitimately.

While none of this is obvious, the text of the Transcendental Ideal section contains a number of indications that this is indeed the structure Kant has in mind. For one thing, Kant returns to PCD at the very end of the section in order to distinguish between a legitimate and an illegitimate version of it. There, Kant claims that PCD is valid for *empirical* objects, which are completely determined with respect to every possible *empirical* predicate (A582/B610; see

---

[7] For Kant's account of concepts in terms of marks, see the brief remarks in Section 6.2 and Watkins and Willaschek 2017.
[8] I assume that 'not-P is true of x' is equivalent to 'It is not the case that P is true of x'; that is, attributing the negated predicate is equivalent to negating the attribution of the predicate.

Rohs 1978; Longuenesse 2005b). With this, Kant can only have a regulative use of PCD in mind since empirical objects, as appearances, are not *given* to us as completely determined; that is, we do not experience them as being determined with respect to every possible empirical property.[9] Rather, Kant's view seems to be that, with respect to any empirical object and any of its empirical properties, it is at least in principle possible for us to find out empirically whether the object has that property. This means that we can use PCD as a regulative principle that generates, for every particular case, the disjunctive hypothesis that the object either has or does not have the property in question (e.g. that this material is either a metal or not; Section 4.2.2).[10]

Even though he does not explicitly invoke the regulative/constitutive distinction, Kant effectively claims that via a "natural illusion" we mistake this regulatively used PCD, restricted to empirical objects, for an unrestricted constitutive transcendental principle:

> consequently, nothing is an object *for us* unless it presupposes the sum total of all empirical reality as condition of its possibility. In accordance with a natural illusion, we regard as a principle that must hold of all things in general that which properly holds only of those which are given as objects of our senses. Consequently, through the omission of this limitation we will take the empirical principle of our concepts of the possibility of things as appearances to be a transcendental principle of the possibility of things in general. (A582/B610)

Even though Kant does not use the full terminological machinery he will employ some sixty pages later in the Appendix (see Section 4.2), we can see the same pattern at work here: there is a logical principle (PD), mentioned at the beginning of the section; there is a transcendental principle (PCD); and there is the distinction between a legitimate (regulative, empirical, immanent) use of that principle ('empirical' only insofar as the principle is applied to empirical objects, not with respect to its origin, which is rational) and an illegitimate (constitutive, transcendent) use. And, as in the case of the principles Kant discusses in the Appendix, the transcendental illusion consists not in the transition from the logical to the transcendental principle (which is

---

[9] Even though Béatrice Longuenesse does not employ the distinction between a regulative and a constitutive use of PCD, she also seems to assume that when applied to empirical objects, it can only be used regulatively: "So, from the standpoint of the Transcendental Analytic, the representation of a totum realitatis as the complete whole of positive determinations of things can only be a goal which reason sets to the understanding for the improvement of its knowledge, not an actually given whole" (Longuenesse 2005b: 220).

[10] In a later section of the Ideal of Reason chapter Kant explicitly claims, not concerning PCD but concerning the closely related proposition that the world was created by a supreme being, that it is a regulative principle of reason, which, however, is naturally mistaken for being constitutive (A619/B647).

Transcendental Ideal and Appendix (8.1.2)

legitimate and necessary), but in the transition from the regulative to the constitutive use of that principle.

While I think that Kant must have something like this structure in mind in the passage under discussion, it is less clear whether he is *justified* in applying it to the case at hand. In analogy to the transition from the Logical Maxim to the constitutive Supreme Principle, two questions arise: is it rationally necessary to make regulative and immanent use of PCD in order to follow PD? And why do we mistake the regulatively valid PCD for a constitutive principle of reason? Kant does not answer these questions, but given our reconstruction of the transition from the Logical Maxim to the Supreme Principle in Chapter 5, the following answers suggest themselves.

First, we must take into account the fact that PD, as Kant states it, is a principle not of reason but of the understanding; as Kant says, it is based on the principle of non-contradiction, which he associates with the latter (A151/B191). Moreover, it is stated not as a prescriptive maxim but descriptively. Thus, we have to take an additional step from PD to a corresponding maxim of reason (Section 4.2.2), which could be:

PD_{max} For every concept C and every possible predicate P (not yet contained in C), either add P to the content of C or add not-P to its content, but not both.[11]

Note that, in contrast to PD, this maxim quantifies over all predicates. (A maxim of adding *any* predicate to a concept hardly makes sense.) The idea behind this maxim is the Leibnizian notion of a 'complete concept,' explicitly mentioned by Kant in our context (A572/B600), which is a concept that represents an individual object by containing *all* predicates that hold of it. If, as Leibniz assumes, no two objects can have exactly the same properties, it follows that there can be only one possible object corresponding to each complete concept.[12] PD_{max} directs us to approximate such a concept by requiring that for every concept and every predicate, we add either that predicate or its negation to the concept's content. Since this is supposed to be a *logical* principle, we abstract from any relation to objects and do not assume a sum total of predicates; that is, we think of 'all' predicates 'distributively,' not 'collectively' (A582/610). This means that we can think of PD_{max} as containing an open-ended series of prescriptions of the form: 'With respect to a given concept C, if P_1 is a predicate, add either P_1 or not-P_1 to its content; and if P_2 is a predicate, add either P_2 or not-P_2; etc.' The aim of this procedure

---

[11] For a similar suggestion, see Klimmek 2005: 172.
[12] See e.g. Leibniz, *Discours de metaphysique*, §8. See Wood 1978: 42–50 for discussion of the Leibnizian background of Kant's PCD.

would be to develop maximally rich and detailed concepts with which to represent objects. We can understand this as part of reason's striving for 'unity of reason,' in line with the logical principle of specification (Section 4.2), which requires us to look for the subspecies of any species, thus developing ever more fine-grained concepts of species. PD_{max} can thus be understood as a means by which reason employs the understanding in its search for unity.

As is the case with other logical maxims (Section 5.1.1), however, reason cannot stop here and restrict itself to its logical use. Rather, we must hypothetically apply the logical maxims to reality itself. This is because, with respect to most empirical objects, we do not know which predicates might actually apply to them. We know that human beings are bipeds but not feathered. But are they electrically charged or neutral? Is their behavior determined by neural activity alone? Are they capable of living peacefully together? And how about this particular human being? Is it irascible or sanguine, physically stronger than average, susceptible to heart disease? In order even to be able to *ask* these questions, we must generate research hypotheses about objects and their determinations. Therefore, in order to apply PD_{max} (with its open-ended prescription to develop ever more determinate concepts) to reality itself, we must hypothetically assume that every object we can encounter – that is, every empirical object – *is* completely determined, which is the regulative version of PCD. But for this, we do not have to accept as true that every object is completely determined, which would be the constitutive version of PCD. All we have to do is adopt PCD as a general non-empirical research hypothesis that allows us to generate more specific empirical hypotheses about natural objects and their properties (Section 4.2.2). Thus, even though Kant does not supply us with the details, there is a plausible route from PD through PD_{max} to the regulative use of PCD, which answers our first question of why it is rationally necessary to make regulative and immanent use of PCD in order to follow PD.

To the second question of why we mistake the regulatively valid PCD for a constitutive principle of reason, Kant himself provides an answer (in the above passage), even though it is highly elliptical: "through the omission of this limitation [to objects of the senses] we will take the empirical principle of our concepts of the possibility of things as appearances to be a transcendental principle of the possibility of things in general" (A582/B610). Not limiting a principle's scope to objects of the senses and applying it to things in general (including things in themselves) is the hallmark of transcendental realism (with its identification of empirical objects with things in themselves) (Section 5.2.3). Thus, on Kant's diagnosis, we illegitimately take the regulative and 'empirical' principle to be constitutive, because we naïvely identify empirical objects with things in themselves – specifically with *noumena* in the positive sense. Given this identification, we take a principle that is valid only regulatively and only with respect to empirical objects to be constitutive and valid of objects in general, because we implicitly assume that reality itself (as a rational order) conforms to the principles of reason, such that the regulative principles of reason also hold constitutively.

In sum, we find that in the passages at the beginning and the end of the Transcendental Ideal section, Kant identifies a logical-transcendental transition that is similar to the transition from the Logical Maxim to the Supreme Principle, as well as a regulative-constitutive confusion similar to the one diagnosed in the Appendix. Moreover, this picture is rather plausible: we start with the idea of the determinability of a concept and move to the idea of a complete concept and a logical maxim of reason aimed at the formation of complete concepts. The application of this maxim to reality requires the hypothetical (regulative) use of the principle of complete determination, which, given transcendental realism, must then appear as a constitutive principle of nature.[13]

8.1.3 Kant's Derivation of the Concept of an ens realissimum

The next three steps from here to the concept of an *ens realissimum* (the transcendental ideal) are more straightforward, if perhaps philosophically less appealing. First, implicit in PCD is the idea of a totality of all possible predicates (step 3). Kant also calls it "the *sum total of all possibility*" (A573/B601), because all possible predicates exhaust all the possible ways things can be: it is the "*material of all possibility*, which is supposed to contain a priori the data for the *particular* possibility of every thing" (A573/B601). 'On closer inspection' of this sum total, however, we find that it does not contain *all* predicates or possibilities after all, but only the *primitive* ones – those that cannot be derived from others. In particular, we do not need to include in the sum total of all predicates those that are mere negations of already included predicates, since these will be automatically considered by PCD as well (because, with respect to every predicate, PCD refers to the disjunction of that predicate and its negation).

Next, Kant assumes (in the role of the transcendental realist) that in each pair of contradictory predicates there is one side that is objectively *positive*, while the other is derived by "transcendental negation" (A574/602). Darkness is only the absence of light, for instance, not itself something positive. In this way, we arrive at the notion of the sum total of *positive* predicates or 'realities' (*omnitudo realitatis*) (step 4).[14] And finally, in keeping with the Leibnizian

---

[13] If this is plausible as a reading of the Transcendental Ideal section, it shows that Kant does not claim that PCD is *true* of empirical objects, as many readers seem to assume (see e.g. Rohs 1978: 175).

[14] One might doubt that there is an objective distinction between 'positive' and 'negative' predicates. Consider, for instance, the predicates 'straight' (as in 'straight line') and 'bent.'

assumption that a complete concept singles out an individual object, the idea of a totality of positive predicates naturally leads to that of an *object* that *has* all these positive predicates: the *ens realissimum* or transcendental ideal (A576/B604) (step 5).

Before we discuss the plausibility of this derivation, let us briefly pause and consider the sense in which the transcendental ideal, like the other transcendental ideas, can count as an 'inferred concept' – that is, a concept derived by way of a 'necessary inference of reason' (see Section 6.2.2). No such inference is formulated in Section Two, where the transcendental ideal is derived. The only hint in the text is Kant's mention of a "transcendental major premise of the complete determination of all things" (A577/B605).[15] Unfortunately, Kant does not elaborate on the inference for which PCD is to serve as a 'transcendental major premise.' In particular, he does not name the minor premise and conclusion of this inference. If we permit ourselves to speculate, the derivation reconstructed here suggests that the essential step from PCD to the transcendental ideal in the conclusion must be the thought that the sum total of possibilities presupposed in PCD is the idea of an individual object. Hence, the inference might be formulated as follows:

P1   Everything is completely determined with respect to every possible predicate (= PCD).
P2   If P1, then there is a sum total of positive predicates (*omnitudo realitatis*).
C1   There is a sum total of positive predicates (*omnitudo realitatis*) (from P1, P2).
P3   The idea of an *omnitudo realitatis* is a complete concept that represents an individual object.
C2   There is a thing that possesses all positive predicates (*ens realissimum*) (from C1, P3).

Does straightness consist in the absence of bends (in which case it is a negative predicate)? Or is bentness a deviation from being straight (so that straightness is a positive predicate)? This question does not make much sense, and there is no reason to expect an objective answer to it. More generally, there will have to be many pairs of contradictory predicates with respect to which neither can plausibly be considered basic while the other is considered to be derived by negation, because it is the *pair* of predicates that is basic. A solution to this problem might consist in admitting disjunctive predicates (e.g. 'either bent or straight') as properly basic and thus as part of the sum total of all realities. For more on the problem of which predicates should be admitted to the *omnitudo realitatis*, see Chignell 2012.

[15] Before, Kant had reminded his readers that the "logical determination of a concept" (according to PD) rests on a disjunctive inference of reason (A576–7/B604–5; see also 9:129–30). Now Kant moves from the *logical* PD to the *transcendental* PCD by noting that the way in which a concept is "divided up" according to PD "agrees with" and is "analogous" to how the sum total of realities is thought of as "divided up" into predicates according to PCD (A577/B605). Thus, Kant is not saying here that the transcendental ideal itself is derived by way of disjunctive inference (see e.g. Wood 1978: 53). As Allison rightly insists, the reference to disjunctive inferences is meant merely as an analogy (Allison 2004: 401); see also Chapter 6, note 14.

Kant makes the move from P1 and P2 to C1 by saying, as already quoted, that PCD "contains a transcendental presupposition, namely that of the material of *all possibility*, which is supposed to contain a priori the data for the *particular* possibility of every thing" (A572–3/B600–1). And he argues for P3 by claiming the following (in the name of the transcendental realist):

> Through this possession of all reality, however, there is also represented the concept of a *thing in itself* which is thoroughly determined, and the concept of an *ens realissimum* is the concept of an individual being, because of all possible opposed predicates, one, namely that which belongs absolutely to being, is encountered in its determination. Thus it is a transcendental *ideal*. (A576/B604)

This means that we can find the elements of this inference, if not the inference itself, in Kant's text. In this sense, the transcendental ideal can plausibly be regarded as an inferred concept in Kant's sense. (Alternatively, as indicated earlier, it might be thought of as derived through an inference from the conditioned – the possibility of things – to the *ens realissimum* as its unconditioned condition.)

It might be objected that this derivation fails to show that an *ens realissimum* is 'really' (as opposed to merely 'logically') possible, since this would require that it does not contain any 'really repugnant' predicates (Wood 1978: 56–7; Klimmek 2005: 211–12; Chignell 2009). As Kant first explained in his 1763 essay *Negative Magnitudes*, real repugnance consists in two forces' being actualized while their effects cancel each other out. This means that God cannot have really repugnant predicates because otherwise he would be characterized by 'privation' (namely the canceled-out effects of the repugnant predicates), which is incompatible with only having positive features (2:85–6). Kant's solution in *Negative Magnitudes* is to insist that even the most real being does not possess *all* realities (all basic positive properties); rather, such a being is the *ground* of all reality (2:85; see also A580/B608).[16]

In the Transcendental Ideal section, Kant likewise claims that the *ens realissimum* grounds all possibility (Allison 2004: 403–4), and real repugnance was discussed in the Amphiboly section (A273/B329). In the first *Critique*, however, Kant does not seem to link these two topics in any way. Real repugnance is neither explicitly mentioned nor implicitly appealed to in the Transcendental Ideal section.[17] The reason, I think, is that Kant does not

---

[16] Andrew Chignell attributes to the Kant of *Only Possible Argument* the claim that all fundamental positive predicates can be co-instantiated in one object (Chignell 2009: 186), but the passage from *Negative Magnitudes* that he quotes as evidence (2:200–1) only contains the weaker claim that God cannot have really repugnant predicates. Kant appears to distinguish between these two claims and to reject the former at 2:85–6. For further discussion, see Chignell 2012.

[17] Kant says that predicates must be excluded from the sum total of possibility either when they are derivable from others or when they "cannot coexist with one another [*neben einander nicht*

need to commit himself to the claim that the transcendental ideal is really possible. In the Transcendental Ideal section, Kant is reconstructing the thoughts of the rational theologian. For this purpose, it is sufficient to show that the transcendental ideal is an idea of reason that can be derived by a 'natural inference of reason.' Of course, in order to count as an idea of reason, the ideal needs to be free of contradiction (logically possible). But it does not need to have objective reality, and, correspondingly, its object does not have to be 'really possible.'[18] At least in the context of the Transcendental Ideal, then, Kant does not need to be concerned with real repugnance, since he can allow that the ideal may well turn out to lack objective reality.[19] It is only when considered in a practical context that the problem of the objective reality of the ideal and the real possibility of its object will become relevant to Kant (and will be established by appeal to the alleged moral necessity of our belief in God).[20]

A further problem with Kant's derivation of the transcendental ideal concerns P3 – the claim that the idea of the totality of all positive predicates (*omnitudo realitatis*), if it represents anything at all, necessarily represents a single individual object (*ens realissimum*). Why should there not be two or more objects that instantiate all positive predicates? The answer, I want to suggest, is that P3 is plausible (only) against the background of a tacit assumption of transcendental realism (Section 5.2.3). Assume with TR$_{pos}$

---

stehen können]" (A574/B602), the latter of which is sometimes read as referring to really repugnant predicates (see e.g. Klimmek 2005: 211). When Kant goes on to explain this in more detail, however, only logical and 'transcendental' negations are discussed, not real repugnance, which suggests that the predicates that 'cannot stand next to each other' are logically contrary predicates (such as 'human' and 'inanimate'), since these logically exclude each other but cannot be 'derived' from each other like contradictory predicates ('human' and 'not-human'). Note that the distinction between logically contrary predicates and really repugnant predicates is vague and depends on the richness of the predicate in question. If the predicate 'human' is defined as 'rational animal,' and 'material being' as 'consisting only of matter,' the two predicates are not logically contrary but may well be really repugnant. If we should find out (empirically or by a priori reflection) that nothing that consists of matter alone can be alive, and if we add this to our concept of an animal (and thus to that of a human being), the two predicates turn out to be logically contrary after all. That our non-mathematical concepts can become more specific through scientific progress is a key element in Kant's account of definitions (A727–8/B755–6).

[18] See the resolution of the third antinomy, where Kant likewise does not commit himself to the real (but only to the logical) possibility of transcendental freedom (A558/B586).

[19] Relatedly, Wood and Chignell argue that in the first *Critique* Kant is agnostic about whether things in themselves can have really repugnant properties (Wood 1978: 59; Chignell 2009: 190). It might be objected that Kant speaks of the ideal as "faultless" (A641/B670). But since Kant goes on to say that he has neither proven nor refuted its 'objective reality,' 'faultless' can only mean that the ideal is not contradictory.

[20] See Kant's discussion of the objective reality of the idea of God in the second *Critique* (5:136), where he effectively says that mere speculative considerations (such as those discussed in the Transcendental Ideal section) do not suffice to establish the objective reality of transcendental ideas; see Willaschek 2010: 190–1.

that empirical objects are *noumena* in the positive sense and as such are parts of a fully rational order of things. If such an order is cognitively accessible to us at all, it is accessible through rational thinking alone, independently of sensible input. This means that if there are *noumena* in the positive sense, it must at least in principle be possible to represent each individual object that is part of that order without appealing to its sensible features. For human beings, this means representing individual objects through concepts alone, so that a maximally specific concept such as that of an *omnitudo realitatis*, if it represents anything at all, must necessarily represent precisely one individual object.

Thus, given transcendental realism, it would appear to follow that the idea of an *omnitudo realitatis*, the sum total of all basic positive predicates, singles out one possible individual object, namely the *ens realissimum*, which has all the positive features included in that sum total. This means that there is an intuitively compelling transition from the Principle of Determination to the idea of an *ens realissimum*. We start from the logical principle that for any given predicate and any concept, only the predicate or its negation can be added to the content of the concept, and we then turn this into a maxim to add, with respect to every predicate and every concept, either a given predicate or its negation to a given concept (PC_{max}). The aim behind this maxim would be the development of maximally specific concepts. In order to follow that maxim, we must assume, as a heuristic hypothesis, that every object is fully determined with respect to every possible predicate (PCD). This principle presupposes that it makes sense to speak of 'all predicates' an object might possibly have. Restricting our focus to predicates that are basic in the relevant sense, we arrive at the idea of the *omnitudo realitatis*, or sum total of all basic (and therefore positive) properties. It certainly *seems* that one can think of such a totality of basic properties. But if that is a possible thought we can think, so is the idea of an object that *has* all these properties. In this rather natural way, we arrive at the idea of an *ens realissimum*. (One may be more doubtful, however, about whether that idea necessarily singles out one individual.)

Now all this might suggest that Kant, in the Transcendental Ideal, has reconstructed an argument for the *existence* of an *ens realissimum*. However, Kant insists that this derivation of the transcendental ideal remains in the realm of concepts and representations and does not concern the *existence* of an *ens realissimum*:

It is self-evident that with this aim – namely, solely that of representing the necessary complete determination of things – *reason does not presuppose the existence of a being conforming to the ideal*, but only the idea of such a being, in order to derive from an unconditioned totality of complete determination the conditioned totality, i.e., that of the limited. (A577–8/B605–6; emphasis added)

Thus, what Kant takes himself to have shown so far is that rational thinkers naturally arrive at the idea of an *ens realissimum* and are thus in a position to ask themselves whether such a being exists, but not that they are necessarily tempted to *believe* that it exists. This may come as a surprise given that the conclusion of the inference presented earlier (C2) is precisely that the *ens realissimum* exists. But note that this conclusion only follows if the major premise of the inference, PCD, is taken to be constitutive and not merely regulative. When Kant says, in the quote, that reason 'presupposes the idea of such a being (*ens realissimum*)' in order to derive the complete determination of finite objects, he may mean that we treat PCD as a regulative principle and the idea of the *ens realissimum* as a regulative idea. If that is correct, Kant's derivation of that idea should be understood as hypothetical: if we want to think of objects as completely determinate, we must presuppose the idea of an *ens realissimum*. That this is indeed Kant's view is confirmed when, two pages later, he says:

Meanwhile this use of the transcendental idea [in transcendental theology] would already be overstepping the boundaries of its vocation and its permissibility. For on it, as the concept of all reality, reason only grounded the thoroughgoing determination of things in general, without demanding that this reality should be given objectively, and itself constitute a thing. This latter is a mere fiction, through which we encompass and realize the manifold of our idea in an ideal, as a particular being; for this [i.e. realizing] we have no warrant, not even for directly assuming the possibility of such a hypothesis. (A580/B608)

While it is not easy to follow Kant's argument, it seems clear that the only legitimate use of the transcendental ideal that he recognizes here is its use as a (heuristic) 'fiction' and that his derivation of that idea should not be misunderstood as establishing its existence. It is only in Section Three of the Ideal of Reason chapter that Kant discusses the argument for the *existence* of the *ens realissimum*.[21]

In this way, the structure of the Ideal of Reason chapter parallels that of the Paralogisms and Antinomy chapters in that it first presents the transcendental idea(s) in question and only then moves to the 'necessary' but 'dialectical' inferences of reason that (a) lead to metaphysical assertions and (b) derive the respective transcendental idea(s). This parallel is obscured by the fact that, at

---

[21] I think the quoted passages show that some of the difficulties of understanding the Transcendental Ideal section come from the same source as those concerning the Transition Passage and the Appendix (4.3.2), namely that Kant in many passages does not explicitly distinguish between the regulative and the constitutive use of transcendental principles and ideas, which allows his exposition to remain neutral with respect to (or worse, to go back and forth between) his own critical take on these principles and ideas (which consists in recognizing only a regulative use as legitimate) and the thoughts of the rational metaphysician Kant reconstructs (who takes these principles and ideas to be constitutive).

the end of the section on the Transcendental Ideal, Kant already mentions the idea of God (but only once) and talks about 'hypostasizing' and 'realizing' that idea (A580/B608). This seems to be a mere anticipation, however, since, as we will now see, the second part of that derivation (the identification of the *ens realissimum* with God) requires more argument than is provided in the Transcendental Ideal section. It is only this additional argument that delivers the transcendental idea of God.[22]

8.1.4 The Natural Argument for God's Existence

This takes us to the second part of Kant's derivation of the idea of God, which he presents in Section Three of the Ideal of Reason. Kant's critical reconstruction of rational theology centers on the notion of an absolutely necessary being and its relation to the concept of an *ens realissimum* (the transcendental ideal). Kant distinguishes between three possible types of speculative arguments for God's existence (A590–1/B618–19).

The Ontological Argument (see A596–7/B624–5)
P1   It is part of the concept of an *ens realissimum* that it necessarily exists.
C1   Denying the necessary existence of an *ens realissimum* involves a contradiction.
C2   The *ens realissimum* necessarily exists (= the *ens realissimum* is an absolutely necessary being).

---

[22] According to Grier, this section of the Ideal chapter continues the derivation of the ideal begun in Section Two by showing "why, given the inappropriateness of hypostasizing the idea, we are nevertheless somehow constrained to do so, and even further, to personify it" (Grier 2001: 233–4, 236). In fact, however, no reference to personification is made in Section Three. Since Kant had insisted that what is at issue in Section Two is only the idea as such, not the existence of its object (A577–8/B605–6), the function of Section Three rather seems to be to transition to the question of God's existence and thus to prepare the discussion of the three proofs of God's existence (see A584/BB612; A586–7/B614–15). In fact, Grier herself suggests a similar picture (Grier 2001: 251) but then reverts again to the two-step derivation picture (Grier 2001: 254). Relatedly, Grier puts much emphasis on the fact that according to Kant we 'hypostatize' the concept of an *ens realissimum* (A580/B608; A583/B611 n.), which she takes to mean that we assume that it represents an existing object, and she explains this as a specific case of transcendental illusion (Grier 2001: 245–50; see also Allison 2004: 405–10). But note that 'hypostasis' literally means 'underlying ground.' Thus, when Kant talks of hypostatizing the *ens realissimum* at A580/B608 he may simply be referring back to what he had said immediately prior, namely that we must regard the "highest reality" not as a sum total of the possibility of things but as their "ground." Similarly, it is possible to read the steps mentioned in the footnote at A583/B611 ('realised, hypostatized, personified') as concerning only the *concept* of the *ens realissimum* and not its existence; that is, we must *think* of the *ens realissimum* as an object that underlies all possibility and as a person, which is not yet to believe that it exists. Allison admits that the hypostatization as an argument for the *existence* of the *ens realissimum* at the end of Section Two is "transparently fallacious" on his reconstruction (Allison 2004: 410). By contrast, I think that any such argument (on behalf of the rational theologian) only comes in Section Three.

The Cosmological Argument (see A604–6/B632–4)
P1   If anything exists, there must be an absolutely necessary being.
P2   I exist.
C1   There is an absolutely necessary being.
P3   If something is absolutely necessary, it is an *ens realissimum*.
C2   The *ens realissimum* exists.

The Physicotheological Argument (see A625–6/B653–4)
P1   There is a qualitatively and quantitatively extensive amount of order and beauty in nature and its objects.
P2   Order and beauty in natural things is contingent and requires a cause that possesses proportionate intelligence and power.
C   There necessarily exists an intelligent and free cause of the world (which is the *ens realissimum*, that is, God).[23]

Kant discusses and rejects each of these arguments. While the Ontological Argument falsely infers from the possibility of an *ens realissimum* that such a being must exist, the Cosmological and Physicotheological Arguments infer from the existence of something contingent (e.g. my own existence or the existence of order in nature) the existence of a necessary being, falsely assuming that only the *ens realissimum* can be this necessary being (A608/B636; A629/B657). Now one might suppose that these three proofs are part of Kant's argument for the Rational Sources Account insofar as they are 'necessary inferences of reason' that arise naturally in the course of rational thinking and lead to metaphysical claims about something unconditioned. This is not the picture Kant presents, however. Rather, Kant makes it very clear that the Ontological Argument is "entirely unnatural, and a mere novelty of scholastic wit" (A603/B631), while he calls the Cosmological Argument an "artifice" (A610/B638) that, moreover, presupposes the Ontological Argument. Both proofs, according to Kant, are philosophical inventions, not natural expressions of common reason. In a sense, this is true even of the Physicotheological Argument, which Kant praises as "the oldest, clearest and the most appropriate to common reason" (A623/B651). As we will see, this praise is restricted to an abductive version of that proof, not to the supposedly deductive argument philosophers have made of it. The latter argument, according to Kant's diagnosis, in fact depends on both the Cosmological and the Ontological Arguments (A629–30/B657–8) and hence cannot be more 'natural' than they are.

According to Kant, there is only *one* 'natural' (speculative) argument for God's existence, which corresponds to the *one* theological idea (the transcendental ideal). Kant presents this two-step argument in Section Three of the Ideal of Reason, emphasizing repeatedly that "this is the natural course taken by every human reason, even the most common" (A584/B612; see also

---

[23] In English, this is commonly called the 'Argument from Design.'

Transcendental Ideal and Appendix (8.1.4)

A586/B614; A589/B617).[24] While the first step deductively infers the existence of a necessary being from the Supreme Principle and the existence of something contingent (A584/B612), the second is an abductive inference (or inference to the best explanation) to the conclusion that only an *ens realissimum* can play the role of a necessary being: "Thus among all the concepts of possible things the concept of a being having the highest reality would be *best suited* to the concept of an unconditionally necessary being" (A586/B614; emphasis added). Kant concludes:

> This, therefore, is how the natural course of human reason is constituted. First it convinces itself of the existence of *some* necessary being. In this it recognizes an unconditioned existence. Now it seeks for the concept of something independent of all conditions, and finds it in that which is the sufficient condition for everything else, i.e., in that which contains all reality [the *omnitudo realitatis*]. The All without limits, however, is absolute unity, and carries with it the concept of one single being, namely the highest being; and thus reason infers that the highest being, as the original ground of all things, exists in an absolutely necessary way. (A586–7/B614–15)

As a first approximation, we can formulate the first step of the 'Natural Argument' for God's existence as follows:

P1   If something exists contingently (the modally conditioned), then there must be something that exists necessarily (the modally unconditioned) (application of the Supreme Principle).
P2   There are objects that exist contingently.
C1   There is at least one necessary being (i.e. a being that necessarily exists).

This may look like a reformulation of the thesis side of the Fourth Antinomy (A452–4/B480–2). As Kant explains a little later, however, reason cannot be satisfied with either side of that antinomy – the thought of a necessary being in the world, on the one hand, and the thought of an infinite regress of contingent objects and events, on the other. He concludes that "you must assume the absolutely necessary *outside* the world" (A617/B645).[25] Thus, the first step of the Natural Argument must look something like this:

P1*   If something in the world exists contingently (the modally conditioned), then there must be something *outside the world* that exists necessarily (the modally unconditioned).
P2*   There are objects in the world that exist contingently.
C1*   There is at least one necessary being (i.e. a being that necessarily exists) outside the world.

---

[24] Recall that this two-step argument itself is only the second part of Kant's overall account of why it must appear rationally compelling to assume that God exists, the first part being the derivation of the transcendental ideal in Section Two.
[25] Here, 'outside' of course does not mean 'located in space outside of the world,' but something like 'distinct from the world and any of its parts.'

To this, Kant adds the second step, which starts from C1*:

C1* There is at least one necessary being (i.e. a being that necessarily exists) outside the world.
P3   The best possible candidate for a necessary being outside the world is the *ens realissimum*.
C2   The *ens realissimum* (= God as necessary being) exists.

P3 uses the transcendental ideal Kant had derived in Section Two and claims, plausibly enough, that it is the only concept we have of something (outside the world) that might conceivably exist with absolute necessity. After all, Kant had argued that the *ens realissimum* can be thought of as the unconditioned condition of all possibility (and hence as necessary) and as the ground and prototype of all things (and hence as distinct from the world that consists of these things).

8.1.5 Kant's Critical Diagnosis of the Natural Argument

As Kant insists, C1* and P3 together, even if true, do not guarantee the truth of the conclusion, because it is still possible that there are *other* necessary beings besides the *ens realissimum*, even if we are not aware of them or not aware that they exist necessarily:

> [I]t still cannot be inferred that therefore the concept of a limited being, which does not have the highest reality, contradicts absolute necessity ... Rather we are still at liberty to count all the remaining limited beings equally as absolutely necessary, even though we cannot infer their necessity from the universal concept we have of them. (A588/B616)

Thus, it does not follow that the *ens realissimum* exists, because we cannot be sure that it, and not something else, is the necessary being reason is looking for. The three possible deductive arguments for God's existence that Kant recognizes – the Ontological, Cosmological, and Physicotheological Arguments – are three different *philosophical* attempts to improve on the Natural Argument. While the Ontological Argument tries to derive the necessary existence of an *ens realissimum* from its very concept, both the Cosmological and the Physicotheological Arguments claim that only the *ens realissimum* can be a necessary being. In fact, the latter two arguments can both be understood as specific versions of the Natural Argument, in which P3 is substituted by a straightforward identification of the absolutely necessary being with the *ens realissimum*.[26] This would explain why Kant's official

---

[26] While the similarities between the Natural Argument and the Cosmological Argument are obvious (to the point that commentators have even identified the two; e.g. Allison 2004: 417),

account of the transcendental illusion involved in the Ontological and Cosmological Arguments (A614–20/B642–8) focuses exclusively on the first step of the Natural Argument. There, Kant locates the transcendental illusion, in a way that is already familiar to us, in the illegitimate transition from a regulative to a constitutive use of the transcendental ideal:

> The ideal of the highest being is, according to these considerations, nothing other than a *regulative principle of reason*, to regard all combination in the world as if it arose from an all-sufficient necessary cause, so as to ground on that cause the rule of a unity that is systematic and necessary according to universal laws; but it is not an assertion of an existence that is necessary in itself. But at the same time it is unavoidable, by means of a transcendental subreption, to represent this formal principle to oneself as *constitutive*, and to think of this unity hypostatically. (A619/B647; emphasis altered)[27]

Thus, Kant's central point is that instead of using the transcendental ideal regulatively, as a hypothesis that guides our search for unity in nature, we assert the existence of its object as 'necessary in itself.' Even though Kant does not explain here what the 'transcendental subreption' that makes us represent a 'formal' (i.e. logical) principle as constitutive consists in, we know from our discussion of the transition from the Logical Maxim to the constitutive Supreme Principle that it is the assumption of transcendental realism that accounts for this transcendental illusion.[28]

Of course, that is not the only fault Kant finds with the Natural Argument. As we have seen, he insists that it is at best an abductive argument and thus does not guarantee the truth of its conclusion. There are more problems with this inference than Kant mentions, which, however, he includes in his discussion of the Cosmological Argument and which apply equally to the Natural Argument (A609–10/B637–8). First, as a specific version of the Supreme Principle, P1* is valid only as a regulative, not as a constitutive, principle and hence cannot be known to be true. Second, the inference from P1* and P2*

---

it is less obvious that Kant also meant the Physicotheological Argument to be a fleshed-out version of the Natural Argument with a strengthened third premise. That this is indeed what Kant has in mind can be seen from the fact that he repeatedly takes care to identify the phenomena from which the Physicotheological Argument infers the existence of God, such as the order and beauty in nature, as "contingent" (*zufällig*) (A627/B655; see also A622/B650; A625/B653; A629/B657). They are contingent insofar as they are conditioned and call for an explanation in terms of a sufficient reason, which according to the Supreme Principle can only be a necessary being. In this way, Kant makes clear that the Physicotheological Argument is only a special form of the Natural Argument (with its focus on a necessary being).

[27] As we have seen, mistaking regulative principles for constitutive ones, according to Kant's own account, is not strictly speaking 'unavoidable.' So by 'representing ... as constitutive' Kant must mean the transcendental illusion (which, according to Kant, *is* unavoidable), not the error it suggests. Thanks to Pavle Kufrin for prompting this clarification.

[28] At A389, Kant calls transcendental realism (the identification of empirical objects with things "truly subsisting independently of us") a "subreption." On Kant's pre-critical and critical use of the term 'subreption,' see Grier 2001: 57–65, 239–47, and Birken-Bertsch 2006.

to C1* rests on the ambiguity of the middle term, since the 'conditioned' in P1* is a thing in itself, while in P2* it is an empirical object.[29] Third, in C1* we falsely assume that we have arrived at a positive conception of a necessary being by simply doing "away with every condition, without which, however, there can be no concept of any necessity" (A610/B638). Finally, the proof confuses a 'logical' with a 'transcendental' concept of necessity.

This latter point is elaborated in Kant's critique of the Ontological Argument, where he insists that the only notion of absolute necessity we have is logical (concerning the necessity of *judgments*), not real or transcendental (concerning the necessity of *objects*): "the absolute necessity of the judgment is only a conditioned necessity of the thing" (A593/B621). For instance, the judgment that all triangles have three angles is absolutely necessary because it rests on the Principle of Non-Contradiction. But the necessity of a particular real triangle is only conditional: *if* it exists, it must have three angles. Therefore, we cannot make coherent sense of the concept of a being that exists necessarily.[30] In fact, according to Kant, the Ontological Argument with its inference to a necessary being from the possibility of an *ens realissimum* provides the only possible way to elucidate that concept (A595–6/B623–4). And since that argument is flawed, so is the concept of absolute *real* necessity.[31]

8.1.6 Conclusion

In this section, we have seen how Kant derives the concept of an *ens realissimum* and reconstructs a 'natural' argument for God's existence based on that concept. Given that reason generates the notion of an *ens realissimum*, Kant provides a plausible route to the claim that such a being exists, and exists necessarily, by linking it to the general thought that if there is something contingent, then there must be something necessary that grounds it. This thought is a version of the Supreme Principle and generates a transcendental illusion in the same way the latter does, namely by being mistaken for a constitutive principle and being made the major premise of a fallacious inference. The concept of God (thought of rather abstractly as the necessarily

---

[29] See Kant's similar critique of the paralogisms and the antinomies, considered in Chapter 7 above.

[30] But see e.g. Stang 2016: 122–28 for a more positive discussion of Kant's conception of absolute real necessity.

[31] Kant's diagnosis of the Ontological Argument is that it involves an illicit transition from the *logical* to the *real* use of reason, in this case from logical to real necessity (A592–6/B620–4), from the logical possibility of a concept to the real possibility of its object (A596/B624 n.), and finally from a logical to a real predicate of existence (A598/B626). Thus, Kant's famous line that being is not a "*real* predicate" (A598/B626; emphasis added) is just another instance of the general pattern Kant uses to reconstruct, and diagnose, traditional metaphysics.

existing *ens realissimum*) is a necessary concept of reason, and under the assumption of transcendental realism we are naturally, though perhaps not inevitably, led to believe that its object must exist.

We found that Kant hints at a transition from a logical to a transcendental principle of reason at the beginning of the Transcendental Ideal section and sees a logical/transcendental transition at work in the Ontological Argument. Kant also mentions a regulative function of the concept of God and seems to allude to a regulative use of the PCD. However, neither the regulative/constitutive distinction nor transcendental realism are very prominent in Kant's reconstruction of the thoughts of the rational theologian. The reason for this is that Kant will explain the regulative role of the idea of God only later, in the Appendix, to which we turn now.

8.2 The Constitutive Use of Ideas and Principles in the Appendix

We finally arrive at the fourth and final level of Kant's development of the Rational Sources Account in the Transcendental Dialectic, namely his account in the Appendix of the constitutive use that we are necessarily tempted to make of transcendental (and other) ideas and of transcendental principles related to them. Since we have already dealt with the first part of the Appendix extensively (Section 4.2), we will only briefly recall those main points from the first part that are relevant here and then turn to the second part. While the Appendix had long been neglected, in recent decades there has been a surge of interest in Kant's philosophy of science and the regulative function it ascribes to principles and ideas.[32] But note that our focus here is different, since with respect to the Rational Sources Account, I am primarily interested not in regulative ideas and principles but in what explains their illusory *constitutive* use in science.

8.2.1 Part One of the Appendix: Principles

In the first part of the Appendix, entitled "Of the Regulative Use of the Ideas," Kant introduces the three principles of *homogeneity* (for every two species, there is a common genus) (A651–4/B679–82), *specification* (for every species, there is more than one subspecies) (A654–7/B682–5), and *continuity* (for every two species, there is a mediating species) (A657–8/B685–6; A660–1/B688–9). Each principle comes in a logical and a transcendental version. While the logical principles concern unity among our cognitions and are subjective and methodological (A648/B676), economical

---

[32] See the literature cited in Sections 4.2.1 and 4.2.2.

(A653/B681), and prescriptive (A652/B680), the transcendental principles concern nature itself (e.g. A653/B681) and are objective and descriptive (A648/B676). Kant insists that the logical principles presuppose the transcendental ones (A654/B682; A656/B684; A660/B688) and points out (toward the end of the section) that the transcendental principles can be legitimately presupposed only when used *regulatively*, not *constitutively*. To use a principle constitutively is to take it to be true of a given domain of objects. To use it regulatively is to assume it hypothetically (without committing oneself to its truth) and to derive empirical hypotheses from it. In this way, the principle can guide our inquiry into nature toward a unified system of natural knowledge (see Section 4.2).

But since a principle must be descriptive if we are to derive hypotheses from it, the regulative principles must not be confused with the logical ones, which are prescriptive and merely tell us to *look* for common genera, subspecies, and mediating species among the concepts and cognitions we already possess (Section 4.2.2). The reason these logical principles presuppose the regulative use of the transcendental ones is that we need to go beyond our current concepts and cognitions in order to achieve what the logical principles aim at, namely the unity of reason: a complete system of scientific knowledge (Section 5.1.1). We need to look for *new* (i.e. as yet unknown to us) genera and species, and in order to look for these we need empirical hypotheses, which are generated in accordance with the regulatively used transcendental principles. All this, according to Kant, is rationally necessary and completely legitimate. We succumb to transcendental illusion only when we take the regulative principles to be constitutive – that is, when we believe that, for all natural objects, there really *is* a common genus, that there *is* a mediating species for any two species, and that for any species there really *is* more than one subspecies.

This is in keeping with Kant's general account of transcendental illusion as mistaking subjective principles for objective ones. This illusion is caused by transcendental realism, that is, by the implicit assumption that nature is a rational order that necessarily conforms to the principles of reason. Put crudely, according to transcendental realism nature really is as reason leads us to expect it to be. Given this assumption, transcendental principles of reason must appear to be not just regulative but constitutive. What drives our falsely taking the principles of reason to be constitutive is reason's interest in a unified system of knowledge, on the one hand, and transcendental realism, on the other, since the latter creates the illusion that nature must necessarily satisfy reason's interest. Nevertheless, Kant insists that the transcendental principles, when used regulatively, make a positive contribution to empirical knowledge and the unity of reason, which secures them some (indeterminate) objective reality.

8.2.2 Part Two of the Appendix: Ideas

Even though the first part of the Appendix bears the regulative use of 'ideas' in its title, after the first couple of pages it is only the three principles of homogeneity, specification, and continuity that Kant seems to be concerned with. It is only in the second part of the Appendix, entitled "On the Final Aim of the Natural Dialectic of Human Reason" (A669/B697), that Kant finally turns to the three ideas of soul, world, and God, arguing that they too have a legitimate regulative use and, because of that, "some, if only indeterminate, objective validity" ("*einige, wenn auch nur unbestimmte objektive Gültigkeit*") (A669/B697).[33] This kind of objective validity or reality

> is not to consist in the fact that it relates straightway to an object (for in such a signification we would not be able to justify its objective validity); rather, it is only a schema, ordered in accordance with the conditions of the greatest unity of reason, for the concept of a thing in general, which serves only to achieve the greatest systematic unity in the empirical use of our reason, in that one derives the object of experience, as it were, from the imagined object of this idea as its ground or cause. (A670/B698)

In other words, ideas of reason gain objective validity by representing not a real object but an 'imagined' one, from which we 'derive' the empirical object in much the same way as we derive empirical hypotheses from regulative principles. As Kant explains this function of ideas at the beginning of Part One of the Appendix, the idea works in analogy with a *focus imaginarius*, that is, with the imagined focal point of light rays *behind* the physical surface of a mirror, where an object seen in the mirror appears to be (although of course it is actually *in front* of the mirror) (A644/B672).[34] Similarly, an idea presents us with an imagined object that, if it were real, would lend unity to *nature*, and that, as imagined, lends unity to our *understanding* of nature. Just like the transcendental principles, the legitimate use of ideas can only be regulative, not constitutive (A671/B699).

Kant then goes on to apply this thought to the three kinds of transcendental ideas (psychological, cosmological, and theological), claiming in each case that we must regard nature *as if* there were a substantial simple, personal, and

---

[33] For helpful discussion that also explicitly considers the second part of the Appendix, see e.g. McLaughlin 2014; Massimi 2017. Unfortunately, Kant does not explain how the regulative function of principles and that of ideas are related. Are the ideas meant to guide the use of the transcendental principles, or are these meant to be two distinct ways of pursuing the unity of reason? Note that the first part of the Appendix picks up where the Introduction to the Transcendental Dialectic ended and adds that the Supreme Principle and the other transcendental principles that fall under it are only of regulative and not of constitutive use. Similarly, part two of the Appendix takes the three kinds of ideas introduced in Book One and adds that they are only of regulative and not of constitutive use.

[34] See Grier 2001: 37–8 for the Newtonian origin of this analogy.

spiritual soul that unifies our psychological states; *as if* there were a world infinite in space, time, causation, and the series of its modal conditions; and *as if* there were a God who lends unity to all possible experience (A672–3/B700–1; A682–6/B710–14). According to Kant, this unifying role is the real cognitive content of our ideas (A674/B702). As he insists, we do not have any understanding of the soul, the world, or God considered as objects in themselves, but only in their relation to the systematic unity of cognition and nature. Thus, we can only assume the existence of these objects "relatively" (that is, in their relation to experience), but not "absolutely" (in itself) (A676/B704) – not because we cannot know whether these objects exist, but because we cannot even make sense of them unless we relate them to what we know: "in a word, this transcendental thing [the object of the idea] is merely the schema of that regulative principle through which reason, as far as it can, extends systematic unity over all experience" (A682/B710). (As we know from Chapter 5, this 'regulative principle' is none other than the regulative Supreme Principle.) As Kant puts it crisply with respect to the relative assumption and regulative employment of the idea of God as the author of a teleologically ordered nature, "in this way we can make a lot of discoveries" (A687/B715), since it makes us look for phenomena we would not have otherwise expected.

Kant warns us against falsely employing the ideas constitutively, since this leads into two false research strategies, which Kant calls "lazy reason" and "perverted reason" (A689/B717; A692/B720). The former consists in appealing to metaphysical explanations without looking for empirical causes, the latter in naïvely projecting a teleological order onto nature. Both mistakes ultimately consist in taking "the regulative principle of the systematic unity of nature for a constitutive one" (A693/B721). Kant offers the following explanation for this mistake:

Hence the idea of it [systematic unity] is inseparably bound up with the essence of our reason. The very same idea, therefore, is legislative for us, and thus it is very natural to assume a corresponding legislative reason (*intellectus archetypus*) from which all systematic unity of nature, as the object of our reason, is to be derived. (A694–5/B722–3)

Even though Kant does not mention transcendental realism explicitly, the explanation of the transcendental illusion involved in the constitutive use of the idea of systematic unity (and with this, of the other regulative ideas) is the same as the explanation at work in the other parts of the Transcendental Dialectic. The idea of systematic unity is essential to human reason since it is already part of the logical use of reason. This idea is 'legislative' for us – that is, it provides us with regulative principles for our inquiries into nature – but it is 'very natural' to take these principles to be constitutive: to believe that there must be systematic order in nature itself because we think of nature as the creation of an *intellectus archetypus*, an intuitive intellect that imposes a rational order on the world that it both represents and, in the same act, creates. In other words, we think of nature as a rational order consisting of *noumena* in the positive sense (which Kant defines as the objects of an intellectual intuition) (B307).[35] Thus, we find that in the Appendix Kant explains the transcendental illusion involved in the constitutive misuse of the (transcendental) ideas by appealing to TR$_{pos}$ (the claim that empirical objects are *noumena* in the positive sense and part of a rational order).

In sum, we are naturally led to assume that there are real objects corresponding to our ideas of soul, world, and God because we are not aware that these ideas are merely products of our own reason that do not respond in any way to objective features of reality, but only to the subjective need of reason for unity and systematicity of knowledge. This illusion can be explained by appeal to transcendental realism, which makes us assume that reality is as reason expects (or needs) it to be and therefore mistake the 'imaginary,' merely intentional 'objects' of these ideas for something real. According to Kant, however, the function of the transcendental ideas is not to represent independently existing objects (A681/B709), but only to guide our search for unity in nature and thus to approximate a complete system of scientific knowledge.[36] Of course, there is much more to be said about the positive role in science that Kant attributes to the transcendental ideas (e.g. Massimi 2017; Kraus in press), but that is a topic that goes well beyond the role the ideas play in Kant's account of the rational sources of metaphysics, which is our focus here.[37]

---

[35] Even if Eckart Förster is right to say that with respect to §77 of the third *Critique* we must distinguish between the concept of an 'intellectual intuition' and that of an 'intuitive intellect' (Förster 2011: 154), it seems that an *intellectus archetypus* will have non-discursive but still non-sensible representations of things in themselves and in this sense is also an intellectual intuition.

[36] This means that I do not agree with Grier and Allison, who claim that transcendental illusion has a positive epistemic function in that it makes possible the regulative use of transcendental ideas (e.g. Grier 2001: 287–9; Allison 2004: 425). The regulative use of these ideas consists in regarding empirical phenomena *as if* they were grounded in the objects of these ideas. There is nothing illusory in this kind of use, as long as we are aware of what we are doing. The illusion sets in only if we are tempted to mistake regulative principles and ideas for constitutive ones, which we are if we implicitly assume transcendental idealism (for a related criticism of Grier's and Allison's reading, see Massimi 2017). Admittedly, Kant does say that the illusion which consists in taking the ideas of reason to represent objects is "indispensably necessary" (A644–5/B672–3), but this may just be the result of his overly literal interpretation of the *focus imaginarius* metaphor.

[37] On the regulative use of the ideas, see also the papers collected in Dörflinger and Kruck 2011.

8.2.3 Conclusion

While the central aim of the Appendix is to lay out the positive use to which the principles and ideas of reason can be put, at the same time it is part of Kant's extended argument for the Rational Sources Account. Kant shows how the metaphysically innocent and rationally necessary use of *logical* principles takes us to metaphysical or *transcendental* principles that are naturally thought of as being constitutive of nature, and he argues that our attempt to unify empirical cognitions into a complete system of scientific knowledge is guided by the ideas of soul, world, and God, which are also naturally mistaken for constitutive ideas (that is, ideas of independently existing objects). The first part of the Appendix argues that rational beings must try to approximate a complete system of scientific knowledge of nature and that this enterprise naturally leads them to accept as true certain metaphysical claims (that nature itself is systematically structured, that there is a common genus for any two species, etc.). The second part argues that in order to approximate such a system of knowledge, we must employ certain ideas of reason, which quite naturally leads us to assume that there are real objects corresponding to them. But it is important to see that this latter step is one that Kant himself does not embrace, because the only legitimate use we can make of these transcendental principles and ideas is regulative, not constitutive. Thus, Kant pursues two aims in the Appendix: outlining the legitimate use we can make of transcendental principles and ideas and reconstructing the thoughts of a traditional metaphysician as part of an apparently rational but deceptive line of reasoning. But while these two projects are clearly distinct, Kant does not always keep them separate insofar as their first step (from the logical to the real use of reason, from logical to transcendental principles, from the logical forms of inference to the transcendental ideas) is the same. It is only in the second step (thinking of the transcendental principles and ideas as constitutive rather than regulative) that the two projects differ. This would seem to explain some of the difficulties readers encounter when trying to understand Kant's position in the Appendix to the Transcendental Dialectic. Given the general interpretation of the Transcendental Dialectic developed here, however, we can see that it exhibits the same structure as the other parts of the Transcendental Dialectic (and Kant's argument for the Rational Sources Account): first, Kant takes us from the logical to the real use of reason; second, the latter is naturally understood to be constitutive but is defensible only when taken to be regulative; and third, it is the tacit assumption of transcendental realism that explains why we move from the regulative to the constitutive use of reason's principles and ideas.

9 Transcendental Realism and Kant's Critique of Speculative Metaphysics

In this book, we have reconstructed Kant's account of the rational sources of speculative metaphysics (the Rational Sources Account). In this final chapter, we will complement our picture by turning to Kant's *critique* of metaphysics insofar as it reacts specifically to features of metaphysical speculation that figure prominently in the Rational Sources Account, namely the tacit assumption of transcendental realism, the discursivity of reason, and the subjective origin of transcendental ideas. In this way, we will return to issues first introduced in Chapter 1 (see particularly Section 1.2.2).

We can distinguish at least three levels in Kant's critique of speculative metaphysics. First, there is the general result of the Transcendental Analytic, according to which human cognition is limited to empirical objects and from which it follows that we cannot have cognition of supersensible objects. Second, there is Kant's critique of the metaphysical arguments (the paralogisms, the arguments for the theses and antitheses of the antinomies, and the arguments for God's existence) and their conclusions in the course of the Transcendental Dialectic. And third, there is his critique of transcendental ideas (conceptions of God, the soul, and the world) as lacking (determinate) 'objective reality,' that is, as not representing objects.[1]

It may seem that all three levels of Kant's criticism of metaphysics depend on his transcendental idealism (TI) – that is, on the claim that empirical objects are mere appearances and not things in themselves (A369; A491/B519). TI may seem to ground the first level of critique because according to Kant it is precisely their status as appearances that makes cognition of empirical objects possible and their status as things in themselves that makes the objects of speculative metaphysics unknowable. TI can seem to ground the second level

---

[1] Saying that transcendental ideas do not represent objects may sound more radical than necessary. Of course, the transcendental ideas, according to Kant, are not inconsistent and thus represent logically possible objects. However, they lack objective reality and therefore do not represent really possible objects (see e.g. A596/B624 n. for the distinction between logical and real possibility and Chignell 2009, 2012, and Stang 2016 for Kant's account of real possibility). Even that latter claim may sound more radical than necessary; I will defend it later, in Section 9.4.

of Kant's critique of metaphysics because that critique consists in unveiling the transcendental illusion at work in the inferences of speculative metaphysics. This illusion depends essentially on transcendental *realism* (see Chapters 5–8), which Kant rejects by relying on his own (independently motivated) transcendental *idealism*. And even the third level of Kant's critique may seem to presuppose TI, since the failure of transcendental ideas to represent objects is explained by the fact that the objects they purport to represent are individual things in themselves, of which, according to TI, we cannot have representations.

Against such a picture, which admittedly captures Kant's own understanding of his critique of speculative metaphysics, I will argue that, as a matter of philosophical argument, all three levels of his critique are independent of transcendental idealism. Rather, the first level depends on a different aspect of Kant's philosophy, namely his claim that cognition (in finite beings) requires sensible intuition, from which it follows that we cannot have cognition of the supersensible. In this way, the first level of Kant's critique of metaphysics responds to a feature of metaphysical speculation that Kant emphasizes in the Introduction to the Transcendental Dialectic, namely its *discursive* character (Section 1.2.1), which is a consequence of the discursivity of reason (Section 1.1.5). The second level, by contrast, responds to the tacit assumption of transcendental realism, the rejection of which, however, does not imply the truth of transcendental idealism. The third level responds to the specifically subjective origin of transcendental ideas and argues that, in the absence of an account of how they can nevertheless represent objects, we must conclude that they do not.

In this way, I will argue that one can share Kant's critique of speculative metaphysics without accepting his transcendental idealism. This is important because transcendental idealism is a highly contentious philosophical doctrine that not many contemporary philosophers accept.[2] By contrast, I will suggest in what follows that the claim that cognition requires sensible intuition, the rejection of transcendental realism, and Kant's 'debunking' account of transcendental ideas, while by no means self-evident, can be argued for in ways that might even appeal to philosophers who remain skeptical about transcendental idealism.

First, I briefly explain how the different formulations of transcendental realism I have worked with in this book are really expressions of the same underlying thesis and how they relate to transcendental idealism (Section 9.1). Next, I offer reasons for rejecting transcendental realism that do not presuppose transcendental idealism, thereby explaining the second level of Kant's

---

[2] For a discussion of different forms of realism and anti-realism in twentieth-century philosophy and a defense of robust realism about common sense objects, see Willaschek 2003.

critique of metaphysics (Section 9.2). I then indicate how the first, most general level of that critique depends not on transcendental idealism but on the much more specific claim that human cognition is limited to sensible objects (Section 9.3). Finally, I distinguish between different interpretations of Kant's account of transcendental ideas and argue for a radical reading according to which, when viewed in a purely speculative context, ideas of reason fail to represent (really possible) objects, which accounts for the third level of Kant's critique of metaphysics (Section 9.4). In this way, I hope to show that Kant develops a challenging critique of speculative metaphysics that does not presuppose his transcendental idealism.

9.1 Transcendental Realism and Transcendental Idealism

In Chapters 5–8, we encountered four different versions of transcendental realism at work in Kant's account of transcendental illusion:

TR   Empirical objects are things in themselves.
TR_{pos} Empirical objects are *noumena* in the positive sense and parts of a rational order.
TR_C There is a necessary correspondence between the principles of reason and the structure of empirical reality.
TR_{rep} Necessarily, if some object o, in order to be represented (by finite beings like us), must be represented as being F, then o is F.

The relation between the first three formulations is largely straightforward: given that the 'things in themselves' mentioned in the generic formulation TR can only be *noumena* in the positive sense, and given that the latter, qua objects of a divine intellect, are part of a rational order of things (see Section 5.2.3), TR_{pos} is just a more explicit formulation of TR. And TR_C is a direct consequence of TR_{pos}: if empirical objects are part of a rational order, then they are necessarily structured in accordance with rational principles.

According to TR_{rep}, by contrast, the necessary conditions of representing an object are conditions of that object itself. But even though TR_{rep} and TR_C are different theses, they are nevertheless closely related, since TR_C follows from TR_{rep}. According to TR_C, there is a necessary agreement between the structures and principles of human reason and those of reality. This can be reformulated as the idea that the subjective conditions of a *rational* representation of reality (in the form of a unified system of reason) are conditions of reality itself. Put crudely, if we, as rational beings, must represent the world as a rational order, then the world is a rational order. This is a specific version of TR_{rep} as applied to rational cognition.

On the other hand, TR_{rep} can be reformulated in a way that brings out its proximity to TR_C. TR_{rep} is the claim that there is a necessary agreement between the properties we must attribute to something in order to represent it, on the one hand, and the properties of the represented object, on the other. Moreover, TR$_{rep}$ in its unrestricted form also presupposes the identification of appearances with things in themselves because, once we distinguish between appearances and things in themselves in the way Kant suggests, it becomes apparent that TR$_{rep}$ is unproblematically true only with respect to representation-dependent appearances, but not with respect to representation-independent things in themselves. After all, there is no obvious reason why things in themselves should conform to subjective conditions of representation. In sum, TR$_{rep}$ can plausibly be regarded as the most general expression of the fundamental meta-ontological background assumption that Kant calls transcendental realism.

But note that transcendental realism on its own, whether understood as TR$_C$ or TR$_{rep}$, is not yet a version of the view, sometimes called 'metaphysical realism' (e.g. Putnam 1981: 49), according to which reality is radically mind-independent.[3] Rather, TR is neutral on this point since it implies neither that reality depends (in some appropriate sense) on human reason or thought nor that it does not. For instance, a proponent of TR$_C$ might hold that TR$_C$ is true *either* because reality in some way depends on human reason *or* because both reality and human reason depend on a perfectly rational being (God). Similarly, TR$_{rep}$ allows but does not require that the necessary conformity of represented objects to the conditions of their representation is explained by the former's depending on the latter. Considered on its own, then, TR is not a claim about the metaphysical dependence or independence of reality on our minds. Rather, it is a version of what is sometimes called 'epistemological realism,' that is, the claim that our cognitive capacities are apt for providing us with knowledge of reality.

This is not to deny, however, that the typical proponent of speculative metaphysics targeted by Kant in the Transcendental Dialectic thinks of TR in combination with some form of 'metaphysical realism.' TR typically comes as part of the view that the reality that reason allows us to cognize is independent of finite minds and their cognitive access to it.

But note that Kant's transcendental idealism (TI) also implies a version of epistemological realism, namely epistemological realism with respect to empirical objects, which is why Kant can insist that his transcendental idealism is a form of 'empirical realism' (A370). Kant's transcendental idealism is the claim that empirical objects are mere appearances and not things in themselves (A490–1/B518–19). It is a long-debated question how this claim is best

---

[3] This generic formulation needs to be restricted to specific domains (e.g. material objects) and qualified in various ways (e.g. in order to allow that artifacts and a divinely created world can be mind-independent in the relevant sense); see Willaschek 2003: ch. 1.

understood. Interpretations vary widely, and no consensus among interpreters is in sight.[4] It seems safe to say, however, that TI minimally implies that all properties of objects we can cognize ('appearances') depend (in some appropriate sense) on the possibility of being represented by finite rational beings like us. This is a paradoxical claim, since we ordinarily assume that most of the properties that we cognize in (empirical) objects are not representation-dependent in this way. For instance, the approximately spherical form of the earth is not normally thought to depend on the possibility of our representing the earth as approximately spherical (or, more generally, on our representing it in space); rather, we would ordinarily think that, conversely, the earth can be correctly represented as having that form *because*, quite independently of the possibility of our representations of it, it does have that form.

Thus, the sense in which transcendental idealism is 'idealist' is orthogonal to the sense in which transcendental realism is 'realist': while TI is *idealist* in that it makes empirical objects depend (in some sense) on the forms in which we necessarily represent them (space, time, categories) and is thus a form of 'metaphysical anti-realism,' TR is *realist* in that it allows for knowledge and cognition of reality and is thus a form of 'epistemological realism.' As I will argue next, this means that TI and TR are not contradictory theses; we can follow Kant in rejecting TR without having to accept TI.

9.2 A Critique of Transcendental Realism

Acceptance of TR_{rep} means that we project the necessary conditions of representing objects onto the represented objects themselves. As I have indicated earlier (Section 7.2), this is an entirely natural attitude, and ridding oneself of it requires critical reflection. As I will argue now, however, we have good reason to do so, even independently of Kant's transcendental idealism.

9.2.1 Kant's Rejection of Transcendental Realism in the Transcendental Dialectic

According to Kant, transcendental idealism (TI) is the 'key' to the resolution of the antinomies (A490/B518) in that TI is both necessary and sufficient for showing how the contradictions between the antinomical pairs of statements are only illusory (Section 5.2.2). Kant argues for TI in the Transcendental Aesthetic, claiming to have proven its truth beyond any doubt (A490/B518). According to Kant, however, the fact that TI is the 'key' to resolving the antinomies is an independent and self-sufficient argument for the truth of TI,

---

[4] See e.g. Schulting 2011; Allais 2015; Willaschek (forthcoming).

since without assuming TI we would have to admit that reason contains contradictory principles (Bxix n.). Since reason – the very faculty of logical reasoning and mediate inferences – cannot be contradictory (5:120), TI must be true.

Kant believes that TI is necessary and sufficient for the resolution of the antinomies because, according to his diagnosis, the antinomies presuppose transcendental realism (TR). According to Kant, TR implies (1) that the world as the sum total of objects (including all empirical objects) has a determinate magnitude (mathematical antinomies) and (2) that causal and modal conditioning relations can hold only between objects belonging to that one world (dynamical antinomies). If we assume TI, by contrast, it turns out (1) that the world of empirical objects does not have a determinate magnitude (because it consists of appearances and is therefore not fully determinate; A499/B527) and (2) that there can be causally and modally unconditioned things in themselves (*noumena* in the positive sense) that are not part of that world of empirical objects but might nevertheless causally and modally condition empirical objects (A530–2/B558–60). In this way, TI allows for the resolution of the antinomies by denying TR.

Even though Kant does not say so explicitly, the same diagnosis applies to the paralogisms and the arguments for God's existence. As we saw in Chapters 7 and 8, they too presuppose TR, since only given TR do the paralogisms and (what I have called) the Natural Argument for God's existence appear to be valid arguments. Once we accept TI, and thus deny TR, the dialectical nature of these inferences becomes apparent, since we can then see that their major premises are true only of things in themselves, while their minor premises are true of appearances (or, in the case of the paralogisms, true of transcendental apperception). This means that the subject term is used to refer to different kinds of objects in the major and the minor premises, so that the conclusion does not follow. Thus, once we accept TI, we can unveil the dialectical character of these inferences.

This suggests that Kant's critique of speculative metaphysics depends on TI in the same way that, according to his reconstruction, the arguments of the traditional metaphysician depend on TR. And of course, that is just how Kant himself presents things: TI is not just sufficient but also necessary for avoiding the dialectical fallacies of pure reason, which is why the Transcendental Dialectic is an indirect proof of the truth of TI (Bxix n.). Given the paradoxical character of TI, however, from a contemporary perspective it would be rather unfortunate if Kant were right on this point. Many, if not most, contemporary philosophers (at least outside the camp of Kant scholars) reject TI.[5] Kant's

---

[5] Of course, there are exceptions. The most prominent of these is Hilary Putnam, who presented his 'internal realism' as a version of Kant's transcendental idealism (Putnam 1981: 60). But in fact, there are huge differences between these views, since internal realism does not attribute any

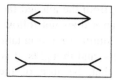

Figure 9.1 The Müller-Lyer illusion.

critique of traditional metaphysics would therefore be much more philosophically attractive (and of greater relevance to the lively meta-metaphysical debate of our time) if it could be shown to be independent of TI.

9.2.2 Rejecting Transcendental Realism without Accepting Transcendental Idealism

As we saw earlier, the most general form of TR that underlies the dialectical inferences is TR_{rep} – the assumption that things must really be as we necessarily represent them to be. TI implies the falsity of TR_{rep}, since TI (the claim that empirical objects are appearances, not things in themselves), if properly understood, implies that only in the case of *appearances* are the conditions of representation also conditions of the represented objects, whereas this is not true of objects in general, in particular of things in themselves. In other words, TI implies the falsity of TR_{rep} by restricting its validity to the realm of empirical objects (appearances) and denying that it holds for things in themselves. TI also implies the falsity of TR_C since TI implies that empirical objects as such cannot be identified with the objects of a rational order, that is, with *noumena* in the positive sense. Importantly, however, neither the falsity of TR_{rep} nor the falsity of TR_C requires the truth of TI, since TI is only the contrary, but not the contradictory opposite, of these theses. In other words, it is possible to reject TR_{rep} and TR_C (and speculative metaphysics as diagnosed by Kant) without accepting TI.[6]

That TR_{rep} in its unrestricted form is false – or at least highly implausible – can be seen, for instance, in the case of optical illusions. If I necessarily visually represent the two lines in the Müller-Lyer illusion as having different lengths (see Figure 9.1), it does not follow that they really have different lengths. And if a white wall under red light is necessarily represented as being

---

particular, "ideal" status to space and time and does not allow for *noumena* in the positive sense, since these would be objects from the "God's Eye Point of View" that Putnam rejects (73–4). Putnam himself returned to a more robust realism in the 1990s.

[6] That the rejection of transcendental realism (and thus the avoidance of the dialectical fallacies Kant analyzes in the Transcendental Dialectic) does not require the acceptance of transcendental idealism has also been argued by Paul Guyer (1987: 385–415).

red, it does not follow that it really is red. Also, from the alleged fact that we necessarily represent physical space as Euclidean it does not follow that it is Euclidean.[7] But even if we set perception and intuitive representations aside and restrict TR$_{rep}$ to discursive judgments, beliefs, and thoughts, it is hardly a plausible claim. After all, it seems possible that, because of the limited capacities of our minds, we as finite cognizers necessarily form false beliefs about some aspects of nature. For instance, it is at least conceivable that we are necessarily led to believe that material objects must *either* consist of simple, indivisible parts *or* be infinitely divisible, while in fact – in a way we cannot fully comprehend – neither option is true (a possibility that seems to be actual according to current physics). Even if there are not any such necessary but false beliefs, ruling out their possibility a priori, as TR$_{rep}$ does, would be unwarranted.[8]

Consider the following analogy. Before Einstein, people believed that physical space was either finite and bounded or infinite and unbounded.[9] But if the structure of physical space is hyperbolic, as Einstein argued, it is possible that space might be finite but unbounded (like the inside surface of a sphere). Now in this particular case, we are in principle able to comprehend the truth (assuming that Einstein was right), even if it has taken human beings millennia to arrive at it. If humans were constitutionally less intelligent (if someone of Einstein's intelligence were biologically impossible), we would never have been able to find out the truth about physical space. This means that there are *actual* features of nature that *possible* human beings cannot represent correctly. But then it follows by parity of reasoning that there are *possible* features of reality that *actual* human beings are not cognitively equipped to represent correctly.[10] And this means that TR$_{rep}$ is false.

This is not to say that some suitably restricted form of TR$_{rep}$ might not turn out to be philosophically defensible. (As we have seen, TI can be understood as a restricted version of TR$_{rep}$.) Nevertheless, we have good reason to reject TR$_{rep}$ at least in its unrestricted form. This does not commit us to accepting TI, since we can deny that the necessary conditions of representing some object in all cases are necessarily conditions of that object without accepting that

---

[7] That the visual representation of space is not in fact Euclidean has been argued persuasively by Thomas Reid; see Matthiessen 2016.
[8] As Ladyman et al. point out in their critique of current mainstream analytic metaphysics, there is no reason to assume that the "generic theory or model of the physical world" that evolution "has endowed us with" is adequate to the task of cognizing the micro and macro structures of nature (Ladyman et al. 2007: 10).
[9] See for instance 20:288, where Kant identifies finitude with boundedness and infinity with unboundedness.
[10] For a similar argument for the possibility of unknowable and unthinkable features of the world, see Nagel 1986; see also Willaschek 2003.

empirical objects are mere appearances. The latter claim is much more specific than is needed for the denial of the former.

Similar remarks apply to TR_C. That there is a necessary correspondence between the principles of reason and those of nature is a daring metaphysical thesis that faces many objections. A version of the traditional problem of evil is one of these: if nature is a rational order, and if evil is contrary to reason, why are there so many ostensible cases of natural and moral evil in the world? But even if we set this problem aside, it seems that there are many aspects of nature that do not permit of rational explanation, such as the exact value of the fundamental physical constants, contingent historical facts such as Kant's birth, and the occurrence of a particular mutation in a genome. Finally, even if we were to grant that it is possible that, unbeknownst to us, these phenomena have a place in a rational order, we would not be rationally *justified* in claiming that TR_C is in fact true. After all, the mere possibility that, against all appearances, TR_C *might* nevertheless be true does not constitute a reason to believe it. In fact, given the speculative character of TR_C, it is difficult to think of a way in which it could possibly be justified.[11] Thus, even if we leave the question of whether TR_C is true undecided, we find that, independently of TI, we have good reason not to accept TR_C.

In sum, while Kant himself believes that TI is necessary for avoiding the fallacies of traditional metaphysics, we can see that in fact all that is required is the rejection of TR_{rep} and TR_C, which are themselves general metaphysical theses of dubious standing that can be rejected without accepting TI.

9.3 Limits of Cognition without Transcendental Idealism

Let us now briefly turn to the first, most general level at which Kant's critique of speculative metaphysics might seem to depend on transcendental idealism (TI). Traditional metaphysics, according to Kant, had attempted to gain cognition of the unconditioned and of the supersensible more generally by means of inferences from a priori premises. As Kant reminds his readers toward the end of the Transcendental Dialectic, we did not have to wait for his detailed critique of the dialectical inferences to know that this endeavour was doomed to fail:

> The outcome of all dialectical attempts of pure reason ... confirms what we have already proved in the Transcendental Analytic, namely that all the inferences that would carry us out beyond the field of possible experience are deceptive and groundless. (A642/B670)

---

[11] But see Della Rocca 2010 for a defense of the Principle of Sufficient Reason that can also be read as a defense of a form of TR_C.

In the Transcendental Analytic, Kant had argued for the following *limits of cognition* claim:

LC Human cognition is limited to empirical objects (e.g. B165–6).

An empirical object is the potential object of an empirical representation, that is, of a representation that involves an element of 'sensation,' which in turn goes back to the object's affecting our minds (A19–20/B34). Because according to Kant the only way in which objects can be 'given' (made cognitively accessible to us) is by affecting our minds (A19/33), which makes them empirical objects, and because objects need to be given in order to be cognized (A50/B74), even cognition a priori is limited to empirical objects. But since the specific objects of speculative metaphysics – the supersensible in general and the unconditioned in particular – are not empirical objects and cannot be given in space and time, it follows from the general restriction of human cognition (LC) that any attempt to gain metaphysical cognition of the soul, the world at large, and God must fail. This second way in which Kant criticizes the pretensions of speculative metaphysics is much more general and potentially more damaging than the one discussed in the previous section, since it targets not only specific arguments that tacitly presuppose transcendental realism but any attempt to gain cognition and knowledge of the supersensible.[12]

This level of Kant's critique might also seem to suffer from the weakness that it presupposes transcendental idealism (TI), for instance by relying on the ideality of space and time. As with Kant's critique of transcendental realism, however, on closer inspection it turns out that LC (the claim that human cognition is limited to empirical objects) can be defended even without TI. In fact, LC follows from two other famous Kantian theorems which are independent of TI, namely:

---

[12] Cognition and knowledge are not the same for Kant. While (theoretical) cognition is a species of representation, namely a representation that conceptually determines an object given in intuition, knowledge is a species of *Fürwahrhalten*, or taking something to be true, which is an attitude directed at representations (judgments) (Willaschek and Watkins 2017). Therefore, even though knowledge typically presupposes cognition, it does not follow from the impossibility of metaphysical *cognition* that metaphysical *knowledge* is impossible. Indeed, Kant is committed to the claim that we do have general knowledge about things in themselves (that they exist, affect our sense, etc.), while this does not contradict his claim that we cannot have cognition of (specific) things in themselves. Thus, the claim in the text that we cannot have metaphysical knowledge of the supersensible is meant to apply only to metaphysical knowledge about specific types and individual instances of supersensible objects, such as God, souls, or the world as a whole.

Kant's Critique of Speculative Metaphysics (9.3)

CI   No cognition without intuition (A51/B75)

and

HIS Human intuition is sensible (A19/B33).

Even though the precise relationship between LC, CI, and HIS in Kant's philosophy is far from clear, the general outline of the story is roughly as follows. Theoretical *cognition* (in the fundamental cases) is a representation in which a *given* object is *determined* as to one or more of its general features (A50/B74; see Watkins and Willaschek 2017). In human and other finite beings, objects can be given only in *intuition*, whereas they are determined by being brought under general *concepts*. Therefore, all (theoretical) cognition requires intuition (= CI), because otherwise no objects that could be conceptually determined would be given to us.[13] According to Kant, human intuition is a kind of 'receptivity,' that is, a capacity to represent individual objects in response to causal impact from the represented object (A19/B33).[14] Since what it means for intuition to be sensible, according to Kant, is simply that it is receptive in this sense, it follows that human intuition is sensible (= HIS) and that its only objects are those that can affect our senses – that is, empirical objects. Since cognitions can only be about objects that are given in intuition (CI), and since objects given in intuition are empirical objects (HIS), it follows that human cognition is limited to empirical objects (= LC).[15]

Nothing in this argument requires or implies TI, since the argument is silent on the question of whether empirical objects are mere appearances or things in themselves. That empirical objects are mere appearances follows, according to Kant, from the ideality of space and time – that is, from the alleged fact that space and time are mere forms of intuition and not things in themselves (nor

---

[13] Moreover, the concepts also need a relation to intuition in order to have 'objective reality.' We can ignore this point for the moment but will return to it later, in Section 9.4.

[14] The fact that human intuition is such a capacity does not exclude its also having a priori forms – space and time – which can themselves be made objects of intuition.

[15] Besides this line of reasoning, which underlies Kant's critique of traditional metaphysics, there is a different (though related) one directed specifically against Leibniz-Wolffian metaphysics, which rejects the idea of a purely conceptual (i.e. analytic) cognition of actual (and even 'really' possible) individual objects. See Anderson 2015, Part IV, for a development of this line of critique. According to Anderson, Kant's "master argument" (Anderson 2015: 286 et passim) against rationalist metaphysics in the Transcendental Dialectic is that although metaphysical claims about the soul, world, and God are claims about the existence of individual objects, these claims cannot be analytic (as the Leibniz-Wolffian metaphysician assumes). While I think that Anderson makes a valid point here, it is somewhat misleading to call this Kant's 'master argument,' given that it targets only a specific kind of rationalist metaphysics and thus does not uncover, as Kant clearly aims to do in the Transcendental Dialectic, a necessary illusion grounded in the structure of rational thinking as such.

properties of or relations between such things) (A42–3/B59–60). But it is not necessary to assume the ideality of space and time in order to arrive at LC, which, as we have just seen, follows from CI and HIS.[16]

9.4 Transcendental Ideas as Empty Concepts

We finally turn to the third level of Kant's critique of metaphysics: his claim that transcendental ideas are cognitively defective in that they do not allow us to represent actual objects, but only objects "in the idea" (A671/B699). Kant's account of transcendental ideas can be understood in at least three different ways. According to what might be called a *conservative reading*, the only thing that is wrong with transcendental ideas is that we cannot use them in synthetic judgments that qualify as cognitions. According to this reading, a judgment such as 'God exists' or 'I am an immortal soul' manages to represent a determinate state of affairs and is either true or false. The only problem is that, because of the limits of human cognition, we cannot find out whether it is true or false. In particular, the concepts of God and soul *possess objective reality*, that is, they manage to represent a class of ('really') possible objects; it is only that we cannot find out whether or not there are any actual objects in that class. The fact that we cannot have cognition of supersensible objects and cannot know whether they exist does not prevent us from having determinate thoughts about them (e.g. Wood 1978: 48; Horgan 2010: 24).

According to the *radical reading*, by contrast, the problem with judgments like 'God exists' is not just that we cannot find out whether they are true. The more fundamental problem is that the concepts of supersensible objects we employ in them are defective in that they *lack objective reality*, that is, a representational relation to really possible objects. Therefore, although they are 'logically possible' (they do not involve a contradiction), these judgments are nevertheless 'empty' and 'without sense and significance.' The transcendental ideas do not represent any objects, so that judgments about their supposed objects are neither true nor false (e.g. Strawson 1966: 16; Bennett 1974: 270; McLaughlin 2014: 568–9).

Between these extremes, there is room for a *moderate reading* according to which we cannot *know* or ascertain whether the transcendental ideas have objective reality. According to this reading, we can use transcendental ideas

---

[16] For Kant, CI is true by definition: cognition just is a cognitive state that requires a relation to some *particular* object (or set of such objects), and intuition just is the kind of representation that provides such a relation to particular objects. Thus, Kant's argument for LC hinges on HIS, that is, the claim that human intuition can only be sensible (and therefore can only 'give' us empirical objects). As central as HIS is to Kant's philosophy in general and to his critique of metaphysics in particular, though, Kant never seems to argue for it explicitly. I have tried to reconstruct such an argument elsewhere; see Willaschek 2015.

and make judgments about souls, the world, and God, but we cannot be sure that by doing so we manage to represent anything, because we *cannot know*, or ascertain, whether these concepts *have objective reality* (e.g. Chignell 2009).

However, this exposition of three apparently incompatible readings of Kant's account of transcendental ideas must immediately be qualified. As we have seen (Sections 4.2.2 and 8.2.2), transcendental ideas do receive some 'indeterminate objective reality' from their regulative role in human cognition, since it is only by means of the transcendental ideas that we can approximate a complete system of scientific knowledge. Further, the lack of objective reality can be balanced by means of *symbols* (sensible representations associated with an idea) which allow us to make legitimate use of transcendental ideas (e.g. 5:352–3; 20:179–80).[17] Moreover, the ideas of God, freedom, and immortality receive objective reality, or a relation to objects, as the content of 'postulates of pure practical reason' – that is, as part of the content of beliefs about the necessary conditions under which we can fulfill our categorical moral obligations (5:134–41).[18] In this latter way, Kant argues, these ideas gain content determinate enough to specify (really) possible objects:

The abovementioned three ideas of speculative reason [of freedom, immortality, and God] in themselves are no cognitions; but they are (transcendent) thoughts in which there is *nothing impossible*. Now they receive, through an apodictic practical law ..., *objective reality*, i.e. it [the law] indicates to us that they have objects, without being able to show how their concept can refer to an object, and that, too, is not yet cognition of these objects ... But nevertheless theoretical cognition ... has been thus extended insofar as, through the practical postulates *objects* were still *given* to these ideas *by lending objective reality to a merely problematic thought*. (5:135; emphasis added)

We will not be able to discuss Kant's reasoning in this passage. I wish only to highlight three points about the resulting picture. First, as far as speculative reason is concerned, the ideas of freedom, God, and immortality lack objective reality. Second, transcendental ideas receive objective reality – that is, a relation to some possible[19] object – only through their relation to the Moral Law and the postulates based on it. And third, even after the second *Critique* Kant insists that the *only* way in which we can *represent* God is by way of analogy and symbolism (5:353; 20:279; see also Chignell 2010: 199). Thus, moral considerations lend 'objective reality' to the ideas of God, immortality, and freedom, but they *represent* their objects only analogically and symbolically.

---

[17] On the role of symbolism in this context, see Recki 2001: 155–77.

[18] For a discussion of these three ways of providing some form of objective reality for transcendental ideas, see Chignell 2010.

[19] Kant leaves out "possible" in the quoted passage, but he uses it two sentences before: "Since hereby nothing further has been achieved by practical reason than that those concepts are real, and really have their (*possible*) objects ..., no synthetic sentence is possible through their acknowledged reality" (5:134; emphasis added).

This means that there is a sense in which the conservative reading is clearly correct, namely once we take into account the indirect ways in which ideas of reason can receive objective reality (regulative use, symbolism, practical grounds). Moreover, it is compatible with both the moderate and the radical reading, as long as these are understood as concerning the transcendental ideas 'in themselves' (as Kant puts it in the passage just quoted), that is, the transcendental ideas in a purely theoretical perspective and in abstraction from moral considerations and indirect means of representation. It is this latter perspective, however, in which I am interested here. Thus, the question is whether, according to Kant, these ideas as such manage to represent any (really possible) objects. With respect to *this* question, the conservative reading is clearly inadequate. This follows from Kant's repeated insistence that it is *only* by indirect means that the ideas of reason gain a relation to objects. This leaves the radical and the moderate readings as possible contenders for an account of transcendental ideas *per se*. So the question is whether transcendental ideas in abstraction from indirect means *lack* objective reality (the radical reading) or whether we *cannot know* whether they have objective reality (the moderate reading).

In what follows, I will defend the *radical* reading, since it follows from a central part of Kant's Rational Sources Account, namely the 'subjective' origin of transcendental ideas.

9.4.1 The Radical Reading Explained

Let us start by characterizing the radical reading more fully. Consider the example of the concept of the soul, understood as an immaterial thinking substance. We are surely thinking *something* when we think that there are souls. Also, we can grant that this thought is logically possible in that the marks included in the concept of a soul (immateriality, thinking, substance) do not involve a contradiction. According to the radical reading, however, this thought is nevertheless cognitively defective because, when used in combination with 'immaterial,' the mark 'substance' lacks any relation to objects. The concept of a substance is a pure concept of the understanding (category) that has 'sense and significance' only when combined with a sensible 'schema,' that is, with a corresponding pattern of sensible data that allows us to apply that concept to an object: "Thus the schemata of the concepts of pure understanding are the true and sole conditions for providing them with a relation to objects" (A145–6/B185). Without such a schema, Kant insists, a category, such as the concept of a substance, is merely a subjective form of thought but not a representation of an object (e.g. A287/B343). Therefore, categories are not "valid" for supersensible objects (A286/B342).

The reason for this is that concepts relate to objects only indirectly, and this in a twofold sense.[20] First, concepts relate to objects – that is, represent them – only through the marks they contain, which are themselves concepts. Let us assume that the concept of dog, for instance, contains the marks 'mammal,' 'has a tail,' and 'barks' (among others). Therefore, it represents dogs by representing everything that has all the features specified in the marks. But how do the marks relate to objects? Ultimately, by being appropriately connected to sensible data Kant calls "sensations" (*Empfindungen*) (A19–20/B34). Therefore, the concept 'dog' relates to objects because there is a characteristic set of empirical features (a 'schema') connected with it – a way that dogs typically look (sound, smell, ...) – and that allows us to apply that concept to dogs (A141–2/B180–1). (This is the second sense in which concepts relate to their objects only indirectly.)[21]

Now this latter account in terms of *empirical* schemata is not available for a category, which is an a priori concept, so that nothing in what is given in sensibility can fully correspond to that concept. (Otherwise, the concept could be acquired by abstraction from empirical data and would not be a priori.) Therefore, Kant argues that the categories must have *transcendental* schemata (A142–7/B181–7), which consist not in patterns of empirical sensations (like the schema of a dog) but in patterns of temporal determinations. Because, according to Kant, time is an *a priori* form of *sensible* intuition, such a transcendental schema is both sensible and a priori. In the case of substance, for instance, this schema is "persistence of the real in time" (A144/B183). The details and plausibility of this account need not concern us here. What matters is that, according to Kant, without such a transcendental schema, a category is not a representation of a class of objects but merely a subjective form of thought:

If we leave out persistence (which is existence at all times), then nothing is left in my concept of substance except the logical representation of the subject ... by means of which no object whatever of the use of this concept is determined. (A242–3/B300–1)

But the concept of a soul (which is the concept of an immaterial thinking *substance*) cannot have a transcendental schema, because a soul is supposed to be a *supersensible* substance. While we can represent substances in the empirical world as objects that 'exist at all times,' this is not possible for supersensible objects such as immaterial souls, since temporal predicates do not apply to them. (According to Kant, space and time are merely subjective forms of sensible representation and not properties of things in themselves.)

---

[20] For a more detailed discussion of concepts in Kant, see Watkins and Willaschek 2017.
[21] Obviously, the story will be much more complicated for concepts such as 'sales agent' and 'democracy.'

The same holds, *mutatis mutandis*, for the concepts of God (as *ens realissimum*) and the world (as containing the unconditioned totality of empirical conditions), which are also concepts without sensible schemata. Recall that transcendental ideas, according to Kant, are "categories extended to the unconditioned" (A409/B436 and earlier, Section 6.1). Given that unconditioned objects are supersensible, it follows that transcendental ideas lack objective reality just as much as 'unschematized' categories do.

This radical reading can appeal to the many passages where Kant insists that a priori concepts have objective reality (relate to possible objects) *only* if their objects can, at least in principle, be given in experience. As Kant repeats again and again, without sensible intuition a priori concepts would be "empty" (B149; see also A51/B75) and "without sense and reference" (B149; see also 8:133; A239/B298): "The merely transcendental use of the categories [i.e. a use not restricted to objects of a possible experience; A238/B298] is thus in fact no use at all, and has no determinate object, nor even an object that is at least determinable as far as its form is concerned" (A247–8/B304). And: "Thus, the categories without schemata are only functions of the understanding for concepts, *but do not represent any object*" (A147/B187; emphasis added). Since Kant defines ideas of reason as concepts whose objects *cannot* be given in experience (A327/B384) and that lack sensible schemata, it follows that the transcendental ideas are also empty, without sense and reference, and lack a (determinate) object. Objects that are thought through concepts alone, "without any schema of sensibility," are "impossible" (A286/B342). Consequently, Kant says of the transcendental ideas that "no object can be determined through them" (A329/B385). By denying that transcendental ideas can have a "constitutive use," Kant explicitly denies that they provide us with "concepts of certain objects" (A644/B672).[22]

9.4.2 The Radical Reading Defended

The radical reading faces two major objections, one from the side of the conservative reading, the other from that of the moderate reading. First, there are those passages where Kant insists that even though we cannot cognize supersensible objects such as God or souls, we can nevertheless think them (Bxxvi; see also B166 n.; Bxxix). Along with his claim that he "had to deny *knowledge* in order to make room for *faith*" (Bxxx), they imply that even though we cannot know that God exists and that our souls are immortal, we can believe in (and hence think of) God and an immortal soul. If the

---

[22] Even though the class of concepts of reason is wider than that of transcendental ideas (Section 6.1), in this chapter I will use these two terms interchangeably (as Kant himself often does; see Chapter 6, note 1).

Kant's Critique of Speculative Metaphysics (9.4.2)

transcendental ideas are empty and without sense and significance, how can they feature in intelligible thoughts and provide the content of our beliefs?

This objection has already been answered, however, by appeal to the indirect means through which transcendental ideas can receive objective reality. As we saw, Kant thinks that the transcendental ideas 'in themselves' lack objective reality, but are 'given' (really possible) objects and acquire objective reality by their role in the postulates of pure practical reason (Willaschek 2010). However, one might worry that the radical reading cannot allow for this possibility. If transcendental ideas as such lack objective reality, it may seem to follow that their objects are 'really impossible,' since Kant seems to identify a concept's having objective reality with its having an object that is really (and not just logically) possible (e.g. Bxxxvi n.; A596/B624). But if the objects of our concepts of God, freedom, and soul were really *impossible*, adding practical considerations or symbolic representations could not change this. Thus, the radical reading may seem to imply the falsity of the conservative reading (which, as I had granted, is clearly correct once Kant's practical considerations are taken into account).[23]

But this consequence does not follow. If the transcendental ideas as such lack objective reality, this means that they *do not have*, or do not relate to, really possible objects. It does not mean that they *do have*, or relate to, objects that are really *im*possible. Moreover, that the transcendental ideas as such lack objective reality does not rule out that they acquire objective reality once they are assigned a practical role (as in the postulates), just as the categories acquire objective reality by being given a transcendental schema. Therefore, the radical reading does not rule out that the transcendental ideas, if combined with practical considerations, have really possible objects.

The second objection, coming from the defender of the moderate reading, concerns the question of whether Kant really means to say that a priori concepts lack a relation to (really possible) objects. While some passages (e.g. from the Phenomena and Noumena and the Amphiboly sections) may suggest the radical reading, Kant's considered view, so the objection goes, is better presented in the following footnote:

> To cognize an object, it is required that I be able *to prove* its possibility ... But I can think whatever I like, as long as I do not contradict myself, i.e., as long as my concept is a possible thought, even if I *cannot give any assurance* whether or not there is a corresponding object somewhere within the sum total of all possibilities. (Bxxvi; emphasis added)[24]

---

[23] Thanks to Andrew Chignell and Tobias Rosefeldt for (independently) raising this objection and to the latter and Stefanie Grüne for discussion about a possible solution.

[24] Also note that in the passage quoted earlier (A243/B301) Kant concludes "one therefore does not even know whether [the unschematized category] means anything at all."

According to passages like this, the problem with a priori concepts such as the transcendental ideas is not that they *lack* objective reality but that we cannot 'prove,' 'give assurance,' or know that they have objective reality. Thus, the point of the transcendental deduction of the categories is to *prove* that the pure concepts of the understanding have objective reality. Since no such deduction is possible for the transcendental ideas, we cannot know whether they have objective reality (a determinate relation to a possible object), which means that we cannot gain cognition of objects by using these concepts. But this does not necessarily mean that they *lack* objective reality.

This second objection thus comes down to a version of the moderate reading that has been suggested by Andrew Chignell, who links it to the claim that "Kant's real worry about the ideas of reason ... is that ... the positive predicates involved may, for all we know, be 'really repugnant' in a way that makes their objects 'really impossible'" (Chignell 2009: 179). Real repugnance consists in the extra-logical opposition of real features, for instance in the case of two opposing forces that in effect 'cancel each other out' (Section 8.1). For example, if a riverboat is propelled upstream by oarsmen but nevertheless does not move forward because of the river's current, the force exerted by the oars and the force of the current are 'really repugnant.' Kant's philosophical point is that in cases like this, even though no effect is observable (the ship does not move), the forces are nevertheless real. Kant discusses this phenomenon in his 1763 essay *Negative Magnitudes* and uses it in the *Critique of Pure Reason* as an argument against Leibnizian rationalism, which, according to Kant, does not have the theoretical means to acknowledge that real repugnance is possible (A272–4/B328–30).

According to Chignell, however, there is a second type of real repugnance (which he calls "subject-cancelling," as opposed to the one mentioned thus far, which is "predicate-cancelling"; Chignell 2009: 172–3). It consists in a logically possible object's being 'really' impossible because its properties are really repugnant. On Chignell's version of the moderate reading, because human cognition is limited to empirical objects, we cannot know whether the features we attribute to supersensible objects are really repugnant (Chignell 2009: 189–90), and hence we cannot know whether these objects are really possible (or, equivalently, whether our concepts of them have objective reality).

As is often the case with aspects of Kant's philosophy whose interpretation depends on terms Kant does not explicitly define but more or less takes for granted (such as 'objective reality'), we can find passages pointing in different directions.[25] While some of the things Kant says suggest a radical reading,

---

[25] See Ferrarin 2015: 304–7, who presents Kant as being entangled in an antinomy about whether the ideas of reason have objective reality.

other passages speak in favor of Chignell's more moderate reading. Kant sometimes says that cognition requires that our concepts *have* objective reality, while at other times he says that cognition requires that we be able to *prove* that our concepts have objective reality.[26]

This kind of textual ambiguity notwithstanding, I think that the radical reading is more adequate to Kant's concerns in the *Critique of Pure Reason* than the moderate one. There are two reasons for this. First, while I agree with Chignell that what he calls 'real harmony' (i.e. absence of real repugnance) is a necessary condition for real possibility and objective reality, it is important to see that it is not sufficient. The 'unschematized' categories, for instance, lack objective reality according to Kant, even though their being really repugnant is not an issue. Rather, the issue seems to be that we cannot simply assume that a priori concepts have objective reality, given that they arise from our own minds independently of the objects they are supposed to represent. Thus, there is a problem with a priori concepts and their relation to objects that remains even if we grant that the concepts in question are not really repugnant.

Second, there are a number of passages where Kant concludes from the fact that transcendental ideas are 'self-made' and 'subjective' concepts that they are 'illusory' and without objects. As we have seen (Chapter 6), Kant offers a subjectivist account of how we come to have concepts such as that of God and of an immortal soul, which explains our having such concepts in a way that is entirely independent of whether there are any objects that correspond to them (A312/B368–A338/B396). Our concepts of God and an immortal soul are not derived from any objective feature of the world but rather respond to a subjective need of our own reason (e.g. A309/B365; A336/B393). But this purely subjective origin of the transcendental ideas undermines their status as 'objective' (that is, object-related) representations. As Kant explains (not with respect to ideas, but with respect to judgments):

If, moreover, one can unfold the subjective causes of the judgment [in a case of illusion or 'mere persuasion'] ... without having any need for the constitution of the object, then we expose the illusion. (A821/849)

This thought also applies to transcendental ideas: if we can show how we come to have these ideas on purely subjective grounds, without any need to refer to

---

[26] In fact, even a single passage can point in opposite ways, such as the footnote just quoted, which first speaks in favor of the moderate reading but then continues as follows: "But in order *to ascribe* objective validity to such a concept ... something more is required" (Bxxvi; emphasis added). Assuming that here, as elsewhere, Kant uses 'objective validity' interchangeably with 'objective reality,' the 'more' that is required, namely 'proof' or 'assurance,' is required not for objective reality itself but for *ascribing* objective reality. This would be compatible with what Kant says in other places, namely that, independently of sensibility, a priori concepts *lack* objective reality.

their supposed objects, we expose any pretense of their relating to objects as illusory. Consequently, Kant repeatedly emphasizes that transcendental ideas are *mere* creations of our own minds: the idea of God ("thought of in the transcendental sense") "is a mere fiction" (A580/B608; see also A584/B612), and its object is "a mere creature of [our] own thinking" (A584/B612) of which we lack any conception of what it might be in itself (A698/B726). However, as Kant points out, "one easily forgets that those ideas are arbitrarily made by us and not derived from objects" (20:300).[27]

The subjectivist account of ideas of reason provides support not just for the radical reading as the most plausible take on Kant's account of transcendental ideas but also for the philosophical claim that ideas such as that of an *ens realissimum* or an immortal soul, when considered only in a speculative metaphysical framework, are cognitively defective. The subjective origin of transcendental ideas establishes a presumption *against* their objective reality – against their being responsive to objects and objective features that exist independently of us. Given their subjective origin, we would need an account of how they nevertheless manage to represent something objective. But as Kant insists in the context of the deduction of the categories, the only way to provide such an account for a priori concepts is by linking them to intuition (in the case of the categories, to possible experience). No such account is to be had in the case of the transcendental ideas. Hence, we are forced to admit that ideas of reason lack objective reality and therefore cannot be used even to speculate about things in themselves, because they fail to represent any such objects and cannot be used to attribute any properties or features to them. Ideas of reason, considered merely from a speculative point of view, lack objective reality and consequently do not represent objects.

9.5 Conclusion

In this chapter, I have argued that Kant's critique of traditional metaphysics (*metaphysica specialis*) in the Transcendental Dialectic is independent of any commitment to his transcendental idealism. Rather, Kant's critique of the specific arguments for the immortality of the soul, the structure of the world as a whole, and the existence of God only requires the rejection of transcendental realism, which can be motivated without accepting transcendental idealism. Moreover, Kant's general critique of metaphysical attempts to gain

---

[27] This is what is sometimes called a 'debunking argument' in contemporary discussions. Such an argument shows that some representation or judgment that we take to be objectively valid is in fact invalid (or at least that we are not justified in assuming that it is) because of how we come to possess that representation or form that judgment. For instance, evolutionary debunking arguments try to undermine the truth of moral beliefs by showing that they are produced by evolutionary processes that are not truth-tracking (e.g. Joyce 2006; Street 2006; Kahane 2011).

cognition and knowledge of the supersensible does not presuppose transcendental idealism either, but only a number of more specific claims about human cognition, most importantly the claim that human intuition is sensible. Finally, I have argued that, according to Kant, the ideas of reason (such as those of God, soul, and world) are cognitively defective in a deeply damaging way since, at least when considered in a purely speculative context, they lack objective reality and a relation to (really, not just logically) possible objects. These considerations result in a critique of metaphysical speculation that targets the very features of metaphysical speculation highlighted by the Rational Sources Account (the tacit assumption of transcendental realism, the discursivity of reason, and the subjective origin of metaphysical ideas).

Conclusion to Part II: Transcendental Illusion and the 'Other Side' of the Transcendental Dialectic

The Transcendental Dialectic is generally read as Kant's demolition of traditional metaphysics.[1] Its 'other side,' which is the topic of the second part of this book, consists in Kant's Rational Sources Account, which explains in a plausible way why and how we inevitably arrive at the idea of something unconditioned and the ideas of soul, world, and God as unconditioned in specific ways. On its most general level, the explanation is this: we start from something conditioned (such as my present mental state, a material object, or a contingent event in the world) and infer that the totality of its conditions exists. This inference is entirely natural and appears to be valid if we assume the Supreme Principle, which tells us that for everything conditioned, there is a totality of its conditions.[2] Since this principle in turn gives expression to the discursive and iterative character of rational questions and reason's interest in completeness and systematicity (see Chapter 2), we can see that the metaphysical questions concerning soul, world, and God, as well as apparently rational answers to them (in the form of the conclusions of the paralogisms, the theses and antitheses of the antinomies, and the conclusion of the Natural Argument for God's existence), arise from the very structure of rational thinking, which is exactly what Kant's Rational Sources Account says.

More specifically, in Chapter 5 I suggested as our guiding interpretative hypothesis that there is a general three-part template underlying Kant's Rational Sources Account in the Transcendental Dialectic: (1) a transition from the logical to the real or transcendental use of reason and its ideas and principles, (2) the tendency to misuse the latter by treating them as constitutive rather than regulative, and (3) the tacit assumption of transcendental realism as

---

[1] But see the work of Karl Ameriks (e.g. Ameriks 1981/2000; 1992; 2006) for a more nuanced reading.

[2] The paralogisms are an exception since, unlike the arguments underlying the antinomies and the Natural Argument for God's existence, they do not explicitly appeal to a version of the Supreme Principle in their major premises and do not name something conditioned in their minor premises. But as I have indicated (Section 7.1.1), even the paralogisms presuppose the Supreme Principle once we make explicit that their conclusions are meant to show that the soul is unconditioned.

Conclusion to Part II

an explanation of that tendency (Section 5.2). Our discussions of Book One of the Paralogisms, Antinomy, and Ideal as well as the Appendix have confirmed this hypothesis.

While not every aspect of the general template is equally prominent in each of these chapters, I have argued that its three elements are (explicitly or implicitly) present in each part of the Transcendental Dialectic. Specifically, we have seen that the 'common title' of all *transcendental* ideas, the concept of the unconditioned, is based on the *logical* form of rational inferences in general and that the derivation of the system of *transcendental* ideas is based on the three *logical* types of rational inference (categorical, hypothetical, disjunctive). (As I have indicated, however, I am skeptical about the cogency of these derivations.) Similarly, the paralogisms rest on an illicit slide from *logical* features of the 'I think' to metaphysical or *transcendental* determinations of the underlying subject; the antinomies presuppose that the *logical* requirement of a complete series of premises for a conclusion is mistaken for the *transcendental* Supreme Principle; the derivation of the *transcendental* ideal starts with a transition from the *logical* principle of determinability to the *transcendental* principle of complete determination; and the Appendix argues that *logical* principles of reason presuppose *transcendental* ones. As I have argued, in most cases these transitions from the logical to the transcendental can be motivated by the thought that in order to follow through on the logical requirement to approximate the unity of reason (a complete system of scientific knowledge), we must adopt the corresponding transcendental principle, which itself results from applying the logical principle to nature and its objects. (This transition from the logical to the transcendental is not just a feature of the Transcendental Dialectic but can also be found in the Metaphysical Deduction in the Transcendental Analytic, where Kant derives the transcendental categories from the logical forms of judgment.)

The transcendental principles and ideas we arrive at can be thought of and used in two different ways, however: *regulatively*, as heuristic devices, or *constitutively*, as true descriptions of nature. Kant briefly invokes this distinction in the Antinomy chapter with respect to the cosmological version of the Supreme Principle and in the Ideal chapter with respect to the idea that the world was created by a supreme being. He does not invoke the distinction in the Paralogisms, however, and fully develops it and its relevance only in the Appendix. As I have argued, deferring discussion of the relevance of this distinction is part of Kant's general strategy in the Transcendental Dialectic of reconstructing the inferences of the uncritical metaphysician in all of us (as part of his Rational Sources Account). While Kant immediately diagnoses the mistakes involved in the relevant rational *inferences* in the same chapter, he fully explains the status of their *conclusions* and the transcendental ideas to which they give rise only later, in the Appendix. There, Kant explains that while transcendental principles and ideas are naturally taken to be constitutive (as truly representing aspects of reality), they are in fact legitimate only when used regulatively (as heuristic hypotheses).

Thus, concerning the first two parts of our general template, we find that Kant indeed develops his Rational Sources Account by moving (1) from logical to transcendental principles or ideas, which (2) are misunderstood as constitutive. This is not to say, however, that Kant's application of this pattern is completely uniform. In the paralogisms, for instance, the logical/transcendental transition does not seem to start from a formal feature of the logical use of *reason*, but rather from transcendental apperception, which Kant aligns with the understanding. And although transcendental apperception is 'logical' (in the sense of being devoid of any content), at the same time it is also 'transcendental' in that, according to Kant, it is a condition of the possibility of objective experience. In the case of the antinomies, it seems that the logical/transcendental transition plays a role only with respect to the cosmological Supreme Principle, but not in the arguments underlying the antinomies or in the antinomies themselves. By contrast, Kant invokes the regulative/constitutive distinction in the context of the resolution of the antinomies, but not in the paralogisms. These differences do not tell against the claim that Kant's argument follows the three-part template, however; they merely show that he allows himself some flexibility in applying it to different topics.

We found that the third element of that template, transcendental realism (TR), is equally at work on each level of Kant's argument in the Transcendental Dialectic. This is least obvious in Book One on the system of transcendental ideas, where Kant does not explicitly appeal to transcendental realism at all. But the reason for this is that, with respect to the Rational Sources Account, Book One only tells us half the story, the other half being supplied much later in the Appendix. While Book One argues that the logical use of reason in rational inferences takes us to the concept of the unconditioned, to the very idea of transcendental ideas, and to the distinction between three classes of transcendental ideas (psychological, cosmological, theological), it is only in the Appendix that we are told that the natural way to think of these concepts and distinctions, namely as constitutive (reflecting objective structures of reality), is mistaken. Even there, Kant does not state explicitly that this mistake is motivated by the tacit assumption of transcendental realism; as I have argued, however, this is the explanation he implicitly relies on. If we combine the scattered parts of that story, we see that TR even plays a role in Book One, since it explains why we naturally assume that the transcendental ideas and the concept of the unconditioned reflect objective features of reality and not just 'needs of reason.' Something similar is true of the Paralogisms chapter, where Kant also does not mention TR,

Conclusion to Part II

since the distinction between the regulative and the constitutive use of the idea of the soul must wait until the second part of the Appendix.

Note that TR features in Kant's argument for the Rational Sources Account in two different ways. First, a tacit assumption of transcendental realism explains why we take the inferences in question (paralogisms, the inferences underlying the antinomies, and the 'natural' proof of God's existence) to be valid, even though, according to Kant, they are really invalid because of the ambiguity of their middle terms.[3] While the major premises are true only of things in themselves, the minor premises are true only of empirical objects (or, in the case of the paralogisms, of transcendental apperception).[4] But the inference *appears* to be valid once we assume transcendental realism, which tells us that empirical objects *are* things in themselves. So one role of transcendental realism according to the Rational Sources Account is to serve as a tacit background assumption that makes invalid 'dialectical' inferences of reason appear *valid*.

The other role of TR is to explain why regulative principles and ideas appear to be constitutive. This explanation appeals to TR_C – the claim that the structure of reason necessarily corresponds to the structure of nature itself. Given TR_C, regulative principles of reason – descriptive principles that are used as heuristic hypotheses – will naturally appear to be constitutive, that is, true of nature itself. It is this role of transcendental illusion that Kant invokes in the Appendix by distinguishing between the regulative and the constitutive use of reason's principles and ideas. It is at work on all four levels of Kant's argument for the Rational Sources Account, however, since it also concerns the Supreme Principle, the derivation of the concept of the unconditioned, and the major premises of the 'necessary inferences of reason' in Book Two (the paralogisms, the arguments underlying the antinomies, and the Natural Argument for God's existence). In all of these cases, we tend to regard the relevant principle as constitutive even though, according to Kant, it can be legitimately used only regulatively, and it is TR_C that explains this tendency. In this way, transcendental realism explains why dialectical inferences appear not only valid but also *sound* – that is, why their major premises appear to be true and hence why we take their conclusions (and the ideas they contain) to be constitutive rather than regulative.

In this way, it has hopefully become clear that in the Transcendental Dialectic Kant indeed presents a highly complex, but also very plausible, argument for his Rational Sources Account. We must ask metaphysical

---

[3] As we have seen, this is true even of the Natural Argument for God's existence, even though this is not the point Kant emphasizes in his diagnosis, presumably because that part of the argument is basically the same as the one for the thesis side of the fourth antinomy.

[4] I bracket here the other possible diagnosis, according to which the inferences are valid but not sound (7.2.3).

questions because the discursive and iterative structure of reason takes us from questions about the specific conditions of empirical objects and events (questions about bearers of properties, causes of events, and the grounds of contingent things) to questions about the totality of their conditions, and thus the unconditioned. This idea of the unconditioned (of a totality of conditions for something conditioned) arises naturally from rational reflection on things that are conditioned. We assume that if some conditioned x exists, there must exist some condition of x. But then it seems that the totality of conditions of x (including, by transitivity, any condition of a condition of x) also exists, since this follows from the natural assumption (the 'principle of comprehension') that, for any non-empty predicate F, there is the set of all objects that are F. And once we possess the concept of a totality of conditions, we are led by the natural tendency of rational thinking toward completeness and systematicity to *look* for the totality of conditions for everything conditioned. Thus, the discursive and iterative character of human reason (its tendency to require explanations, ask questions, and respond to any answer with further questions), together with the rational striving for completeness, inevitably leads us to ask metaphysical questions (RS-1).

Unfortunately, reason does not stop here. Instead, rational reflection on metaphysical questions suggests a priori answers that appear to be rationally warranted. For instance, it appears to follow from a priori premises that, as thinking beings, we are simple, persistent immaterial substances. Although Kant arrives at this point in a slightly different way, we can explain why this consequence appears to be compelling by appealing to the principle that there must be a totality of conditions for everything conditioned (the Supreme Principle). My mental states are conditioned by there being a bearer whose mental states they are. Even if we were to allow that this bearer is itself a mental state, it seems that there must ultimately be some bearer that is not a mental state – a thinking substance. Similarly, it equally appears to follow from a priori premises that there is a necessary being, because for anything contingent happening in the world, there must be something that explains it (its condition or ground), which takes us to the conclusion that there must be some ultimate ground which is not itself contingent and hence necessary. In this way, we arrive at apparently compelling answers to our inevitable metaphysical questions (RS-2).

If all we had were these two types of metaphysical inference, according to Kant, we might never have detected that there is something deeply wrong with them. However, there is a third group of metaphysical inferences, the antinomies, which lead us with apparent rational necessity to contradictory conclusions. For instance, it appears compelling to infer that any series of causes of some event must have begun with some uncaused cause, because an infinite series of causes does not provide an ultimate (complete and unconditional) answer to the question of why the resulting event happened. At the

Conclusion to Part II

same time, reason would not be satisfied even if there was an uncaused cause, because even in that case, we would lack a complete and unconditional explanation of why the resulting event happened; we would still face the questions of why the uncaused cause exists, why it caused something, and why it did so at the particular moment it did. Assuming with TR that there must be answers to all our rationally necessary questions, there thus appear to be compelling arguments both for and against the possibility of uncaused causes. Behind these contradictory considerations lies the Supreme Principle, according to which, if the conditioned exists, then the unconditioned totality of its conditions must also exist. Since this totality can be thought of *either* as an unconditioned condition (UCC) *or* as a totality of conditioned conditions (TCC) but in neither case provides the complete answers we expect, it appears that we can infer the truth of one disjunct from the falsity of the other. Since the conclusions we thus arrive at are contradictory, though, we know that something has gone wrong.

As Kant analyzes this mistake, it rests on falsely assuming that the rational principles that make us ask metaphysical questions (such as the Supreme Principle) are true of reality itself. As we have just recapitulated, the source of this illusion and the errors that result from it lies in the tacit assumption of transcendental realism. As I have argued, we can reject this assumption without relying on Kant's own transcendental idealism.

Even though transcendental realism is not itself a rational principle, it is part of what Kant calls "common human reason" (Aviii) insofar as it is an intuitively plausible background assumption we automatically rely on unless we critically reflect on it. It is our natural understanding of how our rational capacities are geared to reality: reason is a capacity for a priori *cognition*, that is, for objective representation; what could be more natural than the view that its principles are objectively valid? This natural assumption shows up in the intuitiveness of thoughts like the following: 'If the world is not finite, then it must be infinite'; 'If there is thought, there must be someone or something that thinks'; 'If there is something contingent, there must be something necessary that explains it.' These thoughts are expressions of the expectation that reality provides answers to our rational questions (even if we may not always be in a position to know these answers). And this expectation is in turn just an expression of the underlying assumption that reality must conform to reason. According to Kant's analysis in the Transcendental Dialectic, it is this assumption, together with the discursive, iterative, and systematic character of rational thinking, that drives metaphysical speculation (RS-3).

What I hope to have made clear is that this analysis, while no doubt disputable in many of its details, provides an original and plausible picture of the metaphysical urge – one that traces metaphysical thinking back to its sources in reason itself.

Postscript
Kant's Practical Metaphysics

As this book has shown, Kant conceives of human reason as being in a tragic position: its very nature makes it ask metaphysical questions about the unconditioned, but the limitation of human cognition (its dependence on sensible intuition) makes answering them impossible. In this respect, the main result of the *Critique of Pure Reason* is negative: we are barred from having theoretical cognition and specific knowledge of the unconditioned.

As Kant indicates in the Canon section of the first *Critique* and fully explains in the second and third *Critiques*, however, that is not the end of the story of the metaphysical urge. Rather, we are rationally warranted in accepting some of the tenets of traditional metaphysics after all because they constitute necessary presuppositions of moral agency.[1] An adequate discussion of this aspect of Kant's philosophy would require a book of its own. I do not want to close, however, without providing at least a glimpse of Kant's 'practical metaphysics' and how it relates to the account of the rational sources of metaphysics that we have been considering in this book.

In the *Critique of Practical Reason*, Kant introduces the idea of a practical metaphysics (metaphysics based on practical considerations) by observing that "pure practical reason ... likewise seeks the unconditioned for the practically conditioned" (5:108). Kant refers back to the Supreme Principle he had discussed in the first *Critique* (see Chapter 3) and assumes that a corresponding principle also holds for practical reason. But while theoretical cognition of the unconditioned is impossible, according to Kant we do have access to the unconditioned through our consciousness of the Moral Law (5:29–30). As Kant argues, the Moral Law (or, in its prescriptive form, the Categorical Imperative) is the fundamental principle of *practical* reason and the source of unconditional moral obligations (5:30–1).[2] In being aware of these

---

[1] Kant argues for these claims in different ways in all three *Critiques* (A804/B832–A831/B859; 5:107–46; 5:446–74) and in various other works (6:4–8; 8:137–42; 8:396 n.; 8:418–19; 9:67–9 n.; 20:293–301).

[2] This sense of unconditionality is different from the epistemic and inferential unconditionality discussed in Chapter 2 of this book (and of course also from 'real' unconditionality as discussed in Chapter 3). *All* moral laws (e.g. 'Do not lie' and 'Help people in need') are uncondition*al* in

obligations, we are equally aware of our ability to live up to them, which, according to Kant, implies *freedom* in the strongest sense (5:30) and membership in the intelligible world (5:46). Moreover, the Moral Law grounds an obligation to realize what Kant, with the philosophical tradition, calls the 'highest good,' which he understands as happiness conditioned by virtue.[3] This highest good is "the unconditioned totality of the object of pure practical reason" (5:108), that is, the ultimate and inclusive end of rational agency. As Kant argues, it must be considered to be realizable through our own actions, since otherwise we could not be obligated to bring it about. But we can conceive of it as fully realizable only if we believe that our *soul* is immortal (so that we can achieve, by infinitesimal approximation, complete virtue; 5:122–4) and that there is a *God* (who distributes happiness in proportion to virtue; 5:124–32). In this way, acceptance of the Moral Law commits us to three theoretical propositions – three "postulates of pure practical reason" (or 'practical postulates,' for short) – namely that there is a God, that our souls are immortal, and that our wills are free (5:132).[4]

Kant defines a "postulate of pure practical reason" as "a *theoretical* proposition, though one not demonstrable as such, insofar as it is attached inseparably to an a priori unconditionally valid *practical* law" (5:122). Thus, a practical postulate is characterized by three features (Willaschek 2010): (1) it is a theoretical proposition, that is, one that is meant to capture 'what is,' aiming at being true (9:86); (2) it is 'not demonstrable as such,' which means that there can be no conclusive empirical evidence or argument a priori for or against the proposition in question (let us call such a proposition 'theoretically undecidable'); and (3) it is 'attached to a practical law,' by which Kant means that someone who acknowledges the Moral Law as binding must, by a kind of

---

that they hold independently of the contingent motives and ends of their addressees. Only *the* Moral Law (in the singular, the 'fundamental principle') is also epistemically and inferentially uncondition*ed* in that it cannot be derived from a more general or epistemically more fundamental principle (see Kleingeld and Willaschek (forthcoming) on the distinction between moral *laws* and *the* Moral Law and the sense in which the latter is fundamental).

[3] For discussion of Kant's conception of the highest good, see e.g. Reath 1988; Engstrom 1992; Kleingeld 1995; Höwing 2016; and Marwede 2018.

[4] This shows that the distinction between a logical and a real use of reason (see Chapters 1 and 2) also applies to practical reason. The Moral Law is an epistemically and inferentially unconditioned practical cognition (see note 2). As Kant repeatedly emphasizes, it can play this role only because it is a *formal* principle of the will that abstracts from all matter of the will (which matter is the "object of the will" and depends on empirical inclinations) (e.g. 5:27). Thus, the Moral Law belongs to the *logical use of reason* insofar as it abstracts from all objects and serves as an unconditioned *practical cognition*. By contrast, the highest good, since it is the "totality of the *object* of pure practical reason" (5:108; emphasis added), belongs to the *real use of reason*. Thus, even though Kant himself does not put it this way, the transition from Moral Law to the highest good is a *transition from the logical to the real use of pure practical reason*. (See also Watkins 2010: 162–4, who distinguishes between the 'formal' and the 'material' employment of practical reason.)

subjective but still rational necessity, hold that proposition to be true (we can say that such a proposition is 'practically necessary').

By presenting God, freedom, and immortality as practical postulates, Kant can claim to have reconstructed, in a practical mode, the three central tenets of traditional metaphysics, each of which he had criticized as theoretically unwarranted in the Transcendental Dialectic. Since they concern not normative principles but theoretical propositions about non-empirical objects, they belong to the very domain of *speculative* metaphysics, even though our reason for accepting them is ultimately practical and this acceptance must take the form of belief or faith (*Glauben*) rather than knowledge (*Wissen*).[5] It is this combination of speculative content and practical warrant that constitutes what I call Kant's 'practical metaphysics.'[6]

Kant's practical metaphysics is fascinating and highly original, but it faces serious questions and objections. First, there are questions concerning Kant's arguments for his postulates. Do we really have to think of the highest good as being fully realizable? Perhaps approximating it would do just as well. Is the kind of moral perfection required by the highest good (Kant speaks of "holiness," 5:122) such that it cannot be realized by finite beings (so that its realization is possible only in an infinite afterlife)? Perhaps we should rather conclude that if we, as finite beings, cannot possibly realize this kind of perfection, we cannot be morally required to achieve it. And if we tone down the highest good to what is humanly possible, it seems that we do not need God to proportion happiness to virtue, since a good legal system and a just economy might be all that is needed in this respect. For these and other reasons, Kant's arguments for the postulates of God and immortality are not entirely convincing (see also Guyer 2000).

By contrast, there is an excellent case to be made for freedom of the will as a practical postulate. This is not the place to pursue this issue in any detail (see Willaschek 2018) but let me just mention that the proposition 'Human beings have free will' is a theoretical claim that, if suitably interpreted, may well be practically necessary even if it is undecidable on purely theoretical grounds, since it is a presupposition for being the addressee of moral obligations. And once we see that there is a plausible argument for a postulate of freedom, there are other potential postulates that come to mind, for instance the realizability of the highest good (as Kant himself seems to suggest; 5:125) and the possibility of human progress (8:309) and of global peace, which Kant calls the "highest

---

[5] I discuss Kant's account of belief in Willaschek 2016; for alternative readings, cf. Chignell 2007; Stevenson 2011b; Pasternack 2014; and Höwing 2016.

[6] Kant himself, in the unpublished *Progress* essay, speaks of a "practical-dogmatic" metaphysics (20:311; see Caimi 2017). It is 'dogmatic' not because it is uncritical but because it makes positive assertions about the supersensible (as opposed to remaining skeptical).

political good" (6:355). Even the claim that I am not a brain in a vat (or, closer to Kant, that I am not deceived by an evil demon) might count as a postulate in Kant's sense; it is theoretically undecidable, but its truth is a presupposition of taking other people's concerns seriously and is thus practically necessary. These brief remarks are merely meant to indicate that even if we do find Kant's arguments for the postulates of God and immortality unconvincing, the project of a practical metaphysics may still be viable and attractive.

There is a second kind of worry raised by that project, however. It concerns the question of whether it can be rational to believe theoretical claims without sufficient evidence for their truth. Many philosophers, past and present, would object with Hume that "the wise man ... proportions his belief to the evidence" (*Enquiry* X.1.87) and require that, if a proposition is theoretically undecidable, we must withhold judgment. Kant rejects this kind of 'evidentialism' by arguing for what he calls the "primacy of pure practical reason in its connection with speculative reason" (5:119), which in effect consists in the claim that if there are practical postulates (that is, theoretical propositions that are theoretically undecidable but practically necessary), then it is rationally admissible (and even necessary) to accept them.

Kant's argument for this claim (5:119–21) can be outlined as follows. The Moral Law is absolutely binding for every rational being. If there are practical postulates, this means that we are rationally committed to accepting them because they are presuppositions of doing what the Moral Law requires of us. Now speculative reason, considered on its own, requires us to reject (i.e. not to accept) these postulates because they are theoretically undecidable. But we cannot both accept and not accept the postulates, so either speculative reason or practical reason must give. As Kant points out, the requirements of pure practical reason are categorical, whereas those of speculative reason are merely hypothetical (see Section 2.2.3). Since in cases of conflict categorical requirements prevail over hypothetical ones, we must accept the postulates. Thus, practical reason has primacy. Again, much more would be needed to adequately discuss this argument, but I think we can at least see that, given Kant's account of moral obligation as both categorical and rational, there is a plausible case to be made against evidentialism and in favor of Kantian practical metaphysics. Note that this argument is independent of which propositions might qualify as practical postulates.[7] Moreover, it does not require

---

[7] For a detailed reading of the section "On the Primacy of Pure Practical Reason in Its Connection with Speculative Reason" (5:119–21), see Willaschek 2010. For different readings of Kant's general conception of a practical postulate and the primacy of pure practical reason, see Guyer 2000 and Gardner 2006. For recent critiques of evidentialism and a defense of practical reasons for belief, see e.g. Marušić 2015; Leary 2016; and Rinard 2017. Kant's position differs significantly from theirs, however, in emphasizing the categorical character of the practical reasons on which the postulates are based.

Kant's demanding conception of moral obligation and seems to work just as well with a slightly relaxed sense of practical necessity, according to which a proposition is practically necessary if we cannot conceive of ourselves as agents without taking that proposition to be true. I therefore believe that there is much promise in the project of a Kantian practical metaphysics, even from a contemporary point of view.

This finally takes us to the question of whether the postulates (assuming for the moment, with Kant, that all three are well founded) satisfy the interest of reason in the *unconditioned*. Does speculative reason get what it wants after all, only in a different, practical mode of cognition? The answer is: almost, but not quite.

As we have seen, what speculative reason is ultimately after is *complete* explanations of all empirical phenomena and *ultimate* answers to our rational questions. If we start with a given empirical phenomenon and ask why it occurred the way it did, as rational inquirers we ultimately aim for an answer that does not raise further 'why' questions of the same kind. Only recourse to something unconditioned can provide complete explanations in this sense. In particular, according to Kant, a complete explanation of psychological phenomena must appeal to the existence of a soul substance; complete explanations of phenomena in space and time require the existence of a world that is unconditioned in spatial, temporal, mereological, causal, and modal respects; and a complete explanation of everything contingent requires the existence of God (thought of as a necessary and most real being).

Assuming that the postulates provide us with rationally warranted beliefs in the immortality of the soul, freedom of the will, and the existence of God, they allow us to give *some* complete explanations of the required kind. But note, first, that the postulates are silent on the question of whether there is something unconditioned that explains the spatially, temporally, and mereologically conditioned aspects of empirical reality (as discussed in the first and second antinomies), since freedom of the will of the kind Kant envisions ('transcendental freedom,' absolute spontaneity) only concerns causal conditioning relations. Second, even the assumption of freedom of the will does not allow for a complete explanation of *all* causally conditioned phenomena, but only of those that arise from human agency. Therefore, even if we accept Kant's postulates, many phenomena for which reason requires a complete explanation will remain unexplained. And third, even those phenomena that *can* be explained by appeal to the postulates are explained only in a limited sense, since we do not *know*, but only *believe*, that the ultimate *explanans* (God, freedom, immortal soul) exists. Kant distinguishes between the epistemic status of practical postulates and the epistemic status of theoretical hypotheses (5:142), since only postulates warrant subjective certainty and unconditional conviction, while hypotheses do not. In this respect, a practical postulate has a stronger epistemic standing than a mere hypothesis. But when we use the postulates as a basis for speculative explanations, their epistemic status still falls short of the status of the 'absolute' (*schlechthin*) principles Kant discusses in the Introduction to the Transcendental Dialectic (A301/B358), which are supposed to be epistemically and inferentially unconditioned. While the postulates concern the existence of unconditioned *objects*, they themselves are not epistemically and inferentially unconditioned, since their justification depends on the Moral Law (and various other premises). Moreover, the reason why we must accept them is merely subjective in that it responds not to features of the objects in question (God, the soul) but merely to the "need of pure reason" (5:142) to account for the possibility of moral obligation and the realizability of the highest good. (The situation may be different in the case of freedom of the will.) In this sense, explanations based on the postulates remain second-class explanations. As Kant puts it, even though the postulates must be added to the inventory of speculative reason, they remain "exuberant" and "foreign" to it (5:120).

In sum, even if we grant Kant that we must rationally accept the three postulates of God, freedom, and immortality, the rational need for complete explanations will never be satisfied. What Kant says at the very beginning of the first *Critique* remains true: "Human reason has the peculiar fate in one species of its cognitions that it is burdened with questions which it cannot dismiss, since they are given to it as problems by the nature of reason itself, but which it also cannot answer, since they transcend every capacity of human reason" (Avii).

Bibliography

Works Referred to by Short Title

Auszug: Georg Friedrich Meier. *Auszug aus der Vernunftlehre*. Halle: Gebauer, 1752. Cited from *Immanuel Kant's Schriften*. Berlin: Königlich-Preußische Akademie der Wissenschaften, 1900–. Vol. 16, 1–872.

Categories: Aristotle. *Categories*, trans. with notes by J. L. Ackrill. Oxford: Clarendon Press, 1963.

De Anima: Aristotle. *On the Soul*, in Jonathan Barnes (ed.), *The Complete Works of Aristotle. The Revised Oxford Translation*. Princeton University Press, 1984, 641–93.

Deutsche Metaphysik: Christian Wolff. *Vernünfftige Gedancken von Gott, der Welt und der Seele des Menschen, auch allen Dingen überhaupt*. Halle: Renger, 1751. Repr. in Charles A. Corr (ed.), Christian Wolff. *Gesammelte Werke*, section 1, vol. 2.1. Hildesheim: Olms, 2003.

Discours: René Descartes. *Discourse on the Method of Rightly Conducting One's Reason and Seeking the Truth in the Sciences*, in John Cottingham, Robert Stoothoff, and Dugald Murdoch (eds. and trans.), *Descartes. Selected Philosophical Writings*. Cambridge University Press, 1988, 20–56.

Discours de Metaphysique: Gottfried Wilhelm Leibniz. *Discourse on Metaphysics*, in *Discourse on Metaphysics, Correspondence with Arnauld and Monadology*, trans. George R. Montgomery. Chicago, IL: Open Court, 1947, 1–65.

Enquiry: David Hume. *An Enquiry Concerning Human Understanding*, ed. Tom L. Beauchamp. Oxford University Press, 1999.

Entwurf: Christian August Crusius. *Entwurf der nothwendigen Vernunftwahrheiten, wiefern sie den zufälligen entgegen gesetzet werden*. Leipzig: Gleditsch, 1745. Repr. in Giorgio Tonelli (ed.), *Christian August Crusius. Die philosophischen Hauptwerke*, vol. 2. Hildesheim: Olms, 1964.

Ethics: Baruch de Spinoza. *Ethics*, in Michael L. Morgan (ed.), *Spinoza: Complete Works*, trans. Samuel Shirley. Indianapolis, IN: Hackett, 2002, 213–383.

Grimmsches Wörterbuch: Deutsches Wörterbuch von Jacob und Wilhelm Grimm. Leipzig: Hirzel, 1852–1971. (Online at http://woerterbuchnetz.de/cgi-bin/WBNetz/wbgui_py?sigle=DWB.)

Instauratio Magna: Francis Bacon. *The Instauratio Magna*, in Graham Rees and Maria Wakely (eds.), *The Oxford Francis Bacon*, vols. XI, XII, XIII. Oxford University Press, 2000–7.

Bibliography

Meditations: René Descartes. *Meditations on First Philosophy,* in John Cottingham, Robert Stoothoff, and Dugald Murdoch (eds. and trans.), *Descartes. Selected Philosophical Writings.* Cambridge University Press, 1988, 73–122.

Metaphysica: Alexander Gottlieb Baumgarten. *Metaphysica-Metaphysik. Historisch-kritische Ausgabe,* ed. Günther Gawlick and Lothar Kreimendahl. Stuttgart, Bad Canstatt: Frommann-Holzboog, 2001.

Metaphysics: Aristotle. *Metaphysics,* in Jonathan Barnes (ed.), *The Complete Works of Aristotle. The Revised Oxford Translation.* Princeton University Press, 1984, 552–729.

Monadology: Gottfried Wilhelm Leibniz. *Monadology,* in *Discourse on Metaphysics, Correspondence with Arnauld and Monadology,* trans. George R. Montgomery. Chicago, IL: Open Court, 1947, 249–72.

Natürliche Gottesgelahrtheit: Christian Wolff. *Natürliche Gottesgelahrtheit nach beweisender Lehrart abgefasset.* Halle: Renger, 1742–5. Repr. in Jean École et al. (eds.), Christian Wolff. *Gesammelte Werke. Deutsche Schriften. Natürliche Gottesgelahrtheit,* section 1, vol. 23. Hildesheim: Georg Olms, 1994.

Nicomachean Ethics: Aristotle. *Nicomachean Ethics,* in Jonathan Barnes (ed.), *The Complete Works of Aristotle. The Revised Oxford Translation.* Princeton University Press, 1984, 729–868.

Politeia: Platon. *Republic,* in John M. Cooper (ed.), *Plato. Complete Works.* Indianapolis, IN: Hackett, 1997, 971–1224.

Principles: René Descartes. *Principia Philosophiae. Principles of Philosophy,* trans. Valentine R. Miller and Reese P. Miller. Dordrecht: Reidel, 1983.

Regulae: René Descartes. *Regulae ad directionem ingenii. Rules for the Direction of the Natural Intelligence. A Bilingual Edition of the Cartesian Treatise on Method,* ed. and trans. George Heffernan. Amsterdam: Rodopi, 1998.

Other Works

Abaci, Uygar. 2017. 'Kant, the Actualist Principle, and the Fate of the Only Possible Proof,' *Journal of the History of Philosophy* 55, 261–91.

Al-Azm, Sadiq J. 1972. *The Origins of Kant's Arguments in the Antinomies.* Oxford: Clarendon Press.

Allais, Lucy. 2015. *Manifest Reality. Kant's Idealism and His Realism.* Oxford University Press.

Allison, Henry E. 1998. 'The Antinomy of Pure Reason, Section 9 (A515/B543–A567/B595),' in Georg Mohr and Marcus Willaschek (eds.), *Immanuel Kant. Kritik der reinen Vernunft.* Berlin: Akademie, 465–91.

2004. *Kant's Transcendental Idealism.* Revised and enlarged edition. New Haven, CT: Yale University Press.

2012. 'Transcendental Realism, Empirical Realism, and Transcendental Idealism,' in Henry E. Allison, *Essays on Kant.* Oxford University Press, 67–83.

Ameriks, Karl. 1982/2000. *Kant's Theory of Mind. An Analysis of the Paralogisms of Pure Reason.* Oxford University Press.

1992. 'The Critique of Metaphysics. Kant and Traditional Ontology,' in Paul Guyer (ed.), *The Cambridge Companion to Kant.* Cambridge University Press, 249–80.

1998. 'The Paralogisms of Pure Reason in the First Edition (A338/B396–A347/B406; A348–380),' in Georg Mohr and Marcus Willaschek (eds.), *Immanuel Kant. Kritik der reinen Vernunft*. Berlin: Akademie, 371–90.

2001. 'Kant on Science and Common Knowledge,' in Eric Watkins (ed.), *Kant and the Sciences*. New York: Oxford University Press, 31–52.

2006. 'The Critique of Metaphysics. The Structure and Fate of Kant's Dialectic,' in Paul Guyer (ed.), *The Cambridge Companion to Kant and Modern Philosophy*. Cambridge University Press, 269–302.

Anderson, R. Larnier. 2015. *The Poverty of Conceptual Truth*. Oxford University Press.

Barnett, David. 2010. 'You Are Simple,' in Robert C. Koons and George Bealer (eds.), *The Waning of Materialism*. Oxford University Press, 161–74.

Baum, Manfred. 2001. 'Die Kantische Systematik im Umriss. Systemform und Selbsterkenntnis der Vernunft bei Kant,' in Hans Friedrich Fulda and Jürgen Stolzenberg (eds.), *Architektonik und System in der Philosophie Kants*. Hamburg: Meiner, 25–41.

Beckermann, Ansgar. 1998. 'Zum Verhältnis von Kantischer und Fregischer Logik. Kritische Einwände gegen Michael Wolff (II. Teil),' *Zeitschrift für philosophische Forschung* 52, 422–34.

2008. *Analytische Einführung in die Philosophie des Geistes*. Berlin: de Gruyter.

Bennett, Jonathan. 1966. *Kant's Analytic*. Cambridge University Press.

1974. *Kant's Dialectic*. Cambridge University Press.

Bird, Graham. 2017. 'The Antinomies. An Entirely Natural Antithetic of Human Reason,' in James R. O'Shea (ed.), *Kant's Critique of Pure Reason. A Critical Guide*. Cambridge University Press, 223–4.

Birken-Bertsch, Hanno. 2006. *Subreption und Dialektik bei Kant. Der Begriff des Fehlers der Erschleichung in der Philosophie des 18. Jahrhunderts*. Stuttgart, Bad Cannstatt: Frommann-Holzboog.

2015. 'Konstitutiv/Regulativ,' in Marcus Willaschek, Jürgen Stolzenberg, Georg Mohr, and Stefano Bacin (eds.), *Kant-Lexikon*. Berlin: de Gruyter, 1264–6.

Bliss, Ricki, and Kelly Trogdon. 2014. 'Metaphysical Grounding,' in Edward N. Zalta (ed.), *The Stanford Encyclopedia of Philosophy* (winter 2016 edition), plato.stanford.edu/archives/win2016/entries/grounding/.

Boehm, Omri. 2016. 'The Principle of Sufficient Reason, the Ontological Argument and the Is/Ought Distinction,' *European Journal of Philosophy* 24, 556–79.

Brook, Andrew. 1994. *Kant and the Mind*. New York: Cambridge University Press.

2016. 'Kant's View of the Mind and Consciousness of Self,' in Edward N. Zalta (ed.), *The Stanford Encyclopedia of Philosophy* (winter 2016 edition), plato.stanford.edu/archives/win2016/entries/kant-mind/.

Brook, Andrew, and Paul Raymont. 2017. 'The Unity of Consciousness,' in Edward N. Zalta (ed.), *The Stanford Encyclopedia of Philosophy* (summer 2017 edition), plato.stanford.edu/archives/sum2017/entries/consciousness-unity/.

Butts, Robert E. 1997. 'Kant's Dialectic and the Logic of Illusion,' in Patricia A. Easton (ed.), *Logic and the Workings of the Mind*. Atascadero, CA: Ridgeview, 307–17.

Caimi, Mario. 1995. 'Über eine wenig beachtete Deduktion der regulativen Ideen,' *Kant-Studien* 86, 308–20.

2000. 'Einige Bemerkungen über die Metaphysische Deduktion in der *Kritik der reinen Vernunft*,' *Kant-Studien* 91, 257–82.

2012. 'Zur Metaphysischen Deduktion der Ideen in der Kritik der reinen Vernunft,' *Methodus* 7, 23–41.

2017. 'Der Begriff der praktisch-dogmatischen Metaphysik,' in Andree Hahmann and Bernd Ludwig (eds.), *Über die Fortschritte der kritischen Metaphysik. Beiträge zu System und Architektonik der kantischen Philosophie.* Hamburg: Meiner, 157–69.

Callanan, John J. 2017. 'The Ideal of Reason,' in James R. O'Shea (ed.), *Kant's Critique of Pure Reason. A Critical Guide.* Cambridge University Press, 243–59.

Cantor, Georg. 1895. 'Beiträge zur Begründung der transfiniten Mengenlehre,' *Mathematische Annalen* 46, 481–512.

Carruthers, Peter. 2004. *The Nature of the Mind. An Introduction.* New York: Routledge.

Chalmers, David. 1996. *The Conscious Mind. In Search of a Fundamental Theory.* New York: Oxford University Press.

Chalmers, David, David Manley, and Ryan Wassermann. 2009. *Metametaphysics. New Essays on the Foundations of Ontology.* Oxford: Clarendon Press.

Charles, David. 2000. *Aristotle on Meaning and Essence.* Oxford: Clarendon Press.

Chignell, Andrew. 2007. 'Belief in Kant,' *Philosophical Review* 116, 323–60.

2009. 'Kant, Modality, and the Most Real Being,' *Archiv für Geschichte der Philosophie* 91, 157–92.

2010. 'Real Repugnance and Belief about Things-in-Themselves. A Problem and Kant's Three Solutions,' in Benjamin J. Bruxvoort Lipscomb and James Krueger (eds.), *Kant's Moral Metaphysics. God, Freedom, and Immortality.* New York: de Gruyter, 177–209.

2012. 'Kant, Real Possibility, and the Threat of Spinoza,' *Mind* 121, 635–75.

2017. 'Kant on Cognition, Givenness and Ignorance,' *Journal of the History of Philosophy* 55, 131–42.

Cohen, Hermann. 1871. *Kants Theorie der Erfahrung.* Berlin: Dümmler.

Correia, Fabrice, and Benjamin Schnieder. 2012. 'Grounding. An Opinionated Introduction,' in Fabrice Correia and Benjamin Schnieder, *Metaphysical Grounding. Understanding the Structure of Reality.* Cambridge University Press, 1–36.

Dahlstrom, Daniel. 2015a. 'Schluss,' in Marcus Willaschek, Jürgen Stolzenberg, Georg Mohr, and Stefano Bacin (eds.), *Kant-Lexikon.* Berlin: de Gruyter, 2023–9.

2015b. 'System,' in Marcus Willaschek, Jürgen Stolzenberg, Georg Mohr, and Stefano Bacin (eds.), *Kant-Lexikon.* Berlin: de Gruyter, 2238–42.

de Boer, Karin. 2016. 'Categories versus Schemata. Kant's Two-Aspect Theory of Pure Concepts and His Critique of Wolffian Metaphysics,' *Journal of the History of Philosophy* 54, 441–68.

Della Rocca, Michael. 2010. 'Principle of Sufficient Reason,' *Philosophers' Imprint* 10, 1–13.

Dohrn, Daniel. 2015. 'Transzendental,' in Marcus Willaschek, Jürgen Stolzenberg, Georg Mohr, and Stefano Bacin (eds.), *Kant-Lexikon.* Berlin: de Gruyter, 2313–19.

Dörflinger, Bernd, and Günter Kruck (eds.). 2011. *Über den Nutzen von Illusionen. Die regulativen Ideen in Kants theoretischer Philosophie.* Hildesheim: Olms.

Dummett, Michael. 1978a. 'Preface,' in Michael Dummett, *Truth and Other Enigmas*. Cambridge, MA: Harvard University Press, ix–li.
  1978b. 'Realism,' in Michael Dummett, *Truth and Other Enigmas*. Cambridge, MA: Harvard University Press, 145–65.
Dupré, John. 1983. 'The Disunity of Science,' *Mind* 92, 321–46.
Dyck, Corey W. 2014. *Kant and Rational Psychology*. Oxford University Press.
Eidam, Heinz. 2000. *Dasein und Bestimmung. Kants Grund-Problem*. Berlin: de Gruyter.
Emundts, Dina. 2010. 'The Refutation of Idealism and the Distinction between Phenomena and Noumena,' in Paul Guyer (ed.), *The Cambridge Companion to Kant's 'Critique of Pure Reason.'* Cambridge University Press, 168–89.
Engelhard, Kristina. 2005. *Das Einfache und die Materie. Untersuchungen zu Kants Antinomie der Teilung*. Berlin: de Gruyter.
Engfer, Hans-Jürgen. 1989. 'Principium rationis sufficientis,' in Joachim Ritter et al. (eds.), *Historisches Wörterbuch der Philosophie*, vol. 7. Basel: Schwabe, 1325–36.
Engstrom, Stephen P. 1992. 'The Concept of the Highest Good in Kant's Moral Theory,' *Philosophy and Phenomenological Research* 52, 747–80.
  2006. 'Understanding and Sensibility,' *Inquiry* 49, 2–25.
  2009. *The Form of Practical Knowledge. A Study of the Categorical Imperative*. Cambridge, MA: Harvard University Press.
Ertl, Wolfgang. 1998. *Kants Auflösung der 'dritten Antinomie.' Zur Bedeutung des Schöpfungskonzepts für die Freiheitslehre*. Freiburg: Karl Alber.
Falkenburg, Brigitte. 2000. *Kants Kosmologie. Die wissenschaftliche Revolution der Naturphilosophie im 18. Jahrhundert*. Frankfurt am Main: Klostermann.
Ferrari, Jean. 1998. 'Das Ideal der reinen Vernunft (A567/B595–A642/B670),' in Georg Mohr and Marcus Willaschek (eds.), *Immanuel Kant. Kritik der reinen Vernunft*. Berlin: Akademie, 491–525.
Ferrarin, Alfredo. 2015. *The Powers of Pure Reason. Kant and the Idea of Cosmic Philosophy*. University of Chicago Press.
Fine, Kit. 2001. 'The Question of Realism,' *Philosophers' Imprint* 1, 1–30.
Fisher, Mark, and Erik Watkins. 1998. 'Kant on the Material Ground of Possibility. From the "Only Possibe Argument" to the "Critique of Pure Reason",' *Review of Metaphysics* 52, 369–95.
Fodor, Jerry A. 1974. 'Special Sciences (Or: The Disunity of Science as a Working Hypothesis),' *Synthese* 28, 97–115.
Förster, Eckart. 2011. *Die 25 Jahre der Philosophie. Eine systematische Rekonstruktion*. Frankfurt am Main: Klostermann.
Friedman, Michael. 1991. 'Regulative and Constitutive,' *The Southern Journal of Philosophy* 30, 73–102.
  1992. *Kant and the Exact Sciences*. Cambridge, MA: Harvard University Press.
  2001. *Dynamics of Reason. The 1999 Kant Lectures at Stanford University*. Stanford, CA: CSLI Publications.
Fulda, Hans Friedrich, and Jürgen Stolzenberg (eds.) 2001. *Architektonik und System in der Philosophie Kants*. Hamburg: Meiner.
Gardner, Sebastian. 1999. *Kant and the Critique of Pure Reason*. London: Routledge.
  2006. 'The Primacy of Practical Reason,' in Graham Bird (ed.), *A Companion to Kant*. Malden, MA: Blackwell, 259–74.

Gava, Gabriele. 2014. 'Kant's Definition of Science in the *Architectonic of Pure Reason* and the Essential Ends of Reason,' *Kant-Studien* 105, 372–93.
  2016. 'The Fallibilism of Kant's Architectonic,' in Gabriele Gava and Robert Stern (eds.), *Pragmatism, Kant and Transcendental Philosophy*. London: Routledge, 46–66.
  (in press). 'Kant, Wolff and the Method of Philosophy,' *Oxford Studies in Early Modern Philosophy* 8.
Gawlick, Günther, and Lothar Kreimendahl. 2011. 'Einleitung,' in Alexander Gottlieb Baumgarten, *Metaphysica – Metaphysik. Historisch-kritische Ausgabe*, ed. Günther Gawlick and Lothar Kreimendahl. Stuttgart, Bad Cannstatt: Frommann-Holzboog, ix–lxxxiv.
Geiger, Ido. 2003. 'Is the Assumption of a Systematic Whole of Empirical Concepts a Necessary Condition of Knowledge?,' *Kant-Studien* 94, 273–98.
Gerhardt, Volker. 2002. *Immanuel Kant. Vernunft und Leben*. Stuttgart: Reclam.
Ginsborg, Hannah. 2017. 'Why Must We Presuppose the Systematicity of Nature?,' in Michela Massimi and Angela Breitenbach (eds.), *Kant and the Laws of Nature*. Cambridge University Press, 71–89.
Gomes, Anil, and Andrew Stephenson (eds.). 2017. *Kant and the Philosophy of Mind. Perception, Reason and the Self*. Oxford University Press.
Goy, Ina. 2007. *Architektonik oder Die Kunst der Systeme. Eine Untersuchung zur Systemphilosophie der Kritik der reinen Vernunft*. Paderborn: Mentis.
Grier, Michelle. 1993. 'Illusion and Fallacy in Kant's First Paralogism,' *Kant-Studien* 83, 257–82.
  2001. *Kant's Doctrine of Transcendental Illusion*. Cambridge University Press.
  2011. 'Reason. Syllogisms, Ideas, Antinomies,' in Will Dudley and Kristina Engelhard (eds.), *Immanuel Kant. Key Concepts*. Durham, NC: Acumen, 63–82.
Grüne, Stefanie. 2009. *Blinde Anschauung. Die Rolle von Begriffen in Kants Theorie sinnlicher Synthesis*. Frankfurt am Main: Klostermann.
  2017. 'Givenness, Objective Reality, and A Priori Intuitions,' *Journal of the History of Philosophy* 55, 113–30.
Guyer, Paul. 1979. *Kant and the Claims of Taste*. Cambridge, MA: Harvard University Press.
  1987. *Kant and the Claims of Knowledge*. Cambridge University Press.
  1990. 'Reason and Reflective Judgment. Kant on the Significance of Systematicity,' *Noûs* 24, 17–43.
  2000. 'The Unity of Reason. Pure Reason as Practical Reason in Kant's Early Conception of the Transcendental Dialectic,' in Paul Guyer, *Kant on Freedom, Law and Happiness*. Cambridge University Press, 60–95.
  2003. 'Kant on the Systematicity of Nature. Two Puzzles,' *History of Philosophy Quarterly* 20, 277–95.
  2005. 'The Unity of Nature and Freedom. Kant's Conception of the System of Philosophy,' in Paul Guyer, *Kant's System of Nature and Freedom. Selected Essays*. Oxford University Press, 277–313.
Guyer, Paul, and Allen Wood. 1998. 'Introduction to the Critique of Pure Reason,' in Paul Guyer and Allen Wood (eds.), *The Cambridge Edition of the Works of Immanuel Kant. The Critique of Pure Reason*. Cambridge University Press, 1–73.
Haag, Johannes. 2007. *Erfahrung und Gegenstand. Das Verhältnis von Sinnlichkeit und Verstand*. Frankfurt am Main: Klostermann.

Hafemann, Burkhard. 1998. *Aristoteles' Transzendentaler Realismus. Inhalt und Umfang erster Prinzipien in der 'Metaphysik.'* Berlin: de Gruyter.
Hahmann, Andree, and Bernd Ludwig (eds.). 2017. *Über die Fortschritte der kritischen Metaphysik. Beiträge zu System und Architektonik der kantischen Philosophie.* Hamburg: Meiner.
Hawking, Stephen. 2005. *The Theory of Everything. The Origin and Fate of the Universe.* Beverly Hills, CA: Phoenix Books.
Hebbeler, James C. 2012. 'The Principles of the First "Critique",' *The Review of Metaphysics* 65, 555–79.
Heidegger, Martin. 1929. *Kant und das Problem der Metaphysik.* Frankfurt am Main: Klostermann.
Heidemann, Dietmar H. 2017. 'Kants Vermögensmetaphysik,' in Andree Hahmann and Bernd Ludwig (eds.), *Über die Fortschritte der kritischen Metaphysik. Beiträge zu System und Architektonik der kantischen Philosophie.* Hamburg: Meiner, 59–77.
Heimsoeth, Heinz. 1924. *Metaphysische Motive in der Ausbildung des kritischen Idealismus.* Berlin: Pan-Verlag Rolf Heise.
1966–71. *Transzendentale Dialektik. Ein Kommentar zu Kants Kritik der reinen Vernunft*, vol. 1 (1966): *Ideenlehre und Paralogismen*; vol. 2 (1967): *Vierfache Vernunftantinomie; Natur und Freiheit; intelligibler und empirischer Charakter*; vol. 3 (1969): *Das Ideal der reinen Vernunft; die spekulativen Beweisarten vom Dasein Gottes; dialektischer Schein und Leitideen der Forschung*; vol. 4 (1971): *Die Methodenlehre.* Berlin: de Gruyter.
Henrich, Dieter. 1960. *Der ontologische Gottesbeweis. Sein Problem und seine Geschichte in der Neuzeit.* Tübingen: J. C. B. Mohr.
2001. 'Systemform und Abschlussgedanke. Methode und Metaphysik als Problem in Kants Denken,' in Ralph Schumacher, Rolf-Peter Horstmann, and Volker Gerhardt (eds.), *Kant und die Berliner Aufklärung. Proceedings of the Ninth International Kant Congress, Berlin 2000*, vol. 1. Berlin: de Gruyter, 94–115.
Hessbrüggen-Walter, Stefan. 2004. *Die Seele und ihre Vermögen. Kants Metaphysik des Mentalen in der "Kritik der reinen Vernunft."* Münster: Mentis.
2015. 'Vermögen,' in Marcus Willaschek, Jürgen Stolzenberg, Georg Mohr, and Stefano Bacin (eds.), *Kant-Lexikon.* Berlin: de Gruyter, 2481–4.
Hicks, Amanda. 2013. 'Kant's Response to the Principle of Sufficient Reason,' in Stefano Bacin, Alfredo Ferrarin, Claudio La Rocca, and Margit Ruffing (eds.), *Kant und die Philosophie in Weltbürgerlicher Absicht. Proceedings of the Eleventh International Kant Congress, Pisa 2010*, vol. 5. Berlin: de Gruyter, 359–70.
Hinske, Norbert. 1991. 'Die Wissenschaften und ihre Zwecke. Kants Neuformulierung der Systemidee,' in Gerhard Funke, Manfred Kleinschnieder, Rudolf Malter, Gisela Müller, and Thomas M. Seebohm (eds.), *Proceedings of the Seventh International Kant Congress, Mainz 1990*, vol. 1. Berlin, Bonn: Bouvier, 157–78.
1993. 'Kants Rede vom Unbedingten und ihre philosophischen Motive,' in Hans Michael Baumgartner and Wilhelm G. Jacobs (eds.), *Philosophie der Subjektivität. Zur Bestimmung des Neuzeitlichen Philosophierens, Akten des 1. Kongresses der*

Internationalen Schelling-Gesellschaft 1989, vol. 1. Stuttgart, Bad Cannstatt: Frommann-Holzboog, 265–80.
  1998. 'transzendental; Transzendentalphilosophie,' in Joachim Ritter, Karlfried Gründer, and Gottfried Gabriel (eds.), *Historisches Wörterbuch der Philosophie*, vol. 10. Basel: Schwabe, 1359–436.
Hoefer, Carl. 2016. 'Causal Determinism,' in Edward N. Zalta (ed.), *The Stanford Encyclopedia of Philosophy* (spring 2016 edition), plato.stanford.edu/archives/spr2016/entries/determinism-causal/.
Höffe, Otfried. 2003. *Kants Kritik der reinen Vernunft. Die Grundlegung der modernen Philosophie*. München: Beck.
Hogan, Desmond. 2010. 'Kant's Copernican Turn and the Rationalist Tradition,' in Paul Guyer (ed.), *The Cambridge Companion to the Critique of Pure Reason*. Cambridge University Press, 21–40.
Horn, Christoph, and Christof Rapp. 2001. 'Verstand; Vernunft,' in Joachim Ritter, Karlfried Gründer, Gottfried Gabriel (eds.), *Historisches Wörterbuch der Philosophie*, vol. 11. Basel: Schwabe, 748–64.
  2005. 'Intuition und Methode. Abschied von einem Dogma der Platon- und Aristoteles-Exegese,' *Logical Analysis and History of Philosophy* 8, 11–45.
Horstmann, Rolf-Peter. 1997. 'Kants Paralogismen,' in Rolf-Peter Horstmann, *Bausteine Kritischer Philosophie. Arbeiten zu Kant*. Bodenheim: Philo, 79–107
  1998. 'Der Anhang zur Transzendentalen Dialektik (A642/B670–A704/B732). Die Idee der systematischen Einheit', in Georg Mohr and Marcus Willaschek (eds.), *Immanuel Kant. Kritik der reinen Vernunft*. Berlin: Akademie, 525–46.
Höwing, Thomas. 2016. 'Kant on Opinion, Belief, and Knowledge,' in Thomas Höwing (ed.), *The Highest Good in Kant's Philosophy*. Berlin: de Gruyter, 201–22.
Hudson, Hud. 2007. 'Simples and Gunk,' *Philosophy Compass* 2, 291–302.
Jenkins, C. S. 2011. 'Is Metaphysical Dependence Irreflexive?,' *The Monist* 94, 267–76.
Joyce, Richard. 2006. *The Evolution of Morality*. Cambridge, MA: MIT Press.
Kahane, Guy. 2011. 'Evolutionary Debunking Arguments,' *Nous* 45, 103–25.
Kahneman, Daniel. 2011. *Thinking, Fast and Slow*. New York: Farrar, Straus and Giroux.
Keil, Geert. 2000. *Handeln und Verursachen*. Frankfurt am Main: Klostermann.
Kern, Andrea. 2006. *Quellen des Wissens. Zum Begriff vernünftiger Erkenntnisfähigkeiten*. Frankfurt am Main: Suhrkamp.
Kitcher, Patricia. 1982. 'Kant's Paralogisms,' *The Philosophical Review* 9, 515–47.
  1990. *Kant's Transcendental Psychology*. New York: Oxford University Press.
  2011. *Kant's Thinker*. Oxford University Press.
Kitcher, Philip. 1986. 'Projecting the Order of Nature,' in Robert E. Butts (ed.), *Kant's Philosophy of Physical Science. Metaphysische Anfangsgründe der Naturwissenschaft 1786–1986*. Dordrecht: Reidel, 201–35.
  1994. 'The Unity of Science and the Unity of Nature,' in Paolo Parini (ed.), *Kant and Contemporary Epistemology*. Dordrecht: Kluwer, 253–72.
Kleingeld, Pauline. 1995. 'What Do the Virtuous Hope For? Re-Reading Kant's Doctrine of the Highest Good,' in Hoke Robinson (ed.), *Proceedings of the Eighth International Kant Congress, Memphis 1995*, vol. 1. Milwaukee, WI: Marquette University Press, 91–112.

Bibliography

1998a. 'The Conative Character of Reason in Kant's Philosophy,' *Journal of the History of Philosophy* 36, 77–97.

1998b. 'Kant on the Unity of Theoretical and Practical Reason,' *The Review of Metaphysics* 52, 311–39.

Kleingeld, Pauline, and Marcus Willaschek. (forthcoming). 'Autonomy without Paradox. Kant on Self-Legislation and the Moral Law.'

Klemme, Heiner F. 1996. *Kants Philosophie des Subjekts. Systematische und entwicklungsgeschichtliche Untersuchungen zum Verhältnis von Selbstbewußtsein und Selbsterkenntnis*. Hamburg: Meiner.

2010. 'Die rationalistische Interpretation von Kants "Paralogismen der reinen Vernunft." Eine Kritik,' in Jiří Chotaš, Jindřich Karásek, and Jürgen Stolzenberg (eds.), *Metaphysik und Kritik. Interpretationen zur 'Transzendentalen Dialektik' der 'Kritik der reinen Vernunft.'* Würzburg: Königshausen und Neumann, 141–61.

Klimmek, Nikolai F. 2005. *Kants System der transzendentalen Ideen*. Berlin: de Gruyter.

Kneale, William, and Martha Kneale. 1984. *The Development of Logic*. Oxford: Clarendon Press.

Knoepffler, Nikolaus. 2001. *Der Begriff 'transzendental' bei Immanuel Kant. Eine Untersuchung zur 'Kritik der reinen Vernunft.'* 5. überarbeitete Auflage. München: Herbert UTZ.

Kolodny, Niko. 2005. 'Why Be Rational?,' *Mind* 114, 509–63.

König, Peter. 2015. 'Bedingung,' in Marcus Willaschek, Jürgen Stolzenberg, Georg Mohr, and Stefano Bacin (eds.), *Kant-Lexikon*. Berlin: de Gruyter, 223–6.

Kraus, Katharina T. (in press). 'The Soul as the "Guiding Idea" of Psychology. Kant on Scientific Psychology, Systematicity, and the Idea of the Soul,' *Studies in History and Philosophy of Science*.

Kreimendahl, Lothar. 1998. 'Die Antinomie der reinen Vernunft. 1. und 2. Abschnitt (A405/B432–A461/B489),' in Georg Mohr and Marcus Willaschek (eds.), *Immanuel Kant. Kritik der reinen Vernunft*. Berlin: Akademie, 413–47.

Kreimendahl, Lothar, and Jens Oberhausen. 2011. 'Einleitung,' in Lothar Kreimendahl and Jens Oberhausen (eds.), *Immanuel Kant. Der einzig mögliche Beweisgrund zu einer Demonstration des Daseins Gottes. Historisch-kritische Edition*. Hamburg: Meiner, xiii–cccxxxix.

Kreines, James. 2015. *Reason in the World. Hegel's Metaphysics and Its Philosophical Appeal*. Oxford University Press.

Kreis, Guido. 2015. *Negative Dialektik des Unendlichen – Kant, Hegel, Cantor*. Berlin: Suhrkamp.

Kripke, Saul A. 1980. *Naming and Necessity*. Cambridge, MA: Harvard University Press.

Ladyman, James, Don Ross, and David Spurrett. 2007. 'In Defence of Scientism,' in James Ladyman, Don Ross, David Spurrett, and John Collier (eds.), *Every Thing Must Go. Metaphysics Naturalized*. Oxford University Press, 1–66.

Lau, Chong-Fuk. 2015. 'Spekulation, spekulativ,' in Marcus Willaschek, Jürgen Stolzenberg, Georg Mohr, and Stefano Bacin (eds.), *Kant-Lexikon*. Berlin: de Gruyter, 2143–5.

Leary, Stephanie. 2016. 'In Defense of Practical Reasons for Belief,' *Australasian Journal of Philosophy* 95, 529–42.

Levey, Samuel. 2016. 'The Paradox of Sufficient Reason,' *Philosophical Review* 125, 397–430.

Longuenesse, Béatrice. 1998. *Kant and the Capacity to Judge. Sensibility and Discursivity in the Transcendental Analytic of the Critique of Pure Reason.* Princeton University Press.

2005a. 'Kant's Deconstruction of the Principle of Sufficient Reason,' in Béatrice Longuenesse, *Kant on the Human Standpoint.* Cambridge University Press, 117–142.

2005b. 'The Transcendental Ideal and the Unity of the Critical System,' in Béatrice Longuenesse, *Kant on the Human Standpoint.* Cambridge University Press, 211–35.

Lowe, E. J. 2006. 'Non-Cartesian Substance Dualism and the Problem of Mental Causation,' *Erkenntnis* 65, 5–23.

Ludwig, Bernd. 2017. 'Kants Fortschritte auf dem langen Weg zur konsequent-kritischen Metaphysik,' in Andree Hahmann and Bernd Ludwig (eds.), *Über die Fortschritte der kritischen Metaphysik. Beiträge zu System und Architektonik der kantischen Philosophie.* Hamburg: Meiner, 79–118.

MacFarlane, John. 2002. 'Frege, Kant, and the Logic in Logicism,' *The Philosophical Review* 111, 25–65.

Malzkorn, Wolfgang. 1995. 'Kants Kritik an der traditionellen Syllogistik,' *History and Philosophy of Logic* 16, 75–88.

1998. 'Sind Kants Paralogismen ein natürliches und unvermeidliches Problem der Vernunft?,' in Jochen Lechner (ed.), *Analyse, Rekonstruktion, Kritik.* Frankfurt am Main: Peter Lang, 95–111.

1999. *Kants Kosmologie-Kritik. Eine formale Analyse der Antinomienlehre.* Berlin: de Gruyter.

Martin, Raymond, and John Barresi (eds.). 2003. *Personal Identity.* Oxford: Blackwell.

Marušić, Berislav. 2015. *Evidence and Agency. Norms of Belief for Promising and Resolving.* Oxford University Press.

Marwede, Florian. 2018. *Das Höchste Gut in Kants Deontologischer Ethik.* Berlin: de Gruyter.

Massimi, Michela. 2017. 'What Is This Thing Called "Scientific Knowledge"? – Kant on Imaginary Standpoints and the Regulative Role of Reason,' *Kant Yearbook* 9, 63–84.

Matthiessen, Hannes O. 2014. *Epistemic Entitlement. The Right to Believe.* Basingstoke: Palgrave Macmillan.

Matthiessen, Hannes O. 2016. 'Empirical Conditions for a Reidean Geometry of Visual Experience,' *Topoi* 35, 511–22.

McLaughlin, Peter. 2014. 'Transcendental Presuppositions and Ideas of Reason,' *Kant-Studien* 105, 554–72.

Meerbote, Ralf. 1982. 'Kant's Use of the Notions "Objective Reality" and "Objective Validity",' *Kant-Studien* 63, 51–8.

Messina, James. 2014. 'Kantian Space, Supersubstantivalism, and the Spirit of Spinoza,' *Kant Yearbook* 6, 43–64.

Mohr, Georg. 2004. *Kants Grundlegung der kritischen Philosophie. Werkkommentar und Stellenkommentar zur Kritik der reinen Vernunft, zu den Prolegomena und zu den Fortschritten der Metaphysik.* Frankfurt am Main: Suhrkamp.

Mudd, Sasha. 2013. 'Rethinking the Priority of Practical Reason in Kant,' *European Journal of Philosophy* 24, 78–102.

Bibliography

Naeve, Nico, and Hernán Pringe. 2015. 'Antinomie der reinen Vernunft,' in Marcus Willaschek, Jürgen Stolzenberg, Georg Mohr, and Stefano Bacin (eds.), *Kant-Lexikon*. Berlin: de Gruyter, 127–35.

Nagel, Thomas. 1986. *The View from Nowhere*. New York: Oxford University Press.

Neiman, Susan. 1994. *The Unity of Reason. Rereading Kant*. New York: Oxford University Press.
  1995. 'Understanding the Unconditioned,' in Hoke Robinson (ed.), *Proceedings of the Eighth International Kant Congress, Memphis 1995*, vol. 1. Milwaukee, WI: Marquette University Press, 505–19.

Nenon, Thomas. 2015. 'Gültigkeit, objektive,' in Marcus Willaschek, Jürgen Stolzenberg, Georg Mohr, and Stefano Bacin (eds.), *Kant-Lexikon*. Berlin: de Gruyter, 966–7.

Nortmann, Ulrich. 1998. 'Kants Urteilstafel und die Vollständigkeitsfrage. Kritische Einwände gegen Michael Wolff (I. Teil),' *Zeitschrift für philosophische Forschung* 52, 406–21.

Pasternack, Lawrence. 2014. 'Kant on Opinion. Assent, Hypothesis, and the Norms of General Applied Logic,' *Kant-Studien* 105, 41–82.

Peirce, Charles S. 1992. *The Essential Peirce. Selected Philosophical Writings*, ed. Nathan Houser and Christian J. W. Kloesel. Bloomington: Indiana University Press.

Pissis, Jannis. 2012. *Kants transzendentale Dialektik. Zu ihrer systematischen Bedeutung*. Berlin: de Gruyter.

Proops, Ian. 2010. 'Kant's First Paralogism,' *Philosophical Review* 119, 449–95.

Putnam, Hilary. 1981. *Reason, Truth, and History*. Cambridge University Press.

Quine, Willard Van Orman. 1953. 'Two Dogmas of Empiricism,' in Willard Van Orman Quine, *From a Logical Point of View*. Cambridge, MA: Harvard University Press, 20–46.

Reath, Andrews. 1988. 'Two Conceptions of the Highest Good in Kant,' *Journal of the History of Philosophy* 26, 593–619.

Recki, Birgit. 2001. *Ästhetik der Sitten. Die Affinität von ästhetischem Gefühl und praktischer Vernunft bei Kant*. Klostermann: Frankfurt am Main.

Redaktion. 2015. 'Realität, objektive,' in Marcus Willaschek, Jürgen Stolzenberg, Georg Mohr, and Stefano Bacin (eds.), *Kant-Lexikon*. Berlin: de Gruyter, 1897–8.

Renaut, Alain. 1998. 'Transzendentale Dialektik. Einleitung und Buch I (A293/B349–A338/B396),' in Georg Mohr and Marcus Willaschek (eds.), *Immanuel Kant. Kritik der reinen Vernunft*. Berlin: Akademie, 353–71.

Ricken, Friedo. 2010. 'Von der Unentbehrlichkeit der transzendentalen Theologie. Zum "Ideal der Reinen Vernunft",' in Norbert Fischer (ed.), *Kants Grundlegung einer kritischen Metaphysik. Einführung in die 'Kritik der reinen Vernunft'*. Hamburg: Meiner, 313–23.

Rinard, Susanna. 2017. 'No Exception for Belief,' in *Philosophy and Phenomenological Research* 94, 121–143.

Rohlf, Michael. 2010. 'The Ideas of Pure Reason,' in Paul Guyer (ed.), *The Cambridge Companion to Kant's 'Critique of Pure Reason.'* Cambridge University Press, 190–209.

Rohs, Peter. 1978. 'Kants Prinzip der durchgängigen Bestimmung alles Seienden,' *Kant-Studien* 69, 170–80.

1987. 'Philosophie als Selbsterhellung von Vernunft,' in Wolfgang R. Köhler, Wolfgang Kuhlmann, and Peter Rohs (eds.), *Philosophie und Begründung*. Frankfurt am Main: Suhrkamp, 363–91.

Rosefeldt, Tobias. 2000. *Das logische Ich. Kant über den Gehalt des Begriffes von sich selbst*. Stuttgart: Philo.

2017. 'Subjects of Kant's First Paralogism,' in Anil Gomez and Andrew Stephenson (eds.), *Kant and the Philosophy of Mind. Perception, Reason, and the Self*. Oxford University Press, 221–44.

Rosen, Gideon. 2010. 'Metaphysical Dependence. Grounding and Reduction,' in Bob Hale and Aviv Hoffmann (eds.), *Modality, Metaphysics, Logic and Epistemology*. Oxford University Press, 109–35.

Rutherford, Donald. 1995. *Leibniz and the Rational Order of Nature*. Cambridge University Press.

Schafer, Karl. 2017. 'Rationality as the Capacity for Understanding,' *Nous*. Online at https://doi.org/10.1111/nous.12231.

Schaffer, Jonathan. 2010. 'Monism. The Priority of the Whole,' *Philosophical Review* 119, 31–76.

Schmucker, Josef. 1990. *Das Weltproblem in Kants Kritik der reinen Vernunft. Kommentar und Strukturanalyse des ersten Buches und des zweiten Hauptstücks des zweiten Buches der transzendentalen Dialektik*. Bonn: Bouvier.

Schulting, Dennis. 2011. 'Kant's Idealism. The Current Debate,' in Dennis Schulting and Jacco Verburgt (eds.), *Kant's Idealism. New Interpretations of a Controversial Doctrine*. Dordrecht: Springer, 1–29.

Schulting, Dennis, and Jacco Verburgt (eds.) 2011. *Kant's Idealism: New Interpretations of a Controversial Doctrine*. Dordrecht: Springer.

Seeberg, Ulrich. 2015. 'Richtigkeit, objektive,' in Marcus Willaschek, Jürgen Stolzenberg, Georg Mohr, and Stefano Bacin (eds.), *Kant-Lexikon*. Berlin: de Gruyter, 1984–5.

Sider, Theodore. 2011. *Writing the Book of the World*. Oxford University Press.

Stang, Nicholas F. 2016. *Kant's Modal Metaphysics*. Oxford University Press.

Stephenson, Andrew. 2015. 'Kant on the Object-Dependence of Intuition and Hallucination,' *Philosophical Quaterly* 65, 486–508.

Stevenson, Leslie. 2011a. 'A Theory of Everything? Kant Speaks to Stephen Hawking,' in Leslie Stevenson, *Inspirations from Kant. Essays*. Oxford University Press, 63–76.

2011b. 'Opinion, Belief or Faith, and Knowledge,' in Leslie Stevenson, *Inspirations from Kant. Essays*. Oxford University Press, 77–94.

Stich, Stephen P., and Ted A. Warfield (eds.) 2003. *The Blackwell Guide to Philosophy of Mind*. Malden, MA: Blackwell.

Strawson, Peter F. 1959. *Individuals. An Essay in Descriptive Metaphysics*. London: Routledge.

1966. *The Bounds of Sense. An Essay on Kant's Critique of Pure Reason*. London: Methuen.

Street, Sharon. 2006. 'A Darwinian Dilemma for Realist Theories of Value,' *Philosophical Studies* 127, 109–66.

Stuhlmann-Laeisz, Rainer. 1976. *Kants Logik. Eine Interpretation auf der Grundlage von Vorlesungen, veröffentlichten Werken und Nachlaß.* Berlin: de Gruyter.

1990. 'Formale und transzendentale Logik im Paralogismenkapitel von Kants *Kritik der reinen Vernunft*,' in Hubertus Busche, George Heffernan, and Dieter Lohmar (eds.), *Bewußtsein und Zeitlichkeit. Ein Problemschnitt durch die Philosophie der Neuzeit.* Würzburg: Königshausen und Neumann, 61–75.

Sturm, Thomas. 2001. 'Kant on Empirical Psychology. How Not to Investigate the Human Mind,' in Eric Watkins (ed.), *Kant and the Sciences.* Oxford University Press, 163–85.

2009. *Kant und die Wissenschaften vom Menschen.* Paderborn: Mentis.

2015. 'Hypothese,' in in Marcus Willaschek, Jürgen Stolzenberg, Georg Mohr, and Stefano Bacin (eds.), *Kant-Lexikon.* Berlin: de Gruyter, 1059–61.

(in press). 'Kant on the Roles of Ends in Science,' *Kant-Studien.*

Sturma, Dieter. 1998. 'Die Paralogismen der reinen Vernunft in der zweiten Auflage,' in Georg Mohr and Marcus Willaschek (eds.), *Immanuel Kant. Kritik der reinen Vernunft.* Berlin: Akademie, 391–412.

Tahko, Tuomas E. 2015. *An Introduction to Metametaphysics.* Cambridge University Press.

Tetens, Holm. 2006. *Kants 'Kritik der reinen Vernunft.' Ein systematischer Kommentar.* Stuttgart: Reclam.

Theis, Robert. 2010. 'Kants Ideenmetaphysik. Zur "Einleitung" und dem "Ersten Buch" der "transzendentalen Dialektik",' in Norbert Fischer (ed.), *Kants Grundlegung einer kritischen Metaphysik. Einführung in die 'Kritik der reinen Vernunft.'* Hamburg: Meiner, 197–214.

Thöle, Bernhard. 2000. 'Die Einheit der Erfahrung. Zur Funktion der regulativen Prinzipien bei Kant,' in Rainer Enskat (ed.), *Erfahrung und Urteilskraft.* Würzburg: Königshausen und Neumann, 113–34.

2010. 'Kants Diagnose der Illusionen der rationalen Psychologie,' in Jiří Chotaš, Jindřich Karásek, and Jürgen Stolzenberg (eds.), *Metaphysik und Kritik. Interpretationen zur 'Transzendentalen Dialektik' der Kritik der reinen Vernunft.* Würzburg: Königshausen und Neumann, 99–116.

Timmermann, Jens. 2009. 'The Unity of Reason. Kantian Perspectives,' in Robertson, Simon (ed.), *Spheres of Reason. New Essays in the Philosophy of Normativity.* Oxford University Press, 183–98.

Tolley, Clinton. 2007. 'Kant's Conception of Logic.' Dissertation, University of Chicago, Department of Philosophy.

2012. 'The Generality of Kant's Transcendental Logic,' *Journal of the History of Philosophy* 50, 417–46.

Verburgt, Jacko. 2011. 'How to Account for Reason's Interest in an Ultimate Prototype? A Note on Kant's Doctrine of the Transcendental Ideal,' in Dennis Schulting and Jacko Verburgt (eds.), *Kant's Idealism. New Interpretations of a Controversial Doctrine.* Dordrecht: Springer, 237–54.

Wartenberg, Thomas E. 1992. 'Reason and the Practice of Science,' in Paul Guyer (ed.), *The Cambridge Companion to Kant.* Cambridge University Press, 228–48.

Watkins, Eric. 1998. 'The Antinomy of Pure Reason. Sections 3–8 (A462/B490–A515/B543),' in Georg Mohr and Marcus Willaschek (eds.), *Immanuel Kant. Kritik der reinen Vernunft.* Berlin: Akademie, 447–65.

2005. *Kant and the Metaphysics of Causality.* Cambridge University Press.

(ed.) 2009. *Kant's Critique of Pure Reason. Background Source Materials.* Cambridge University Press.

2010. 'The Antinomy of Practical Reason. Reason, the Unconditioned and the Highest Good,' in Andrews Reath and Jens Timmermann (eds.), *Kant's Critique of Practical Reason. A Critical Guide.* Cambridge University Press, 145–67.

2013. 'Kant on Infima Species,' in Stefano Bacin, Alfredo Ferrarin, Claudio La Rocca, and Margit Ruffing (eds.), *Kant und die Philosophie in Weltbürgerlicher Absicht. Proceedings of the Eleventh International Kant Congress, Pisa 2010,* vol. 5. Berlin: de Gruyter, 283–94.

2016a. 'Kant on Materialism,' *British Journal for the History of Philosophy* 24, 1035–52.

2016b. 'The Unconditioned and the Absolute in Kant and Early German Romanticism,' *Kant Yearbook* 8, 117–42.

(in press). 'Kant on Real Conditions,' in Margit Ruffing and Violetta Waibel (eds.), *Natur und Freiheit. Proceedings of the Twelfth International Kant Congress, Wien 2015.* Berlin: de Gruyter.

Watkins, Eric, and Marcus Willaschek. 2017. 'Kant's Account of Cognition,' *Journal of the History of Philosophy* 55, 83–112.

Willaschek, Marcus. 1992. *Praktische Vernunft. Handlungstheorie und Moralbegründung bei Kant.* Stuttgart, Weimar: J. B. Metzler.

1998. 'Phaenomena/Noumena und die Amphibolie der Reflexionsbegriffe (A235/B294–A292/B349),' in Georg Mohr and Marcus Willaschek (eds.), *Immanuel Kant. Kritik der reinen Vernunft.* Berlin: Akademie, 325–51.

2003. *Der mentale Zugang zur Welt. Realismus, Skeptizismus und Intentionalität.* Frankfurt am Main: Klostermann.

2006. 'Practical Reason. A Commentary on Kant's Groundwork of the Metaphysics of Morals (GMS II, 412–417),' in Christoph Horn and Dieter Schönecker (eds.), *Groundwork for the Metaphysics of Morals.* Berlin: de Gruyter, 121–38.

2007. 'Contextualism about Knowledge and Justification by Default,' *Grazer Philosophische Studien* 74, 251–72.

2008. 'Kant on the Necessity of Metaphysics,' in Valerio Rohden, Ricardo R. Terra, Guido A. Almeida, and Margit Ruffing (eds.), *Recht und Frieden in der Philosophie Kants. Proceedings of the Tenth International Kant Congress, Sao Paulo 2005,* vol. 1. Berlin: de Gruyter, 285–307.

2010. 'The Primacy of Pure Practical Reason and the Very Idea of a Postulate,' in Andrews Reath and Jens Timmermann (eds.), *Kant's Critique of Practical Reason. A Critical Guide.* Cambridge University Press, 168–96.

2012. 'Non-Relativist Contextualism about Knowledge,' in Christoph Jäger and Winfried Löffler (eds.), *Epistemology: Contexts, Values, Disagreement. Proceedings of the 34th International Ludwig Wittgenstein Symposium in Kirchberg.* Frankfurt: Ontos, 53–62.

2013. 'Kant's Two Conceptions of (Pure) Reason in the "Critique of Pure Reason",' in Stefano Bacin, Alfredo Ferrarin, Claudio La Rocca, and Margit Ruffing (eds.), *Kant und die Philosophie in Weltbürgerlicher Absicht. Proceedings of the Eleventh International Kant Congress, Pisa 2010,* vol. 2. Berlin: de Gruyter, 483–93.

2015. 'The Sensibility of Human Intuition. Kant's Causal Condition on Accounts of Representation,' in Rainer Enskat (ed.), *Kants Theorie der Erfahrung*. Berlin: de Gruyter, 129–49.

2016. 'Kant and Peirce on Belief,' in Gabriele Gava and Robert Stern (eds.), *Pragmatism, Kant, and Transcendental Philosophy*. New York: Routledge, 133–51.

2017. 'Kant on Real Conditioning,' *Studi Kantiani* 30, 29–44.

2018. 'Freedom as a Postulate,' in Eric Watkins (ed.), *Kant on Persons and Agency*. Cambridge University Press, 102–19.

(forthcoming). 'Transcendental Idealism,' in Julian Wuerth (ed.), *Cambridge Kant-Lexicon*. Cambridge University Press.

Willaschek, Marcus, and Eric Watkins. 2017. 'Kant on Cognition and Knowledge.' *Synthese*. Online at https://doi.org/10.1007/s11229-017-1624-4.

Williams, Michael. 2001. *Problems of Knowledge. A Critical Introduction to Epistemology*. Oxford University Press.

Wilson, Jessica M. 2014. 'No Work for a Theory of Grounding,' *Inquiry* 57, 535–79.

Wolff, Michael. 1995. *Die Vollständigkeit der kantischen Urteilstafel. Mit einem Essay über Freges Begriffsschrift*. Frankfurt am Main: Klostermann.

1998. 'Erwiderung auf die Einwände von Ansgar Beckermann und Ulrich Nortmann,' *Zeitschrift für philosophische Forschung* 52, 435–59.

2000. 'Kantische Urteilstafel und vollständige Induktion. Nachtrag zu meiner Kontroverse mit Ulrich Nortmann,' *Zeitschrift für philosophische Forschung* 54, 86–94.

Wood, Allen W. 1978. *Kant's Rational Theology*. Ithaca, NY: Cornell University Press.

2010. 'The Antinomies of Pure Reason,' in Paul Guyer (ed.), *The Cambridge Companion to Kant's Critique of Pure Reason*. Cambridge University Press, 245–66.

Wuerth, Julian. 2010. 'The Paralogisms of Pure Reason,' in Paul Guyer (ed.), *The Cambridge Companion to Kant's Critique of Pure Reason*. Cambridge University Press, 210–44.

Wundt, Max. 1924. *Kant als Metaphysiker. Ein Beitrag zur Geschichte der deutschen Philosophie im 18. Jahrhundert*. Stuttgart: Enke Verlag.

Young, John M. 1992. 'Functions of Thought and the Synthesis of Intuitions,' in Paul Guyer (ed.), *The Cambridge Companion to Kant*. Cambridge University Press, 101–22.

Zöller, Günther. 1984. *Theoretische Gegenstandsbeziehung bei Kant. Zur systematischen Bedeutung der Termini "objektive Realität" und "objektive Gültigkeit" in der "Kritik der reinen Vernunft."* Berlin: de Gruyter.

Index of Names

Abaci, Uygar, 220
Al-Azm, Sadiq J., 212
Albert the Great, 144
Allais, Lucy, xii, 247
Allison, Henry E., 11, 64, 87, 95, 103, 111–12, 116, 123, 137–8, 143, 170, 179, 184, 209, 219–20, 226–7, 231, 234, 241
Ameriks, Karl, 11, 69, 156, 189, 195, 197, 264
Anderson, R. Lanier, 11, 34, 104, 154, 197, 253
Aristotle, 2, 29, 38, 51, 144–5, 147, 169, 190
Augustine, 143

Bacon, Francis, 6, 51
Barnett, David, 194
Barresi, John, 194
Baum, Manfred, 62
Baumgarten, Alexander Gottlieb, 31, 38–9, 58, 60, 78, 82, 98, 144–5, 190
Beckermann, Ansgar, 173, 194
Bennett, Jonathan, 8, 11, 22, 83, 173, 185, 190–1, 195, 254
Benson, Carolyn, xii
Bertea, Stefano, xii
Bird, Graham, 209
Birken-Bertsch, Hanno, 110, 235
Bliss, Ricki, 75, 79
Blöser, Claudia, xii
Boehm, Omri, 99, 101
Breitenbach, Angela, xii
Brook, Andrew, 194–5
Burt, Fabian, xii, 168, 196
Busse, Ralf, xii
Butts, Robert E., 137

Caimi, Mario, 32, 112, 116–17, 171, 272
Callanan, John J., 219
Cantor, Georg, 95–6
Carruthers, Peter, 194
Chalmers, David, 37, 194
Chaplin, Rosalind, xii, 87

Chignell, Andrew, xii, 30, 72, 99, 115, 220, 226–8, 243, 255, 259–61, 272
Cohen, Hermann, 36
Correia, Fabrice, 74, 216
Crusius, Christian August, 30

Dahlstrom, Daniel, 50, 54
Della Rocca, Michael, 98, 216, 251
Descartes, René, 29–30, 32, 145
Dohrn, Daniel, 113
Dörflinger, Bernd, 241
Dummett, Michael, 149, 215
Dupré, John, 66
Dyck, Corey W., 189–90, 202

Eidam, Heinz, 99
Emundts, Dina, 141
Engelhard, Kristina, 209, 212
Engfer, Hans-Jürgen, 98
Engstrom, Stephen P., 24, 271
Ertl, Wolfgang, 209

Falkenburg, Brigitte, 11, 209
Ferrari, Jean, 219
Ferrarin, Alfredo, 24, 81, 260
Fine, Kit, 74, 80
Fodor, Jerry A., 66
Förster, Eckart, 141, 241
Frege, Gottlob, 96
Friedman, Michael, 67, 108, 110, 173
Fulda, Hans Friedrich, 53

Gardner, Sebastian, 156, 273
Gava, Gabriele, xii, 38, 54, 62, 67–8, 204
Gawlick, Günther, 39
Geiger, Ido, 117
Gerhardt, Volker, xi, 11
Ginsborg, Hannah, 117
Gomes, Anil, 195
Goy, Ina, 54

Index of Names

Grier, Michelle, 11, 63, 103, 111–13, 117, 122–3, 136–40, 170, 184, 189, 196–7, 219–20, 231, 235, 239, 241
Grüne, Stefanie, 72, 175, 259
Guyer, Paul, ix, 11, 22, 26, 32, 53, 92, 105, 113, 117, 129, 141, 155, 172, 174, 183, 209, 249, 272–3

Haag, Johannes, 140
Hahmann, Andree, 90
Hawking, Stephen, 66
Hebbeler, James C., 33
Heidegger, Martin, 36
Heidemann, Dietmar H., 24
Heimsoeth, Heinz, 11, 36, 178
Henrich, Dieter, 53, 219–20
Hessbrüggen-Walter, Stefan, 24
Hicks, Amanda, 99
Hinske, Norbert, 62, 113, 179
Hoefer, Carl, 216
Höffe, Otfried, 11
Horn, Christoph, 29
Horstmann, Rolf-Peter, 108, 110–11, 170, 189
Höwing, Thomas, 271–2
Hudson, Hud, 216
Hume, David, 6, 148, 273
Hüwelmeyer, Kai, xii

Jenkins, C.S., 100
Joyce, Richard, 262

Kahane, Guy, 262
Kahneman, Daniel, 24, 137
Keil, Geert, 216
Kern, Andrea, 24
Kitcher, Patricia, 189, 195
Kitcher, Philip, 53, 67, 108, 117
Kleingeld, Pauline, xii, 24, 28, 271
Klemme, Heiner F., 189, 196
Klimmek, Nikolai F., 10–11, 50, 63, 72, 139, 169–71, 174–5, 177, 184–5, 187, 189, 203, 219, 223, 227–8
Kneale, Martha, 51
Kneale, William, 51
Knoepffler, Nikolaus, 113
Kolodny, Niko, 25
König, Peter, 78
Kraus, Katharina T., xii, 40, 241
Kreimendahl, Lothar, 39, 209, 220
Kreines, James, 11, 99, 103
Kreis, Guido, 95
Kruck, Günter, 241
Kufrin, Pavle, xii, 235

Ladyman, James, 250
Lau, Chong-Fuk, 26
Leary, Stephanie, 273
Leibniz, Gottfried Wilhelm, 29, 98, 144, 147, 223, 253
Levey, Samuel, 92, 98, 216
Longuenesse, Béatrice, 99, 219, 222
Lowe, E.J., 194
Ludwig, Bernd, 37, 90

MacFarlane, John, 48
Malzkorn, Wolfgang, 11, 50, 90, 139, 171, 189, 195–6, 203, 206, 209–10
Martin, Raymond, 194
Marušić, Berislav, 273
Marwede, Florian, xii, 271
Massimi, Michela, 108, 112, 116, 239, 241
Matthiessen, Hannes O., 69, 250
McLaughlin, Peter, 112, 116, 239, 254
Meerbote, Ralf, 105
Meier, Georg Friedrich, 30–1, 51, 55, 61–2, 120
Messina, James, 144
Mohr, Georg, xi, 11
Mudd, Sasha, 112, 116
Müller, Andi, xii
Müller-Hornbach, Maria, xii

Naeve, Nico, 209
Nagel, Thomas, 250
Neiman, Susan, 11, 53, 144
Nenon, Thomas, 105
Nortmann, Ulrich, 173

Oberhausen, Jens, 220

Pasternack, Lawrence, 272
Peirce, Charles Sanders, 69
Pissis, Jannis, 10–11, 110
Plato, 32
Pringe, Hernán, 209
Proops, Ian, 58, 64, 103, 126, 137, 189, 195, 197, 200
Putnam, Hilary, 246, 248

Quine, Willard Van Orman, 67

Rapp, Christof, 29
Reath, Andrews, xii, 271
Recki, Birgit, 255
Renaut, Alain, 103, 171
Ricken, Friedo, 219
Rinard, Susanna, 273
Rohlf, Michael, 58, 138, 170–2, 184
Rohs, Peter, xi, 38, 219, 222, 225

Index of Names

Rosefeldt, Tobias, xii, 11, 174, 189, 191, 196–7, 200, 259
Rosen, Gideon, 78, 80
Russo, Maria, xii
Rutherford, Donald, 144

Schafer, Karl, xii, 58, 148
Schaffer, Jonathan, 78
Schmucker, Josef, 203, 209
Schnieder, Benjamin, 13, 74, 216
Schulting, Dennis, 138, 247
Seeberg, Ulrich, 105
Sider, Theodore, 145
Spinoza, Baruch de, 100, 144, 191
Stang, Nicholas F., 72–3, 103, 220, 236, 243
Stephenson, Andrew, 72, 195
Stevenson, Leslie, 66, 272
Stich, Stephen P., 194
Stolzenberg, Jürgen, 53
Stratman, Joseph, xii, 87
Strawson, Peter Frederick, 173, 194, 219, 254
Street, Sharon, 262
Stuhlmann-Laeisz, Rainer, 50, 195
Sturm, Thomas, xii, 38, 40, 53, 55, 62, 108, 115
Sturma, Dieter, 189

Tahko, Tuomas E., 37
Tetens, Holm, 211

Theis, Robert, 171
Thomas Aquinas, 144
Thöle, Bernhard, 110–13, 117, 129, 189, 196
Tolley, Clinton, xii, 38, 48, 73, 173
Trogdon, Kelly, 75, 79

Verburgt, Jacko, 138, 219

Wartenberg, Thomas E., 117
Watkins, Eric, xi–xii, 2, 30, 41, 46, 55, 72, 74–6, 78, 80, 85, 100, 109, 139, 156, 189, 209, 220–1, 252–3, 257, 271
Williams, Michael, 69
Wilson, Jessica M., 80, 133
Wolff, Christian, 29–31, 38, 51, 62, 98, 143–4
Wolff, Michael, xii, 48, 73, 173
Wood, Allen W., ix, 11, 22, 26, 83, 92, 105, 141, 155, 174, 183, 209, 211–12, 219–20, 223, 226–8, 254
Wuerth, Julian, 189
Wundt, Max, 36

Young, John Michael, ix, 173

Zöller, Günther, 105

Index of Subjects

a priori, purely, 27
ambiguity, 123–5, 139–41, 146–7, 195–6, 201, 236
answer, ultimate, 1, 5–6, 133–4, 160, 176, 213–15, 274
antinomies, 84, 91, 149, 187, 203–4, 208–16, 265–6, 268
  general schema, 210
  generated by three-step procedure, 209
  involving sophisma figurae dictionis, 207
  and necessary inferences of reason, 209–12
  resolution of, 138–9, 154
  synthesis either too big or too small, 212
  and transcendental realism, 212–16
appearance/thing in itself, 42, 138, 140, 246
Appendix to the Transcendental Dialectic, 107–20, 124, 237–42
  ambiguity in, 124
  two projects, 242
apperception, transcendental, 200–1
assuming, 115, 117–18, 123–4

belief/knowledge, 272, 274; *see also* knowledge
biology, 66
bivalence, 149, 215
  Bivalence$_w$, 149–50
brain in a vat, 273

category, 42–3, 82, 256
  objective validity of, 106
  relational, 75, 80–4, 86, 183
  transcendental deduction of, 106, 198, 260
  (un)schematized, 80–2, 86, 258, 261
causation, 42, 74, 80–1, 83, 89, 106
  uncaused cause (as inferred concept), 176
certain, certainty, 54, 57–8, 61–3, 67
  empirical/rational, 61
chemists, 145–6
cognition, 2, 41, 46, 59, 253
  epistemically/inferentially (un)conditioned, 56–63, 70, 87–8, 158

and knowledge, 252
limits of, 251–4
from mere concepts, 34
no cognition without intuition (CI), 253
synthetic, 34
system of, 53
community (causal interaction), 76–7, 80, 82–3
complete, completeness, 1, 6, 54, 61, 69–70, 92, 158, 160, 173, 264, 268
  of conditions, 94
  and totality, 91–4
compositum/totum, 77
comprehension, principle of, 94–6, 98, 101, 153, 155, 158, 180, 268
concatenation, inferential, 51–3
concept, complete, 223
concurrence, 82–3, 86–7, 97
condition, 4, 73–86, 101; *see also* conditioning, real
  analytic/synthetic link between conditioned and condition, 153–4
  ascending/descending series of conditions, 94
  complete series of conditions, 93, 207, 209
  complete series of conditions (finite/infinite), 210, 213, 215
  coordinated/subordinated, 83, 91, 93, 97
  epistemic/inferential, 63
  logical/real, 49, 52, 131, 133, 178
  necessary/sufficient, 78–9
  of the possibility of experience, 86
conditioned, 4, 46, 73–86; *see also* cognition
conditioning, real, 73–86, 158, 160
  (a)symmetry of, 75–8, 83
  as disjunctive concept, 75, 78–83
  intelligibility of, 75, 83
  (in)transitivity of, 75–8, 83, 86, 89, 93
  (ir)reflexivity of, 76–7, 83, 86, 89
  three fundamental relations, 82, 86–7, 158
constitution, material, 83, 89

294

Index of Subjects

constitutive/regulative, 110, 202, 222, 238, 242, 265, 267; *see also* principle
contingent/necessary, 74, 81–3
cosmology, rational, 39, 166

De Mundi, 143
debunking argument, 262
deduction, metaphysical, 170; *see also* idea, transcendental
dependence, 82–3, 86–7
descriptive/prescriptive; *see* principle
dianoia/noêsis, 29, 32
discursive/discursivity, 1, 6, 22, 34, 36–7, 50, 69–70, 158, 160, 244, 264, 268
Dreams of a Spirit Seer, 125

ens realissimum, 74, 166, 220, 226–7, 229–34, 258, 262
evidentialism, 273
explanation, 58, 85–6
   complete, 91, 273–5
   inferential, 52
explanatory, 75, 78, 85–6

faculty, 21–3
False Subtlety, 22, 50
focus imaginarius, 239, 241
freedom as practial postulate, 272

given, 71–3, 84, 152
   epistemic/ontological meaning, 72
God, 87–9, 92–3, 99–101, 141–4, 231, 236, 258, 271, 274; *see also ens realissimum*; ideal, transcendental
   cosmological argument, 232, 234
   idea of, 184, 231, 239–41
   natural argument, 166–70, 233–6
   objective reality of the idea of, 228
   ontological argument, 231–2, 234–5
   physicotheological argument, 232, 234–5
good, highest, 271
gravitation, 67
ground, grounding (metaphysical), 74–80, 99–102, 216
   irreflexivity of, 100
   transitivity of, 101
Groundwork, 28, 35, 40, 43–4, 148

Hechsel Logic, 195
hypostatizing, 231

idea, 167–8; *see also* idea, transcendental
   cosmological, 187, 202–8
   cosmological (system of), 203
   guiding (in a system), 54
   practical, 167
   psychological, 187–95
idea, transcendental, 167–70, 239, 241, 244, 254–62; *see also* idea
   concept of soul/world/God (no transcendental idea), 170
   conservative/moderate/radical reading of, 254, 256–62
   as inferred concept, 168, 172–7, 227
   as mere creation of our minds, 262
   metaphysical deduction of, 170–7
   objective reality of, 254–6, 259
   and really possible objects, 258–60
   as result of series of prosyllogisms, 174
   subjectivist account of, 261–2
   system of, 7, 165, 168–9, 186, 266
   three classes, 168, 182–5
ideal, transcendental, 166, 219–20
   as inferred concept, 226–7
   as really possible, 227–8
idealism, transcendental (TI), 138–9, 199, 243–51
   as key to resolution of antinomies, 138–9, 247
illusion, logical/perceptual, 135–6
illusion, transcendental, 103, 126, 135–8, 147, 150, 159, 161, 164, 241
   in Appendix, 238, 240–1
   explanation of, 137
   and ideal of reason (God), 235
   in paralogisms, 195–202
imperative, categorical, 64, 70, 121, 270
inference, 22
inference, rational (inference of reason), 22, 48–51, 63, 70, 86
   cosmological, 139, 146, 154–5, 204, 208
   forms of (categorical/hypothetical/disjunctive), 49–50
   necessary inference of reason, 168, 176–7, 179, 188–9, 216, 232
inherence, 80–3, 86–7, 192–3
intellect, intuitive, 141, 241
intellectus archetypus, 240–1
interaction, causal, 76, 80; *see also* community
intuitive, intuition, 22, 29–31, 34, 36
   human intuition as sensible (HIS), 253
   intellectual intuition, 141, 241
iterative, iterativity, 1, 6, 23, 69–70, 93, 158, 160, 216, 264, 268

Jäsche Logic, 59, 120
judgment, relational (logical forms of), 80–2, 86, 183
justification, epistemic, 67–9

Index of Subjects

knowledge, 58, 143, 252; *see also* belief/knowledge
  philosophical, 37–8
  scientific, 54, 57, 59, 63–70, 128, 157

law, moral; *see* Moral Law
logic, 48, 62
  Aristotelian, 51
  formal, 48
  general, 48
  logic textbook as a model, 62
  transcendental, 48
logical/real, 32–3
logical/transcendental, 32, 113
Logical Maxim, 6–8, 46–7, 56–71, 128, 158
  'becomes' principle of pure reason, 103–4, 121–2
  no categorical imperative, 64
  subjective validity of, 107
logos, 29

Metaphysical Foundations, 39–41, 43–4
metaphysics, 12, 36–44
  critique of, 15, 124, 243–63
  critique of (three levels), 243
  immanent/transcendent, 39–41, 43–4
  metaphysica generalis/specialis, 39
  as a natural predisposition, 3
  of nature/of morals, 39
  practical, 44, 270–5
  as a science, 3, 40–1
  speculative, 39, 272
Moral Law, 270–5
Müller-Lyer illusion, 249
mundus intelligibilis, 143

necessary/sufficient, 86; *see also* condition
necessary being, 231–6
necessity
  absolute, 234, 236
  logical/real, 236
negation, transcendental, 225, 228
Negative Magnitudes, 133, 227, 260
noumenon, 140
  in the negative sense, 140–2, 154
  in the positive sense, 140–2, 147, 152, 154, 159, 162, 164, 207–8, 224, 229, 241, 245, 248
noêsis, *see* dianoia/noêsis
nous, 29, 32, 140, 144
Nova Dilucidatio, 33, 99

omnitudo realitatis, 81–3, 220, 225–9, 233
On a Discovery, 33, 77, 100
Only Possible Argument, 220, 227

ontology, 39–40, 43
order, rational; *see* world
organism, 77, 129

paralogism, 173, 187–202, 265–6
  diagnosis of, 199–202
  as necessary inference of reason, 191–4
  and recent philosophy of mind, 194
  as *sophisma figurae dictionis*, 195–6
  and Supreme Principle, 192
  and transcendental illusion/realism, 195–202
parents/children, 74, 207
parts/whole, 74, 77–8, 82–3, 93
periodic table of elements, 114
possibility
  logical/real, 228, 243, 259
  sum total of, 81, 220, 225–7, 231
postulate of pure practical reason, 40, 255, 259, 271–5
predicate, *see* subject/predicate
prescriptive, *see* descriptive/prescriptive
principle, 33, 59
  of complete determination, 221–6
  of comprehension, 94–6, 98, 101, 153, 155, 158, 180, 268
  of continuity, 108, 110, 117, 120, 131–2, 136, 237
  constitutive/regulative, 110–18, 124, 164, 217, 230
  descriptive/prescriptive, 111, 113–15, 119–20, 129
  of determinability, 219–25
  epistemically/inferentially first, 59
  of homogeneity, 108, 110, 114, 131, 145, 237
  logical/transcendental, 108–10, 115, 117, 129
  logical, becomes transcendental, 121
  of non-contradiction (PNC), 60, 98
  of specification, 108, 110, 120, 131–2, 136, 237
  of sufficient reason (PSR), 98–102, 102, 216, 251
Progress, 37, 90, 96, 181, 199, 272
Prolegomena, 76, 170
psychology, rational, 39–40

quantum mechanics, 66
question, rationally necessary, 160

ratio, 29
Rational Sources Account, 3–6, 9, 18, 26, 32, 35, 39, 43–4, 47, 65, 71, 124, 134, 148–51, 157, 164–7, 171, 173, 179, 184–6, 190, 216, 232, 242, 263–4, 267
  argument for, 160
  (four) levels, 6, 65, 165, 216, 218, 237

Index of Subjects

fundamental level of, 127
general template, 14, 151, 165, 264, 266
and rationalism, 147
RS-1, RS-2, RS-3, 5, 157, 160–2, 268–9
realism, epistemological/metaphysical, 246–7
realism, transcendental, 9, 138–51, 159–60, 162, 164, 180, 196, 207–8, 217, 224, 235, 238, 240–2, 245–51, 266, 269
and cosmological ideas, 207–8
in paralogisms, 195–202
in Rational Sources Account, 267–8
TR_c, 144–50, 196–7, 206, 245, 249, 251
TR_{neg}, 142
TR_{pos}, 142, 208, 228, 245
TR_{rep}, 198–200, 202, 245, 249–51
and ultimate answers, 215
real, *see* logical real
reality, objective, 105, 113, 118–9, 254–62; *see also* validity, objective; idea, transcendental
reason, 1, 3, 21–2, 52, 62, 65, 264
as capacity for mediate inference, 22–3
common human, 26
considered objectively/subjectively, 25
defined in terms of aprioricity, discursivity, mediate inference, 22
as entire higher faculty of cognition, 22
as a faculty, 23–6
as faculty of principles, 33
as having ends, needs, interests, 24
hypothetical use of, 54–5, 113–14, 118
lazy/perverted, 240
logical/real use (*in abstracto/concreto*), 31–5, 45–8, 55, 58, 61–2, 68, 70, 74, 82, 130, 132, 157–8, 178, 271
maxim of, 56, 64, 125, 136
Meier's definition of, 30
normative and teleological conception of, 25
practical/theoretical, 26
pure, 3, 26–7
pure practical, 270
pure practical (primacy of), 273
pure speculative, 35
speculative, 26, 44, 65, 273
as system of a priori principles and cognitions, 25
two aspects of a priori reasoning, 30
and understanding, 22, 29–31
unity of, 53–4, 116, 128, 157–9, 162, 192, 224, 265
universal human, 3, 26, 44, 64–5, 68–70, 150, 159
uses of, 28
regulative, *see* constitutive/regulative
representation, *see* subject/representation

relativity theory, 66–7
repugnance, real, 33, 227–8, 260–1
rule, 49, 114–15

schema, transcendental, 81, 256–7
science, 53–6, 62–3, 65–8
empirical/historical, 61
holistic character of scientific theories, 67–8
rational, 60–1, 63
and certainty, 54–5, 61–2, 67
and systematicity, 37–8, 54, 62
sensibility/understanding, 36
soul, 87, 271, 274
idea of, 184, 239–41, 256–7
as person, simple, spirit, 193
as substance, 190
space
Euclidian, 67
finite/infinite, 250
regions in, 81
speculation, 26, 69
speculative; *see* metaphysics
subject/predicate, 81–3, 190–1
subject/representation, 76, 81–2
subreption, 235
substance
concept of, 256
$substance_1/substance_2$, 191
substance/attribute, 74, 82
substance/inherence, 80
as unconditioned, 192
sufficient; *see* necessary/sufficient
Supreme Principle, 7–8, 46, 65, 71–3, 83, 86–7, 91, 93, 96, 98–102, 126, 158–60, 162, 192, 233, 264, 268
about appearances/things in themselves, 152–6
analytic/synthetic, 153
argument for, 97–8, 152–3
correspondence to Logical Maxim, 131–4
final formulation of, 97
objective validity of, 106–7, 123, 126, 159
regulative use of, 118–20
syllogism, 48, 50, 52, 57, 69; *see also* inference
episyllogism, 51
polysyllogism, 50, 52, 70
prosyllogism, 51, 56–7, 174, 203
symbol, 255
synthesis, 50
system/systematicity, 23–5, 53–6, 173; *see also* idea, transcendental (system of)
of scientific knowledge, 37–9, 62–70

taking something to be true (*Fürwahrhalten*), 115, 123, 252
theology, rational, 39, 218
theory of everything, 66, 216
thing in itself; *see* appearance/thing in itself
TI; *see* idealism, transcendental
time
   moments in, 74, 81–2, 136
   succession, temporal, 81, 83, 194
totality, 91–7, 101
   absolute, 94
   of conditions; *see* unconditioned
transcendental, 32, 49, 111–13; *see also* logical/transcendental
Transcendental Dialectic, 9, 43, 164, 264
   two projects/sides/strands of, 9–12, 124, 165, 264
transition
   from logical to real/transcendental, 8, 125, 164, 197, 202, 216–17, 222, 225, 236–7, 242, 265, 271
   from logical features of 'I think' to real predicates of soul, 202
   from Logical Maxim to Supreme Principle, 7, 103, 125–6, 134, 137, 148–51, 160
   from regulative to constitutive, 127–52, 223, 225, 235
Transition Passage, 120–6
   deliberate ambiguity, 123–5
   Transition$_i$, 122

unconditioned, 35, 46–7, 56, 87–8, 101, 159–61, 168, 213, 268, 270, 274; *see also* cognition
   absolutely unconditioned, 88
   complete series of conditioned conditions, 91
   concept of, 168, 177–82
   epistemically/inferentially, 275
   as totality of conditioned conditions (TCC), 96–7, 182, 192, 210, 269
   totality of conditions, 90–7, 159–60, 178–82, 203–4, 213, 264, 268
   totality of coordinated conditions, 93
   two distinct senses of, 91
   as unconditioned condition (UCC), 87, 96–7, 182, 192, 210, 269
   as unconditioned totality of conditions (UTC), 96–8, 182, 213
understanding; *see* reason
unity, 61
   of reason, 53–4, 116, 128, 157–9, 162, 192, 224, 265
   systematic; *see* system/systematicity

validity, objective, 65, 105–7, 110–11, 116–19, 126, 239, 261
   indeterminate/indirect, 116, 239

whole, *see* parts/whole
world, 87, 149, 274
   idea of, 184, 239–41
   as rational order, 143–4, 154, 159, 206, 229, 245
   as sum total of (empirical) objects, 87, 170, 183–5, 248
   as unconditioned, 206